Theories of Justice

California Series on Social Choice and Political Economy

Edited by Brian Barry (1981 to 1991), Robert H. Bates, James S. Coleman (from 1992), and Samuel L. Popkin

A Treatise on Social Justice,
Volume I

Theories of Justice

Brian Barry

UNIVERSITY OF CALIFORNIA PRESS
Berkeley · Los Angeles

This book is a print-on-demand volume. It is manufactured
using toner in place of ink. Type and images may be less
sharp than the same material seen in traditionally printed
University of California Press editions.

University of California Press
Berkeley and Los Angeles, California

Library of Congress Cataloging-in-Publication Data

Barry, Brian M.
    Theories of justice.

    (A Treatise on social justice; v. 1) (California
series on social choice and political economy; 16)
    Bibliography: p.
    Includes index.
    1. Social justice. I. Title. II. Series.
III. Series: Barry, Brian M. Treatise on social
justice; v. 1.
JC578.B37 vol. 1   320'.01'1 s   [320'.01'1]   88-27764
ISBN 0-520-03866-5 (cloth)
ISBN 0-520-07649-4 (ppb.)

Printed in the United States of America

For H. L. A. Hart

The principles of justice may . . . be regarded as those principles which arise when the constraints of having a morality are imposed upon parties in the typical circumstances of justice.

These ideas are, of course, connected with a familiar way of thinking about justice which goes back at least to the Greek Sophists, and which regards the acceptance of the principles of justice as a compromise between persons of roughly equal power who would enforce their will on each other if they could, but who, in view of the equality of forces amongst them and for the sake of their own peace and security, acknowledge certain forms of conduct insofar as prudence seems to require. Justice is thought of as a pact between rational egoists the stability of which is dependent on a balance of power and a similarity of circumstances. (Perhaps the best known statement of this conception is that given by Glaucon at the beginning of Book II of Plato's *Republic*. . . . In modern times elements of the conception appear in a more sophisticated form in Hobbes *The Leviathan* and in Hume *A Treatise of Human Nature*. . . .) While the account [in "Justice as Fairness"] is connected with this tradition and with its most recent variant, the theory of games, it differs from it in several important respects. . . .

[T]he acceptance of the duty of fair play by participants in a common practice is a reflection in each person of the recognition of the aspirations and interests of the others to be realized by their joint activity. . . . [The] main purpose [of these remarks] is to forestall . . . the misinterpretation that on the view presented, the acceptance of justice and the acknowledgement of the duty of fair play depends in every day life solely on there being a *de facto* balance of forces between the parties. It would indeed be foolish to underestimate the importance of such a balance in securing justice; but it is not the only basis thereof. The recognition of one another as persons with similar interests and capacities engaged in a common practice must, failing a special explanation, show itself in the acceptance of the principles of justice and the acknowledgement of the duty of fair play.

John Rawls, "Justice as Fairness,"
Philosophical Review 67 (1958)

Contents

Preface

The three volume *Treatise on Social Justice* of which this is the first represents a new departure for me. Hitherto, I have specialized in making fairly brief forays into problems before they got too overcrowded, whereas the present work is a sustained attack on the oldest problem in political philosophy (with an enormous recent literature to boot), the nature of justice in society. The reason for the change in strategy is that I felt a need to dig deeper into the foundations of a theory of justice, but also to carry it further in terms of institutional specifics.

The present volume is an exposition and critical analysis of the two theories of justice that seem to me the leading contenders: one that I call justice as mutual advantage and the other justice as impartiality. Volume II will be devoted to defending justice as impartiality, to laying out the theory in more detail, and to drawing attention to some of its implications for the distribution of benefits and burdens in a society. Volume III will endeavor to arrive at specific conclusions about what justice entails for economic institutions, both within countries and between them.

In the course of writing this volume I have incurred many debts, and it is a pleasure to have the opportunity to acknowledge at any rate some of them. The Center for Advanced Study in the Behavioral Sciences in Stanford must come first. Although it is ten years since I took up my year of residence at that wonderful institution, this book still qualifies for inclusion in the Ralph Tyler Library of books initiated at the Center. (I hope it makes up in bulk for what it lacks in timeliness.) When I went to the Center in July 1976, I had no plans to return to the topic of distributive justice. However, in the liberating atmosphere of the Center I found, during the latter half of my stay, that some new ideas (or at any rate new variations on old ideas) were stirring. Though I do not think that a single paragraph of what I wrote during that period survives into this book, I can certainly date my work on it from then. Although I got a lot out of talking to a number of the Fellows (and particularly to the other participants in the informal seminar on Inequality that ran through most of the year), I want to single out Robert Simon who, thanks to the wisdom of Gardner Lindzey and Preston Cutler, was assigned the office next to mine and with whom I enjoyed many lengthy and illuminating discussions of the questions dealt with in this book.

The University of Chicago provided a marvellously stimulating environment for me in the next five years, during which the basic ideas that appear in this book were worked out in a series of papers.[1] I must express my special thanks to the graduate students, from the departments of sociology, philosophy, and political science, and from the schools of law, business, theology, and public policy, whose acuity made my courses on distributive justice so valuable to me in testing my ideas. I must also warmly acknowledge the criticism and encouragement of the members of the Tuesday Group, and particularly Charles Silver and Russell Hardin, whose ideas about utilitarianism form a subterranean current in this book.

During the academic year 1979–80, I was fortunate enough to be free of teaching duties, thanks to fellowships from the Rockefeller Foundation and the American Council of Learned Societies. The former grant also allowed me to spend the first three months of 1980 in Oxford, where I particularly appreciated the opportunity of talking to Tim Scanlon and Derek Parfit.

From the beginning of 1983, the California Institute of Technology removed most of the excuses for not finishing the book by providing a working environment that it would be hard to equal. The mainstay of the Caltech setup has been Kathryn Kurzweil, whose goodwill and effectiveness have reduced the toll—what Robert Pirsig called the seepage of gumption[2]—exacted by other projects to a level below anything one could ever reasonably hope for. Later chapters of the book have benefited from discussion in the Caltech Tuesday Group and the Social Theory Seminar organized by Marshall Cohen. I had much encouragement from Bruce Cain, Randall Curren, Alan Donagan, Leonid Hurwicz, Arthur Kuflik, Talbot Page, Bart Schultz, Alan Strudler, and

James Woodward. Will Jones in addition provided me with extensive and valuable detailed comments in writing. It is also a pleasure to acknowledge a large debt to the Huntington Library in San Marino for offering a haven from the heat and the telephone—with a congenial scholarly community as a bonus.

John Gillroy helped greatly with references and bibliography. Janet Casebier, the Head of Humanities and Social Sciences in the Caltech Library, expended a great deal of time and effort on my behalf to obtain copies of articles that I needed to see. Almost all the typing, draft after draft, was done by Joanna Barry. She has done so much to make the book possible as to make even that two million or so words a minor part of it—she alone knows quite how much. My son Austin was in his first year of junior high school when the book was begun and graduated from college last year. This book has therefore been a condition of most of his existence and his contribution, in the form of having to put up with a father preoccupied much of the time with the finer points of bargaining theory, was no less great for being not altogether voluntary.

Russell Hardin's comments on the complete book, commissioned by the University of California Press, were both encouraging and astute in suggesting room for improvement. The final revisions were made, in spite of all the obstacles put in the way by what is laughingly called the administration, at the European University Institute. My secretary, Marlies van Hoof, gave valuable help in the preparation of the final draft.

The dedicatee of this book, Herbert Hart, did not contribute directly to it. But if the argument is now more solidly worked out and more lucidly expressed than it was half a dozen drafts ago, the reader as well as I has reason to thank him for his example, imperfectly as I have succeeded in emulating it.

Most of this book was written to the accompaniment of those excellent radio stations WFMT in Chicago and KUSC in Los Angeles. Richard Capparela and his colleagues became ethereal friends who helped alleviate the tedium that seems inseparable much of the time from literary composition. Equally important was the more tangible though (mostly) silent companionship of George, who until his death in 1983 was rarely more than a few feet away, and latterly of Tom, Orly, and Rover.

Florence, March 1987

PART I

Don't Shoot the Trumpeter! Problems of Fair Division

CHAPTER I

The Case of the Noxious Neighbors

1. TWO THEORIES OF JUSTICE

A Treatise on Social Justice is addressed to the question that Plato asked in the *Republic* two and a half thousand years ago: What is justice? The asking of that question by Plato may be said to have inaugurated political philosophy in the Western world. But the question itself is one that arises inevitably in any society whenever its members start to think reflectively about the arrangements within which their lives are lived. Through contact with other societies, people come to realize that social arrangements are not a natural phenomenon but a human creation. And what was made by human beings can be changed by human beings. This realization sets the stage for the emergence of theories of justice. For a theory of justice is a theory about the kinds of social arrangement that can be defended.

In Plato's time as in ours, the central issue in any theory of justice is the defensibility of unequal relations between people. Like the Athenians, we see all around us in our societies huge inequalities in political power, in social standing, and in the command over economic resources. The degree of inequality on each of these dimensions is different in different societies, and so is the extent to which a high position on one is associated with a high position on the others. South Africa is not easily confused with Scandinavia. Nevertheless, in every society there are those who give orders and those who obey them, those who receive deference and those who give it, those who have more than they can use and those who have less than they need.

3

Moreover, even if there is some tendency for those with superior personal characteristics to occupy the higher positions, the correlation is manifestly a weak one, and in any case the height of the social pyramid seems out of all proportion to the range of talent and achievement actually found among people. The implication of this (as Hobbes and Hume both recognized) is that if any existing society is to be deemed just as it stands, the defense will have to be indirect. It will have to take the form of an argument that these gross inequalities are inescapable consequences of the operation of social arrangements with advantages such as liberty, security, or prosperity. Whether or not arguments on these lines are valid is one of the key questions that any theory of justice must reach a conclusion about. (The answer I shall give is a very qualified yes.) But whether or not inequalities of the kind I have described can be defended, there can be no doubt that their existence poses the issue of justice inescapably.

At the time when Plato wrote the *Republic*, nobody seriously questioned the idea that the bounds of justice were the bounds of the state. Then, as now, the violation of treaty obligations was denounced as injustice. But the framework within which the domination and exploitation of one society by another took place was not regarded as open to scrutiny on a charge of injustice. The assertion that Plato put into the mouth of Thrasymachus in the *Republic*—that justice is what is to the advantage of the powerful—was rather shocking as a statement about justice among fellow citizens. But it is exactly this same sentiment that Thucydides has the Athenian envoys put forward in their dialogue with the leading citizens of the island of Melos: "the question of justice only enters where there is equal power to enforce it, and . . . the powerful exact what they can, and the weak grant what they must."[1] And although the dialogue itself is, of course, fictitious, it seems to represent well enough the dominant attitude among the Athenians, if we judge by actions rather than words.

Plato's neglect of (or disbelief in) justice beyond state borders has been pretty faithfully followed by subsequent philosophers who have applied themselves to the topic of justice. What is especially noteworthy is the long-continued failure even to consider the justice of the distribution of wealth in the world as a whole. Indeed, to the best of my knowledge the first extended treatment of this topic by a political philosopher dates from as late as 1979.[2]

In earlier times, this neglect of international distribution was more excusable, for two reasons. First, the means of redistribution were feeble. News traveled slowly and supplies even slower. Only two hundred years ago, Adam Smith could write:

> Whatever interest we take in the fortune of those with whom we have no acquaintance or connection, and who are placed altogether out of the sphere of our activity, can produce only anxiety to ourselves, without any manner of advantage to them. To what purpose should we trouble ourselves about the world in the moon? All men, even those at the greatest distance, are no doubt entitled to our good wishes, and our good wishes we naturally give them. But if, notwithstanding, they should be unfortunate, to give ourselves any anxiety upon that account seems to be no part of our duty. That we should be but little interested, therefore, in the fortune of those whom we can neither serve nor hurt, and who are in every respect so very remote from us, seems wisely ordered by Nature; and if it were possible to alter in this respect the original constitution of our frame, we could yet gain nothing by the change.[3]

Now that men can walk on the moon and send back photographs of the earth from space, this all sounds very quaint. Nor is distance nowadays a bar to the ability to help—or harm. If there are no duties to aid the misfortunate at a distance this will require a moral argument. The plea of incapacity will not work.

The second reason for a new salience to the issue of international redistribution is that it is only in the past two hundred years that the processes of unequal economic development have opened up such enormous international disparities. Even a century ago, the standard of living of the average European industrial worker or agricultural laborer—measured in life expectancy, adequacy of diet, quality of housing, hours of work, and so on—was not outstandingly better than that of a moderately prosperous Asian peasant.

Now, however, the degree of economic inequality of the world population taken as a whole is more extreme than that in all but a very few states in Latin America, the distribution of whose wealth almost everyone would agree to be intolerably inequitable. The justice of the international distribution of economic resources cannot therefore be left aside in any general treatment of justice. I shall discuss some of the issues raised by international justice briefly in chapter 5, and then return to discuss the international situation more extensively in the final volume of this work.

In the *Republic*, Plato discussed two main theories of justice. One is his own, a hierarchical notion according to which a just society is one modeled on a well-ordered human soul. For reasons that will become clear in Part III, I totally reject the presuppositions of this theory and shall say no more about it. However, the theory against which Plato pits his own—the theory that he presumably regarded as the one to beat—continues to be a live option, and is one of the two theories around which *Theories of Justice* is constructed. Like Plato, I shall eventually reject this theory as inadequate, but I hope to give it a better run for its money than it got from Plato. This is in fact far easier to do than it was when Plato wrote, because the theory has been developed so much further. Hobbes and Hume restated it at length in the seventeenth and eighteenth centuries, and in the past thirty years or so, with the advent of game theory and its application to problems of fair division, it has become possible to work with it in a far more sophisticated way than before. This in turn has stimulated philosophers, of whom David Gauthier is the best known, to recast the theories of Hobbes and Hume taking advantage of the technical refinements now available.[4]

The theory in question is the one that is introduced in the *Republic* by Glaucon:

> People say that injustice is by nature good to inflict but evil to suffer. Men taste both of its sides and learn that the evil of suffering it exceeds the good of inflicting it. Those unable to flee the one and take the other therefore decide it pays to make a pact neither to commit nor to suffer injustice. It was here that men began to make laws and covenants, and to call whatever the laws decreed "legal" and "just." This, they say, is both the origin and the essence of justice, a thing midway between the best condition—committing injustice without being punished—and the worst—suffering injustice without getting revenge. Justice is therefore a compromise; it isn't cherished as a good, but honored out of inability to do wrong. A real "man," capable of injustice, would never make a pact with anyone. He'd be insane if he did. That, Socrates, is the popular view of the nature of justice and of the conditions under which it develops.[5]

This idea is introduced shortly after Thrasymachus has withdrawn from the discussion, and is recognizably an offshoot of his view that justice is what is to the advantage of the stronger. It concedes the central point that justice is founded in advantage, but argues that, in the actual conditions of human life, people can expect to advance their interests more effectively through cooperating with other members of their society than through all-out conflict with them. In Hobbes's terms: peace is better for everyone than a war of all against all.

It should be noticed as a feature of this theory of justice that no special motive for behaving justly has to be invoked. Justice is simply rational prudence pursued in contexts where the cooperation (or at least forbearance) of other people is a condition of our being able to get what we want. Justice is the name we give to the constraints on themselves that rational self-interested people would agree to as the minimum price that has to be paid in order to obtain the cooperation of others.

The alternative to this that I shall be putting forward is less conceptually parsimonious. Followers of this second approach hold that there has to be some reason for behaving justly that is not reducible to even a sophisticated and indirect pursuit of self-interest. It is thus incumbent upon them to explain what the appeal of justice can be, either to human beings in general or at least to those raised under conditions favorable to moral education. I shall give my own answer later (see especially section 35). However, an outline of the answer can be arrived at by considering the function that, on this alternative view, justice is taken to have in human society.

Let us approach this answer by looking at the common ground between the two theories. They share two features. First, they have in common the idea that questions of justice arise when there is a conflict of interest between different people or groups of people. Second, they also share the idea that justice is what everyone could in principle reach a rational agreement on. Both approaches therefore lend themselves to formulation in terms of some kind of social contract, though the contractual apparatus is not essential and in fact both approaches have been developed in noncontractual forms. (I shall have more to say about the relation to contract in chapter 7.)

How then do the two approaches differ? Very schematically, we can locate the difference in this way. Under the first approach the agreement is allowed to reflect the fact that some people have more bargaining power than others. It is bound to do this because it appeals to self-interest as the motive for behaving justly. If the terms of agreement failed to reflect differential bargaining power, those whose power was disproportionate to their share under the agreement would have an incentive to seek to upset it. The second approach, however, is not constrained by the requirement that everyone must find it to his advantage to be just. It can therefore afford the luxury (which it has to pay for, of course, by finding an alternative motivation for behaving justly) of detaching justice from bargaining power.

This gives us the defining characteristic of the second approach, namely, that justice should be the content of an agreement that would be reached by rational people under conditions that do not allow for bargaining power to be translated into advantage. Obviously this is very vague as it stands. Everything turns on the way in which the conditions of agreement are filled in, and a whole variety of specific theories of justice have been constructed by building up the conditions in different ways. (See especially chapter 9.) What I want to emphasize here is simply that according to the second theory a just state of affairs is one that people can accept not merely in the sense that they cannot reasonably *expect* to get more but in the stronger sense that they cannot reasonably *claim* more.

The motive for behaving justly is, on this view, the desire to act in accordance with principles that could not reasonably be rejected by people seeking an agreement with others under conditions free from morally irrelevant bargaining advantages and disadvantages. I shall postpone until section 35 my discussion of the strength of this motive and the kinds of social situation in which it is most likely to develop. Here all I need to do is emphasize that, on the second approach, we are not bound by the assumption that the answer to the question "Why should I be just?" must appeal to self-interest.

I shall call this second approach "justice as impartiality," in contrast to the first, which I shall call "justice as mutual advantage." The significance of speaking of "justice as impartiality" is that this approach, however it is worked out in detail, entails that people should not look at things from their own point of view alone but seek to find a basis of agreement that is acceptable from all points of view. The general approach, which calls on people to detach themselves from their own contingently given positions and take up a more impartial standpoint is, of course, a product of the Enlightenment, and everyone who follows it acknowledges a debt to Kant. By far the most significant contemporary figure in that tradition is John Rawls, whose monumental *A Theory of Justice*[6] is in my judgment a work of major and enduring significance. Most of Part II will in fact be largely devoted to a critical exposition of and reflection upon certain central themes in his work.

The two approaches have, as I have made clear, been around for quite a long time. However, in the course of the last thirty years or so a good deal more rigor and precision has entered into the analysis. This is partly the result of the already mentioned technical advances in game theory and decision theory and their assimilation into the literature of political philosophy. But what is equally important is simply that a lot of time and effort has gone into working through alternative ways of setting up the problem of justice within the two approaches and arguing about the pros and cons of each. My object in *Theories of Justice* is to examine this work and in the course of doing so to argue toward some general conclusions of my own.

Part I is concerned with analyses of justice on a small scale—in fact most of the time the smallest scale on which problems of justice can arise at all, namely, two people. In Part II, I shall move on to the larger context and talk about justice within societies. I shall try to show that the two theories of justice are both to be found within David Hume's theory of justice and also both to be found within John Rawls's. I hope by looking with a fresh perspective at these two master political philosophers to gain light on the subject of justice in society. Then in Part III, I shall pull together the discussion of small- and large-scale justice in Parts I and II. I shall seek to show how each of the theories of justice is in fact a family of theories, each member of the family defined by the way in which it specifies key components in the theory. I shall use this scheme to locate the solutions discussed earlier, and thereby I hope make clearer what is at issue in the disputes among recent writers on justice.

2. BARGAINING AND ARBITRATION

In this chapter and the next I shall take up the notion of justice in the simplest possible kind of case: a conflict between two parties over the division of some particular scarce resource. This chapter will be confined to justice as mutual advantage. In the next chapter I shall introduce justice as impartiality by looking at the criticisms that have been made of solutions embodying justice as mutual advantage. I think it is as well at this point to emphasize rather than to gloss over the artificiality of any such analyses. We shall be taking the situations of the two parties as given, without any inquiry into the origins of those situations, and we shall be asking what it would be fair for an arbitrator to decide in this one case considered in isolation from all similar ones. Natural objections arise at once. Should we not talk about the justice of social positions before we can sensibly discuss the fairness of particular decisions? And how can we reasonably ignore the fact that conflicts are normally dealt with by rules covering cases of a certain general kind rather than by one-off arbitrations?

If the purposes of the book were purely practical, these objections would be decisive. But if our purpose is first of all to understand as fully as possible the alternative conceptions of justice, there is much to be said for beginning with the simplest cases, and accepting the inherent artificiality. The rest of the story can then be filled in later. Indeed, the third chapter, which completes Part I, is devoted precisely to asking what happens when we shift our perspective from one in which we look at conflicts between two people on a one-off basis, asking what a fair arbitrated solution would be, and instead think of rules and institutions whose function is to lay out in advance the terms upon which disputes are to be settled. And the relation of small-scale justice as analyzed here and the justice of the institutions that allocate social positions will be taken up extensively when the groundwork has been laid, in chapter 9.

With this by way of preface, let me now turn to justice as mutual advantage in the context of a two-party dispute over a single issue. The idea of justice as mutual advantage is that the just outcome should represent for both parties a gain over what they would have acquired from a continuation of the conflict. This immediately implies that the process of determining a fair outcome has to be split into two parts. The first consists of establishing a nonagreement point: an outcome that the parties will arrive at in the absence of agreement. The second consists of a prescription for moving the parties from there to a point that preserves their relative advantage at the nonagreement point but is in the set of outcomes that are "efficient," meaning that one party cannot be made better off without the other being made worse off. There are, as we shall see, two competing rationales for this prescription for the move from the nonagreement point to one that is efficient in the sense specified. One, which is most fully within the spirit of justice as mutual advantage, says that the move should be made in a way that reflects the relative bargaining power of the parties. The other appeals to an intuitive notion of fairness and claims that a fair division of the "cooperative surplus" is one that divides it equally between the parties. We shall see, however, that many theorists put forward a criterion of equal gain which has the effect of producing the same outcomes as the rationale that appeals to relative bargaining power.

The present section will follow up the first alternative. According to this, the role of an arbitrator is simply to simulate the results of bargaining. It might be asked why there is any point in bringing in an arbitrator in that case. I shall explain later in this section, under "The Uses of Arbitration," where the arbitrator comes in. But there is no point in even raising that question unless we conclude that it makes sense to talk about a bargaining solution—that is to say, an outcome that rational actors, given their respective strategic advantages and disadvantages, ought to reach. Doubts can be, and have been, raised about the possibility of carrying out this program in any plausible way, and these doubts are fundamental to the whole enterprise. Of course, it is open to anyone to object that we do not get fairness by asking what ideally rational actors would finish up with if they bargained with each other. But it is not even worth asking that question unless we think it makes sense to produce a formula and say that this tells us what ideally rational bargainers would finish up with in any given situation. Still less, I need hardly say, is it worth arguing about the relative merits of alternative proposals for the formula.

As so often happens, the technical discussion with which economists and game theorists are most at home has overwhelmed the discussion of fundamental issues. There is a plethora of competing operationalizations of relative bargaining power—the world is full of so-called "bargaining solutions"—but there is a dearth of serious discussion of the very idea of a bargaining solution. Surprisingly, perhaps, philosophers have been little help here. In fact, they have tended to be more uncritical than many of the more technically equipped people. As I shall show in the next chapter, this is a pattern: philosophers tend to show more confidence in the constructs of game theory than do the more sophisticated game theorists. Thus, David Gauthier, in his *Morals by Agreement*, devotes one sentence to observing that "whether there are principles of rational bargaining with...context-free universality of application...has been questioned." He then goes on to say that "undaunted by...scepticism" he will set out his own theory and say why he prefers it to the Nash solution.[7]

I shall in Appendix B refute Gauthier's criticism of the Nash solution and his defense of his own alternative. However, before such questions are even worth discussing we must first address the notion of a bargaining solution itself. In order to have a definite example of a bargaining solution to hand, I shall explain the earliest and most popular of such solutions, the Nash solution. I shall then, using it as my illustration, ask what can be said in favor of bargaining solutions, what can be said against them, and what can be said in reply to skeptical attacks. I shall argue for the realism of bargaining solutions, so long as they are not made to do too much, and I shall show how the practice of arbitration naturally lends itself to the use, implicitly if not explicitly, of bargaining solutions.

Let me begin, then, by setting out as clearly and untechnically as possible the operation of the Nash solution. Anyone who understands the workings of the Nash solution can without loss skip the exposition of it given below under the heading "The Nash Solution," though I hope that what follows in the rest of the section will still be of interest. However, I should emphasize that those who feel they "have the general idea" of the Nash solution are precisely those for whom the exposition is designed. I make so bold as to maintain that much of the discussion of bargaining solutions (such as Nash's) by philosophers has been vitiated by their neglecting to obtain an intimate acquaintance with the workings of these solution concepts. A clear sign of this is the tendency of philosophers to take over an interpretation from some game theorist of what it is about a solution concept that makes it come out the way it does and then quote it from one another without examining it for themselves. The interpretation thus becomes like a parcel that is passed from hand to hand and never unwrapped. I shall seek to substantiate this in relation to the notion of a "threat advantage" in the next chapter (see section 8).

THE NASH SOLUTION

For our purposes, there are two key dates in the analysis of fair division between two people in terms of bargaining. These are 1950 and 1955. In 1950, the mathematician J. F. Nash published an article in *Econometrica* entitled "The Bargaining Problem."[8] Five years later, R. B. Braithwaite, a philosopher at Cambridge University who had worked in philosophy of science and decision theory, was elected to the chair of moral philosophy and published, as his first (and, as far as I know, last) contribution to the subject of his chair, an inaugural lecture entitled *Theory of Games as a Tool for the Moral Philosopher.*[9] In this section I shall say something about the context and significance of Nash's article and explain his solution. In the following section I shall do the same for the brief monograph that Braithwaite based on his lecture.

Until Nash came along, the standard view among game theorists and economists was that bargaining problems had no determinate solution. Thus, John von Neumann and Oskar Morgenstern, in their pioneering work in game theory, *The Theory of Games and Economic Behavior,*[10] maintained that it is possible to say only two things about rational bargaining: first, that, if the parties are rational, neither will accept an agreement giving it less than it could obtain in the absence of agreement; and second, that the parties will not reach an agreement such that there is an alternative agreement available under which one would be able to do better without the other doing worse. This corresponded exactly to the standard economic view according to which we can say that rational trading partners will reach the contract curve but we cannot say where on it they will finish up. Subject to those restrictions, the outcome could be anywhere: its location was held to depend on the "psychology of the parties."

In the usual terminology, all we are supposed to be able to say in general is that the outcome of bargaining will, if the parties are rational, lie on that portion of the Pareto frontier that is above the nonagreement point for both parties. I can explain the notion of the Pareto frontier by saying that it is the set of Pareto-optimal points, and that a Pareto optimum is an outcome such that it is not possible to move away from it in a way that makes one party better off without making another worse off.[11] Thus, take the simplest possible kind of case, in which two people can share $100 in any way that they can agree upon. If they fail to agree neither gets anything. Then the requirement that any agreement must be better for each than the nonagreement point has here the trivial implication that neither will actually hand over money to the other. (The Pareto frontier may well include such transfers.) And the requirement that the outcome should be on the Pareto frontier rather than inside it simply entails that they will agree to divide the whole of the money between them rather than, say, only $90 of it.

It is a good question what the meaning of "rationality" is in this context but one that I shall have to be brief and dogmatic about. I think it is clearly a normative or prescriptive concept rather than a positive or descriptive one. It is, however, a minimally prescriptive or normative concept in that it attempts to deduce the implications of the efficient pursuit of utility. Thus, it would be irrational individually to accept as the outcome of bargaining less than the nonagreement utility because that would be a gratuitous loss of utility; and it would be jointly irrational for the parties to settle for an agreement that was suboptimal because they would be giving up an attainable increase in utility.

Common sense, however, revolts against the conclusion that within the limits I have stated the outcome must turn entirely on the personal characteristics of the parties and nothing else. Suppose that one of the parties is very rich and the other very poor. The rich person, let us suppose, will be little affected by how much or how little of the money he gets, whereas the poor one desperately needs a small portion of it but is much less concerned about getting larger amounts. We have an intuitive feeling that the rich person has an advantage in bargaining here that flows from his position. It remains true that a particularly skillful poor person in this situation might do well against an ineffective rich one. But we feel that there is an objective inequality in bargaining power here that, with rational bargainers, will result in the rich person getting more than half the money.

Nash's solution to the bargaining problem may be seen (and I suggest should be seen) as an attempt to capture this elusive notion of unequal bargaining power formally. For this he needs a measure of utility, and makes use of the measure that von Neumann and Morgenstern constructed making use of hypothetical choices among lotteries. Thus, if the rich person is indifferent between a certain $50 and an equal chance of nothing and $100, we say that, setting no money at 0 utility and $100 at unity, the utility of $50 is 0.5. And if the poor person is indifferent between a certainty of $25 and an equal chance of nothing and $100, we shall say that the utility of $25 is 0.5. That he derives the same utility (within this system of normalization) from $25 as the other does from $50 reflects his relatively greater anxiety to be sure of getting something. The rich man can afford the luxury of accepting a fair gamble.

This method of representing utilities has come in for a good deal of criticism on the grounds, among other things, that it cannot separate out attitude toward risk. But in the present case that is not an objection because, as we shall see later in this section, the best rationale for the Nash solution incorporates a reference to risk in it. According to this, the Nash solution is a point such that the parties are equally averse to risking the nonagreement outcome by holding out for more than the solution offers. Thus, the parties' attitudes to risk constitute the driving force behind the solution.

The actual form of the Nash solution is that rational bargainers will finish up at the point where the product of the utilities of the parties is maximized, when the nonagreement outcome is assigned zero utility to each party. (I shall henceforward assume that the nonagreement payoffs have been set at zero without making it explicit on each occasion.) I should, however, emphasize that the rationale of the Nash solution is not that it is designed to maximize joint efficiency, except in the uncontroversial sense that it gets the parties to the Pareto frontier. (This point will be taken up in Appendix B.) It is not to be seen as a backdoor way of getting utilitarianism without interpersonally comparable utilities. It is intended rather to represent the results of rational agents trying to do the best for themselves individually.

TABLE 1.1.   AN ILLUSTRATION OF THE NASH SOLUTION

Rich		Poor		
Money	Utility	Money	Utility	Product of utilities
$100	1.0	$ 0	0	0
90	0.9	10	0.4	0.36
80	0.8	20	0.6	0.48
70	0.7	30	0.7	0.49
60	0.6	40	0.78	0.468
50	0.5	50	0.85	0.425
40	0.4	60	0.91	0.364
30	0.3	70	0.96	0.288
20	0.2	80	0.98	0.196
10	0.1	90	0.99	0.099
0	0	100	1.0	0

To illustrate the Nash solution at work, I have in Table 1.1 assigned utilities to our rich and poor people at intervals of $10. The highest product of these $10 intervals comes at a 70/30 split in favor of the rich person; the actual maximum is a little more favorable to the rich person, at about 73/27. The same information is represented in Figure 1.1. The Nash solution comes where the rectangle with the largest area can be drawn within the Pareto frontier, and the outcome is again where the rich person gets $73 to the poor person's $27.

I have devoted some time to setting out the Nash solution because the ideas that it incorporates are crucial in understanding later developments. To review them once more, there are four elements that make up the Nash solution. First, there is the nonagreement point as the point from which the gains derived from agreement are to be calculated. Second, there is the Pareto frontier as the set of points from which the solution must be drawn. Third, there is the solution concept itself, which is designed to allocate the gains in moving from the nonagreement point to the Pareto frontier in a way that reflects relative bargaining power. And fourth, there is the assumption that the only information required to operate an adequate solution concept is information about the von Neumann/Morgenstern utilities of the parties. These features are in fact common to almost all the bargaining solutions that have been proposed as variants on Nash: they differ in the way in which they manipulate the utility information to arrive at an outcome.

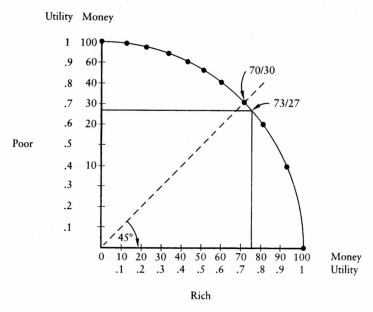

Figure 1.1.   An Illustration of the Nash Solution

THE IDEA OF A BARGAINING SOLUTION

I am not particularly interested in the Nash solution for its own sake. What I am primarily concerned with is the whole idea of a bargaining solution, since it is this that underlies all the work in the past thirty years on so-called fair division. But it is better to talk about a particular bargaining solution than about bargaining solutions in the abstract. I shall therefore say something first about the rationale of the Nash solution, and then move on to the more general question of the value of solution concepts for bargaining games, using the Nash solution as my example.

Two main lines of justification for the Nash solution have been offered. The first is the one advanced by Nash himself in "The Bargaining Problem" and consists in a proof that the Nash solution uniquely satisfies a number of formal conditions. In addition to the familiar minimum conditions—that the solution should lie on the Pareto frontier and dominate the nonagreement point—Nash stipulates three further conditions. The first is that the solution should be invariant with respect to the units in which utility is measured. Given that the units of von Neumann/Morgenstern utility are arbitrary, this seems reasonable. The

Nash solution deals with the problem of units by multiplying the utilities together. (Thus, if we had increased all of the poor man's utilities by a factor of ten, the solution would have come to the same division of the money because the products of the two men's utilities would have stayed in the same ratio. The only difference would have been that every product would have been ten times larger.)

The second condition is one of symmetry: if the utility schedules of the players are identical then the outcome should yield equal utility, measured in the same terms as those that made the utility schedules identical. This requirement too seems hard to fault.

The third requirement is less intuitively compelling. It is the independence of irrelevant (or, better, infeasible) alternatives. What this means is that if the negotiation set is increased, the solution can legitimately move to a point in the new area, but it cannot change to a different one of the outcomes that were available originally. Conversely, restricting the negotiation set can legitimately remove the original solution point and compel the movement of the outcome to another; but if the original solution is still available, the subtraction of other alternatives should not result in a shift from it. This is a rather strong condition, and rules out all kinds of schemes for "splitting the difference." (I shall discuss this point further in section 5.)

However, although this set of conditions is quite interesting for the light it throws on the properties of the Nash solution, I have to confess that I am unable to see how it can be thought to amount to a recommendation for it, considered as a bargaining solution. For we can surely imagine a solution uniquely satisfying a number of nice-sounding *a priori* conditions of this kind and still being quite absurd in its implications for bargaining situations. What matters is not coming up with a unique solution but providing reasons for believing that someone would do better (in terms of that person's own utility function) by following its prescriptions than by following some alternative rule of conduct.[12]

This demand is to some degree met by an alternative rationale of the Nash solution, which is due to John C. Harsanyi.[13] This might be thought to capture formally the intuitive notion giving rise to our feeling that the poor person had less bargaining power than the rich one and should therefore be expected to get less than half the legacy. It derives the Nash solution from a rule specifying which party should make the next concession in a sequence of offers and counteroffers. The rule says that the party with more to lose by holding out should be the one to make a more attractive offer to the other. "More to lose" should not be taken to require interpersonal comparisons of utility. Rather, we are to compare the relationship among one party's von Neumann/ Morgenstern utilities with the relationship among those of the other party.

Let us imagine, then, that each of the parties engaged in a Nash bargaining game has proposed to the other a certain division of the resource in dispute. Setting the nonagreement point at zero, call the utility of player 1's proposal to himself u_1' and the utility to player 2 of this same proposal u_2'. Similarly, call the utility of player 2's proposal to himself and to player 1 u_2'' and u_1'' respectively. Now, the rule telling us who is to make the concession requires us to compare $u_1' - u_1''/u_1'$ with $u_2'' - u_2'/u_2''$. Whichever player has the lower ratio should be the one to offer the next concession. The idea behind this rule is that the player with the lower ratio has more to lose from the breakdown of negotiations (and hence the nonagreement payoff of 0) in comparison with the amount to be lost by accepting the other's offer instead of holding out for its own. The connection with the Nash solution arises from the fact that the concession rule is equivalent to the rule that we compare $u_1' u_2'$ with $u_1'' u_2''$ and stipulate that the player whose proposal has the lower product should make the next concession. Thus, by following the concession rule (whichever way we write it) the players will converge on the Nash solution, provided only that they move in suitably small steps.

It may be helpful to illustrate the concession rule at work in our example of the rich and the poor man dividing $100. (See Table 1.1 for the relevant utility figures.) Suppose that each opens the bidding by offering a 90–10 division of the money in his own favor. Then the Harsanyi formula as applied to R gives us $0.9 - 0.1/0.9 = 0.89$. As applied to P it gives us $0.99 - 0.4/0.99 = 0.6$. The rule then tells us that P should make the next concession, and we can verify from Table 1.1 that the product of utilities from P's offer (0.099) is less than the product of utilities from R's offer (0.36). If P is to force R to make the next offer, he must make an offer that gets the product of utilities above 0.36 and we can see from Table 1.1 that to achieve this (if divisions are in $10 intervals) P must propose a 50–50 division. The Harsanyi formula gives us 0.44 for R and 0.53 for P, which confirms that R has to make the next offer. R can now reply with the proposal of a 60–40 division in his own favor, which raises the product of utilities from 0.425 to 0.468. The

Harsanyi formula gives us 0.17 for R and 0.08 for P, which means that P must make the next move. This must be to a 70–30 division in R's favor, which is (within the limitation of $10 intervals) the highest product of utilities possible and is hence the Nash solution.*

Let us stand back from the detail and ask how compelling this style of reasoning really is. Can we say that one could never do better than to follow it against a rational opposite number in a bargaining game? That would be nice, but we clearly cannot. (In this respect it contrasts with the minimax strategy for a two-person zero-sum game. It can be shown that a party can do no better than by playing this strategy unless it thinks it can outguess its opponent. Thus, the strategy can be recommended to two parties each of which believes its opponent to be as rational as itself.)[14]

The notion underlying the second rationale of the Nash solution is that the probability of a party's making a concession is proportional to its relative loss from not making a concession. And if each party uses this notion as the basis on which to assign a subjective probability to the other's making a concession, we get the required prescription.[15] But a great variety of decision rules will produce *some* determinate outcome if followed by both players. If each thinks that there is some outcome

---

* An alternative rationale for the Nash solution (under certain conditions) is derived from the idea that an agreement reached later is worth less to both parties than the same agreement reached earlier. Owing to time discounting, the value of the resource diminishes with each successive offer. We can alternatively imagine the parties as dividing a pie that shrinks more the longer the parties argue about its division. If the parties discount time at different rates, there is a greater pressure on the one with the higher discount rate to reach an agreement. All else being equal, he is hence in a weaker bargaining position, and this will bias the division of the resource against him. Suppose, however, that the parties have the same time discount rates, so that their relative bargaining power is affected only by the utilities that enter into the Nash solution. Then there is still a strategic inequality within the structure of the game in that the player who makes the first offer has an advantage. This advantage is bigger the bigger the loss of utility at each stage. If we think of the offers and counteroffers occurring at short intervals (and it is in the interest of each player to move quickly) then it can be shown that the outcome asymptotically approaches that of the Nash solution. Thus, the Nash solution may be seen as the limit of a bargaining game with moves extending over time at progressively shorter intervals. (See A. Rubinstein, "Perfect Equilibrium in a Bargaining Model," pp. 47–60 of *The Economics of Bargaining*, edited by Ken Binmore and Partha Dasgupta [Oxford: Basil Blackwell, 1987] and Ken Binmore, "Nash Bargaining Theory II," pp. 61–76 in Binmore and Dasgupta.) Binmore elsewhere in the same volume remarks that Rubinstein's result is "strongly related to Harsanyi's rationalization of Zeuthen's principle" ("Perfect Equilibrium in Bargaining Models," pp. 77–105, quotation from p. 94). We can see Rubinstein's time discounting as supplying the incentive that is otherwise lacking to make the parties offer concessions rather than sitting on their own offers indefinitely.

X that the other party will settle for and that the other party will not accept less, then X, whatever it is, is likely to emerge as the outcome. But there is no guarantee that X will be the Nash solution.

There is of course nothing to stop you from assigning a probability to the other person's making the next concession by using Harsanyi's formula. But the trouble is that your estimate has no coercive force in itself, and it may be plain wrong. If your bargaining partner could somehow convince you that it *was* wrong, you would do well to revise it.

Harsanyi defends the link between the concession rule and the probability of concession by deriving it from several axioms one of which he calls the "symmetric-expectations postulate." This runs as follows: "You cannot choose your bargaining strategy...on the expectation that a rational opponent will choose a *different* bargaining strategy from your own and, in particular, that he will choose a bargaining strategy *more concessive* than you yourself would choose in the same situation."[16] Now suppose that Harsanyi is in the position of the rich person (R) and that both Harsanyi and the poor person (P) understand and acknowledge the way in which P's utility function places him at a strategic disadvantage. P might still somehow manage to make it sound really convincing that he will never settle for a penny less than an equal split of the money. What is Harsanyi to do? There may be a good deal of weeping and wailing and gnashing of teeth; but if he is really persuaded, he has no alternative, as a rational maximizer, to conceding P's demand. If he is such a slave to his theory as to insist on the Nash solution or nothing, then, if P meant what he said, he will get nothing. He may, of course, say that his theory predicts that P will not, when it comes to the crunch, stick to his "final offer." But, to repeat, that theory has no coercive power over P and may simply turn out to have made a false prediction in this case.

We can see, then, that the Nash solution is no panacea, but it can be rehabilitated if more modest claims are made for it. The point that I first want to make is that in bargaining it pays to be tough—so long as the other party isn't tough as well. A rational maximizer may insist that his "final offer" is really final; but two rational maximizers engaging in the same strategy are liable to find themselves deadlocked. This, however, contradicts elementary rationality as conceived of here. For the non-agreement point, so far from being Pareto optimal, is dominated by *every* agreement on the division of the $100 that gives each player something. Suppose that both of the parties are aware of the problem.

Might it not be prudent of them to seek a way of avoiding a showdown?

If once they see the danger of losing everything from actual bargaining, they may be attracted to the idea that they should look for some formula by which the dispute can be settled. If they can agree on a formula with the property that, when applied, it gets them to the Pareto frontier, they can avoid the risk of getting the nonagreement outcome as a by-product of their bargaining strategies. But what formula? Let us in this context examine the claims of the Nash solution for adoption.

One approach would be to say that what really matters is reaching an agreement on some terms that are mutually advantageous in comparison with the nonagreement outcome. The problem then is to find a formula on which the parties can agree. Anatol Rapoport, in his discussion of solutions such as those of Braithwaite and Raiffa (which will be discussed below), apparently takes this line. "The essence of fair compromise," he says, "is not in this formula or that but in the willingness of both parties to commit themselves in advance to abide by the consequences of *some* formula, which seems fair to them independently of the particular situation in which they may find themselves."[17] How do we look for a formula that is to be agreed upon in advance of any particular dispute that may arise? One answer is that proposed by Nash: we stipulate a number of apparently reasonable conditions that any solution should meet. If we can then show that one and only one formula satisfies these requirements, we can say that it has a unique claim. The claim is based on what Thomas Schelling called "mathematical esthetics."[18]

The Nash solution is, in this way of thinking about it, a "prominent solution" in a coordination game, and Schelling, who pioneered the study of such prominent solutions, actually canvassed the idea of bargaining solutions as proposed "prominent solutions" by virtue of their appeal to mathematical esthetics.[19] There are two objections to this approach. The first is that, if the players are simply looking for a prominent solution, the one that requires recourse to utility estimates hardly fills the bill. The von Neumann/Morgenstern utilities that are needed to apply the Nash solution are slippery things. It is difficult enough to form an honest estimate of one's own utilities; far more difficult to convince somebody else that one is telling the truth and not putting forward an estimate that is calculated to improve one's position in the Nash formula. (The question of strategic misrepresentation of preferences is of great importance and will be taken up at some length in chapter 3.) Even if only mathematical properties are to be used (and this seems reasonable when what is to be divided is a sum of money), it would surely be a good deal more obvious to take the money itself as the basis for applying mathematical esthetics than to take something as elusive and problematic as utilities. And then, I take it, the symmetrical properties of an equal division of the money would exert a powerful force on the imagination. "Prominence," or "obviousness," is in the eye of the beholder. The Nash solution and the competing utility-based solutions we shall go on to discuss are anything but obvious to most people. Perhaps we might sum up the first point, then, by saying that the Nash solution could function as a prominent solution only for a pair of mathematicians.

The second objection is that the problem of dividing the $100 is, after all, not a pure coordination game. (A pure coordination game is one in which the payoffs depend purely on the players' ability to reach an agreement, not on the form the agreement takes. The usual example is of two people who want to meet in some public place such as a store or an airport: it doesn't matter to either where they go so long as they both go to the same place.) It is true that a bargaining situation has something in common with a coordination game, namely, that there is a great premium on reaching agreement. Within limits, one might say, it is more important that an agreement be reached than that it be reached at one point as against another. But the limit of the truth of that is imposed precisely by the fact of a bargaining situation's not being a coordination game, so that it does make a difference at what point the agreement comes. Thus, we could imagine R saying that, much as he admires the esthetics of a fifty-fifty split, he is inclined to think that P will eventually come to see the practical attractions of a split that gives him only $30.

With this, we get back to the real strength of the Nash solution: that it is not simply a unique point recommended by mathematical esthetics, but does have some real claim to capture our intuitive sense of what makes for a strong or a weak bargaining position. It may appear that what I said a little while ago knocked the bottom out of this assertion; but this would, I believe, be a misconception. I have indeed denied that a rational maximizer can be advised with complete confidence that he or she has no chance of ever doing better than to settle for the Nash solution. Obstinacy may, if it is convincing enough, make up for a weak bargaining position. But that does not mean that the concept of a weak bargaining position has no application.

Suppose we up the stakes in the division of the money and make the story as follows. An eccentric millionaire has left the whole of his fortune—a million dollars exactly—to two people, to be shared between them in any way that they can agree upon. The will further states that if, within three months of probate, they do not reach an agreement on some division of the money, the entire million dollars shall be given to the government for the purpose of reducing the national debt. If they reach an agreement such that the sum of their two claims amounts to less than a million dollars, each shall inherit the amount specified in the agreement and the residue shall be applied to reducing the national debt.

Now let us say that P has borrowed from the Mafia a hundred thousand dollars and had no hope of repaying it. Until the millionaire died, he was resigned to the prospect of being added to the foundations of some building when the loan became due for repayment. R is already so rich that the odd hundred thousand dollars will not make a noticeable impact on his way of life, but for nine hundred thousand dollars he can fulfill a long-standing desire to run an Onassis-style cruising ship. He also knows about P's predicament and has no moral scruples about taking advantage of it. Surely we must admit that P really is in a weak position to hold out for an equal share of the million dollars. He may, indeed, be able to convince R that he would sooner have a concrete overcoat than settle for less than half, and he may thus prevail. But I must say that, if I were in his shoes, I would accept an unequal division; and I wonder how many readers of these words are really prepared to say that they would do otherwise.

Let us review the situation. It should be borne in mind that we are not now asking how rational actors will actually go through a process of negotiation, making offers and counteroffers, with the implied threat always in the background that unless the other party makes a concession no agreement will be reached and neither will get anything. We are now supposing that the parties have become sufficiently alarmed by the possibility of deadlock to break off direct bargaining over alternative divisions and instead retreat for a period to arguing over a formula that will divide all the money between them. They are now trying to see if they can agree on one.

In putting forward the Nash solution as such a formula, my reasoning is as follows. Each of the parties can, by refusing to accept any formula, push them both back into direct negotiation over the outcome. Assuming (as we are throughout) that the parties are rational utility-maximizers, neither will accept a formula providing less utility than it can expect to obtain from such direct negotiations. But how should that amount be estimated? A plausible answer is: Neither can expect to get more than the payoff associated with the Nash solution, and both have some chance of getting the nonagreement payoff. The Nash solution represents the outcome from among the set of Pareto optimal outcomes that corresponds to the balance of bargaining strength inherent in the situation. Neither party has any reason for conceding to the other party in advance more than the Nash solution provides for, and each stands to gain from eliminating the risk of nonagreement.

In practice, however, the unavailability of even approximately veridical estimates of utility makes all this appearance of exactitude quite misleading. This means that what has just been said can be translated into terms that sound much more appealing to common sense. We can say simply that rational parties will look for a formula that gives each of them as much as could have been expected from direct bargaining (allowing for the possibility of nonagreement), and anything which produces outcomes in the general area of the Nash solution should satisfy this requirement.

THE USES OF ARBITRATION

Back at the beginning of this section of the book I said that in the most straightforward conception of justice as mutual advantage the division proposed as fair by an arbitrator would correspond to the outcome of rational bargaining. I raised at that time the question of what in such a case would be the point of having an arbitrator, and promised to deal with it when I had explained the notion of a bargaining solution, using the particular example of the Nash solution. Having now done that, I can return to the original question.

In this subsection, then, I shall offer an analysis of the ways (for there are several) in which bargaining outcomes can play a part in the work of an arbitrator who is called upon to offer a solution to a conflict. I shall begin by arguing that the pursuit of individual advantage may well lead both parties to wish to call in an arbitrator. The simplest argument here is that in real life it may easily happen that the process of bargaining will fail to get the parties to the Pareto frontier. If each would lose too much in future credibility, for example, by backing away from his "final offer," the parties will just remain at the nonagreement point. It may be said that "rationality" is defined to preclude such a possibility.

But then we must point out that the conditions for it are extraordinarily strong. For the parties must somehow know enough about each other to guarantee that they will not become irrevocably committed to incompatible "final offers." The status of the concept of rationality as an ideal becomes very clear in this light.

One possibility that presents itself at this point is that the parties might recognize the danger of deadlock and agree to implement, say, the Nash solution. However, such an agreement is very far from bringing about by itself a determinate settlement. They must now agree on a pair of utility functions to be plugged into the formula. This, however, is simply the occasion for another bargaining game, which may prove just as intractable as the original one. Each party has an incentive to declare a utility function that puts it in as strong a position under the formula as it can possibly hope to get away with. There may be a wide gap between what each party declares about itself and what the other is prepared to accept from him; and there is no mechanism for resolving the dispute automatically. In the end, the credibility of a declared utility function can be maintained only by being willing to go to a showdown in defense of it. But it was precisely the risk of losing all in a showdown that we supposed would drive the parties to agree on applying the Nash formula in the first place.

A way out of this difficulty that might naturally occur to them would be to bring in a neutral third party to make the utility estimates. If they agree at the outset to abide by whatever determination she makes, they can assure themselves that their first agreement, on the Nash formula, will not be voided by lack of agreement on its implementation. We might suppose that, to make her task more feasible, they agree to turn over to her whatever financial information she asks for, to provide evidence about choices that they have actually made in the past in the face of uncertainty, and (if she thinks it worthwhile) to answer questions about the choices they would make among hypothetical lotteries.

Strictly speaking, we should probably not describe someone with such a limited mandate as an arbitrator at all. She is not being invited to propose a division of the money but simply to answer what is, in principle, an empirical question, even if it is one no answer to which is beyond challenge. We might without too much stretching compare the situation to one in which a buyer and a seller agree that if the picture is a genuine so-and-so it is worth one amount and if it is not then it is worth some other, lesser amount, and agree to accept as authoritative a certain art expert's judgment. There is, of course, an undeniable sense in which the art expert is deciding on the price at which the picture will change hands, but only in virtue of being entrusted with the task of making a determination of fact.

We can now imagine a further development. The parties might ask the arbitrator to estimate the terms of agreement that they would most likely have reached in direct negotiations. Clearly, if the argument up until now has been correct, the arbitrator should apply the Nash solution or at any rate work with some intuitive notion of relative bargaining strength roughly corresponding to that of the Nash solution. Since, as I have already observed, estimating utilities is not a precise art, there would be far less difference in practice than one might naively think between putting rough-and-ready numerical estimates into the Nash formula and going straight to a judgment about the balance of bargaining strengths.

The next step up in the arbitrator's discretion would be for the disputing parties to agree simply to put the decision in her hands without specifying the basis on which she is to resolve the issue: they simply bind themselves in advance to accept whatever decision she reaches. Now it might be thought that this step totally transforms the state of the question. For the arbitrator is now free, we might think, to impose whatever solution appeals to her own sense of justice. Since the parties have committed themselves to accepting her decision and have not stipulated that it should approximate the outcome of direct negotiation, she can ignore considerations of bargaining strength completely. Suppose she believes that P obviously needs the money far more than does R, or finds P a more deserving case than R. Then, we might say, she is free to award the whole million dollars to P, even while acknowledging that such an outcome could never have arisen out of a process of bargaining.

Before we get carried away by this, however, we should take account of constraints that operate even where the arbitrator is given complete discretion. We must bear in mind that the arbitrator can get appointed in the first place only with the consent of the parties. This is crucial, as we can see if we ask what qualities rational disputants would look for in an arbitrator. It would not, for a start, be rational for either of them to buy a pig in a poke. If they had wanted to turn the negotiation into a gamble they could have spun a coin rather than bothering to call in an arbitrator. They will, then, look at people with settled and known principles or (even better) an extensive record of previous decisions in somewhat similar cases.

Each side will, we may suppose, make an estimate of the likely outcome of having the dispute adjudicated by one proposed arbitrator or another. Each will then press the claims of those whom it expects to be favorable and veto those whom it expects to be unfavorable. Perhaps it will turn out that no appointment can be made: it is possible that all those who are not vetoed by one side will be vetoed by the other. In that case, the parties must revert to direct bargaining. But since each side will refuse to accept any arbitrator whose decision it expects to be less favorable than the outcome of direct bargaining, this suggests that an arbitrator who is acceptable to both sides must be one whose decisions approximate the Nash solution.

Thus, there turns out to be less than meets the eye in the apparently significant differences between (a) agreeing on the Nash solution and appointing an arbitrator to apply it, (b) agreeing that the outcome should reflect relative bargaining strength and appointing an arbitrator with instructions to approximate the results of bargaining, and (c) agreeing on the appointment of an arbitrator without any specified limits on her discretion.

It is true that in the third case the parties will no doubt put forward whatever arguments they think may have an influence with the arbitrator, and these will usually include many points that have little or no bearing on the location of the bargaining outcome. Moreover, we should not be surprised if such arguments have some effect on the arbitrator's decision. For arbitrators do not normally simply announce a bare number such as, in a wage dispute, a number of dollars and cents per hour for the members of each occupational group. Rather, the concrete results tend to be derived from some general formula—for example, one taking account of the pay received by comparable workers in other firms, or of increases in the cost of living since the previous settlement. The skillful choice of a formula to propose to the arbitrator may therefore be instrumental in obtaining a marginally more favorable outcome.

The point I want to emphasize is, however, that an arbitrator will not be acceptable to both sides unless she is expected to stay within the range of outcomes that both prefer to the bargaining outcome discounted by the risk of nonagreement. Where, as in labor negotiations, the nonagreement outcome can be a strike crippling to both sides, the range within which the arbitrator can work will sometimes be quite wide. But even then any arbitrator whose decisions are consistently to the same side of the Nash solution must, as soon as this tendency is clearly established, be vetoed by the other side in future choices of an arbitrator.

Arbitrators who want to continue to be called upon thus have a good motive for approximating the Nash solution. For if they deviate from the Nash solution in a systematic way, one party will always veto them in future; and if they depart from it in an unsystematic way, both may veto them as too unpredictable. However, even if arbitrators were entirely unmoved by the desire to be reemployed later, we should still be on safe ground in predicting that most arbitrators at any given time will tend to produce adjudications that approximate the bargaining outcome, so long as the rate of entry is not too great. The argument is the familiar one from natural selection. Suppose that new-fledged arbitrators come with a wide assortment of principles: those who succumb to vetoes will be winnowed out, with the result that only those whose decisions approximate the bargaining outcome will, over time, stay in business.

The final stage in the sequence of increasing autonomy for the arbitrator is externally imposed arbitration. Here the parties cannot choose whether or not their dispute should be settled by arbitration, nor does the choice of an arbitrator depend on their agreement. This stage differs from the preceding ones in that the outcome of rational bargaining no longer exerts the same constraining force on the range of plausible arbitrated outcomes. For it is no longer possible for either party to insist on bargaining as an alternative to arbitration by an acceptable arbitrator. Even if one side is able to predict with confidence that it could do better by direct bargaining than it can expect to do from the award of a certain arbitrator, that makes no difference. The arbitrator can still be appointed, and her decision will be enforced on the parties by the authority that imposed arbitration in the first place.

What can we say in this case about the constraints on the arbitrated outcome? At first blush we might be tempted to say that arbitration imposed on the parties means that there are no constraints. But this would be to overlook constraints that, although easily taken for granted, are of enormous significance.

Let us imagine a law to the effect that wills of the kind that caused so much trouble earlier in this section shall in future be overridden. This law says that whenever a will specifies the heirs but does not specify a particular division among them, an arbitrator, whose decision shall be final, shall be appointed by the government to divide the money between the heirs. Suppose that the arbitrator who is appointed has strong egalitarian commitments and thinks wealth should be distributed equally. Or suppose she is a utilitarian and thinks that money should be distributed in whatever shares will maximize aggregate happiness. In either case, if R is enormously wealthy she may well award the whole legacy to P.

But we should notice two constraints that nevertheless operate to set bounds on the decision. Both constraints limit the scope of the decision to what is in dispute between the parties. First, the outcome lies on the Pareto frontier defined by the interests of the two parties. An egalitarian or utilitarian arbitrator not constrained in this way would very likely decide that the best thing to do is to give at least some—perhaps all—of the money to people other than the two legatees. And, second, the outcome lies on that segment of the Pareto frontier that is no worse for either party than the nonagreement point. Yet an arbitrator given only the restriction that the outcome must be on the Pareto frontier would have no reason to stop at awarding the whole legacy to P. She might well decide that in addition R should hand over a large part of his preexisting fortune to P.

A government could, of course, appoint a Commissioner for Redistribution who would be empowered to do either of the things that I have just said were excluded by the two constraints. (Post-revolutionary land reform or reallocation of housing space sometimes takes this *ad hoc* form. In more settled regimes, one would expect redistribution of this kind to occur via general rules.) But the point is that we would then have moved beyond arbitration altogether. Thus, although imposed arbitration removes the constraint set by the outcome of rational bargaining, we can see that it still occurs within the bargaining framework, which we may take to be specified by two features. First, there is a nonagreement point, and the payoff at this point sets a floor under what either party can finish up with. And second, the cooperative surplus to be achieved by moving from the nonagreement point to the Pareto frontier is to be shared among the parties.

In the next chapter I shall introduce challenges to this framework. The remainder of the present chapter, however, will be devoted to exploring it further. By bringing in a more complicated example than that of the legacy (though still one involving only two people), I shall be able to introduce two new problems. First, I shall show that the definition of the nonagreement point may be a good deal more difficult than it was in our legacy example. And, second, I shall show that there are alternatives to the Nash solution as a way of dividing the cooperative surplus.

I can also promise that the word "fair" will make an appearance. The main work of this chapter is, however, expository. I shall therefore postpone until chapter 2 a systematic discussion of the case for and against regarding any of these solutions as fair.

3. TWO LECTURES

The title of Part I, "Don't Shoot the Trumpeter!" unites two lectures, one given to a mining community in the Rocky Mountains, the other to an academic community in the Cambridgeshire fens. The first lecture was given by Oscar Wilde when, during his tour of America, he visited Leadville, Colorado, the mining town of legendary violence. After his return to England, Wilde recounted his experiences under the title "Impressions of America."

> They are miners—men working in metals, so I lectured to them on the Ethics of Art. I read them passages from the autobiography of Benvenuto Cellini and they seemed much delighted. I was reproved by my hearers for not having brought him with me. I explained that he had been dead for some little time which elicited the enquiry "Who shot him"? They afterwards took me to a dancing saloon where I saw the only rational method of art criticism I have ever come across. Over the piano was printed a notice:

> PLEASE DO NOT SHOOT THE
>
> PIANIST.
>
> HE IS DOING HIS BEST.

> The mortality among pianists in that place is marvellous.[20]

Wilde's account has been denounced by a historian of the Colorado gold rush as "stupid and almost incredibly naive."[21] And the authors of a book about Wilde's trip describe him returning to his hotel after the lecture and a tour of the sights for "a few hours of sweet dreams about a preposterous Leadville which would grow more preposterous as his dreams, his wit, his drinks, and his imagination played upon it."[22] Doubt has been cast on the veracity of the story about Benvenuto Cellini.[23] And although nobody denies that violence was endemic—the local newspaper waggishly "ran a daily column called 'Breakfast Bullets,' tabulating the night's crimes"[24] —we are assured that Wyman's Great Saloon was "orderly and well run" and that it "witnessed few brawls and caused no public scandals."[25] In one respect, however, Wilde seems to have cleaned up the facts, for according to contemporary records Wyman's notice had the more robust wording: *"Don't Shoot the Pianist—He's Doing His Damnedest."*[26]

The other lecture was the inaugural lecture by R. B. Braithwaite mentioned earlier. The lecture, whose title was *Theory of Games as a Tool for the Moral Philosopher*, was constructed around the problem of a pianist named Luke and a trumpeter named Matthew with the common misfortune of living in adjacent unsoundproofed rooms and having only the same one hour a day in which to practice their instruments. Given that each finds it distracting to have to practice while the other is also practicing, the Pareto frontier is defined as Matthew playing solo every evening, Luke playing solo every evening, and every ratio in between. The question posed to an arbitrator is: What would be a fair way of dividing up the precious playing time between the two men?

Braithwaite, who acknowledges that his interest in the so-called problem of fair division was aroused by Nash's article "The Bargaining Problem," follows Nash in stipulating a two-stage process of arbitration. First, a nonagreement point has to be established. The utilities at this point, which functions as an origin, can be set at zero, subtracting each man's utilities at the nonagreement point from all others. At the second stage, the arbitrator moves the parties out from the nonagreement point to the Pareto frontier in accordance with some formula—the particular solution concept that she regards as appropriate.

Braithwaite's own characterization of his procedure runs as follows:

> The neither wholly competitive nor wholly non-competitive collaboration between Luke and Matthew may thus be regarded as a competition between them for relative advantage, followed by a wholly non-competitive collaboration between them for maximizing their utilities on condition that the relative advantage given by the prudential strategy recommendation for the wholly competitive part of the situation is preserved. In economic language, the problem of fair distribution will first be solved, and its solution will enable us to solve the problem, otherwise insoluble, of how production should be maximized.[27]

In more precise economic language, it should be said that "maximization" is a misleading word in the context, since there is never any question, for Braithwaite, of *adding* the utilities of the two men. What he has in mind is Pareto optimality.

Fairness is to be defined, then, in terms of a two-step procedure. First, we have to define a nonagreement point, which tells us what the parties could get without cooperating, and then we move from that point to one on the Pareto frontier. But how do we establish a nonagreement point for the case of the trumpeter and the pianist? In the problem of dividing up the money, the nonagreement point was specified in the description of the situation: in the absence of agreement neither party got any money. Nash, in "The Bargaining Problem," had in mind as a paradigm of a bargaining problem an ordinary case of contract where the nonagreement point is the *status quo*. But it is, of course, also possible to have a bargaining problem with threats: in the absence of moral or legal constraints the poor person might threaten to put a dent in the rich one's new Mercedes unless he agrees to a favorable division of the $100, and the rich person might threaten to call in some previous debt of the poor person's. (Nash himself in fact developed an extension of the original analysis to incorporate a theory of "optimal threats.")[28]

In Braithwaite's story there is no built-in nonagreement point. He therefore suggests that the nonagreement point should be determined on the basis of optimal threats. That is to say, each of the two musicians tries to create a nonagreement outcome that is as favorable as possible to him when the formula for a move to the Pareto frontier is applied to it. What constitutes an optimal threat depends on the preferences of the two men. Braithwaite stipulates that their preference orderings are as follows. Each would prefer most to play alone and each would next prefer to be silent while the other plays. Matthew, the trumpeter, would next prefer that both play and he puts silence last, while Luke, the pianist, prefers silence to cacophony. Each man will make the arbitrated outcome more favorable, from his own point of view, by getting his own utility at the nonagreement point as high as possible or the other's as low as possible. More precisely, each wants to maximize his relative advantage at the nonagreement point. The "threat game" is thus a zero-sum game: whatever is an improvement in the nonagreement point for one is a deterioration in it for the other.

In the case postulated by Braithwaite, this prescription has the implication that the nonagreement outcome should be one in which both men play every evening. For if one of them does not play on any evening he lets the other improve his starting point by giving him the outcome (playing solo) he most likes. Admittedly, cacophony is the worst outcome only for the pianist, Luke, but there is no way in which he can bring about the worst outcome for Matthew, the trumpeter. What Matthew dislikes most is silence, but if Luke tries to bring this about by not playing himself, all he does is to give Matthew the opportunity of playing his trumpet without interference and thus getting the outcome he likes the most.

This conception of the way to arrive at the nonagreement point is common to Nash and Braithwaite (as Braithwaite himself notes). Where he departs from Nash is in proposing a different formula for moving from the nonagreement point to the Pareto frontier. I shall examine it, and the rationale for it offered by Braithwaite, in the next section. For the present purpose, all that we have to keep in mind is that the adjudicated outcome depends on relative advantage at the nonagreement point. Because the nonagreement point of cacophony is worst for Luke and only next worst for Matthew, Matthew finishes up playing his trumpet over half the time. If the preferences of Matthew and Luke between silence and cacophony were reversed, Luke would play the piano over half the time. And if they both put the nonagreement point of cacophony in the same position in their utilities, Braithwaite's formula would have each of them playing solo half the time.

Within Braithwaite's solution, then, Matthew does better than Luke because he has the "threat advantage": he wins the "threat game" which defines the nonagreement point. Many commentators regard this as an outrageous reason for letting the trumpeter play more often, as we shall see in section 8. But the fault lies not in the trumpeter but in the theory. So don't shoot the trumpeter for doing his best. If we dislike the outcome we ought to conclude that he should never have been placed in a position where doing his best—which here amount to doing his worst—improves his prospects for playing solo when the arbitrator makes the award.

4. BRAITHWAITE VERSUS NASH

THE NASH SOLUTION
TO BRAITHWAITE'S PROBLEM

Since Braithwaite's solution was developed from Nash's, and Braithwaite explicitly criticizes the arbitrated division of playing time given by the Nash solution, we should begin by seeing how the Nash solution applies to Braithwaite's problem. As we have seen, the Nash solution requires that we have von Neumann/Morgenstern utility information, and so does Braithwaite's own solution.

Braithwaite gives us for each man the ratios of the utilities of the four

Matthew

		Play	Not play
Luke	Play	1, 2	7, 3
	Not play	4, 10	2, 1

Figure 1.2.   Payoff Matrix for Braithwaite's Problem

possible outcomes. For ease of exposition, I shall follow Luce and Raiffa and turn Braithwaite's ratios into numbers by calling the lowest payoff to each man one unit of utility and then scaling up the other payoffs appropriately.[29] This gives us the payoff matrix shown in Figure 1.2.

The matrix exhibits Luke's alternative choices, of playing and not playing, one above the other. This shows that he can determine whether the outcome will be in the top row or the bottom row. Matthew's two options are arranged side by side, showing that he can determine whether the outcome lies in the left-hand column or the right-hand column. The utilities arising from each of the four possible combinations of choices are displayed in the cells. Luke's are in each case represented by the first number, Matthew's by the number after the comma.

It should be emphasized that the numbers can be given only as much meaning as is permitted by their method of construction out of a series of lotteries over the pure outcomes. The only aspect of the numbers that must be preserved to avoid changing the information is the ratio between each man's most preferred outcome, next most preferred, and so on. (I shall, to avoid circumlocution, talk in what follows of "Braithwaite's utilities" when I refer to the numbers in the payoff matrix. It should, however, be borne in mind that the numbers are those of Luce and Raiffa: only the ratios can be attributed to Braithwaite. This caution will be especially pertinent when I ask, as I shall from time to time, what would be the implications of taking the numbers in the payoff matrix as representing full-blown interpersonally comparable utilities.) It is worth making explicit here an assumption that Braithwaite makes about these ratios, since it strongly affects the results. This is that the same ratios hold good for any evening regardless of what has happened on preceding evenings. Neither of the two men becomes increasingly satiated by playing, for example, or increasingly tired of listening to the other play.

Matthew

		Play		Not play	
	Play	0,	0	6,	1
Luke	Not play	3,	8	1,	−1

Figure 1.3.   Transformed Matrix for Braithwaite's Problem

As I have already mentioned, Nash himself recommended that his solution, when extended from simple bargaining situations to those like that of the two musicians, should take as the origin the point corresponding to the outcome of optimal threats. We should therefore take as our origin the outcome where both men play, and subtract from each man's payoffs the amount that he gets from this outcome. This gives us the transformed matrix shown in Figure 1.3, which sets the utility that each man derives from the nonagreement point at zero.

The Nash solution picks out the division of playing time that maximizes the product of the two men's utilities. Thus, if Matthew plays all the time, he always gets eight units from playing and Luke always gets three units from listening, for a product of twenty-four. If Matthew plays nine-tenths of the time and Luke the remaining one-tenth, Matthew gets eight units from playing nine-tenths of the time and one unit from listening one-tenth of the time, so his utility is $(0.9 \times 8) + (0.1 \times 1) = 7.3$. Luke's utility, arrived at similarly, is 3.3 units. The product is 24.09—a little higher than when Matthew plays all the time. As Matthew plays less, beyond this point, the product of utilities falls. (When he plays 80 percent of the time, for example, the product of utilities declines to 23.76 units.) Thus we can see that the product of utilities must reach a maximum somewhere around a nine-to-one division of playing time in favor of Matthew. In fact, the maximum occurs at a point a little more favorable to Matthew than that. The Nash solution tells us that Matthew should play about 93 percent of the time. (The product of utilities at this point is slightly in excess of 24.1 units.)

The lopsidedness of this division may seem surprising. But it is, after all, a virtue in a theory that it should yield surprising conclusions, so long as they can be shown on further reflection to be reasonable. I believe that our confidence in the soundness of the Nash solution as a way of representing bargaining power will be increased when we look carefully at the way in which it works here.

Wherein, then, lies Matthew's strategic advantage? The answer may be obtained by comparing the payoffs that enter into the solution: those of cacophony (the nonagreement point) and those of playing solo and listening to the other play solo (the possible constituents of the Pareto set). If we compare the ratios we shall see that whereas Matthew derives eight times as much utility from playing himself as from listening to Luke playing, Luke derives half as much utility from listening to Matthew as he does from playing himself.

Pushing the analysis back to the lotteries that underlie such statements about utility, we can express the comparison in the following terms: Matthew would accept a lottery giving him anything better than one chance in eight of playing solo himself (the other seven chances being of cacophony) rather than listen to Luke. But Luke would rather listen to Matthew play than take anything less than a fifty-fifty chance of playing solo himself (the other outcome again being cacophony). We can if we like express the same relationships in terms of frequency: Matthew would be as willing to have one evening of solo practice at the price of seven nights of cacophony as to listen to Luke play every evening; Luke would be as willing to listen to Matthew every evening as he would be to play himself half the time and endure cacophony the other half.

If we do find the Nash solution surprising, I think the main reason is that it is hard to put ourselves into the shoes of Luke. It would be unusual enough to find two amateur musicians next door to one another who both preferred to listen to the other practice over having silence. But what are we to say of a classical pianist who enjoys listening to the efforts of a jazz trumpeter so much that he would prefer to listen every evening if the alternative is playing solo just under half the time and playing simultaneously with him just over half the time? He surely would be a rare bird. Suppose, however, that the utilities really are as stated, and furthermore that both parties know that they are as stated. Then I think the Nash solution is, on reflection, quite intuitively acceptable as a surrogate for the outcome of an actual bargaining process.

The requirement that each party or the arbitrator knows the utilities of both is, of course, a big hurdle. It is, certainly, an even bigger hurdle when, as here, the utilities depend on personal taste than when (as in our examples in section 2) they are largely determined by objective financial circumstances. But we do not have to be too literal about it. It might, after all, be really quite clear that Luke likes to listen to Matthew a good deal more than Matthew likes to listen to Luke. (Suppose, for example, that Matthew is very good and Luke painfully bad.) We could then imagine Matthew saying to Luke (assuming he was not constrained by moral scruples, friendship, or the need for Luke's cooperation or forbearance in some other matter) something on these lines: "It's really silly our both playing every evening like this. Neither of us enjoys it. The question is what to do. Now the fact is that I like listening to you playing very little more than I enjoy the present racket every evening. But you, I happen to know, have told people that you quite like listening to me practice—not as much as you like practicing yourself when you can hear yourself play, but a great deal more than you like to play at the same time as me. In the circumstances, there's very little in it for me in not playing rather than playing but a lot in it for you. If we don't reach an agreement, I expect I'll just go on playing every evening anyway, and I think that you'll eventually get tired of making yourself miserable just to annoy me, and will settle for listening. But out of the goodness of my heart I'll offer you one evening in every two weeks to yourself if you'll leave me with the rest. Take it or leave it!"

One does not have to like what is going on here to see that Matthew has a strong position. And if he has a strong position, then the Nash solution, in spite of the highly unequal division of playing time it generates, is indeed plausible as an arbitrated outcome that approximates the outcome that one might expect rational actors to arrive at by bargaining.

BRAITHWAITE'S CRITICISM AND ALTERNATIVE

In one of the endnotes to *Theory of Games as a Tool for the Moral Philosopher*, Braithwaite devotes almost a page to the Nash solution.[30] He points out that Nash and he have the same procedure for establishing the origin as "the solution of a 'threat game'" and then describes the differences between Nash's way of getting from the origin to the Pareto frontier and his own. Nash's solution, he observes, "would work out at dividing the playing time in the ratio of 1 for Luke to 13 for Matthew." And he points out that if Luke's payoffs were just a little different, so that his utility from listening to Matthew play were $4\frac{1}{2}$ instead of 4, "Matthew would play every evening and Luke never." (This is true: the product of utilities for this case reaches a maximum when Matthew plays all the time.) Braithwaite concludes the footnote by saying: "These recommendations seem to me clearly unfair on Luke."

But why does Braithwaite find these implications so clearly unfair? The text to which the note is attached suggests that he has some independent standard of fairness according to which a split of thirteen to one (or *a fortiori* all to nothing) is an intrinsically unfair division of playing time.

> My recommendation as to how Luke and Matthew should maximize production while maintaining a fair distribution is, of course, not the only recommendation that can be made. . . . Nash has proposed a general form of recommendation and I have tried out other general forms, all of which would give different results in our example. But my common-sense judgement of fairness is against all of them. So my recommendation has, I think, the negative virtue of being superior to the alternative recommendations that have been worked out.[31]

The natural way of reading this is that Braithwaite has an intuitive idea of what a fair division of playing time would be and that the task of the theorist is to come up with a formula that will approximate these results in a variety of cases. His own solution produces an adjudicated outcome in which Matthew plays on 27 evenings to every 16 on which Luke plays, thanks to Matthew's "threat advantage."[32] This suggests that Braithwaite's intuitions are against any extremely unequal division of playing time: his own solution has Matthew playing about 63 percent of the time, as against about 93 percent under the Nash solution.

But we must recognize that there is absolutely nothing in Braithwaite's solution, any more than in Nash's, to guarantee that there be any limits on the inequality between the shares of Matthew and Luke. By adjusting the silence/cacophony ratios so as to increase Matthew's "threat advantage" we could give him any proportion of the playing time, including the 93 percent that Braithwaite finds so clearly objectionable. Indeed, just as the Nash solution could have Matthew playing all the time, so could Braithwaite's solution. All we have to do (as Rawls noted in a discussion to which we shall return in section 8)[33] is to make Matthew indifferent between playing solo and playing at the same time as Luke. Matthew can now obtain his maximum possible utility by playing all the time, whether Luke plays or not. He therefore has no need of Luke's cooperation; or, to put it the other way round, Luke has nothing to offer to Matthew in return for which Matthew might be induced to let up on some evenings. A Braithwaitean arbitrator would therefore have to say that Matthew must play all the time, and

Luke will have to make the best of it by listening all the time. (Note that this solution is on the Pareto frontier, which means that one person's position could be made better only if the other's were made worse.)

It should, however, be said that the rationale in terms of some intuition about a fair division of playing time is not central to Braithwaite's lecture. This comes out even in the paragraph from which I have quoted all but the last sentence. For, after he has said that his own theory has the virtue of according best with his commonsense judgment of fairness, Braithwaite concludes: "But I cannot expect Luke and Matthew to agree to it merely on that account."[34]

What then is the primary reason that Braithwaite offers for calling his own solution a fair one? In the pages following that sentence, Braithwaite develops an answer on these lines. A solution is fair if it has the property that Matthew and Luke gain equally in the move from the nonagreement point to the Pareto frontier. The division of playing time generated by his own formula, Braithwaite claims, has this property.

Now to say that both men gain equally from a certain outcome implies that one has a way of bringing their utility schedules into some relation with one another. There is nothing in von Neumann/Morgenstern utilities themselves that enables us to do this. They are simply ratios giving each person's relative preference for outcomes. Braithwaite maintains, however, that he has a way of bringing the two men's utilities into relation with one another, using the strategic structure of the game as his guide. Thus, he says that his solution does indeed involve "making a comparison between Luke's and Matthew's preference scales," but that it is one which "is limited to the question of their fair collaboration in this particular example. I am not asserting that [Luke's] utilities should be related in this way to [Matthew's] utilities for all purposes, but only for assessing the fairness of their shares in one particular common task."[35]

Because Braithwaite's way of comparing the utilities makes use of the strategic aspects of the situation, it is hard to distinguish it from a straightforwardly strategic rationale. For to say that each party gains equally when the formula for comparing utilities is based on strategic considerations may be no more than a fancy way of saying that the solution corresponds to the bargaining power of the players. Indeed, as we shall see in the next section, the Nash solution can also be presented as fair in virtue of giving equal gains in utility to both parties. But it is, I think, clear there that this is simply a restatement, invoking the concept of fairness, of the rationale developed by Harsanyi for saying that the

Nash solution would fall out of a strategically motivated rule for making concessions.

I conclude that we can best regard Braithwaite as offering two justifications for his solution. The first, which occupies roughly the second third of Braithwaite's book (the first third is devoted to laying out the problem), emphasizes the strategic rationale. The line here is that the adjudicated outcome is fair because it gives the parties as much as they could reasonably hope to obtain by bargaining. It is worth noticing that, in "The Bargaining Problem," Nash offered precisely this justification (in a very perfunctory way) for the claim that his solution was fair. Thus, he wrote:

> Now since our solution should consist of *rational* expectations of gain by the two bargainers, these expectations should be realizable by an appropriate agreement between the two. Hence, there should be an available anticipation which gives each the amount of satisfaction he should expect to get. It is reasonable to assume that the two, being rational, would simply agree to that anticipation, or an equivalent one. Hence, we may think of one point in the set of the graph [i.e., the Nash point] as representing the solution, and also representing all anticipations that the two might agree upon as *fair bargains*.[36]

The second argument offered by Braithwaite for his solution occupies most of the last third of the lecture. This claims that the structure of the game generates a certain way of bringing the two men's utility scales into relation with one another, and that in terms of this common measure each gains equally in the move from the nonagreement point to the utility frontier. It is therefore, he says, fair because both can be said to do equally well out of it.

Braithwaite's solution is quite complex, as is his rationale for it. It has a certain perverse ingenuity that makes it worth investigating, for those who like that sort of thing. But for those who do not it is probably not worth the toil of working through it all. I have therefore put my exposition and critique of Braithwaite's theory into an appendix, Appendix A. I hope that this represents a reasonable compromise between scholarly integrity and humanity. All that is essential to grasp from the discussion of Braithwaite is that there are two closely related but distinct ideas now in play about the way in which the move should be made from the nonagreement point to the Pareto frontier: reflection of relative bargaining power, and preservation of relative positions at the nonagreement point, that is to say, equal utility gain.

5. BARGAINING AND
EQUAL UTILITY GAIN

It is not hard to see why two quite different rationales for picking an outcome in a game of fair division—that it represents an intrinsically fair division of the gains from cooperation and that it simulates the results of rational bargaining—should lead to the same set of solution concepts. For there is a common element that unites the solution concepts and fits in with both rationales, namely, the notion of an equal gain over the nonagreement point.

If we start by asking what would be an intrinsically fair division of the gain, it seems reasonable that, in the absence of some special claim by one of the parties, we should say that the fair division is an equal one. This might indeed be regarded as a tautology. The only question remaining is then in what units equal gain is to be measured, and all the solution concepts we are examining in this chapter take the relevant units to be units of utility constructed by some transformation of the parties' von Neumann/Morgenstern utilities so as to be comparable. Now suppose instead that we wish to simulate the results of rational bargaining. It is surely again plausible that we shall look for an outcome that is marked by equality—measured in some appropriate units, of course—since it is in the nature of a bargaining solution that it should balance the gains of the parties. That is to say, a bargaining equilibrium should occur at a point where both parties are equally satisfied with the outcome when they compare it to the alternative of the nonagreement point. Unless the outcome gives the parties equal gains in this sense it is not an equilibrium, because the one relatively less satisfied with it has less to lose than the other from upsetting it. It will therefore hardly be surprising to find that the Nash solution has itself been promoted as being fair in the sense that it provides the parties with equal utility gains over the nonagreement point. I shall follow the form of the argument put forward by Otomar Bartos.[37]

Let us begin by going back to the rationale of the Nash solution that was presented in section 2 above. There the Nash solution emerged as the conclusion of a sequence of moves made in accordance with the rule that the party with more to lose by holding out should always be the one to make the next concession. So we may describe the Nash solution as the point at which both parties are risking the same utility loss (in terms of their own utilities) from pressing for more rather than

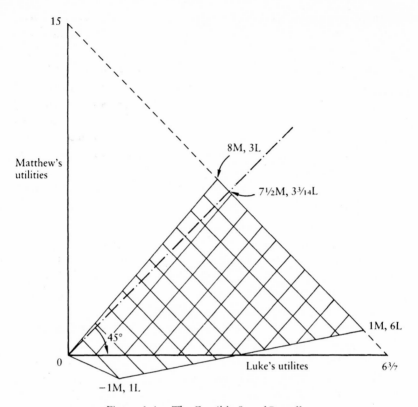

Figure 1.4.   The Feasible Set of Payoffs

accepting it. We can say that utility gain is equal if we transform the utilities in a certain way. In Figure 1.4, the payoffs for the range of possible outcomes make up the whole of the shaded area. The cross-hatched area within this corresponds to a subset of all possible outcomes known as the "feasible set." This is the set of outcomes that dominate the nonagreement point. The rationale for saying that other possible outcomes are infeasible is plainly the thought that nobody would voluntarily accept an agreement worse for him than he could get by refusing to agree. The northeast edge of the feasible set (and of the more inclusive set of possible outcomes) is the Pareto frontier. We construct the figure in such a way that when the Pareto frontier is extended to the axes the extended line cuts both axes at the same distance from the origin (the nonagreement point). We then draw a line from the origin that bisects the angle and divides the (extended) Pareto frontier into two equal parts. Where this 45° line crosses the Pareto frontier is the Nash solution. If it crossed the frontier outside the crosshatched area, the Nash solution would be the point within the crosshatched area closest to that point.

This construction enables us to check visually that the Nash solution is far closer to Matthew's end of the Pareto frontier than to Luke's. Matthew's maximum, when he plays all the time, gives him 8 units of utility to Luke's 3 and, as we see, the point at which the 45° line cuts the Pareto frontier is very close to this, at about 7.5 units for him and 3.2 for Luke. Translated into playing time, this allows Matthew to play about 93 percent of the time, as we already know.

This graphical method of presenting the Nash solution is, I think, valuable in helping to show how it works. It enables us, for example, to see just why it does not make any difference to the outcome picked by the Nash solution how much of the line joining the axes is in the cross-hatched area. All that matters is whether or not the crosshatched area includes within it the point on the Pareto frontier that is cut by a line at an angle of 45° from the origin.

However, I do not believe that the figure has much power to per-suade us that the Nash solution embodies an idea of equal gain over the nonagreement outcome. We can, indeed, define the units of utility so that the distance from the origin to the point where the extended Pareto frontier cuts the axis is one unit, and then it will necessarily turn out to be true that, in that measure, each participant obtains one-half of a unit at the Nash point. But the question is obviously left: Why should we define our units in that way? And it seems to me that there is really no answer that does not repeat the initial idea, namely, that at the Nash point each player has an equal relative amount to lose by going for more, compared with what he has already.

How convincing is this as a defense of the Nash solution's claim to be an embodiment of the criterion of equal gain? I have to confess that this seems to me a difficult question to answer, because it requires us to have an independent criterion of what constitutes an equal gain, whereas I take it that what constitutes an equal gain is precisely what is at issue. However, I think that, when we reflect on the way in which the primary rationale of the Nash solution is that it reflects relative bargaining strengths, we may be led to feel that this is not what we had in mind if we were attracted to the idea of equal gain as a criterion of fair division.

A little reflection on Figure 1.4 above may easily suggest a modifica-tion to the construction that will generate a variant on the Nash solu-tion. Instead of extending the Pareto frontier to the axes and making the

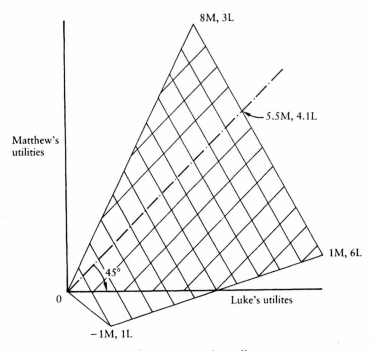

Figure 1.5.   Splitting the Difference

distances from the origin to the intersection equal, we might simply arrange things so that the maximum possible utility of each party is the same distance from the origin. We would then, as before, draw a 45° line from the origin and say that the solution lies where that line intersects the Pareto frontier. It will be seen in Figure 1.5 that this procedure is more favorable to Luke than was the Nash solution in the division of playing time it implies: the point of intersection is less close to Matthew's optimum. In fact, it allows Matthew to play about 63.5 percent of the time, which happens to be about where Braithwaite's solution came out.

The rationale for this procedure is, pretty plainly, that it is a method for "splitting the difference." What we are in effect doing is taking as our extremes at one end the most that each could achieve with the utmost cooperation of the other (playing on every evening while the other is silent) and at the other end the nonagreement point (the outcome of noncooperation). We are then saying that the fair outcome is one that gets each participant the same relative distance from his minimum to his maximum, when the minimum and maximum are defined in this way.

Obviously, saying that the nonagreement point within the game specifies the worst outcome reflects the ethical underpinnings of the two-stage approach. There may well be many ways in which Luke could make Matthew worse off than by resorting to the rather piddling expedient of playing the piano every evening. If he is a big burly fellow he might, for example, be able plausibly to threaten to knock Matthew's front teeth in, thus (among other things) ruining his trumpeting for good. But this is ruled out by the terms of the problem, which require that the nonagreement point be set within the game itself.

The nonagreement point also plays a part in defining the maximum that each can get, for the purposes of the equal-gain computation. In the Braithwaite example, the best that each can do for the other—remain silent while the other plays—is well above the nonagreement point of cacophony, so the proviso that no extra-game moves are allowed guarantees that neither can be made worse off than at the nonagreement point by doing the maximum amount for the other.

In the legacy examples that we analyzed earlier, the nonagreement point exactly coincides with what each gets when (within the limits of the game) he does the best he can possibly do for the other—that is, let him have the whole million dollars. Again, therefore, no additional limit is set on the maximum by the proviso that one person's maximum must be consistent with the other's getting the nonagreement payoff.

To see how the proviso that nobody should be made worse off than at the nonagreement point can have some bite even when we rule out extra-game moves, we need a case where the Pareto frontier runs to the left of the vertical axis or below the horizontal axis. Points beyond the axes are not in the feasible set (by definition) but may still be possible, in the sense that there are ways in which they could be brought about if the parties chose to do so. In fact, there is no difficulty at all in offering examples. They are usually ignored because we (quite reasonably) confine our attention normally to the feasible set, that is to say, to possibilities that are mutually advantageous to the parties in comparison with the nonagreement point.

To illustrate the point, consider the case of buying and selling a house. What are the maxima and minima in the game here? If we were simply to go by the light of nature, we would surely be inclined to say that the best deal that the owner of the house could offer the potential purchaser would be to give him the house free, and that the best deal the potential purchaser could offer the owner would be all the money he could possibly raise. We would then apply the principle of splitting the difference by finding a price for the house that would get each party an equal distance (measured in terms of utility) from its minimum to its maximum. However, the logic of the two-stage approach immediately imposes a discipline on the choice of minimum and maximum, giving us a theoretically grounded range that is in principle precisely defined. For the seller, the nonagreement point is the price below which he would sooner not sell; and for the buyer, it is the price above which he would sooner not buy.

If the least the seller would take for the house rather than keep it is $140,000 and the most the buyer would give for the house rather than lose it is $160,000, the best the buyer could do is to pay $140,000 and the best the seller could do is get $160,000. The criterion of splitting the difference says that the parties should get equally far from their minimum to their maximum. This means that each should gain equally in terms of utilities normalized so that the nonagreement utility is 0 and the maximum attainable (in the relevant sense) is 1.

What this implies for the sale price of the house cannot be determined without information about the parties' utility functions. We cannot assume that the price will be $150,000. The way in which the division diverges from inequality will take the same form as it does under the Nash solution: whichever party has most need of the money that is at stake (in this case the difference of $20,000 between seller's reservation price and buyer's highest bid) will get less than an equal share of it.

The point can be extended. We must observe that there is nothing in the nature of splitting the difference that leads automatically to a more equal division of the resource in dispute than the Nash solution. We might be tempted, by observing that splitting the difference was a good deal more favorable to Luke in Braithwaite's example than was the Nash solution, to conjecture that this is true in general. But if we look back at Table 1.1 and Figure 1.1 we see that splitting the difference gives a division of $70 to $30, which is very close to the Nash solution of $73 to $27. And we could easily construct an example in which the division arising from splitting the difference was *more* unequal than the one given by the Nash solution.

As I have pointed out, the Nash solution satisfies the condition that the contraction of the set of feasible alternative outcomes does not alter the outcome selected so long as that outcome remains available. It also satisfies the condition that when the feasible set is expanded the outcome selected either remains the same or shifts to one that is newly available. Whether or not these conditions (which are one possible interpretation of the notion of the "independence of irrelevant alternatives") are reasonable criteria to impose on a solution is not, I believe, something into which we have any immediate insight by the light of nature. All we can do is compare the Nash solution, which satisfies the conditions, with the solution of splitting the difference, which does not.

In order to come up with an example that will show as clearly as possible what is going on, let us assume that utility is linear with money. Where the sums involved are large, this is not a very plausible assumption, but it is reasonable enough if we imagine a case of a hundred dollars to be divided between two people each of whom is quite comfortably off. To put this in concrete terms, it implies that the people involved would be indifferent between, say, receiving ten dollars with certainty and a one in ten chance of receiving a hundred dollars. (Substitute a hundred thousand dollars for the first figure and a million dollars for the second figure and for most of us it would no longer be true that we would regard the alternatives with equal favor. But for ten dollars and a hundred dollars it may be approximately correct.)

Let us take up again our standard legacy case, with a nonagreement payoff of nothing but this time with only a hundred dollars to be divided. If the utilities of the parties are linear with money, we shall get an equal division of the hundred dollars out of the Nash solution and the same answer from the method of splitting the difference. To drive a wedge between the two solutions, we have to modify the standard story along the following lines. Suppose that the eccentric testator adds the stipulation that, whereas one of the legatees (call him U for Unlimited) can receive any amount agreed upon, in the usual way, the maximum amount that the other legatee (call him L for Limited) can receive out of the hundred dollars is fifty. If U and L reach an agreement on terms that yield more than one-half of the total to L, that agreement is null and void and neither gets anything. It is important to be clear that the modification takes exactly this form. The nonagreement point stays at nothing for both. We must be careful not to think of the case as one in which U is somehow guaranteed fifty dollars come what may. He is guaranteed nothing, and if he fails to reach an agreement with L (within the terms stipulated) nothing is what he will get.

It is not hard to see how the two solutions diverge in what they prescribe as the outcome of this case. The Nash solution says that the fifty-fifty split that would be prescribed in the standard case continues to hold good in this one. For the solution prescribed in the standard case is still available after the feasible set has been truncated by the stipulation that Matthew can receive no more than fifty dollars. Admittedly, the prescribed solution is now at a corner of the feasible set, but the Nash solution takes no account of such a consideration.

In contrast, splitting the difference prescribes that each person should get an equal distance from the nonagreement point to the maximum amount he could possibly get. The theory tells us that distance is to be measured in terms of utility. But since we have specified that in the present case utility is linear with money, we can say that they should get equally far along in terms of money. The minimum for each is zero; the maximum for U is a hundred dollars and for L fifty dollars. What division of a hundred dollars (we want a Pareto-optimal solution that will divide the whole amount up between the legatees) will give L and U the same proportion of fifty and a hundred dollars respectively? The answer is, obviously, that L should get one-third of the legacy and U two-thirds. Thus, rounding to the nearest penny, the splitting-the-difference solution awards \$33.33 to L and \$66.67 to U.

I must confess to being at a loss to discern the superior claim to fairness that some have claimed to discern here in splitting the difference. Insofar as I can say that I have any feelings about equity in this case, it seems to me a positive advantage of the Nash solution that, having established a fifty-fifty split as the fair outcome in the standard case, it does not alter its prescription merely because that outcome in the modified case represents the most that one of the parties could get. In the special sense defined by the Nash solution, each has an equal utility gain when the legacy is split equally in the one case as well as the other.

In case it is not apparent, I should perhaps add that, in the comparison of the way in which the two solutions respond to a truncation of the feasible set, nothing turns on the form of the utility functions that are assumed. I chose to make utilities linear with money in order to illustrate the contrast in the simplest possible way. I did not want the effect of truncating the feasible set to be confounded with effects flowing from the peculiarities of the utility functions. But it can be said with complete generality that, whatever the shapes of the utility functions, truncating the feasible set so that L's maximum becomes fifty dollars will always work to his disadvantage. He will finish up with less than he would have received on the splitting-the-difference formula in the standard case.

I should also observe that there is no special significance in the level at which L's maximum was set in the case as stated. Thus, for example, suppose that L's maximum were ninety dollars. On the formula for splitting the difference, L would still lose from such a proviso—though less, of course, than if the maximum were fifty dollars. (To be precise, L would now receive $47.37 to U's $52.63.) Or suppose that L's maximum were $10. The Nash solution would prescribe that, if the feasible set is truncated so as to exclude the Nash point, one should get as close to it as possible, so L would get his maximum of ten dollars under it. But splitting the difference means that, even here, each should receive the same proportion of his maximum. Thus, U would finish up with $90.91 and L with $9.09. I am inclined to think that this is a particularly awkward example for anyone who wishes to claim that we have some intuitive notion of fairness that should lead us to accept splitting the difference as a formula of fair division, even against the limited competition offered by the Nash solution.

I have pointed out that the Nash solution, originally introduced as a bargaining solution, has been argued for as an equal-gain solution as well. Symmetry would therefore lead us to predict that splitting the difference would be defended as a bargaining solution, and so we find. David Gauthier has argued in some detail for the superiority of splitting the difference to the Nash solution as a way of simulating rational bargaining. I find his arguments unpersuasive. But they raise a number of interesting and important questions about the appropriate criteria for evaluating proposed bargaining solutions. They are therefore worth discussing, but what comes later in this book does not turn on the details of the case for preferring the Nash solution to splitting the difference as a simulation of rational bargaining. I have for this reason put the discussion in a second appendix, Appendix B.

CHAPTER II

What Is a Fair Solution?

6. FAIR DIVISION
OF THE COOPERATIVE SURPLUS

We have seen that arbitration can most straightforwardly be seen as (to adapt Clausewitz) a continuation of bargaining by other means. The object of the arbitrator is to resolve a conflict on terms acceptable to both parties, when the parties consult their own interests in deciding what is acceptable. This entails that the arbitrator should seek to arrive at an adjudication that will as far as possible mimic the outcome of rational bargaining. If we want to formalize this process in a solution concept we shall look for one that captures the notion of relative bargaining strength and makes the outcome depend upon it. The rationale for such a solution is not hard to understand. As I pointed out in section 2, bargaining takes time and effort and even then may in the end fail to get the parties to the Pareto frontier. But saying that was to understate the true case for arbitration. For, at the point the analysis had reached in section 2, I had still not even introduced the kind of situation in which bargaining has the greatest potential for being costly. This is the kind where there is an advantage to be gained by making threats.

In the simple games dealt with in Nash's "The Bargaining Problem," the worst thing that could happen was that the parties might lose the chance to improve on the *status quo* and waste on the fruitless pursuit of an agreement the time and effort involved in the bargaining process. But where threats are made, the outcome may be that the parties are far worse off after the bargaining process has worked its way through than they would have been if the opportunity for mutual gain had never presented itself at all. For, if the parties get locked into their threats rather than moving to an agreement, they may well damage or even destroy one another in the process of carrying out what they have threatened to do.

All this makes it clear enough why rational people pursuing their own interests might wish to have their dispute settled by an arbitrator. But where does fairness come in? Why should we be inclined to think that an outcome reflecting bargaining strength in getting from the origin (i.e., the nonagreement point or threat point) to the Pareto frontier should be reckoned a fair one? Is it simply a mistake to call a solution concept whose claim is to simulate rational bargaining a solution to a problem of *fair* division? In putting this question to academic audiences in recent years, I have found that the overwhelmingly most common reaction of philosophers and nonphilosophers alike is to say that it is a mistake to talk about fairness here. Let me therefore put as persuasively as I possibly can the case for saying that there is indeed a sense, albeit attenuated, in which the simulated outcome of rational bargaining can in some contexts be regarded as fair.

The argument begins by asking us to accept that in certain situations no outcome of actual bargaining would be unfair. Both parties have certain rights whose exercise they can insist on, and nobody can say that any use they make of those rights is unfair. They can make use of them if they choose, or they can give them up in exchange for something they want more. (Thus in Braithwaite's example the two musicians give up the right to play every evening in return for a guarantee that they will be able to play solo on some evenings.) Unless one is prepared to concede this premise, I have to say that I do not see how the argument for the fairness of bargaining solutions can get started. Let us therefore for the sake of the argument concede it and move on. (I shall return to the question in section 38.)

The second leg of the argument now runs as follows. Although no outcome of actual bargaining would be unfair, this does not mean that no decision by an arbitrator can be unfair. And in fact what makes the arbitrator's decision fair is that it gives the parties as much as they could reasonably have hoped to obtain from actual bargaining. Thus, an arbitrator should use (or at any rate should behave as if using) a solution concept that mimics the results of rational bargaining.

The question that is still left hanging by this move is, obviously: Why should we call such an adjudication fair? The economists and game theorists who have addressed themselves to the so-called problem of fair division have tended to take over the presuppositions underlying the framework without questioning them and to concentrate on the technical issues involving the choice of solution concepts. However, if we try to reconstruct an argument for it we cannot, I think, do better than consult Thomas Hobbes, the supreme political theorist of rational prudence.

For our present purpose, two things are relevant in Hobbes's theory. The first is that, like Nash and Braithwaite, Hobbes allows threats to enter into the baseline from which agreements are to be made for mutual advantage. Agreements entered into out of fear—including fear deliberately created by the other party to induce compliance with the terms it offers—are valid, according to Hobbes. The second relevant point is that for Hobbes there is no independent standard by which the fairness of *agreements* can be assessed, but at the same time it is possible for an *arbitrator* to behave unfairly.

> Justice of Actions, is by Writers divided into *Commutative*, and *Distributive*: and the former they say consisteth in proportion Arithmeticall; the later in proportion Geometricall. Commutative therefore, they place in the equality of value of the things contracted for; and Distributive, in the distribution of equall benefit, to men of equall merit. As if it were Injustice to sell dearer than we buy; or to give more to a man than he merits. The value of all things contracted for, is measured by the Appetite of the Contractors: and therefore the just value, is that which they be contented to give. And Merit (besides that which is by Covenant, where the performance on one part, meriteth the performance of the other part, and falls under Justice Commutative, not Distributive,) is not due by Justice; but is rewarded of Grace onely. And therefore this distinction, in the sense wherein it useth to be expounded, is not right. To speak properly, Commutative Justice, is the Justice of a Contractor; that is, a Performance of Covenant, in Buying, and Selling; Hiring, and Letting to Hire; Lending, and Borrowing; Exchanging, Bartering, and other acts of Contract.
>
> And Distributive Justice, the Justice of an Arbitrator; that is to say, the act of defining what is Just. Wherein, (being trusted by them that make him Arbitrator,) if he performe his Trust, he is said to distribute to every man his own: and this is indeed Just Distribution, and may be called (though improperly) Distributive Justice; but more properly Equity; which also is a Law of Nature. . . .
>
> Also if *a man be trusted to judge between man and man*, it is a precept of the Law of Nature, *that he deale Equally between them*. For without that, the Controversies of men cannot be determined but by Warre. He therefore that is partiall in judgment, doth what in him lies, to deterre men from the

use of Judges, and Arbitrators; and consequently, (against the fundamentall Lawe of Nature) is the cause of Warre.

The observance of this law, from the equall distribution to each man, of that which in reason belongeth to him, is called EQUITY, and (as I have sayd before) distributive Justice: the violation, *Acception of persons.*[1]

Thus, if the parties reach an agreement, there is no way of challenging it: justice is the carrying out of the contract or covenant and has no applicability to its terms. But if, to avoid having to fight about it, the parties turn their dispute over to an arbitrator, that arbitrator has to behave impartially. Otherwise the institution of arbitration, which is so useful as a means to the advantages of peace, will be discredited and will be less likely to be resorted to in future.[2]

Hobbes takes the idea of "dealing equally" quite literally, so that equity entails equal distribution. Thus, immediately after the passage quoted, Hobbes says that

from this followeth another law, *That such things as cannot be divided, be enjoyed in Common, if it can be; and if the quantity of the thing permit, without Stint; otherwise Proportionably to the number of them that have Right.* For otherwise the distribution is Unequall, and contrary to Equitie.

But some things there be, that can neither be divided, nor enjoyed in common. Then, The Law of Nature, which prescribeth Equity, requireth, *That the Entire Right; or else, (making the use alternate,) the First Possession, be determined by Lot.* For equall distribution, is of the Law of Nature; and other means of equall distribution cannot be imagined.

Of *Lots* there be two sorts, *Arbitrary,* and *Naturall.* Arbitrary, is that which is agreed on by the Competitors: Naturall, is either *Primogeniture,* (which the Greek calls κληρονομία, which signifies, *Given by Lot;*) or *First Seisure.*

And therefore those things which cannot be enjoyed in common, nor divided, ought to be adjudged to the First Possessor; and in some cases to the First-Borne, as acquired by Lot.[3]

What exactly is the link for Hobbes between equity—the justice of an arbitrator—and equality? I believe that the answer most in line with Hobbes's overall theory would go as follows: human beings are too close to equality in natural powers to enable any rule other than equality to have any prospect of general acceptance in a state of nature;[4] therefore, an arbitrator must make an equal division of what is in dispute. If this is a correct interpretation of Hobbes's case for equality, then it must follow that, if the relative power of the parties were very unequal, the division would have to be correspondingly unequal.

Suppose that people are in a society, so that Hobbes's argument about the rough natural equality of strength and intellect is no longer decisive. The state sets limits on the means that people can use to advance their interests, and it is this that, for example, enabled the rich man to gain at the expense of the poor man in the case of the legacy analyzed in chapter 1. The force of the state stands behind the rich man to protect him against the threats of physical violence by which the poor man might otherwise seek to equalize their positions. At the same time, the state does not make all allocations. It sets up a framework specifying legitimate and illegitimate moves but, within the limits of what is allowed, people are left to bargain with one another. (This is true for all societies; the difference is in the amount left for bargaining, which is greater in the United States than in the Soviet Union, for example.) Where an allocation is subject to bargaining, the case for arbitration is still strong in a society—it is not confined to a Hobbesian state of nature. In situations of unequal power, then, it would seem, as we saw in section 2, that the arbitrator should not depart too far from the balance of power between the parties in making her award. For if she does not give the stronger party what it could reasonably have hoped for from direct bargaining, she makes agreed resort to arbitration less likely in the future. The party that feels itself to be the stronger will be less willing to submit a future dispute to arbitration.

With this in mind, we can return to our original question: In what sense can a bargaining solution be said to be fair? Suppose it is claimed that the Nash solution yields to the parties what they could reasonably expect to get in a process of bargaining. How does this constitute an argument for its fairness? The answer is not exactly that it is its satisfying reasonable expectations that makes the solution fair. Rather, it is that a bargaining solution is one that rational actors can endorse— because it satisfies reasonable expectations. It is what an arbitrator acceptable to both sides would come up with, and this gives it a claim to be considered as fair.

As I said in introducing this conception of a fair division, it appears to me to depend absolutely on the assumption—made explicit by Hobbes —that nothing the parties themselves arrived at could be unfair. If we reject this then it seems to me that we are inevitably led to the view that the rationale of a fair adjudication cannot be that it mimics the results of rational bargaining. We shall then have to propose some independent notion of what constitutes a fair way of dividing the cooperative surplus, such as the criterion that the parties should gain equal relative amounts of utility. As we saw in the previous chapter, it is possible to make the argument that a fair adjudication, understood in this manner, will in fact always correspond to a bargaining solution. But then it is a matter of establishing the correspondence, as Bartos attempted to do for the Nash solution and Gauthier for splitting the difference (see section 5). The two rationales for the same solution remain separate.

In interpreting Hobbes's claim that equity called for equality, I took him as making only a contingent claim: that where the bargaining power of the parties was approximately equal the arbitrator should divide the thing in dispute equally. It may have been felt that this interpretation was somewhat strained and that the natural way to read Hobbes was to take him as saying that, if the parties agree to hand over their dispute to an arbitrator, the arbitrator should act equitably, which always entails equality in the division of the thing in dispute, either by actually splitting it or, where this cannot be done, giving the parties an equal chance of getting it. I have already explained sufficiently, I hope, why such a universal prescription of equal division would not seem to me to fit Hobbes's own account of the importance of equity in an arbitrator, namely, that an equitable decision will encourage people in future to submit their disputes to an arbitrator, thus reducing the occasions for open conflict.

Hobbes's approach, however, can be advocated as a way of producing a fair outcome, without regard to its tendency to reproduce the outcome of bargaining between the parties. In the last section of this chapter I shall in fact put forward a "resourcist" solution to the problem of Matthew and Luke proposed by Braithwaite. By calling it resourcist what I mean is that, as Hobbes envisaged, it takes the thing in dispute (in this case solo playing time) as the subject of division, and moves directly to a solution that divides it equally. It should be clear that this is a quite different approach from any so far considered. All the solutions we have so far reviewed—the Nash solution, Braithwaite's solution, and splitting the difference—have in common the assumption that what is to be divided equally is the gain in utility. They then differ in the way in which they propose to normalize the utilities of the parties. Until I get to section 10 at the end of this chapter, I shall continue to assume that, if a fair division is one that divides gains equally, the measure of equality is to be that the parties gain equally in utility. Most of the discussion has been carried out on the basis of this assumption and I want in sections 7, 8, and 9 to follow up controversies that have been pursued within that framework.

I shall not focus here on ways of operationalizing the notion of an equal utility gain as I did in section 5. Rather, I shall be attending to the first stage in the two-stage sequence, namely, the definition of a nonagreement baseline. This will be the subject of sections 7 and 8. Then in section 9 I shall consider a challenge to the whole two-stage approach. This is the argument that there is no reason for supposing that the ethically defensible outcome must be preferred by both parties to the noncooperative baseline. Why, the question is here asked, should we accept the constraints on redistribution imposed by the whole "fair division" approach? I shall first explain how one might come to deny the relevance of the noncooperative baseline, and then in the second half of section 9 I shall state the case for baseline-dependence.

7. ALTERNATIVE BASELINES

One way of looking at bargaining problems is to see them as representing in microcosm the kind of issue to which social contract theory was addressed. That is to say, we start from a "state of nature" in which people, acting independently, frustrate the satisfaction of one another's desires. We then argue that everyone could gain from a move to a situation in which behavior is authoritatively coordinated, and say that what has to be allocated is the surplus from cooperation—the amount left over when all have been given resources yielding the same amount of utility as they would have had in the "state of nature."

The connection between the classical social contract theories and the modern theories of so-called fair division has been made explicitly by David Gauthier. He argues that "rational men" would not accept principles of distribution that take no account of what people could obtain for themselves in the absence of social cooperation. Rather, "viewing society as the means for producing and distributing an optimal social surplus, [they] will only accept principles of distribution if they restrict their scope to the surplus, and apportion it in accordance with the contribution that each makes to its production."[5] I shall discuss Gauthier as a theorist of justice in whole societies in sections 30 and 37. For the present, I focus on the application of his ideas in the context of small-scale problems. Gauthier has in fact taken Braithwaite's story about the trumpeter and the pianist and applied his ideas to it. As we already know, he favors splitting the difference as the method for allocating the surplus. But he also departs from Braithwaite by proposing an alternative way of establishing the baseline.

It is, of course, notorious that one of the main issues in social contract theory has always been how to conceive of the state of nature. Now a state of nature corresponding to the baseline we have posited up to now is, we might say, super-Hobbesian. For the parties are not trying to do as well for themselves as possible in the absence of cooperation, as Hobbes supposes, but are concerned to attain the best possible position *relative to one another*. (Hobbes does say that the desire to do better than others is a source of conflict, but this is not the driving force in his theory.) Each is prepared to do things he himself dislikes (e.g., bring about cacophony by playing at the same time as the other) so as to make the other party suffer. If the parties know that the arbitrated solution will be one that retains their relative positions, it is clear that they would lose by doing anything else. But we might urge that an arbitrator dedicated to seeking a fair outcome should take some other point as the baseline from which the parties are to gain equally.

THE "SECURITY LEVEL" AS BASELINE

A more Lockean way of conceiving the baseline is to say that it is the point at which Matthew and Luke are each doing as well for themselves as they can in the absence of cooperation. The gain from cooperation over the utility at that point is then to be divided equally. This is Gauthier's idea, and it was also that of Braithwaite's earliest critic, J. R. Lucas. Lucas's article remains, as far as I know, the only one solely devoted to analyzing Braithwaite's inaugural lecture and it is worth some attention. Unlike the critics of Braithwaite to be discussed in the next section, Lucas fully accepts the logic of Braithwaite's position that the relative advantage of the parties at the baseline should be preserved in the solution. He agrees that the utilities of the two men have to be brought into alignment via some method of normalization. (He even accepts Braithwaite's way of doing it.) And he agrees that each should gain an equal amount of utility in the move from the baseline to the Pareto frontier. The only quarrel—a family quarrel—is over the baseline from which equal gain shall be measured. His objection is to the arbitrator's taking account of the damage each can gratuitously inflict on the other. Lucas suggests, instead, that an ethically acceptable baseline would be one where "Luke...would...pursue the prudential strategy, the one best designed to secure his own interests, and would not depart from this merely in order to retaliate on Matthew [and vice versa]."[6]

At the time when he wrote the article that includes his discussion of

Matthew and Luke, Gauthier seems to have similarly regarded the pre-scription for the nonagreement point as one derived from ethical con-siderations. Since then, however, he has tried to tighten up his theory so that there are no constraints that are not ultimately derivable from the sophisticated pursuit of self-interest. At the same time, he has sought to retain unchanged the criterion for the nonagreement point. This entails his arguing that actors rationally pursuing their interests would not make threats. Therefore, he claims, we can ignore threats in arriving at a nonagreement baseline.

Gauthier writes that threats "play a purely hypothetical role in the Nash-Harsanyi analysis, since [the parties] do not actually choose them, but merely appeal to them to determine the costs that each could im-pose on the other in a strict competition for bargaining advantage."[7] This is true, but does not distinguish the pursuit of relative advantage from independent maximization as a baseline. The essence of the two-stage approach is that all we should ever see (if it works perfectly) is behavior that puts the parties somewhere on the Pareto frontier. The nonagreement point plays a purely hypothetical role, whether it be defined along Nash/Braithwaite lines or along Lucas/Gauthier lines. We are not supposed to have to go back to a state of independent maximization before we can get to Gauthier's utopia of a point on the Pareto frontier corresponding to the criterion of splitting the difference. We are supposed to move straight to the point that preserves the posi-tions of the parties in the hypothetical state of nature in which each party independently pursues its own interests.

So far, then, Gauthier has not advanced his case. He goes on to say the following: "Maximally effective threat strategies would not be chosen by [the parties] were they to find themselves unable to co-operate; the threat point bears no particular relationship to the non–co-operative outcome."[8] Now it is quite true that it would be pointless to threaten unless there were some possible action by the other party that would be beneficial to one. But what has this to do with cases where threats do have a chance of improving the outcome? Gauthier's response is that "if [the parties] would not choose these strategies, then they cannot credibly threaten with them. Maximally effective threat strategies prove to be idle."[9] But what Gauthier has failed to show is precisely that it would not be rational to employ threats. Suppose we were to concede that it would be idle to make threats unless there were a possibility of cooperation. (We should not in fact concede it, since threats can be advantageous in zero-sum situations.) It still would not follow that the relevant baseline for cooperation is what each would do if there were no possibility of cooperation. For once the possibility of cooperation exists, one may be able to shift its terms in one's favor by the use of threats.

A better argument, which Gauthier may have in the back of his mind, though it does not correspond to anything he says, would be to say that since it would not be rational to *carry out* a threat it would not be rational to *make* one. That he may be thinking along these lines is suggested by his next remark, which is not strictly related to the content of the preceding ones. For he now says: "Bargaining theorists generally suppose that individuals are in a position to make their threats binding. But this is an unrealistic supposition in most situations."[10]

I fully agree that the "theory of optimal threats" is defective. It was for that reason that I did not attempt to derive the Nash/Braithwaite baseline of cacophony from a general theory but simply said that in the case of the particular problem posed by Braithwaite it seemed fairly clear where the pursuit of relative advantage would lead. But this does not mean that threats would never be used by rational actors trying to do as well as possible for themselves in setting the stage for a move to the Pareto frontier.

It is an old chestnut in the analysis of threats that if a threat is costly to carry out there is no incentive for the threatening party to carry out the threat if it fails to elicit the desired response. But the force of this idea, which may be what Gauthier intends to rely on here, is quite weak. The argument applies only to cases where the threat is in relation to a single action and where (a) there is no expectation of interaction in the future with the same party and (b) there is no chance of any other potential subject of future threats finding out what happened. Provided either of these conditions is met, there is a future-oriented self-interested reason for carrying out the threat, even at some cost, namely, the advantage of appearing credible. Carrying out a threat is, if you like, an investment in the enhanced effectiveness of future threats—perhaps indeed in their continued effectiveness at all.

Now in the case of Matthew and Luke—and very many real-life cases—we need not invoke demonstration effects on third parties to show that carrying out a threat can be rational. Matthew and Luke are engaged in a continuous relationship, so we can envisage the threat game as extending over any amount of time. The incentive for engaging in it is the hope of shifting the eventual "efficient" outcome in one's own direction. Of course, it may not work. There may simply be deadlock and one or the other party may give up and maximize independently taking the behavior of the other as a given. But that does not mean that it is not a rational calculation to try first.

It must be observed here that if we rule out any such strategic play as irrational and insist on nonstrategic maximization as the only form of rational action, we automatically eliminate the rationale for any bargaining solution. For what drives every bargaining solution is the notion that rational actors will refuse any offer that they consider to be inadequate, even though it represents an improvement over the nonagreement point. Only by assuming that people will act strategically in this way can we arrive at a determinate outcome. Otherwise either party to the problem of splitting the hundred dollars will accept an offer of one dollar rather than get nothing, and this obviously leaves it almost entirely open where the outcome will fall. We are back at the pre-Nash situation (see above, section 2, under "The Nash Solution") in which it is said that, so long as the outcome is Pareto optimal and preferable to the nonagreement point for both parties, we have to relegate the location of the outcome to "psychology."

In the case of Matthew and Luke, if we omit strategic considerations then the best thing for Matthew to do if Luke plays every evening is to be silent; and the best thing for Luke to do if Matthew plays every evening is to be silent. If we say, then, that it is irrational to make oneself worse off simply in order to improve one's bargaining position, we have to say that independent maximization, where each does the best for himself given the action of the other, can bring about outcomes at either end of the Pareto frontier—Matthew playing solo all the time or Luke playing solo all the time—so that the whole Pareto frontier can be reached by independent maximization. Only if the two men deliberately do something that is disadvantageous in the short run for themselves—spoiling the setup in which one gets his first preference and the other his second preference, and in its place creating a cacophony which is the third preference of one and the fourth preference of the other—can we obtain a determinate nonagreement point and hence a determinate outcome on the Pareto frontier.

How do Lucas and Gauthier manage to overlook this rather obvious point and still maintain that they can come up with a single nonagreement point that is inside the Pareto frontier? The answer is that both of them say that Matthew and Luke should follow what they call their "prudential strategies" in the absence of an agreement, but they then concur in identifying the "prudential strategy" with one that is actually quite bad for both men.

What both Lucas and Gauthier do is pick a pair of payoffs, namely, the so-called security level of each player.[11] This term will become familiar to anyone who works through Appendix A, since it forms an element in Braithwaite's system for bringing the two men's utilities into alignment. Indeed, Braithwaite himself sinned first by equating the strategy designed to attain the "security level" with the "prudential strategy," which is a gross piece of persuasive definition in that it simply begs the question of whether there is anything prudent about it or not.*

The "security level" is the highest level of utility that can be achieved under the most unfavorable circumstances. To equate prudence with this is to assume that it is always prudent to play completely safe—never to take a chance in pursuit of some greater good. It is true that "prudence" in popular use tends to suggest a strong bias against risk-taking; but even so it is not, even in common speech, considered necessarily imprudent to accept the possibility of a worse outcome in pursuit of a better one. And if we take "prudence" as the rational pursuit of one's own good, it is surely plain that one should not invariably act so as to avoid the worst possible outcome, regardless of the possible gains foregone.

I can best explain exactly what is involved in the attainment of one's security level by talking about the payoff matrix for Matthew and Luke in Braithwaite's story. Figure 1.2 is therefore reproduced here for convenient reference as Figure 2.1. Now, to choose to act in a way that guarantees one one's security level is, as I have said, to act in the most

---

* In Braithwaite's defense it should be said that he calls the maximin strategy in the situation of Matthew and Luke the "prudential strategy" only once. (R. B. Braithwaite, *Theory of Games as a Tool for the Moral Philosopher* [Cambridge: Cambridge University Press, 1955], p. 30). He introduces the notion of a prudential strategy in the context of a zero-sum game, where it makes perfect sense to say that one cannot do better than play the maximin strategy against an equally rational opponent (ibid., pp. 16–20). The maximin strategy is here necessarily identical to the minimax strategy, that is to say, the strategy that holds the other player down to the lowest possible payoff. (Since it is a zero-sum game, what is best for oneself must be worst for the other person, so the maximin and minimax strategies have to coincide.) He then treats the prudential strategy not as the maximin strategy but as the minimax strategy in the game that Matthew and Luke play in order to establish the baseline from which the move to the Pareto frontier will be made. Here, we "reduce the difficult part of the problem to that of a situation in which Luke will be trying to increase, and Matthew to decrease, this relative advantage, which is a wholly competitive situation [i.e., a zero-sum game]" (ibid., p. 28). Given that Braithwaite has already specified that the arbitrated outcome will preserve the relative advantage of the two men when they play this game, it is correct to regard it as zero-sum. Therefore, to say that whatever increases relative advantage (a zero-sum concept) is prudent seems reasonable enough. But this, as Braithwaite himself points out, entails that they choose strategies (playing all the time) that will produce an outcome worse than either could get by playing his maximin strategy (ibid., p. 30).

Matthew

		Play		Not play

		Play	Not play
Luke	Play	1, 2	7, 3
	Not play	4, 10	2, 1

Figure 2.1.   Payoff Matrix for Braithwaite's Problem

cautious way possible. To arrive at this choice requires asking what one should do so as to ensure that one gets the most in the worst circumstances. The strategy is therefore known as the maximin strategy: it seeks to maximize the minimum payoff.

Let us begin by confining our analysis to pure strategies—that is to say, always doing the same action in a situation marked by a particular structure of payoffs—and ask what the maximin strategy is in the case described by Braithwaite. Imagine Matthew wondering what to do. Scanning Figure 2.1, he notices that whether he finishes up by being in the upper or lower row of the payoff matrix is out of his control. It depends on what Luke does. And to follow the maximin strategy he must assume that Luke will do whatever is most disadvantageous to him, even if it is also highly disadvantageous to Luke himself. (It should be borne in mind that the *probability* of finding oneself in the worst situation is irrelevant. The object is simply to ensure that the worst is as good as *possible*.) Matthew therefore asks himself what Luke would do if his sole aim were to keep Matthew's payoffs as low as they could be made. He may be tempted to conclude from such an inquiry that Luke will play rather than not play. For he can then hold Matthew down to a payoff of 3 utility units, whereas if he does not play he leaves it open for Matthew to get a payoff of 10.

But the trouble with this is that if Matthew can make that calculation so can Luke. So perhaps Matthew will finish up not playing (the best response to Luke's playing) but Luke will get the last laugh by not playing after all, reducing him to his lowest possible payoff of 1 unit. (Recall that Matthew dislikes silence above all things.) This suggests that to avoid the worst he should play anyway. He cannot then do worse than get a payoff of 2 units. By parity of reasoning, Luke should choose not to play, since this will ensure that he avoids his worst payoff, which comes from cacophony. With pure strategies, then, Matthew will play and Luke will not play, yielding each a minimum payoff of 2 units. (Of course, if they both actually follow these strategies they will each do a good deal better than that.)

However, both of them can improve on these minimum payoffs by using a mixed strategy. This means making a choice on each occasion by some random means according to pre-established odds. The odds constitute the strategy. Thus, if Matthew plays on one randomly chosen evening in every five, he can ensure himself an average long-run payoff per evening of 2.8 units, whatever Luke does. In fact, this strategy has the great disadvantage that, while it is not possible to do worse than get 2.8, it is also not possible to do better. The strategy has the property (which is not inherent in maximin strategies, as we have just seen) of producing a payoff that is invariant with respect to the other party's choices. Thus, suppose Luke plays every evening. Then Matthew's payoff from playing one-fifth of the time is $(0.2 \times 2) + (0.8 \times 3) = 2.8$. And if Luke never plays, Matthew's payoff is $(0.2 \times 10) + (0.8 \times 1) = 2.8$. Obviously, therefore, any mixture of playing and not playing on the part of Luke will also yield 2.8 units to Matthew.

Luke's maximin mixed strategy is to play one evening in every four. This gives him an average long-run payoff of 3.25 units, which is again invariant with Matthew's choices. Naturally, since the payoffs are not affected by what the other person does, these strategies produce 2.8 for Matthew and 3.25 for Luke when played against each other—figures which may be compared with the 10 for Matthew and 4 for Luke that resulted when the pure maximin strategies were played against each other.

The obvious objection to a maximin strategy as a rule for independent decision-making is that there seems no very good reason for equating "strategy that does the best" with "strategy that avoids the worst." As Gauthier says, the maximin strategy gives each player his "minimal utility," which is "the worst he can do, whatever the circumstances and actions of the others."[12] But is that always a prudent goal?

Suppose Matthew knows that Luke is playing his maximin strategy: he knows, let us say, that at nine o'clock every evening Luke flips two pennies and then plays the piano for an hour if and only if both pennies come up heads. Matthew's obviously best move is to wait until just after nine each evening, and adapt his behavior to Luke's. If he does this, playing only when he has ascertained that Luke will not play, he can get 10 units on an average of three nights in four, and 3 units on an average of one night in four. This yields an expected utility of 8.25

units, as against the 2.8 that is all he would get in this situation by playing his own maximin mixed strategy. Even if, for some reason, Matthew has to decide whether to play or not without waiting to see what Luke does, the information that Luke is playing his maximin strategy should lead him to depart from his own. He is much better off with a strategy of playing every evening for an average utility of 8.0 units than with the average of 2.8 units that his maximin mixed strategy would yield.

The trouble is, of course, that Luke is symmetrically placed in this respect. If he can count on Matthew pursuing *his* maximin mixed strategy, he can improve on the utility derivable from playing his own maximin mixed strategy (3.25) by playing only when Matthew does not (6.4) or, if he has to choose a strategy in advance, by playing every evening (5.8). But if *each* starts acting on the expectation that the *other* will pursue a maximin mixed strategy, they are both bound to be disappointed. If they both decide in advance on a strategy rather than wait and see what the other does each evening, they both play all the time, so we are back with the original baseline of cacophony. Thus, any situation in which each plays his maximin mixed strategy is highly unstable, because it always pays to depart from one's strategy provided the other does not.

We could still, if we wished, specify that, as a matter of principle, the payoffs arising from both parties pursuing their maximin mixed strategies (hereafter "joint maximin payoffs") are to be taken as baseline values as the first step in the construction of a fair procedure. But the question is: Why should we accept that principle? Lucas suggests that the joint maximin payoffs are what would come about "if neither party realized that the musical interference was attributable to a person, and each assumed it was a natural phenomenon." For under these beliefs, "each would pursue a prudential policy; on discovering that it was a colleague who was making the noise, and in coming to an agreement with him to remedy matters the *status quo ante* would be a natural starting point for arranging how matters should be improved."[13] But if Matthew believes that the noises that sometimes emanate from the wall between nine o'clock and ten o'clock in the evening are natural phenomena, he will have *less*, not *more*, reason to adopt a maximin strategy, for he can rule out the possibility that the sequence of noises and silences is specifically designed by a malevolent or strategic neighbor bent on minimizing his utility.

In fact, the way to maximize his utility if Matthew thinks nothing he

TABLE 2.1.   PERCENTAGE OF TIME MATTHEW PLAYS:
NASH SOLUTION VS. SPLITTING THE DIFFERENCE
WITH ALTERNATIVE BASELINES

	Baseline		
	Cacophony	Silence	Security level (joint maximin)
Nash solution	93	70	60
Splitting the difference	63½	56½	56

does will alter the frequency of sounds in the wall is simply to wait each evening and see whether they occur. If they do, he listens; if not, he plays. If for some reason he has to commit himself in advance to a strategy (though why should he?) it should be not a maximin mixed strategy—in fact, neither a maximin strategy nor a mixed strategy—but a decision either to play every evening or never to play. Which of the two pure strategies he should choose depends on the estimate he makes of the future frequency of the mysterious noises.

Although I have criticized the rationale offered by Gauthier and Lucas for the security level as the appropriate nonagreement baseline, I want to round out the discussion by taking note of the answers they give to the question of the division of playing time between Matthew and Luke. In the case of Gauthier, the answer can be found in Table 2.1. We know that Gauthier is an enthusiast for splitting the difference as a method of moving from the baseline to the Pareto frontier, so we have only to look at the bottom right-hand corner of the table to see the outcome he supports: it has Matthew playing 56 percent of the time.

Lucas, however, retains Braithwaite's method of normalizing the utilities. This means that, in Figure A.1 in Appendix A, we take the line of equal advantage (the so-called isorrhope) passing through O, the joint maximin payoff, and see where it cuts the Pareto frontier. It will be seen that this point, marked D on Figure A.1, lies between the midpoint (marked E) and the outcome with a baseline of silence, which is C. The implication of combining the security level with Braithwaite's method of moving from the origin to the Pareto frontier is therefore to shift the solution toward Luke. He now plays over half the time—the split is about 55/45 in his favor. However, the rationale for Braithwaite's system of normalization is so intimately connected with the idea of what the parties can do to one another if they want to be nasty (for what else is the minimax strategy?) that it is hard to see why, rejecting that rationale, one should retain his system for bringing the utilities into alignment.

It is perhaps a tribute to the persuasive force of Braithwaite's inaugural lecture that the two philosophers who have rejected the baseline constituted by Matthew and Luke gratuitously inflicting injury on one another for strategic ends should nevertheless take as baseline a position in which Matthew and Luke are still inflicting injury on one another, though only incidentally to the pursuit of their maximin strategies. Surely there is an obvious alternative that one might take as the baseline, namely, the outcome in which neither plays.

In the case as stated by Braithwaite, of course, silence is ranked below either playing or listening by both men and is below the so-called security level for each. One might be led by that to say that the baseline should not be something that neither would choose. But consider for a moment a case in which Luke has little interest in either playing or listening: he most wants silence and least likes cacophony. (It is immaterial how he orders the intermediate pair of listening to Matthew and playing himself.) Matthew, let us say, most likes to play solo but is prepared to endure cacophony rather than abandon his trumpet. His preference order is: himself play, both play, Luke play, neither play. If, as Gauthier and Lucas propose, the baseline is established by each doing the best for himself without regard to the other, Matthew will play every evening while Luke (reluctantly) listens. For the preferences have the structure that, whatever Luke does, Matthew is better off playing; and, whatever Matthew does, Luke is better off not playing.

There are in this case no gains to be had from cooperation because any move away from the outcome where each is independently doing the best for himself must make Matthew worse off. By playing solo every evening he is already getting what he most wants. If Luke appeals for an adjudication to provide a fair division of evenings between what Matthew wants (to play the trumpet) and what he wants (silence), he will have to be told that the outcome is already Pareto-optimal so there is no room for "fair division" to enter in. (Notice that Luke's position is weakened by his being condemned to maximize: if he were allowed to create an inefficiency by gratuitously playing himself, even when he would prefer to listen, he could set the stage for a "fair division." See above in this section, under "The 'Security Level' as Baseline.")

Whether or not Luke actually prefers listening to Matthew to silence, one might suggest that he should be able to insist on silence if he wants it, and the same for Matthew. Each, on this view, should be able to veto the making of noise of a kind that many people find objectionable, and the availability of this right should not vary with their own preferences. This is after all the way affairs are normally conducted: I have a right against my neighbor to stop his (say) putting up a structure that will block my light, because many people would not wish to have their light blocked; and my neighbor still has to get permission to build it even if he happens to know that I am an eccentric who keeps the blinds down all day and would perhaps even prefer to have him block out the light. I shall go into these matters further later in the chapter (see section 9, where I shall ask why one might wish to set things up in this way).

Lucas recommends his baseline as what would be appropriate if "Dr. Matthew and Professor Luke are fellows of one of those colleges where the fellows are not friends but not enemies either, and treat one another in a distant though not discourteous fashion."[14] I agree that it would be inappropriate for them to make life unpleasant for one another merely to gain a bargaining advantage. But would it not be most appropriate for each of them not to make a noise that the other might find disagreeable unless they reach an agreement otherwise? Colleges do, in fact, have such rules; and even if the college of Dr. Matthew and Professor Luke does not, there is no reason why a moral philosopher called in to adjudicate should not take as a *status quo* point what would happen if such a rule were enforced.

From this perspective, we can see that the dispute between Braithwaite on the one side and Gauthier and Lucas on the other is not exactly about what is the right baseline. Rather, it turns on the legitimacy of the parties' using their rights in different ways in order to improve the eventual outcome. Braithwaite would let them do anything permitted within the framework of the game to get the most favorable possible nonagreement baseline. Lucas, however, without challenging Braithwaite's description of the legal-institutional setting, says that it would be wrong to play all the time merely to make the other man suffer and thus improve one's own initial bargaining position. This leads to the proposal, also endorsed by Gauthier, that the appropriate noncooperative baseline should be one where each person is independently doing as well for himself as possible. I shall not repeat my criticisms of the "security level" as a way of operationalizing this. The point to emphasize here is that Lucas and Gauthier want to constrain the nonagreement baseline by specifying acceptable motives for playing, but not by limiting the range of nonagreement points directly.* Thus, I take it that neither Lucas nor Gauthier would be able to find any objection to Matthew's playing every evening if he were indifferent between playing solo and playing at the same time as Luke, for they would have to admit that he was doing as well as he could for himself by playing all the time.

8. WHAT'S WRONG WITH THREAT ADVANTAGE?

Lucas and Gauthier, as we have just seen, objected that the outcome in Braithwaite's solution depended upon the use of threats. They complained about the way in which this solution (and the same complaint could have been lodged against Nash) took as the noncooperative baseline a situation in which the parties would go in for gratuitous efforts to make each other suffer simply in order to improve their bargaining position vis-à-vis each other. This precision in the concept of a threat is lost by the other two commentators on Braithwaite whose criticisms I want to discuss, John Rawls and Amartya Sen. They too say that what is objectionable in Braithwaite's solution is Matthew's being able to use his "threat advantage." But, unlike Lucas and Gauthier, they employ the term in a way that is liable to mislead us as to the nature of their real objections.

By way of preliminary, I want to trace the history of the term "threat

---

* It is interesting to note that Robert Nozick makes the same distinction in *Anarchy, State, and Utopia.* (New York: Basic Books, 1974). He thinks that people should not blackmail others (i.e., threaten to publicize information unless paid, simply in order to extort money) but that if someone has information about another of an identical kind that he could use profitably in a book, he can legitimately charge the person who would sooner not have it made public "an amount of money equal to his expected difference in royalties between the book containing this information and the book without it" (p. 85). The crassness of this is hardly worth remarking on, but the point to note here is that Nozick shares with Gauthier and Lucas the idea that so long as something obnoxious is done in pursuit of nonstrategic self-interest that makes it all right, whereas the same act carried out (or threatened) on the basis of strategic self-interest is not. As a critic has observed, from the point of view of the victim it makes little difference whether the motive for spreading the information is profitable use in a book, "sadistic joy from divulging it," or the hope of being paid off to suppress it (Thomas R. De Gregori, "Market Morality: Robert Nozick and the Question of Economic Justice," *American Journal of Economics and Sociology* 38 [1979]: 26). But for these metaphysicians of the market, self-interest washes whiter—so long as it does not involve strategic considerations.

advantage." The expression apparently first occurs in 1957, two years after Braithwaite's inaugural lecture was published. Luce and Raiffa, in their discussion in *Games and Decisions* of Braithwaite's lecture, noted that his solution produces the result that Matthew is to play solo more often than Luke. They then quoted Braithwaite's own explanation of this in the following terms: "Matthew's advantage arises purely from the fact the Matthew, the trumpeter, prefers both of them playing at once to neither of them playing, whereas Luke, the pianist, prefers silence to cacophony." And they followed up the quotation with the pregnant remark: "Matthew has the threat advantage."[15]

The reference to threats is, in this exact context, well placed. To threaten somebody is, generally speaking, to attempt to affect his behavior by stating a conditional intention: that, unless he does some specified thing (or refrains from doing some specified thing) you will do something that he will not like. The conditional intention has to be of the if-and-only-if form: a threat to do so-and-so unless the other performs includes the tacit promise that you will not do it if the other does perform.

In the case of Matthew and Luke, each threatens to play all the time even if the other is playing all the time, thus creating the cacophony that neither likes. This threat, in common with most threats, is costly to carry out. The motive for making the threat is to set the stage for negotiations: the optimal threat is whatever will put one in the best position to strike an advantageous bargain. So far so good. Moreover, Braithwaite is also obviously correct in his own text in pointing to an asymmetry in this threat point—that cacophony is the worst of the four possible outcomes for Luke, whereas it is only the next to worst for Matthew. But, as Luce and Raiffa use the expression "threat advantage," it has built into it that the asymmetry in payoffs causes the inequality of playing time. Is it true that Matthew's advantage (in playing time) arises purely from the difference between his preference ordering between cacophony and silence and the preference ordering of Luke over those two outcomes? The answer is that it is true for Braithwaite's own solution, though not for others.

As Braithwaite observes, if we were to exchange the preferences of Matthew and Luke for silence and cacophony while leaving the rest of the utilities the same, "the coupled strategy determined by the new outcome point will be that Luke should play 26 evenings to Matthew's 17. Exchanging [the payoffs for silence and cacophony] has exactly reversed the distribution of time between Luke and Matthew."[16] It is also relevant to observe that we would get exactly the same result if we were to substitute a nonagreement baseline of silence for that of cacophony. For this obviously amounts to exactly the same thing as keeping the baseline of cacophony and reversing the preferences of Matthew and Luke for silence and cacophony. (In Figure A.1 in Appendix A, this entails taking the isorrhope passing through T_{22}, which cuts the Pareto frontier at the point marked C.)

It is, however, a peculiarity of Braithwaite's own solution that the nonagreement point completely determines the outcome in the way correctly claimed by him. This is not so for the other solutions we have examined in detail, the Nash solution and splitting the difference. The simplest way to demonstrate this is to refer again to Table 2.1 in the previous section. If Matthew's "threat advantage" solely determined his advantage in the outcome, making silence the nonagreement baseline should turn the tables and have Luke playing more often—as it would in Braithwaite's own formula. Yet we see in Table 2.1 that Matthew in fact plays more often whatever the baseline is.* The reason for this is that Matthew has another advantage under both formulae: he is less tolerant of Luke's playing solo than Luke is of his playing solo.[17]

My reason for this excursus will, I hope, shortly become apparent. For I believe that a good deal of the subsequent discussion has uncritically taken over Braithwaite's claim that Matthew's success in playing more often arises solely from his threat advantage, which is true for his own theory, and has extended it to all two-stage theories, as if this were the only explanation of an unequal division of the scarce resource in the adjudicated outcomes. Rawls provides us with a good example of this process.

"Justice as Fairness" was John Rawls's first full-dress statement of the ideas later to appear in *A Theory of Justice*. Although "Justice as Fairness" was published only a year after *Games and Decisions*, Rawls footnoted it as "comprehensive and not too technical" and mentioned

---

* We can discern several systematic tendencies in Table 2.1. First, holding the baseline constant, the Nash solution is always more favorable to Matthew than is splitting the difference. Second, holding the solution concept constant, there is an invariable progression among the baselines in the degree to which they favor Matthew: cacophony is the most advantageous baseline for Matthew, followed by silence, and then finally by the joint maximin payoffs as baseline. There is also, third, a striking interaction effect between the two factors: the more favorable a baseline is to Matthew, the bigger the gap between the proportion of the time Matthew plays under the Nash solution and the proportion of the time he plays under the solution of splitting the difference. Or, looking at it the other way round, we can say that the solution concept (Nash) that is invariably more favorable to Matthew accentuates Matthew's advantage from a more favorable baseline.

that chapters 6 and 14 "discuss the developments [in game theory] most obviously related to the analysis of justice."[18] (Chapter 6 of *Games and Decisions* contains the discussion of Braithwaite from which I have already quoted.) In his criticism of Braithwaite's use of game theory to establish a fair division, Rawls did not cite the analysis of Luce and Raiffa. But it seems safe to assume in the circumstances that when he attacked Braithwaite's solution for giving more playing time to Matthew on account of his "threat advantage" he had Luce and Raiffa in mind.

In *A Theory of Justice*, Rawls substantially reproduced his criticism of Braithwaite from "Justice as Fairness" but added the comment that "a similar objection to Braithwaite's analysis is found in J. R. Lucas, 'Moralists and Gamesmen.'"[19] (Lucas's article did not appear until a year after "Justice as Fairness.") This would lead us to believe that Rawls is going to criticize Braithwaite's solution on the same ground as did Lucas: for its dependence on Matthew's "threat advantage." And indeed Rawls does begin by sounding as if this is exactly the line he is pursuing in the lengthy footnote he devotes to Braithwaite in *A Theory of Justice*:

> On the analysis he presents, it turns out that the fair division of playing time between Matthew and Luke depends on their preferences, and these in turn are connected with the instruments they wish to play. Since Matthew has a threat advantage over Luke, arising from the fact that Matthew, the trumpet-er, prefers both of them playing at once to neither of them playing, whereas Luke, the pianist, prefers silence to cacophony, Matthew is allotted twenty-six evenings of play to Luke's seventeen. If the situation were reversed, the threat advantage would be with Luke.[20]

On the basis of these remarks, we might reasonably anticipate that Rawls would ally himself with Lucas in suggesting that the baseline should be one that does not depend upon threats. However, his next move has the effect (whether he realizes it or not) of divorcing him from Lucas's line of attack. What he does is to put forward a modification of Braithwaite's story that is designed to point up the unacceptability of the "threat advantage" element, by making it even more excruciating than in the original version. Yet in fact it leaves no room for threats. He says that "we have only to suppose that Matthew is a jazz enthusiast who plays the drums, and Luke a violinist who plays sonatas, in which case it will be fair on this analysis for Matthew to play whenever and as often as he likes, assuming as it is plausible to assume that he does not care whether Luke plays or not. Clearly something has gone wrong."[21]

Maybe it has, but if so it has nothing to do with threat advantage, or for that matter with threats at all.

A threat, to repeat a point made already, occurs when you attempt to obtain something of value from someone by stating that if he does not comply with a certain demand you will do something which he dislikes. Thus, in the case as set out by Braithwaite, both Matthew and Luke have threats available because each can harm the other by playing every evening and there is some concession each could hope to obtain from the other in return for not playing every evening. In the alternative case, as stated by Rawls, where Matthew plays the drums, it is plain that Luke has no threat against Matthew within the framework of the game; but it is equally true that Matthew has no threat against Luke. Matthew is not *threatening* Luke by playing all the time: he is simply obtaining his highest possible payoff.

Now because Luke cannot move Matthew below his highest payoff even at a cost to himself, Braithwaite would have to say that the "fair division" already exists at the nonagreement point. Rawls is thus quite correct in saying that Braithwaite's analysis produces the answer that Matthew should play all the time. But what we must also observe is that Braithwaite's answer would have to be endorsed by Lucas and Gauthier. Their criterion for the nonagreement point is different from Braithwaite's, but they cannot deny that Matthew should play all the time in the case as stated by Rawls.

On Braithwaite's criterion an adjudication permitting Matthew to play all the time follows from the fact that, even when Luke is doing his worst, he cannot prevent Matthew from getting as high a level of utility as he could obtain under any circumstances. (The worst he can do to Matthew is play all the time himself; but cacophony, by Rawls's stipulation, is as good for Matthew as playing solo.) On the criterion espoused by Lucas and Gauthier, the same adjudication follows from the fact that when Matthew plays all the time he is doing as well for himself as he possibly can, whatever Luke does—and this necessarily includes (since it includes everything) Luke's doing the best for himself that he can.

In spite of the reference to Matthew's threat advantage, Rawls's objection to Braithwaite's solution to the problem of Matthew and Luke does not, however, lie in the dependence of the baseline on threats. Although he represents quite accurately the way in which threat advantage (precisely as defined by Luce and Raiffa) drives Braithwaite's division of time, Rawls's complaint is not to this specific feature of

Braithwaite's solution but to its having anything to do with real bargaining considerations at all. This comes out clearly in what Rawls goes on to say in *A Theory of Justice*: "What is lacking is a suitable definition of a status quo that is acceptable from a moral point of view. We cannot take various contingencies as known and individual preferences as given and expect to elucidate the concept of justice (or fairness) by theories of bargaining. The conception of the original position is designed to meet the problem of the appropriate status quo."[22]

This passage shows how sweeping is Rawls's dissent from Braithwaite's whole approach. What he objects to is our taking into account the strategic features of the situation and then seeking to elucidate the concept of fairness from the contemplation of the kinds of bargain that might be struck by people in that situation. The reference to his own construction, the "original position," shows what he has in mind. This puts people behind a so-called veil of ignorance which conceals from them all information about their personal characteristics and social positions, even the time and place in which they live. From this position they are supposed to choose principles for regulating their affairs with one another that will, very roughly speaking, advance their interests as far as possible, given the informational constraints. The resultant principles are principles of justice. (All this will be discussed in chapter 9.)

Rawls is not against making fair outcomes depend on a process of bargaining: the people in his original position are to play the cards they have to the best advantage. What he is against is allowing them to gain advantageous outcomes as a result of their own superior bargaining strength. Thus, the passage in the text to which the footnote to Braithwaite is appended runs as follows:

> [I]t is to avoid the appeal to force and cunning that the principles of right and justice are accepted. Thus I assume that to each according to his threat advantage is not a conception of justice. It fails to establish an ordering in the required sense, an ordering based on certain relevant aspects of persons and their situation which are independent from their social position, or their capacity to intimidate and coerce.[23]

Now, as it turns out, the implication of Rawls's stringent restrictions on the information available is that the parties are identically situated. There is therefore nothing for them actually to bargain about because there is no basis for ascribing conflicting interests to them. It therefore becomes redundant to have all the members of a society in the original position, since they are interchangeable. The choice of principles thus in practice reduces to a decision-theoretic problem of individual choice under uncertainty. Rawls wants to get "morally irrelevant" considerations out of the process of bargaining, but he believes that *everything* about people is morally irrelevant when it comes to choosing principles of justice for a society. Thus, he starts from the idea that the principles of justice should arise from bargaining, but he then insists that it must be bargaining purged not only of threats but of all other strategic considerations.

When Rawls says that what we need to deal with the problem of Matthew and Luke is "a suitable definition of a status quo that is acceptable from a moral point of view," this might suggest that he is complaining about the nonagreement baseline established by Braithwaite. Bargaining, on this view, would be all right if it started from a morally acceptable nonagreement point. This would, of course, tie in with the preceding complaint about the way in which "threat advantage" enters into Braithwaite's solution. But it would be a mistake to interpret Rawls in this way. Although he misleadingly talks the language of a "status quo," what he means must be understood in the light of what he says in the next sentence about the characteristics an ethically acceptable *status quo* would have. "We cannot take various contingencies as known and individual preferences as given." The objection is not, then, just that strategic considerations enter into the determination of the nonagreement point but that they enter into the solution at all.

I shall give a second illustration of the abuse of the notion of a "threat advantage" by taking up Amartya Sen's discussion of Braithwaite's example in *Collective Choice and Social Welfare*. (He has not, as far as I know, returned to the subject since.) Sen quotes the same passage from Braithwaite that Luce and Raiffa did and, like Rawls, adds that "Matthew has the threat advantage."[24] But, like Rawls in this respect too, what he really wants to complain about is that particular bargaining advantages should enter into the outcome at all. Where he differs from Rawls is in making it explicit that what he objects to is not only bargaining from a nonagreement point but the relevance of a nonagreement point at all. Among the objectionable features of "the solutions put forward by Nash, Braithwaite, and others in similar models" is "the special importance attached to the status quo point," by which Sen (misleadingly) means the nonagreement point. (A nonagreement point need not correspond to the actual *status quo*, though it often will, as in our legacy cases.)

Is this dependence on a precisely defined noncooperative outcome justifiable? The answer to this question seems to depend a great deal on the objective of the exercise. In *predicting* the actual outcome of a bargaining battle, the status quo is clearly relevant, for it defines what will happen in the absence of the parties agreeing to a cooperative solution. There is always the threat that this outcome, which is inferior for both, will emerge as the actual outcome. . . .

This does not, however, mean that the Nash solution is an ethically attractive outcome and that we should recommend a collective choice mechanism that incorporates it.[25]

Sen thus rejects the entire framework of moving from a nonagreement point to the Pareto frontier. His idea is that instead of this we should, if we are talking about the morally right outcome, simply ask what features that outcome should have. For example, we might say that the best outcome is the one that maximizes aggregate utility, or the one that equalizes utility, or the one that maximizes the utility of whoever gets the least. It would only be by pure accident that these criteria would pick out the same outcome as would any technique for preserving relative positions at a nonagreement baseline while moving to the Pareto frontier.

There is an obvious attractiveness to the notion that the rightness of an outcome should not depend on how the parties would fare in some baseline condition. Indeed, one might be brought by prolonged attendance to the case for baseline-independence to wonder how on earth anyone had ever come to think that baseline-dependent conceptions had any moral validity. I shall therefore in the next section follow through the line of argument leading to baseline-independence.

Before turning to that, however, it may be useful to pull together the discussion in this section by observing that Braithwaite's solution can be criticized in several distinct ways. There is the point, to begin with, that the inequality in playing time is *purely* the consequence of Matthew's preference for cacophony over silence. As we have seen, this is true of Braithwaite's own solution but is not true of other two-stage solutions. But we could object to the outcome's depending *at all* (even if other factors enter) on the payoffs arising from mutual threats—what happens when each is doing his worst as against (as Lucas and Gauthier propose) doing his best independently of the other. Then we could object not only to the way in which the baseline depends on threats but to the way in which the solution depends on any kind of factor that reflects bargaining strength in the particular situation at all. And, finally, we could object specifically to the way in which the outcome depends on a baseline. It is to that line of criticism that I now turn. If we abandon baseline-dependence, what do we get?

9. BASELINE-INDEPENDENCE

THE CASE IN FAVOR

Having criticized the dependence of Braithwaite's solution on a baseline in the form of the nonagreement point, Sen commended as an alternative John Harsanyi's theory of ethical judgments and suggested that it would lead to a more equitable outcome in the case of Matthew and Luke.[26] Although I rather doubt if Sen would be as keen on Harsanyi's moral theory nowadays, his suggestion points us in a useful direction. For Harsanyi offers in its most straightforward and perspicuous form a way of approaching issues of fairness and justice that will be elaborated later in this book. We therefore do well to look at the approach in the form worked out by Harsanyi.[27]

So far Harsanyi has appeared, in the first chapter of this book, as the sturdiest defender of the Nash solution as a bargaining solution. However, Harsanyi, unlike others, insists that it has no ethical significance. The Nash solution is simply what two rational utility-maximizers will finish up with. It is a pure accident if the results of such bargaining coincide with what an impartial observer would regard as an ethically desirable outcome, and it is this that is for Harsanyi the criterion of a moral judgment.

For Harsanyi, a moral judgment is still, indeed, one made in pursuit of utility-maximization. (Hence, inevitably, its conclusions will be expressed in terms of utility.) But the pursuit of utility must be hedged around by constraints that represent the requirements of morality. The crucial feature of morality that Harsanyi seizes on is impartiality: an ethical judgment should be one that does not reflect the particular position of the person making it. That one arrangement will be more favorable to me and another more favorable to you should not make me more likely to support the first and you the second.

How could such impartiality be assured? In theory, though not of course as a practical matter, it could be achieved by denying the person making the judgment the knowledge of his or her own identity. This device is what Rawls called a "veil of ignorance" but, in contrast to the form of it proposed by Rawls, Harsanyi's is the thinnest possible veil consistent with ensuring impartiality. (This will be expanded on later—see especially section 41.) That is to say, the person making the ethical judgment knows everything about the situation there is to know—with one big exception. He knows the tastes, capacities, and beliefs of the parties, the predicted consequences of implementing alternative moral principles, and so on. But he does not have knowledge of personal identity, only that there is an equal probability of being any of the parties. In the case of the two musicians, this obviously reduces to our saying that the person making the choice of a distribution of playing time should think of himself as having a fifty-fifty chance of being Matthew or Luke.

Although we cannot in practice construct any such veil of ignorance, we can conduct an intelligible inquiry into what, in the stipulated conditions, would be the principles chosen. And if we assume, with Harsanyi, that the judgment will be made in such a way as to maximize expected utility within the constraint on information, the answer becomes quite determinate. For there is only one principle that will maximize the expected utility of the person one turns out to be, given that one has an equal chance of being anyone, and that is the principle of maximizing the average utility of all the people concerned. If we leave aside complexities arising from variable populations, we can alternatively put this in classical Benthamite utilitarian terms and say that total utility is to be maximized.*

In order to operationalize the principle of maximizing aggregate util-

---

* It is interesting to note that R. M. Hare, in his review of *A Theory of Justice*, criticized Rawls for making the veil of ignorance thicker than the minimum necessary to ensure impartiality (see R. M. Hare, "Rawls' Theory of Justice, I and II," *Philosophical Quarterly* 23 [1973]: 144–55, 241–52, reprinted with minor revisions in Norman Daniels, ed., *Reading Rawls: Critical Studies of A Theory of Justice* [New York: Basic Books, 1975], pp. 81–107). Since Rawls shares with Harsanyi the idea that moral principles are those that a rational maximizer would choose behind a suitably conceived veil of ignorance, Hare was, I think, correct to argue that with a thin veil of ignorance Rawls's premises would lead him to utilitarianism. Hare's own method of arriving at utilitarianism does not employ the formal device of a veil of ignorance but comes to much the same thing. For Hare, the mark of a moral principle is that it is one that someone (again assumed to be a rational maximizer) would be prepared to have applied in all cases falling under it. But the range of imperatives that Hare will allow to be so "universalized" is restricted in ways that reintroduce constraints equivalent to those imposed by a veil of ignorance. Thus, in *Freedom and Reason* (Oxford: Clarendon Press, 1963), Hare takes up Braithwaite's problem of the two musicians, though the pianist for some reason becomes an enthusiast for listening to records of chamber music. He rules out the trumpeter's putting forward the universal prescription "that people should play trumpets when they live next door to other people who are listening to classical records" on the ground that this turns on Matthew's particular tastes (ibid., p. 113). Clearly, however, as soon as we say that people can take account of the fact that they have likes and dislikes but not of the specific content of their own likes and dislikes, the only plausible self-interested universalizable imperative is "Let everyone's wants be satisfied as much as possible," which is the utilitarian criterion.

ity, we need cardinal utility measurements that enable us to compare different people's utilities directly, not merely to compare one person's ratios with another. Let us suppose that the numbers we have been using until now represent such interpersonally comparable utilities. Then by looking at Figure 2.1 we shall immediately see that aggregate utility will be maximized when Matthew plays on every evening. Any evening when Matthew plays will yield an aggregate of 4 more units of utility than any evening when Luke plays. When Matthew plays, the total is 14 (10 to Matthew, 4 to Luke), whereas when Luke plays the total is 10 (7 to Luke, 3 to Matthew). It may be intuitively repugnant to conclude that average utility is maximized if Luke never plays, but the reader should again be reminded that it is specified in Braithwaite's statement of the case that the utility of playing is linear with frequency of playing; in other words, there is no diminishing marginal utility of playing. (In von Neumann/Morgenstern terms, this means that each is indifferent between the certainty of playing on one evening and a $1/n$ chance of playing on n evenings.)

Sen, having complained about the dependence of Braithwaite's solution on bargaining considerations and commended Harsanyi's approach, wrote that "Matthew himself might concede that if he did not know whether he was going to be Luke or Matthew before deciding on a system of distribution of time he might well have ignored the threat advantage and recommended a more equal sharing of time."[28] Yet, as we see, there is no particular connection between what Sen misleadingly called removing Matthew's threat advantage (more accurately, eliminating any reference to a baseline, whether Braithwaite's or anybody else's) and arriving at a more equal distribution of time than that proposed by Braithwaite. On Harsanyi's analysis, Matthew would propose, if he didn't know which man he was, that Matthew should play every evening, and Luke, if he didn't know either, would agree enthusiastically. For any shift from that arrangement would lower their expected utility.

Harsanyi's argument is entirely valid, and anyone who wishes to dissent from its conclusions must say which of the premises he rejects. Suppose we accept provisionally Harsanyi's view that a moral judgment must have the attribute of impartiality, and also accept that the thought-experiment of asking whether one would make the same judgment if one were ignorant of one's own position and characteristics is as good a way as any of getting at what impartiality entails. There remains the objection that no adequate reason has ever been given (by Harsanyi or anybody else) for identifying moral judgments with those made by someone trying to maximize his own prospects from behind a veil of ignorance. This issue will be taken up in chapter 9 and I shall not enlarge on it here (see especially section 41). But it may be seen that, unless we add self-interested motivation to the information conditions, Harsanyi's demonstration of utilitarianism will fall short of being conclusive. If we no longer attribute utility-maximizing motivations to these rational choosers who are unaware of their identities, we cannot deduce that they will light on the principle that aggregate utility should be maximized.

Even so, the attractiveness of the utilitarian solution should not be slighted. Any person of goodwill, presented with the problem of Matthew and Luke, should in my view take very seriously the consideration that any deviation from the solution that has Matthew playing all the time will produce an avoidable loss of utility. For any move toward having Luke play will make Matthew worse off to a greater extent than it makes Luke better off. We may in the end still conclude that on balance the right distribution of playing time is different from that mandated by utilitarianism. But we should not pretend to deny that there is a real cost in discarding the utilitarian solution.

The prescription that aggregate utility should be maximized is the simplest and the best-known example of a principle that is not baseline-dependent. But it is by no means the only possible one. A commonly suggested modification flows naturally from the idea that what is wrong with utilitarianism is its exclusive emphasis on maximizing the total amount of utility at the expense of any concern with the way in which utility is distributed among individuals. It would scarcely be plausible to propose in response to the objection to pure maximizing that we should switch instead to pure equalization. For the principle of equal utility, if interpreted strictly, would require us to say that a situation of equally shared misery was morally preferable to a situation in which everyone was very happy but some were a little more so than others. It would seem more reasonable to say that we should be concerned with both the total amount of utility *and* its distribution, permitting a trade-off between the criteria of maximization and equalization. Another possibility which has received attention recently is to say that the utility of the person with the least utility is to be maximized. In accordance with established usage, I shall call this the principle of maximin utility.

In what follows I shall not bother to analyze the implications of hybrid principles. Obviously someone might propose any number of alternative weightings of maximization and equalization, or maximizing and maximining, or of equalizing and maximining. I shall here confine myself to saying a few words about the implications of equal and maximin utility.

If we take the problem of Matthew and Luke as the domain of these two principles, we shall find that they come to the same thing. This is so because this is a case where the point of equal utility is on the Pareto frontier, which entails that there is no way of making one better off without making the other worse off. As we move along the Pareto frontier from Matthew playing all the time to Luke playing all the time, Matthew loses utility and Luke gains it, so the highest minimum occurs where the curve (actually a straight line) of Matthew's declining utility cuts that of Luke's increasing utility. If we assume for the purpose of illustration that the numbers in Figure 2.1 represent interpersonally comparable cardinal utilities, the solution comes where Luke plays three-fifths of the time. This gives the two men an average of 5.8 units. The split is thus roughly in the same ratio as that proposed by Braithwaite, but it goes in the opposite direction. Once again, it should need no elaborate proof that there is nothing in the principle that utility should be equalized that has any general tendency to result in playing time being equalized. Nor, of course, is there any reason why a sincere proponent of the principle of equal utility should be worried by this.

The exercise that I have just carried out is, however, somewhat beside the point. For it is hard to see why anyone committed to equal or maximin utility would propose that the principle be applied in this fashion. The driving force behind a commitment to equal or maximin utility is the sense that over the course of people's lives they should, as far as possible, do equally well or that the worst off should over the course of their lives do as well as possible.* This clearly requires that

---

* Thus, in *Freedom and Reason* Hare responded to criticisms of pure maximization by stipulating that the equality with which utility is distributed should also be taken into account (p. 121). (I should add that I can find nothing except pure maximization in Hare's more recent *Moral Thinking: Its Levels, Method and Point* [Oxford: Clarendon Press, 1981].) Ted Honderich enunciated a "Principle of Equality" to the effect that we should arrange things so that there should be, as far as possible, "equality in satisfaction and distress" (*Three Essays on Political Violence* [Oxford: Basil Blackwell, 1976], p. 41). Although this sounds like a straightforward espousal of equality, on the next page he remarked ("too briefly") that "equality of distress in a society is not preferable to an inequality of satisfaction." In a later reworking of the same book, Honderich appears to have settled on a vague statement of maximin utility: the Principle of Equality is now reformulated to read that "we should improve the lot of those who are badly off, those in distress, even if this does not produce the greatest possible total of satisfaction or the least of distress" (*Violence for Equality* [Harmondsworth, England: Penguin, 1980], pp. 54–

particular issues, such as the division of playing time between Matthew and Luke, should be determined with an eye to the effect of alternatives on the overall distribution of utility between the two men. Only if their lifetime prospects happened to be equally promising would the right thing be to seek a division of playing time yielding equal utility from the playing time itself. (This would be true whether one's principle for lifetime distribution were equal utility or maximin utility.)

Moreover, since utility arising from the division of playing time will constitute only a drop in the bucket in relation to utility over a whole lifetime, even a small overall difference will require that in compensation the utility of one or the other man from playing should be maximized by letting him play all the time. It is fairly hard to imagine that there could be enough difference in the overall prospects of two people to permit one to say with confidence that they really were unequal and yet not so much as to leave them still unequal after letting one of them play every evening. (Again, the same point applies to maximin lifetime utility. To maximize the utility of the person with the least it will normally be necessary to allocate all the playing time to the person otherwise worse off.)

It is natural to wonder whether in the light of this we need to go back and reconsider our treatment of utilitarianism. Surely, it is just as true there that the principle should apply to utility from all sources: the object should be to maximize the total amount of utility, however derived. Does this entail that a utilitarian will want to do something other than maximize the aggregate utility that the two men get from the division of playing time? The answer is that, within certain restrictions, no such breach between maximizing overall utility and maximizing utility in a particular case can open up. If we take all other arrangements as fixed, then, given the problem of Matthew and Luke, we can maximize overall utility only by maximizing the utility they derive from the division of playing time. So far, then, our analysis earlier in this section can stand.

---

55). (I do not claim to understand the last phrase.) Amartya Sen, in his unreconstructed "welfarist" phase, also toyed with the idea of maximin utility. The route by which he arrived at this was the typical economist's misinterpretation of Rawls, which ignores his explicit statement that the difference principle is defined over "primary goods" (such as income) and reads him as advocating maximin utility. Thus, Sen wrote that "on Rawls's analysis it turns out that the proper maximand is the welfare [i.e., utility] of the worst-off individual" (Amartya K. Sen, *Collective Choice and Social Welfare* [San Francisco: Holden-Day, 1970], p. 136). See also Sen's "Welfare Inequalities and Rawlsian Axiomatics," *Theory and Decision* 7 (1976): 243–62.

We might say perhaps that equal and maximin utility are principles that are baseline-independent in a much more radical way than maximum utility. For at least the principle of maximum utility can be applied (so long as other things are held constant) on a case-by-case basis, whereas the principles of equal or maximin utility cannot be applied at all until we know about the utilities that the parties derive from all other sources. Thus, we must conclude that if all we are given is information about the utility for each of playing and listening, we have insufficient information to say what the principles of equal or maximin utility, properly understood, mandate for the problem of Matthew and Luke. We would need to know how well off they were in all other respects, and then use playing and listening as a makeweight to improve the overall outcome.

Before closing this discussion, I must return briefly to the qualification that I introduced a moment ago without discussing its significance. I said that maximizing *on a case-by-case basis* would result in maximizing overall so long as all other arrangements were taken as fixed. But this is the kind of artificial restriction with which utilitarians are always, rightly, impatient. Why couldn't the two men manage to play at different times? Couldn't the partition between the flats be soundproofed? Is it really impossible for one of them to move? Couldn't one of them hire a music studio for the hour? Or might not one of them take up an alternative form of recreation that avoids the problem altogether? As I shall argue in the next chapter, utilitarianism gains greatly in plausibility when we add some realism of this kind.

THE CASE AGAINST

I now want to turn around and set out what I conceive to be the strongest case for saying that a fair solution to the problem of Matthew and Luke must have the characteristic of baseline-dependence. Let us begin with the negative side of the argument. What, then, is the case against baseline-independence? A quite common move against the utilitarian criterion (maximizing aggregate utility) is to say that it demands "too much sacrifice" on behalf of others to be acceptable.[29] And, although the details in the argument would have to change, it requires little imagination to see how the same sort of argument could be deployed against equal or maximin utility.

The objection may immediately be made that any such line of criticism consists in arguing in a circle. Saying that something involves an

excessive sacrifice implies that you already know what the right answer
is: it makes sense to speak of giving something up only against the background of some standard. But if you already have that standard (for
example, that each person has a "natural right" to whatever he can
make in the market) then the criticism to be made of other criteria
should be that they happen to be incompatible with it. Nothing is added
to this by talking about the "sacrifice" called for by utilitarian or other
criteria.[30]

Such an objection is in my view compelling. But we may still be able
to extract something from the idea. Let us look at things from the
perspective of a certain given actor, say, Matthew in Braithwaite's
story. What we can say is that, under a baseline-independent solution,
how often Matthew is going to be allowed to play—or even whether he
will be allowed to play at all—will depend on the specific circumstances
of his neighbor Luke. To be more precise, it will depend on the claims
Luke can make on the lines of "I get more utility from playing than you
do" or "I get less utility from other things in my life besides playing
than you do."

Thus, without any change in his own life, Matthew's morally
permissible share of playing time can change drastically as a result of
changes in Luke's life. Suppose that Luke breaks up with his girlfriend.
It could well be that he now has fewer alternative sources of enjoyment
so that playing the piano makes a much bigger difference to his utility
than before. Then he will be able to claim a good deal more time on the
utilitarian criterion than he had before. And it is quite conceivable that
on the equal or maximin utility criterion he can flip from never having a
chance to play to being able to play every evening.

We should be careful not to overdraw the contrast between this and
what can happen under baseline-dependency. For here, too, the adjudicated division of playing time between Matthew and Luke obviously
could change to Matthew's detriment purely as a result of changes in
Luke—or, of course, Luke's replacement by another tenant. It must
indeed be trivially true that any scheme for dividing up the time that
depends at all on the characteristics of the two occupants of the apartments (as against one that is totally invariant whatever their characteristics) will have this potential. But the way in which the characteristics
of the actors affect the adjudicated outcome differs from one solution to
another.

If we ask ourselves how one might come to favor baseline-dependent
solutions, we should ask what kind of attitude to one's fellows would

naturally give rise to such an approach. Among those who have discussed the case of Matthew and Luke, Lucas and Gauthier are explicit
about the underpinnings of baseline-dependence. Lucas, in defending
his version of an equal-gain solution, writes: "Thus my external'morality. It is hard, as are all legalistic moralities in which people do not care
for one another and extend to one another only that consideration
which is due to all men merely for being human, but it is less harsh than
Professor Braithwaite's. There is no vindictiveness, only indifference."[31]

Gauthier's scheme is designed explicitly, he says, to be appropriate to
"civil society," the kind of society whose characteristic institution of
social cooperation is the market,[32] and the psychology that Lucas
depicts fits in well with this kind of society. It is therefore hardly surprising that Lucas's proposed solution to the problem of Matthew and
Luke is identical in essentials to that of Gauthier, differing only in that
Lucas takes over Braithwaite's transformation of utilities while Gauthier, as we know, uses the method of splitting the difference. They
agree in stipulating that Matthew and Luke should divide the time so as
to retain the same relative advantage as they would have at the joint
maximin point. I have argued that the joint maximin may not be the
best way of getting the kind of solution they want. The important point
for the present, however, is that both accept that it is really fair for the
division of time to be determined by taking the division that preserves
equal advantage over an appropriate baseline.

Gauthier's general argument is that if people do not care about
one another, they will insist on not finishing up worse off as a result of
cooperation than they could make themselves if they did not cooperate.
Cooperation must be for some gain over what one could obtain without
it. The only question about distribution that is open therefore is how
the gains from cooperation are to be divided up, and this of course
entails baseline-dependence. "Viewing society as the means for producing and distributing an optimal social surplus, rational men [in the
original position] will only accept principles of distribution if they
restrict their scope to the surplus, and apportion it in accordance with
the contribution that each makes to its production."[33] In the case of
Matthew and Luke, that means an equal distribution of the "surplus,"
where the measure of equality is an equal gain in normalized utility,
the normalization being carried out in the way required for "splitting
the difference."

If we want to dig deeper into the origins of this kind of outlook, we
might say that it starts from a picture of a society as made up of indi-

viduals who are conceived of as having their own independent goals in life.

> A just society has no aim beyond those given in the preferences of its members. As a co-operative venture for mutual advantage, it enables each to promote what she holds good. An essentially just society does not introduce a social good as a function of individual goods. This distinguishes it most clearly from a utilitarian society, which also rejects any substantive conception of the good, or any aim beyond those based on the preferences of its members, but which supposes a social good as the sum of individual goods. A utilitarian society lacks any substantive aim but is concerned to realize the greatest sum of individual goods. A just society is concerned only to enable each person to realize the greatest amount of her own good, on terms acceptable to all.[34]

Presumably if all the members of a society were united in wanting to maximize aggregate utility, Gauthier would not be able to gainsay them. Each would be maximizing his own utility by cooperating in the pursuit of the society's aggregate utility. But if any members of the society do not wish to share in the project of "rearing the fabric of felicity," they cannot justly be coerced into joining in. They can insist on their "fair share" of the society's resources, as defined by Gauthier.

How do these ideas apply to Matthew and Luke? The implication is that if they had a common object in maximizing the quality of music produced in the two apartments, then they might be able to agree on the most effective means to that end; for example, that the more talented musician should practice all the time. But if they do not happen to share this goal, it cannot be introduced to form a basis for settling their dispute. And, by the same token, if they do not share the goal of maximizing the total utility experienced in the two apartments, that criterion cannot be used as a basis for determining who should play when.

10. A RESOURCIST SOLUTION

We finished the previous section with a rationale for baseline-dependence: that it is what people without any common purposes might be attracted to as a way of dealing with conflicts. But let us now ask this question. If we were to accept the arguments that led to baseline-dependence, should we not also be led by them to reject equal utility gain as the criterion for a fair way of moving from the nonagreement point to the Pareto frontier? If once we say that fair division of a scarce resource should be distinguished from the pursuit of large-scale purposes such as the maximization or equalization of overall utility, must we not be carried further by that same logic into denying that utility should come into the specification of a fair division at all?

We are, *ex hypothesi*, starting from a situation in which the parties have no concern for one another's welfare. That does not mean that we have to envisage them as rapacious egoists: we may suppose that they are capable of being motivated by considerations of fairness. But what, for such people, will fairness require? The suggestion here to be considered is that they will not accept that the division of the scarce resource in question should be set up with an eye to providing an equal gain in utility. Rather, they will think that what is fair is an equal division of the scarce resource (time, money, or whatever) itself.

It might be said, perhaps, that the resource is in dispute only because both parties want to have it. Since it is its utility-yielding characteristic that makes its division an issue, utility provides a natural common denominator in which to express a fair division. But the reply is that there is nothing natural about that conclusion, given what we are already postulating about the relations between the parties. If they do not share ends then why should they accept utility as a common denominator to determine how far each is going to be able to advance his own ends? Recall that we have assumed, in order to get a case for baseline-dependence, that the parties would not be prepared to subordinate the division of the thing in contention to the achievement of some over-arching distribution of utility. But then why should they accept the achievement of a certain distribution of utility as relevant to fairness, even in the limited sphere of dividing the gains over the noncooperative outcome?

Suppose we agree that I get as much utility gain (measured in a way we both accept as appropriate) from one quarter of a certain resource (e.g., time or money) as you do from three-quarters of it: that does not necessarily move me to acknowledge that it is fair for you to get three-quarters of the resource. Our dispute is, after all, over the division of the resource. The assumption is that we have equally good claims on it. Why not, then, divide the actual stuff in contention equally? This, we may recall, was Hobbes's suggestion about the appropriate way in which to divide a scarce resource between claimants who stand on an equal moral footing with one another (see above, section 6).

The argument against equal utility gain can be seen as one of consistency. As people with no interest in one another's welfare, we are not going to count claims arising from utility comparisons of the kind that would give more to someone who is more efficient at deriving utility from the resource, or more to someone who is overall worse off in utility terms. Why, then, should we accept the relevance of the more limited utility comparison involved in ascribing equal utility gain? Why should I agree that you have a fair claim to a larger share of the scarce resource simply because you happen to have a utility function of a certain shape and I have a utility function of some other shape and when these utility functions are plugged into some formula for equal utility gain it turns out that you do better?

The alternative is, then, that we do not look behind the division of the resource to ask what people will do with it or what they will get out of it. Once they have their "fair share" they can do what they like with it. Each person has purposes of his or her own, and the fair way of dividing scarce resources is to give each person an equal chance to use those resources to fulfill his purposes, whatever they are. Equal opportunity to benefit, equal access to the means of satisfaction, is the relevant equality here. This position is surely in line with commonsense thinking on the subject: I do not think anybody who had escaped long exposure to modern economics or modern philosophy would suppose for a moment that the fair distribution of money is anything but a fair distribution of the chance to buy things or that the distribution of playing time is anything but the distribution of time in which to play.

What is distinctive, then, about what we may call a resourcist solution to problems of fair division is this: the nonagreement point and the gain (if any) to be achieved by moving from it to some mutually advantageous alternative are to be defined right from the start in terms of the distribution of the scarce resource itself. In the case of Matthew and Luke that resource is, of course, solo playing time. It is worth emphasizing that this marks a clean break with all the other solutions so far considered in this book, whether baseline-dependent or not. In all the solutions discussed up to now, the significant question is taken to be how much utility (measured in one way or another) Matthew and Luke should finish up with. It is true, of course, that when the answer to that question has been determined, every solution translates it into a division of playing time. Such a translation from utilities to rights, opportunities, and so forth is standard practice. No utilitarian, for example, has ever proposed that laws and institutional rules should be expressed in terms that make explicit mention of utility. Thus, what makes a resourcist solution distinctive is not that the solution itself should be expressed in terms of playing time but that the division of playing time is not to be justified by reference to the utility that it generates. Rather, we talk about a fair division of the resource itself, without looking behind it to see what distribution of utility is implied by any given distribution of it.

To generate a specific resourcist solution, we need two things: a nonagreement baseline and a rule for moving away from it. In applying the resourcist solution to the problem of Matthew and Luke, I shall make use of a nonagreement baseline already canvassed in this chapter. This is the one that divides the resource of playing time under conditions of nonagreement in a way analogous to that in which money was divided at the nonagreement point in our legacy examples. That is to say, the starting point is that neither party gets any of it. At the end of this section I shall consider the implications of some alternative nonagreement baselines.

As before, our criterion for a fair division of the cooperative surplus is that the parties gain equally from it. What is distinctive is that equality is here to be measured in terms of the resource rather than the utility derived from it. Thus, in the present case we stipulate that any time that is allocated for solo playing must be divided so as to give Matthew and Luke the same amount.

It will simplify the exposition, without any loss of generality, if we consider divisions of playing time that can be contained within six evenings. The accompanying story might be that for some reason—legal imposition or prior agreement, for example—Sundays are out of the reckoning, so that only six evenings in the week are available for practicing; and that Matthew and Luke agree that any division of time must be contained within a single week. Since the proposed solution mandates equal playing time, this means that there are only four possible outcomes consistent with it: Matthew and Luke play three evenings a week each, two evenings a week each, one evening a week each, or not at all.

We can derive the preferences of Matthew and Luke among these valid alternatives from Braithwaite's payoff matrix. Once we have these purely ordinal preferences we need make no further use of the properties of Braithwaite's numbers in arriving at our solution. For convenience, however, I use these numbers as the coordinates in Figure 2.2. As can be seen, Matthew and Luke both prefer three evenings of playing apiece to two, two to one, and one to none. The imposition of an equal distribution of playing time thus eliminates the conflict of interest that is otherwise inherent in the situation with Braithwaite's payoffs. Among the admissible alternatives, both most prefer the same one, which is the one the solution picks.

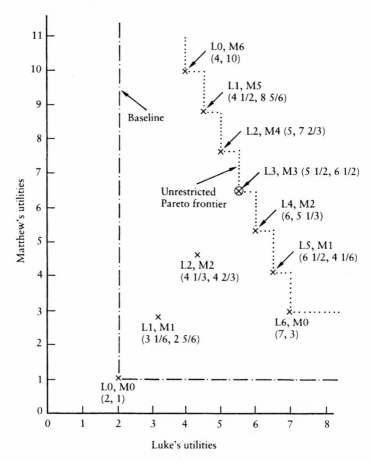

Figure 2.2.   The Resourcist Solution

To put the proposed solution through its paces we need to see how it works when we modify the payoffs given in Braithwaite's story. Suppose now that we change the payoff matrix so that Luke, instead of getting 4 units of utility from listening to Matthew, gets −4. (He may perhaps dislike cacophony even more than listening, but his utility from cacophony plays no part in the solution, so we can disregard it.) This means that he now prefers silence to an equal mix of playing and listening. With Matthew's utilities unchanged, we get Figure 2.3.

As before, we make no use of the utility numbers themselves in applying our solution. Their only function is to illustrate that a consistent story can be told about the orderings of outcomes. Luke's preference ordering among the available alternatives is now the opposite of what it

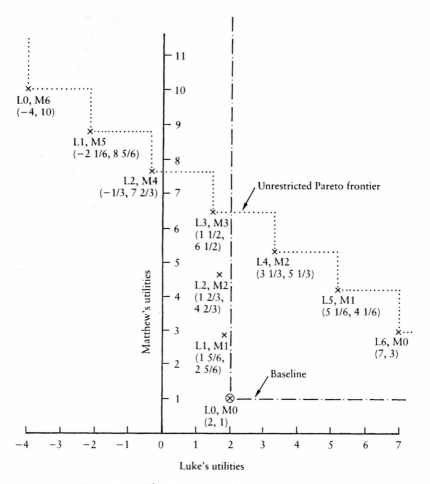

Figure 2.3.   The Resourcist Solution, First Variation

was. He most likes silence and, if there is to be any playing at all, he prefers one evening apiece to two, and two to three. Since we have postulated a baseline of silence, and silence is what Luke prefers to any admissible alternative, there is no mutually advantageous move away from it. The outcome chosen by our solution in this case is therefore no playing.

It may be seen, however, that this outcome is not Pareto-optimal in that there are ways of dividing up the playing time *unequally* that both Matthew and Luke would prefer to silence every evening. In Figure 2.3 the Pareto frontier contains the outcomes in which Luke plays four times out of six, five times out of six, and six times out of six. An obvious question that this presents us with is the following: should we insist on ruling out a move to the Pareto frontier that both prefer to the outcome prescribed by the requirement of equality? If we take problems of strategic behavior into account it is possible that we should. (I shall enlarge on this point in the next chapter.) But if we ignore strategic considerations it does look like a piece of collective irrationality for Matthew and Luke never to play when there is at least one alternative that both would prefer. We should bear in mind here that the resourcist solution is predicated as much as the equal-utility solution on the assumption that it is a good thing for the parties' wants to be satisfied. It differs only in defining fair shares directly in terms of resources.

In the light of what has just been said, I propose to call the solution put forward so far in this section the *strict solution* and to talk of an *extended solution* as well. To obtain the extended solution we first establish the outcome prescribed by the strict solution. (I shall assume for now that this is a unique outcome.) Then we see if it is inside the Pareto frontier. If it is, we replace it with the outcome or outcomes that are on the Pareto frontier and preferred by both Matthew and Luke to it. In the present case, as we have seen, there are three such points on the Pareto frontier and any of them is, in the extended sense, a fair outcome.

Let us now consider a second variation on the payoffs stipulated by Braithwaite. I want to drop Braithwaite's assumption that the desire to play (or listen) on any given evening is completely unaffected by what has happened on previous evenings. This assumption has the effect of forcing all-or-nothing preferences for playing on the parties when they are faced with the equal-time constraint of the strict solution. Either the average payoff of playing and listening for equal periods exceeds that of silence, in which case more playing time is always preferable to less, or silence is superior to a fifty-fifty mix of playing and listening, in which case the less playing the better. (If the average of playing and listening for equal time is the same as silence, any amount of playing time that satisfies the equal-time constraint is equally good.)

To get in a possibility that someone might prefer an intermediate amount of playing time within the constraint of equality, we have to allow the utility of playing, listening, or silence (or more than one) to depend on the frequency with which they occur. Let us again change Luke's payoffs from those in Braithwaite's original payoff matrix, this time so that the value to him of an evening of playing varies inversely with the number of evenings in a week that he plays. Specifically, one evening per week of playing yields 12 units of utility, a second evening 9 units, a third 6 units, a forth 3 units, and additional evenings nothing. We shall retain the payoff of -4 units from listening to Matthew.

Once more, it should be emphasized that the utility numbers are merely a help in visualizing the situation and ensuring that the story is internally consistent. All we actually use from this are the preferences between outcomes that we now attribute to Luke. His highest preference (among the equal-time possibilities) is now that he and Matthew should play on two evenings each per week, with two evenings of silence. His next preference is for one evening each of playing, with four evenings of silence. This is followed by three evenings each of playing. And in last place comes no playing at all.

If Matthew has the same utilities as usual, we have Figure 2.4. We can see that silence comes in last place for both, and also that playing one evening per week each is dominated by playing two evenings per week each. We can therefore eliminate these as outcomes under the strict solution. But playing two evenings per week each does not dominate playing three evenings per week each, nor is it dominated by it. Luke prefers the first and Matthew the second. Both outcomes therefore have to stay in under the strict solution. The strict solution thus cannot be depended on to generate a unique outcome.

We can ask whether the extended solution has any application here. We need first to redefine it for the case of multiple outcomes under the strict solution. We now say that *any* outcome not on the Pareto frontier is to be replaced by the outcome or outcomes that dominate it and are on the Pareto frontier. Let us now look at the two outcomes produced by the strict solution. As we can see from Figure 2.4, the outcome preferred by Matthew, where both play on three evenings a week, is already on the Pareto frontier. But the outcome preferred by Luke, where they both play on two evenings a week, is inside the Pareto frontier. It is dominated by the outcome on the Pareto frontier where Luke plays four times a week and Matthew two. Thus, the extended solution gives us two outcomes both of which utilize all the time available for playing: a three-three split and a four-two split in Luke's favor.

What should happen when either the strict or the extended solution generates more than one outcome? Our resourcist theory simply tells us that these alternatives are fair. But only one of them can be implemented. How can we decide which it should be? We could resort to the line of reasoning followed in the first section of this chapter. If either of two outcomes is fair, we might say, then it is presumably legitimate

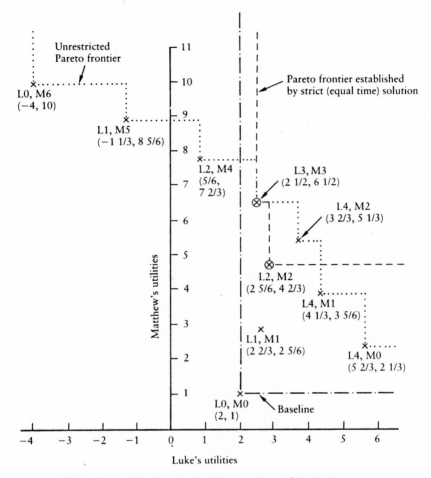

Figure 2.4.   The Resourcist Solution, Second Variation

for the parties to bargain over them. So an adjudicator might apply a bargaining solution in order to reach a decision. This is not, however, the only possible way of dealing with the problem. Taking a lead from Hobbes, we might suggest flipping a coin to settle the issue. Or, by violating the requirement that any solution should fit into a single sequence of six days, we could propose splitting the difference between the two outcomes by implementing them in alternate weeks. Thus, in the case just discussed, the extended solution would let Matthew play on five evenings in every twelve and Luke play on the remaining seven evenings.

I promised to say something about alternatives to the nonagreement baseline used in the main analysis of Braithwaite's example, and I shall finish this discussion of resourcist solutions by doing so. The nonagreement baseline used so far presupposed that the right not to have noise imposed on one should have absolute priority. But it could be suggested that self-expression by playing a musical instrument is also worthy of protection. In the next chapter I shall look at the choice of baselines in a broader context. For the present, however, let us simply complete the analysis by asking how a more permissive nonagreement baseline would work out within a resourcist framework.

It will be most economical to go to the opposite extreme and ask what would happen if the nonagreement baseline were that Matthew is to play for an hour on Mondays, Wednesdays, and Fridays, while Luke is to have Tuesdays, Thursdays, and Saturdays. Obviously they can, by mutual agreement, rearrange the evenings, either permanently or from week to week. But what about the actual numbers of evenings that each gets under this arrangement? Is there any reason to depart from it?

Given the payoffs attributed to the two men in the Braithwaite example and our two variations on it, the answer is no. This is, I take it, easy enough to see when we retain Braithwaite's own payoffs, since both men prefer the new nonagreement point to any equal-time alternative. And although each would, of course, prefer unequal-time alternatives to it, there is none that both would simultaneously prefer. This follows from the fact that the new nonagreement point is already on the Pareto frontier.

In the first variant, it will be recalled, Luke preferred silence to any equal-time alternative, so on the strict solution the baseline of silence was also the outcome. With the new nonagreement baseline, Luke loses his veto on playing. Instead, Matthew gets a veto on any arrangement that lets him play less often than three evenings per week. Since the more he plays the better he likes it, he will obviously take the three evenings he is offered. And although Luke would prefer silence to any equal mix of playing and listening, that preference is now irrelevant and the only question for him is whether to play or not. He prefers playing to silence, so he plays. A solution with both playing half the time is on the Pareto frontier: there are, again, many alternatives that one or the other would prefer but there is none that would be preferred by both of them.

Exactly the same can be said of the second variant on Braithwaite's payoffs. Luke would prefer two evenings of playing per week to three among the equal-time alternatives, but Matthew has no reason for mov-

ing away from the three evenings of playing that he is guaranteed—
except in an upward direction. But Luke would sooner use the three
evenings per week that he is allocated initially to play himself than
either do nothing or cede the time to Matthew. Thus once again the
nonagreement point is on the Pareto frontier.

In order to get our equal-time solution to bring about a departure
from the new nonagreement point we have to change the payoffs. The
simplest way of illustrating this is to imagine that in our first and second
variations on Braithwaite's payoffs those that we have attributed to
Luke are shared by Matthew as well. Consider, then, the first variant.
Both now have the following preference order for equal-time solutions:
no playing, each play one evening, each play two evenings, each play
three evenings. The nonagreement outcome of each playing on three
evenings per week is thus dominated by all the alternatives permissible
under the strict solution. The strict solution therefore mandates that
neither should play, since this is the outcome most preferred by both. It
is clear that there is no departure from this that both would prefer
simultaneously, so we can add that there is no room for the extended
solution to operate here.

In the second variant on Braithwaite's payoffs, we now attribute to
both Matthew and Luke a common preference ordering among permissible alternatives that goes as follows: play two evenings per week
each, play one evening per week each, play three evenings per week
each, not play at all. Since both prefer two evenings of silence to the
nonagreement baseline that allocates all the available time to playing,
the strict solution says that that is what should happen. And, once
again, there is no alternative that both would prefer to that one, so it
remains unchanged when we open up the possibility of moving to an
extended solution.

It would, obviously, be possible to pursue indefinitely the analysis of
alternative nonagreement baselines under different utility assumptions.
I believe, however, that what has been done here should give the reader
a feel for resourcism and the distinctive way in which it approaches the
problem of fair division. The time has now come to assess the various
solution concepts from a broader perspective, and to start looking at
the conditions under which conflicts such as those between Matthew
and Luke actually occur.

CHAPTER III

Fair Division from a Wider Perspective

11. INTRODUCTION

When introducing Braithwaite's problem in chapter 1, I confined myself to presenting only the features—in particular the payoffs—that were essential for getting the analysis off the ground. Now that we are ready to take a wider view of the problem, we can do no better than to look at Braithwaite's original presentation of the case in his inaugural lecture. Braithwaite is quite conscientious in setting out all the assumptions that are required to create the problem, and the result is to bring home in a dramatic way its extreme artificiality. No doubt it is only fair to add that not every problem of fair division will be as artificial as Braithwaite's. But much of the artificiality is inherent in the whole class of problems to which Braithwaite's belongs. For the biggest contribution to lack of realism simply consists in starting the analysis with the problem as stated, with two people locked into a conflict where no solution is very satisfactory. The Pareto frontier defines a set of satisfactory (i.e., efficient) alternatives and the question is supposed to be which one to pick as the most fair. Quite often, however, it is a mistake simply to take the problem as given. It may be possible to find ways of relaxing the constraints that create the problem so that it either disappears or at least becomes less severe.

A nice illustration of what I have in mind is provided by Arthur Caplan's account of his experiences as an "ethical consultant" to a large hospital in New York City. He describes one of the problems he was presented with as follows:

> Every summer the emergency room of the hospital filled up with persons suffering from emphysema and other respiratory ailments. The hot weather made it very difficult for such persons to breathe comfortably, and they came to the emergency room to receive oxygen. Unfortunately, there were only two oxygen units available, and there were often a dozen or more persons seeking to use them at various times during the day and night. The staff of the emergency room asked my help in developing a set of criteria for deciding what would be a fair and equitable allocation of their scarce medical resources.[1]

As he tells it, Caplan's first reaction was to treat this as a problem in fair division of a scarce resource. He therefore consulted various anthologies of medical ethics to see "what various philosophers and theologians had to say about issues of micro-allocation and ethics." The result was what one might expect: "some defended a criterion of merit, some a criterion of need, some a criterion of social utility, and some a random lottery." At this point, however, Caplan thought of a different way of approaching the problem. It occurred to him "that it might be possible to solve the allocation problem by ameliorating the source of the scarcity." Happily, it was. "I asked some of the emergency room staff if Medicaid/Medicare covered the provision of air conditioners in the homes of persons suffering from respiratory ailments. It turned out, much to everyone's surprise, that the machines could be prescribed and the cost reimbursed. I ascended to the status of moral guru in the emergency room, famous as the man who had solved the oxygen machine crunch."[2]

Here, now, is Braithwaite's own account of the problem of the two musicians. In introducing it, Braithwaite says, with unconscious irony, that he will "try to make it as realistic as possible," while cautioning that "of course various simplifying assumptions will have to be introduced in order that the example may be paradigmatic of the collaboration situation in general."[3] The example itself is now stated as follows:

> Suppose that Luke and Matthew are both bachelors, and occupy flats in a house which has been converted into two flats by an architect who had ignored all considerations of acoustics. Suppose that Luke can hear everything louder than a conversation that takes place in Matthew's flat, and vice versa; but that sounds in the two flats do not penetrate outside the house. Suppose that it is legally impossible for either to prevent the other from

making as much noise as he wishes, and economically or sociologically impossible for either to move elsewhere. Suppose further that each of them has only the hour from 9 to 10 in the evening for recreation, and that it is impossible for either to change to another time. Suppose that Luke's form of recreation is to play classical music on the piano for an hour at a time, and that Matthew's amusement is to improvise jazz on the trumpet for an hour at once. And suppose that whether or not either of them performs on one evening has no influence, one way or the other, upon the desires of either of them to perform on any other evening; so that each evening's happenings can be treated independently. Suppose that the satisfaction each derives from playing his instrument for the hour is affected, one way or the other, by whether or not the other is also playing: in radio language, there is "interference" between them, positive or negative. Suppose that they put to me the problem: Can any plausible principle be devised stating how they should divide the proportion of days on which both of them play . . . , Luke alone plays . . . , Matthew alone plays . . . , neither plays . . . , so as to obtain maximum production of satisfaction compatible with fair distribution?[4]

Rather than plunge in and ask what adjudication Braithwaite should make, it would surely be sensible to ask first if it is really necessary to divide up the time at all. Why cannot the soundproofing be improved? Why cannot at least one of them move? Might not one of them rent a studio for an hour each evening (perhaps with a financial contribution from the other)? Is it really impossible for one of them to rearrange his schedule so as to play at some other hour? Or, going further away from the case as stated, might not one of them spend his free hour practicing some other hobby (reading, building model ships, or whatever) while listening to the other play? Braithwaite's remark that he has tried to make the example as realistic as possible consistently with its being paradigmatic of the type of problem might lead us to conclude that there must be something fishy about the type of problem.

Pointing out the peculiarities of the situation depicted by Braithwaite as the setting of the problem is only the beginning, however. Braithwaite asks us to "[s]uppose that it is legally impossible for either to prevent the other from making as much noise as he wishes." Where, then, are we supposed to imagine this as taking place? In a Hobbesian state of nature? In all civilized countries it would be possible to obtain an injunction to prevent a next-door neighbor from making "as much noise as he wishes." There are often in addition local rules more restrictive than those the courts would enforce under tort law, as I pointed out in my discussion of Lucas's proposal to make Matthew and Luke Fellows occupying adjacent sets of rooms in a college.

It is, of course, true that such rules would not do anything to solve the particular problem of Matthew and Luke presented by Braithwaite. But in conceding that, we should at the same time observe that their problem is a highly unusual one, arising from their eccentric preferences in conjunction with the extraordinary rigidity of their timetables. The standard problem with noise from neighbors is that of simple excess. But Matthew and Luke actually like to hear each other practice: "Luke's first preference is for him to play . . . , his second preference is for Matthew alone to play . . . (since he quite likes jazz when he is not playing himself)," and silence comes only after that, followed by cacophony.[5] Similarly, "Matthew . . . has as first preference his playing the trumpet while Luke is silent, his second preference Luke's alone playing, his third preference both of them playing, while the thing he likes least is that neither of them should play (since he likes a cheerful noise about the house)."[6] Thus, if it were not for the time constriction, there would be no problem, since each would enjoy hearing the other when not playing himself. The usual limitations on playing time are therefore neither necessary nor sufficient to solve their problem. But such limitations do speak to the problems that people with less peculiar preferences have.

Leaving all of these points aside, and taking the problem as presented by Braithwaite as the one to deal with, there is a grave practical objection to Braithwaite's proposed solution. This is that it needs a Braithwaite to do the calculations. (It also needs a Braithwaite to understand their rationale, but let us waive that for the present.) That, however, is still not the worst. The insuperable practical objection to Braithwaite's solution is that it requires, in order to put it into effect, utility information which may well not be obtainable in principle, which would be exceedingly laborious to collect even with the honest cooperation of the subjects, and which they both have an incentive to falsify if they can understand the formula into which the information is to be fed sufficiently to realize how they can make the outcome more favorable by strategic misrepresentation. Moreover, this same disability equally hampers the application of all of the solutions that have been discussed in the first two chapters, with the sole exception of the one that was introduced at the end of the previous chapter. (Even that one is not without its problems, as I shall explain in section 13.)

Braithwaite disarmingly dismisses the whole problem of obtaining the required information about utilities by saying: "Suppose that Luke . . ." has a set of preferences over lotteries involving the four possible outcomes that would define von Neumann/Morgenstern utilities for them, and similarly for Matthew.[7] How this information is to be ascertained by Braithwaite, once he is appointed arbitrator, is a problem that is finessed by using the utility information already "assumed" without any discussion of the way it is come by. Indeed, the power of supposition to solve intractable problems is apparently boundless. According to Braithwaite, the utility scale

> is able to allow for envy, malice and all uncharitableness. For we shall suppose that Luke knows Matthew's preference scale, and vice versa. If Matthew has constructed his preference scale in the first instance without considering Luke's valuations, he is at perfect liberty to modify it when he knows these. Thus it may relatively diminish his satisfaction in trumpeting while Luke is silent if he knows how much Luke would enjoy playing the piano. Or, if he is a disagreeable man, the prospect of thwarting Luke may increase his satisfaction. We will suppose that these adjustments have all been made, so that the L-utilities measure Luke's preferences and the M-utilities measure Matthew's preferences when each knows the other's valuations.[8]

We must surely regard as suspect any solution that could be put into effect accurately only by Almighty God, unto whom all hearts are open, all desires known, and from whom no secrets are hid. Much of this chapter will consist essentially of an elaboration of that point and an attempt to see where we are led if we take it really seriously. I shall begin by explaining more fully the problems of obtaining information about utilities. This will take up the next section. I shall then argue (in section 13) that solutions should be judged by the degree to which they depend on utility information and, especially, the degree to which they lend themselves to manipulation by people who succeed in misrepresenting their utilities. Solutions along the lines of the resourcist one put forward at the end of the previous chapter become more attractive when we take such considerations into account. And the same considerations, I shall suggest later in section 13, make the strict solution more advantageous in relation to the extended one than was allowed to appear when they were presented as alternative resourcist solutions in section 10.

In the course of this discussion, I shall often look beyond problems of fair division taken individually and ask what social rules would be best fitted to dealing with whole classes of such problems. This will be the explicit subject of section 14. Here I shall return to the contention with which I began the present section: that we should often refuse to accept that the conditions creating a problem of fair division are unalterable. I shall in particular argue that fixed rules to which people can over time adapt their behavior can avoid a lot of problems. Section 15 extends the discussion by taking up a case of small-scale conflict of interest that is currently a matter of real controversy, namely, the competing claims of smokers and nonsmokers over the scarce resource constituted by their common air supply. The chapter ends with a section containing some concluding remarks about Part I as a whole.

12. THE ELUSIVENESS OF UTILITY

There is a great tendency for theorists of fair division to follow Braithwaite in adopting a God's-eye view. They simply assume right at the outset that we (and—more to the point—the person who has to arbitrate) have access to reliable information about the choices of the parties over hypothetical lotteries and that this information permits the construction of consistent utility schedules. Most often this information simply appears in the text as if by magic. If it does not come from the Almighty in person then we have to take it that (as was at one time said of off-the-record briefings by Richard Nixon) it comes from an unimpeachable source. But this hopelessly skews the whole analysis, since we are looking at numbers representing the utilities of the parties that neither they nor an arbitrator would ever have. (Even if they had some numbers, they could never be certain that they were *the* numbers. But this is exactly what we are invited to assume when we are presented with a payoff matrix in an article about fair division.) Thus, solutions that might seem attractive enough with all the problems about "how do we know" cleared away by fiat are liable to lose their shine when we take account of the inherent unreliability of any such information and the costs that would be involved in collecting even highly imperfect versions of the utility schedules that we find taken for granted in the literature of fair division.

The great exception is provided by Luce and Raiffa, who sensibly warn that "there is always the fear that the real problem may have been abstracted away" if we assume

> that each player knows the true tastes—the utility functions—of the others. For example, suppose that in a bargaining situation the players agree to submit to an arbiter who is committed to Nash's assumptions. To resolve the conflict, the arbiter must first ascertain their utility functions; hence the situation deteriorates into a game of strategy where each player tries to solve the problem of how best to falsify or exaggerate his true tastes. In most

situations, a player's preferences are only partially known to his adversary, and falsification of one's true feelings is an inherent and important bargaining strategy. An arbiter, to be successful, must skillfully ferret out at least a part of the truth.[9]

All these remarks obviously apply with redoubled force to solutions that demand utility information of a more elaborate kind than that needed to put into effect the prescriptions of the two-stage solutions, such as a prescription of maximizing or equalizing overall utility.

Let us look a bit more systematically at the problems that arise in making estimates of cardinal utility, whether interpersonally comparable or not. Collecting the information would, to begin with, be time-consuming. It would also require a good deal of intrusion into private affairs. Whether it is the parties themselves who are seeking to apply a formula or some arbitrator to whom they have turned over the job, if they want a baseline-independent outcome involving interpersonal utility comparisons they are going to have to disclose a lot about their general level of satisfaction with life or about the increment that such things as playing a musical instrument on an extra evening per week would provide. Even the von Neumann/Morgenstern utility information required for the Nash solution or for splitting the difference could be obtained only with a lot of digging to make the relevant estimates.

What makes the problem of obtaining information particularly recalcitrant is that the parties have no incentive to cooperate wholeheartedly with efforts to establish the truth about themselves. On the contrary, assuming that they know how the solution varies according to the utility data fed into the formula, they will, as Luce and Raiffa pointed out, be aware that they can shift the outcome in their own favor by successful dissimulation. Not only does this make the task more difficult—the point seized on by Luce and Raiffa—but it also makes it more unpleasant. If there is enough at stake to make the outcome matter, the relations between the parties, or the parties and the arbitrator, are liable to be poisoned by a miasma of suspicion.

Even if we shove all these difficulties aside, we are still left with the problem that utility estimates are bound to be approximate and, within certain limits, open to controversy. The implication is, however, that both parties can finish up simultaneously feeling that they should have got more out of the application of the formula. Even if the parties reach the Pareto frontier, there is still a psychic loss from the indeterminacy of the utility estimates on which the outcome was based.

All this presupposes that there is a stable structure of preferences waiting to be discovered and that the only difficulty lies in actually finding out what it is. But work by cognitive psychologists in the past two decades is often taken as establishing that this is an illusion. To quote a recent summary of this research: "evidence is mounting in support of the view that our values are often not clearly apparent, even to ourselves; that methods for measuring values are intrusive and biased; that the structure of any decision problem is psychologically unstable; and that the processes whereby elusive values are integrated into decisions within such unstable structures lead to actions that differ in dramatic ways from the predictions of utility theory."[10]

It has thus been found, for example, that what is essentially the same hypothetical choice problem is answered differently according to the way in which it is framed.

> Tversky and Kahneman . . . have presented numerous illustrations of framing effects, one of which involves the following pair of problems, given to separate groups of respondents.
>
> 1. Problem 1. Imagine that the United States is preparing for the outbreak of an unusual disease, which is expected to kill 600 people. Two alternative programs to combat the disease have been proposed. Assume that the consequences of the programs are as follows: If Program A is adopted, 200 people will be saved. If Program B is adopted, there is 1/3 probability that 600 people will be saved, and 2/3 probability that no people will be saved. Which of the two programs would you favor?
>
> 2. Problem 2. (Same cover story as Problem 1.) If Program C is adopted, 400 people will die. If Program D is adopted, there is 1/3 probability that nobody will die, and 2/3 probability that 600 people will die. Which of the two programs would you favor?
>
> The preference patterns tend to be quite different in the two problems. In a study of college students, 72 percent of the respondents chose Program A over Program B and 78 percent chose Program D over Program C. Another study, surveying physicians, obtained very similar results. On closer examination, we can see that the two problems are essentially identical. The only difference between them is that the outcomes are described by the number of lives saved in Problem 1 and the number of lives lost in Problem 2.[11]

These findings and many others related to them have been taken to show that the utility functions postulated by economists and game theorists simply do not exist.[12] For the very definition of von Neumann/Morgenstern utilities depends on the transitivity of preferences over lotteries, and this is violated by these so-called preference-reversal results.

To assert this may, however, be somewhat to overstate the position. The results are characteristically derived from the answers to hypothetical questions about what subjects would choose or would prefer, but nothing actually turns on what answers are given. Thus, the only direct evidence that these experiments provide is about what people say—about "verbal behavior," as behavioralistically inclined psychologists quaintly call it.[13] When experimental subjects are asked to make choices that have actual consequences (typically financial), it has been found that their choices tend to fit the axioms of rational choice better the more money there is at stake.[14]

Results of this kind, supported by common observation, suggest that we do not go too far wrong in attributing to human beings a set of reasonably consistent underlying preferences. At the same time, it is clear that asking about choices over hypothetical lotteries is a very poor method for finding out about the strengths of people's preferences. How important this qualification is taken to be depends on the spirit in which one took the definition of utilities in terms of choices over hypothetical lotteries in the first place.

For the adherents of the principle of meaning as verification, who first popularized the idea that these responses are hard data, it is very serious indeed. Braithwaite belongs to the generation of true believers in logical positivism, so it is naturally put forward by him as a great advantage of von Neumann/Morgenstern utilities that they do not "presuppose any inter-personal comparison of utilities by means of a unit of utility common to both Luke and Matthew, still less any possibility of transference of units of utility from one to the other. Thus, [the use of von Neumann/Morgenstern utilities] avoids the most serious criticism levelled against the assumptions of welfare economics."[15]

What Braithwaite is here referring to is the criticism first made by Lionel Robbins of the kind of welfare economics that culminated in A. C. Pigou's magisterial *The Economics of Welfare*.[16] Thus, Braithwaite tells us that welfare economists "have come in for a great deal of criticism recently from their fellow-economists based largely upon the impossibility of any inter-personal comparison of utilities."[17] With the qualification that "recently" is a rather belated adverb for someone writing in 1954 to apply to a prewar phenomenon, this is accurate enough. Robbins explicitly made the verificationist argument that assertions about utility were meaningless because there was no empirical evidence for them. At best, an assertion about utility was a "value judgment"—construed on standard logical positivist lines as the expression of an attitude rather than as something that could be true or false.[18] The basic notion at work here was that other people are inscrutable: we can never really know what anyone else is feeling, because feelings are internal and all we have direct access to is external movements.[19]

This view rests on an assumption about the relation between observation and knowledge that is untenable. Not merely judgments about utility but judgments about anything else of any complexity would fall before this standard of verification. Of course, there is no relation of entailment between any collection of statements about someone and an assertion about the person's pains and pleasures or likes and dislikes. No more is there a set of rules telling us how, in general, to get from a collection of bits of information about the world to an estimate of how likely something is to happen. But we know, in both cases, what kind of thing counts as evidence and we may well be able to narrow down the range of judgments that are compatible with the evidence. And in addition to judgments about people taken one at a time, I believe that we can sometimes be quite confident in maintaining, say, that one person has a more satisfying life than another, and that one person gets more pleasure from a given activity than another person does.

The idea that extreme skepticism about "other minds" could be met partially by identifying intrapersonal utilities with patterns of choice was foolish from the start. If there is some insuperable difficulty in inferring psychic states from bodily movements (e.g., pain from cries and grimaces), then the difficulty is in no way ameliorated when the movements happen to consist of making marks on a piece of paper by manipulating a pencil or making sounds by moving the vocal cords. The theorist has to interpret the marks or sounds as meaningful responses. Having done that, it is still necessary to decide whether they constitute good evidence about the subject's preferences or not.

If the responses form a consistent pattern, the theorist can construct a utility schedule from it. But to say that what one now has is the subject's *utility schedule* is to claim more than that it is a compact representation of the responses. It is supposed to be a prediction about the way the person would actually behave when faced with situations of choice. But that is a bold leap of inference—from one kind of behavior to another entirely different kind—that no well-brought-up verificationist ought to dream of countenancing (if verificationists ever dream).

In spite of its perennial attractions, it is a muddle, or a family of muddles, to suppose that von Neumann/Morgenstern utilities are "observable" in a way that intensities of preference, thought of in the ordinary way, are not. It cannot be emphasized enough that it has never been suggested that von Neumann/Morgenstern utility schedules were to be established as a practical matter by placing people in real choice situations, where their choices would have real consequences for them. Yet the claims sometimes made for such utility schedules would, it seems to me, be valid only if they were constructed in that way: by observing choices rather than by asking questions.*

If a utility schedule had been constructed by observing a large number of actual choices, the inference from utility schedule to future behavior would be reasonably well supported. One would be saying that a person who makes a certain choice in a given situation is likely to choose the same way again if the situation recurs. But the connection between responses to questions about hypothetical lotteries and actual behavior is obviously more tenuous. The news that most people's responses to pencil-and-paper tests do not even form a consistent pattern, so that no utility schedule can be constructed out of them, is simply the last nail in the coffin of an idea that should already have been pronounced dead.

How, then, should we understand the utility numbers that were thrown around in the preceding two chapters in the course of the exposition and analysis of the Nash solution, splitting the difference, and Braithwaite's own solution? For an answer I would suggest that we revert to a commonsense way of thinking about preferences from the highly artificial one imposed by the verificationists. Ordinarily, we would say that if someone strongly prefers A to B that *explains* why the person chooses an action with a low probability of producing A to one

---

*Actually, even the supposition that a strict verificationist could observe choices is invalid. For to say that someone is making a certain choice in a certain situation is to say something that goes enormously far beyond anything that can be identified with a set of bodily movements. If the information is to be any use for constructing a utility schedule one must attribute to the agent a mass of complex beliefs about the nature of the situation—that if he does this it has a certain probability of resulting in one thing, a certain probability of resulting in another, and so on and so on. Similarly, the use of the utility schedule, once constructed, in order to predict an action in a certain situation requires that the situation be identified not by its physical characteristics but by the beliefs about its properties that the agent holds. Suppose the verificationist responds by saying "I didn't mean to be *that* strict. Surely we arrive at estimates of what people believe on the basis of observation—how else could we? So ultimately our estimates about von Neumann/Morgenstern utilities do rest on observation." The only possible reply is "Welcome to the human race." There is of course a sense in which everything we know about people is based on observation (unless you believe in thought-transference by some means that bypasses the ordinary processes of perception). But in that sense we can know a lot else besides von Neumann/Morgenstern utilities. For example, we can say that a kick on the shin is more painful than having the skin on the back of the hand pinched, and this holds not only for comparisons within persons but across persons.

with a much higher probability of producing B, where these choices are mutually exclusive. The verificationist invites us to construe the statement that the person strongly prefers A as simply the equivalent of the statement that the person chooses A in the conditions specified. Saying that the person chose A because A was strongly preferred would be, if we accepted the verificationist's invitation, exactly like saying that someone is a bachelor because he is unmarried. The two are simply different ways of saying the same thing.

If we reject the verificationist's invitation, as I urge we should, then we shall regard the notion of a preference and the derived notion of utility as broad-gauge concepts that play a central role in our thinking about human life. Contrary to the verificationists, there is no unique set of observations equivalent to any statement about preferences or utilities. There is a whole variety of relevant evidence, from what people do and what they say, and what other people apparently somewhat similar do and say. This evidence is rarely conclusive but is quite often good. At the same time, preferences also explain a wide variety of phenomena, including actions and emotions.

It will be recalled that in chapter 1, I followed the orthodoxy in defining utilities in terms of choices over hypothetical lotteries. Where is that left now? The answer I propose is that we should think of choices among lotteries not as constitutive of utility but as one of its expressions. To repeat: if someone does strongly prefer A to B, then this ought to have some consequences for the person's choices when A and B come with probabilities attached to them. We can if we like use this implication in order to represent our guess about the strength of someone's preferences for various alternative outcomes as a set of choices over hypothetical lotteries. But this is not to be regarded as the canonical interpretation of the notion of strength of preference. To present someone's preferences in this form, as a set of choices satisfying the requirements of consistency that enable a utility schedule to be constructed out of it, is simply to offer an idealization that may be useful for some purposes. As we know from the work of the cognitive psychologists, however, it could never actually be constructed by asking the subject questions about hypothetical lotteries.

What does all this mean for the various solution concepts that made use of von Neumann/Morgenstern utility? It seems to me that much depends on the interpretation that is given to the solution. Let us go back to the discussion of the Nash solution in section 2, and think of it as (a) a prediction about what two people engaged in actual bargaining would finish up with, to the degree that they were rational, (b) a pre-scription for an arbitrator who, for one reason or another, wishes to produce an adjudication that will stimulate the outcome of rational bargaining, or (c) as an adjudication put forward as fair because it gives the parties an equal gain in utility.

In case (a), a theorist, standing outside the negotiation, assigns utility schedules to the parties by some means or other (past experience, sheer guesswork, or whatever) and then cranks out a prediction by applying the Nash formula. There is nothing in the Nash solution itself that requires the utility schedules to be interpreted in the von Neumann/Morgenstern manner. Any set of numbers that the theorist believes to represent relative preference for the outcomes can be used.

In case (b), the outside theorist making a prediction is transformed into the arbitrator making an adjudication based on an estimate of what rational bargaining would produce. Obviously, everything that was said about case (a) applies equally here: what matters is that the utility schedules attributed to the parties should work when fed into the Nash formula, so that each of the parties has some sense that (allowing for the possibility of failing to reach an agreement) it was unlikely to have done better from direct bargaining.

When I discussed arbitration as a substitute for bargaining, I made two points that are relevant here. One was that the arbitrator may use any methods she likes for trying to determine the strength of the parties' preferences for alternative outcomes. These could include asking them questions about choices over hypothetical lotteries, but need not. In practice, although a skillful arbitrator will talk extensively to the par-ties, questions about choices over hypothetical lotteries are not, as far as I know, ever asked. We might find here some confirmation of the cogni-tive psychologists' findings from the accumulated wisdom of arbitra-tors. The second point that is relevant is that arbitrators do not simply announce an award as representing the Nash solution or some other bargaining solution. We do not, in other words, find them stating baldly that, having made the best utility estimates they can, they have con-cluded that such-and-such a figure accurately reflects the balance of power between the parties. Rather, they come up with some formula for relating the award to some principle, some comparison, or some prece-dent. The inevitable fuzziness of utility estimates does not therefore undermine the legitimacy of the adjudication, because it is not overtly and officially put forward as a surrogate for the outcome of bargaining.

Finally, we have (c), where solutions employing von Neumann/

Morgenstern utilities, such as the Nash solution, are used with the justification that they are fair because they give each party an equal share (in terms of some appropriately normalized utility measure) of the gains from cooperation. The problem of indeterminacy carries over from the second case to this third one, but it causes far more trouble here. For in this case the arbitrator is, we are to suppose, to defend the allotment reached by an explicit appeal to the criterion of equal utility gain. The obvious problem here is that, once the determinacy of the utility figures and hence of the arbitrated outcome disappears, the ability of the adjudication to settle disputes is at risk. The arbitrator is left saying rather lamely that her best guess is that doing so-and-so would equalize utility gain. But the parties may well feel unhappy with this because it makes the outcome turn on the arbitrator's unsupported judgment. As soon as the illusion that utility is capable of precise and undisputable measurement goes, we can no longer say that the equal-gain solution provides a way of reaching a definite answer which the parties can accept.

The closest cousin to equal utility gain is equal resource gain. The resourcist solution sketched in section 10 is also a two-stage theory. It too starts from a baseline and moves from there to the Pareto frontier. It too is based on the notion that the parties should gain equally in the move from the baseline to the Pareto frontier. The only point of difference lies in what is to be divided: for a resourcist theory the equal gain should be an equal gain in access to the resource (the right, opportunity, money, and so on) whose distribution is in dispute, and not an equal gain in the utility arising from the enjoyment of the resource, normalized in some appropriate way.

It may be recalled that I argued in section 10 that the ethical assumption commonly advanced in favor of equal utility gain as a solution to problems of fair division seemed to point more naturally to equal resource gain. We can now add, in case that argument was not persuasive, a practical argument for moving from equal utility gain to equal resource gain: that equal resource gain is far easier to implement and leaves less room for dispute about whether or not it has been implemented correctly.

Thus, in the problem of dividing the legacy, the criterion of equal division of the gain from agreement leads quite unambiguously to an equal division of the money. There is nothing either of the parties can say about its utility schedule that will change that outcome to its advantage, assuming that each party prefers more money to less. Braithwaite's problem of the two musicians is more complex and I shall analyze it from this point of view in section 13. But I can anticipate one conclusion of that analysis by saying that, if the parties actually have the utility schedules attributed to them by Braithwaite, then the strict solution provides no incentive for dissimulation.

13. IMPLICATIONS

EQUAL-GAIN SOLUTIONS

In the previous section, I looked at the conclusions that might be drawn from the view that von Neumann/Morgenstern utilities have no privileged epistemic status in relation to any other estimates of the strength of people's preferences. One conclusion was that equal utility gain is an inappropriate, because inherently disputable, basis for adjudicating conflicts over scarce resources if the decision is presented as embodying intrinsic fairness rather than simulating the results of rational bargaining. However, the breaking down of the division between von Neumann/Morgenstern utilities and other utility estimates may also be seen in a more positive light. Instead of looking on the dark side and saying that von Neumann/Morgenstern utilities are no better than others, we might instead look on the bright side and say that other utility estimates are no worse than von Neumann/Morgenstern utilities. Once we throw off old-fashioned verificationism, perhaps we should admit that that leaves other forms of utility estimate in not too bad a position.

This thought could be brought to bear on equal utility gain to cut away at it from the opposite side. Suppose someone were to resist the argument of the previous section and say that it is better to have the right criterion (equal utility gain) applied approximately than the wrong one (equal resources) applied exactly. The natural response would seem to be: once you are prepared to make that kind of trade-off, why stop there?

Let us assume you believe that an ideally fair solution would be for the parties to gain an equal amount of utility over their baseline level, measured in units of interpersonally comparable utility, but that you have settled *faute de mieux* for equal utility gain measured in von Neumann/Morgenstern utilities that have been brought into relation with one another by some more or less arbitrary normalization procedure. We now point out that, once verificationist scruples are laid aside, you may as well admit that it is quite often possible to be confident that one person is in more pain than another—more confident than it is possible much of the time to be about the choices someone would make when faced with some complicated decision involving uncertainties. If you think, then, that it is worth going for the best criterion and accepting difficulties of implementation, why not reinstate equal gain in interpersonally comparable utility as the criterion of a fair division in place of a criterion employing ersatz interpersonally comparable utilities created out of von Neumann/Morgenstern utilities?

One line of reply might take the form of a challenge to the assumption made here to the effect that normalized von Neumann/Morgenstern utilities are really a surrogate for the supposedly unattainable interpersonally comparable utilities. When we look at the arguments put forward in favor of equal-gain solutions as intrinsically fair, we find that some authors treat normalized von Neumann/Morgenstern utilities as a second best while others regard them as embodying the appropriate basis of comparison.

Thus, those who have proposed the Nash solution or splitting the difference as ways of instantiating the ethical idea of equal utility gain are often fairly clear that using von Neumann/Morgenstern utilities is not to be seen as a second best. The justification offered by Bartos (section 5) for calling the Nash solution an equal-utility-gain solution was that the parties had an equal amount to lose from a reversion to the nonagreement point from the Nash outcome. That is not the logic of equal interpersonally comparable utility gain. Similarly, to the extent that Gauthier calls splitting the difference fair because it provides equal utility gain, he quite explicitly appeals to the idea that the parties should finish up an equal distance between the nonagreement point and the maximum they could possibly get out of the game, and this again does not suggest that what we would really like is an equal gain in interpersonally comparable utilities.

On the other side, Luce and Raiffa, in the discussion of so-called games of fair division in their treatise *Games and Decisions*, invariably write as if the normative problem (as distinct from that of simulating the outcome of rational bargaining) ideally requires interpersonal comparison of utilities. We can see this approach at work in Raiffa's own proposed "fair division" solution, which they describe. This is a variant of splitting the difference in which we create an *ad hoc* utility scale for each player by setting the worst outcome that he could possibly obtain within the game at zero and the best possible outcome at unity. With the utilities thus normalized, we aim to find a solution that will give each player the same utility—that is, get him an equal distance from his worst possible outcome to his best possible outcome.*

The obvious objection to this method for normalizing the utilities is that it seems quite arbitrary to use the most disliked outcome to establish the scale. Luce and Raiffa, in introducing the method, call it "an 'ad hoc' method to do interpersonal comparisons of utilities for a given game," and say disarmingly that "although there is no adequate rationale for doing so, one can assume that this [utility transformation] establishes an interpersonal comparison of utility (for the purposes of this game!).[20] The disclaimer is only too appropriate. To see how arbitrary the method is, let us suppose that Matthew absolutely hates silence. He hates it so much that, relative to that outcome, listening to Luke yields a utility of 0.99 on a scale where playing himself counts at 1.0. Raiffa's solution would have Luke playing almost all the time. Yet it is hard to see what attraction this outcome has, if we want something to be fair. Luce and Raiffa would, I think, have to say that this is simply a case where using Raiffa's method of normalization as a substitute for the direct comparison of utilities slips up badly. But I think that anyone who really wanted to ensure an equal gain in interpersonally comparable utilities would be very ill advised to use Raiffa's "ad hoc" system of transformation.

Another example of the same syndrome is provided by Anatol Rapoport's treatment of Braithwaite's problem in his *Fights, Games, and Debates.* Rapoport accepts without a murmur the argument in favor of cacophony as the nonagreement point. But as a way of moving from there to the Pareto frontier he does not even consider the Nash solution (indeed, the name of Nash does not appear in the index). Instead, he

---

* This is obviously a variant of splitting the difference as we have defined it: in fact its maximum is always the same, and its minimum will often be the same as the nonagreement point. In the game of splitting the legacy, for example, the nonagreement point must be the *status quo,* so the arbitrated outcome will always be the same for Raiffa's solution and that of splitting the difference. Now consider the Braithwaite problem with cacophony as the nonagreement point. Raiffa's proposal of setting the worst outcome as zero would not change the scaling of Luke's utilities, since cacophony is the worst for him anyway. But this nonagreement point of cacophony is not the worst thing that could happen to Matthew: his lowest payoff comes from silence. Raiffa's solution will therefore entail our setting silence at zero for Matthew and adjusting the other utilities accordingly. The result is that when we put through a zero-one normalization, Matthew's utilities for every outcome except that where he plays all the time (which of course remains at unity) are slightly raised, and this works to his disadvantage in the computation of equal gain. For he now does better than before from each combination of listening and playing. The point of exactly equal gain will thus be a little closer to equal playing time than when we split the difference with the usual normalization.

assumes that the outcome should provide equal utility gain. As a first move he assumes that the transformation of Braithwaite's ratios into whole numbers by Luce and Raiffa (these are the numbers I have been using) gives us interpersonally comparable units of utility. And he then shows that, for these particular numbers, Matthew and Luke play half the time each. (In order to retain his "threat advantage," Matthew should finish up with one more unit of utility than Luke. The point on the Pareto frontier corresponding to this is 6.5 for Matthew and 5.5 for Luke, and this translates into equal playing time.) Rapoport then goes on to point out that if Matthew's utilities were multiplied by two, we would get a quite different result, in which Luke plays on 15 evenings out of 17.[21] And he says that we could "with equal justification" have taken these numbers.[22] This obviously sets the problem up as one of turning the von Neumann/Morgenstern utilities given by Braithwaite into interpersonally comparable numbers in some nonarbitrary way. "The principle by which such a common utility scale is established is the principle of arbitration."[23] We need not therefore be surprised to find that Braithwaite's own solution is treated in this spirit and that the only alternative considered is that of Raiffa.[24]

If we ask where Braithwaite himself stands we are, I think, liable to have to retire with a feeling of bafflement. I have already (in section 4) said that it is not altogether clear whether Braithwaite sees his solution as justified because it reflects bargaining power or because it provides equal normalized utility gain. However, since the later part of the lecture stresses the second point I incline to the second interpretation. But that still leaves open the question of whether the method of normalization is to be taken as defining fairness or whether ideally one would compare utilities and find a solution from which each party gained an equal amount of utility. My hunch is that in the end Braithwaite sees his own method of normalization as a way of producing an *ad hoc* normalization for the particular game.

Braithwaite imagines Luke complaining that he does not see why he should accept that Braithwaite's solution gives him and Matthew an "equal benefit" over what they would get at the baseline of cacophony. Notice that Braithwaite does not depict Luke as either complaining of cacophony as a baseline or complaining that equal gain over a nonagreement baseline, however defined, has nothing to do with fairness. The only complaint Braithwaite can imagine him making is, apparently, about the geometrical construction that defines lines that preserve relative advantage ("isorrhopes").

What I have done, he will say, is to introduce surreptitiously, distracting attention by all my fine talk about parabolas, a *yardstick* for comparing his preference scale with that of Matthew, and this involves all the absurdities of Bentham's felicific calculus.

Luke is quite right in thinking that my choice of lines parallel to the parabola's axis as the isorrhopes is equivalent to an inter-personal comparison of utility scales. But the fairness of the distribution is concerned with its being equally fair to both parties, and nothing can be said about what it is to be equally fair to both parties in the situation in question without some method of comparing their preference scales for the alternatives in the situation. . . .

If every such comparison is to be forbidden, the moral philosopher asked by Luke and Matthew to advise them in their particular predicament can do no more than repeat the platitude-paradox proclaimed by the pigs in George Orwell's *Animal Farm*: "All animals are equal, but some animals are more equal than others"—a not very helpful remark. But one of the questions which I took it that Luke and Matthew were asking me was: "Can you detect, and explain to us, any feature inherent in our situation which gives to one of us a natural advantage over the other; and, if so, can you attach to this natural advantage any number which we can use for fairly dividing our playing time?" Since the relevant features in the situation are solely their two preference scales, clearly there is nothing that can be said about the advantage which one may have over the other by having a different preference scale that does not involve an inter-personal comparison, by one means or another, of the two preference scales.[25]

This sounds very much like saying that we have somehow to compare von Neumann/Morgenstern utilities, and the way proposed is simply a device for exploiting the utility numbers to arrive at a unique transformation. And the best evidence for this is what Braithwaite has to say about Raiffa. Braithwaite, as we have seen, refers to Nash as a predecessor, but there is one other who is mentioned and that is Raiffa. Describing "non-zero-sum two-person games" as "almost virgin forest," he goes on to say: "Two pioneers, John Nash and Howard Raiffa, have recently attempted to cut tracks through this forest. Nash has hacked out a bold path . . . , but his path seems to me to go in a manifestly wrong direction." (As will be recalled, Braithwaite complained that Nash's solution was "clearly unfair on Luke" because it had Matthew playing almost every evening—see section 4.)

Independently of [Nash], Raiffa has cut several openings in the forest, including Nash's path, but does not think any of them attractive enough to put his faith in. The limited exploration of mine which I shall now report to you—limited in that I am confining myself in this lecture to the case in which there are only two pure strategies open to each of the collaborators, whereas

Nash's and Raiffa's treatments consider the most general cases, finite and infinite—owes much to my two predecessors, and in particular to Raiffa, one of whose openings in the forest I shall cut a new way into.[26]

Unpacking Braithwaite's grossly overworked arboreal metaphor, I take him to be saying that he sees Raiffa's approach to the problem of fair division as more congenial than that of Nash.

Toward the end of the lecture, still in the defense of his method of comparing the utilities, Braithwaite says that his solution makes use of "natural" utility units. We need not go into his reason for saying this. But it leads us to his key reference to Raiffa:

The principle of equating natural utility units enables me directly to connect my treatment of the problem with that given by Raiffa for situations in which the utility scales of the two collaborators can be measured in terms of a common unit (e.g. a monetary unit) so that it makes sense to speak of the *difference* between a utility of Luke's and one of Matthew's. For this situation Raiffa proposes that the two parties should first solve their zero-sum "non-co-operative relative game" (in which the outcomes are the differences between the utilities yielded to Luke and to Matthew by the outcomes of the collaboration situation), and then improve on this solution by advancing to the upper right-hand boundary of their total strategic region by a route which yields equal increments of utility to each party. This corresponds exactly to my method of selecting the prudential isorrhope [i.e., the line of equal advantage with its origin at the nonagreement point], and then of advancing up this isorrhope to the boundary (and I owe the method to Raiffa's paper, though I justify it, and therefore expound it, somewhat differently). Raiffa, however, did not see any way of dealing with situations in which the utility scales were not expressible in terms of a common unit [Braithwaite does not refer to the method of normalization discussed above]; here my idea of a natural utility unit, imposed upon the two parties by the logic of the collaboration situation, which also makes it plausible to equate these units for the purpose of making a recommendation, is complementary to Raiffa's idea as to how to treat a collaboration situation in which common units are given from the beginning.[27]

This suggests very clearly that, if we had a direct measurement of interpersonally comparable utility, we should obviously equalize the gain in utility, and that we use normalized von Neumann/Morgenstern utilities only as a substitute. The snag with this is that Braithwaite, even in this passage, continues to emphasize that the "natural units" are derived from strategic considerations.

I show in Appendix A that the method of normalization proposed by Braithwaite compares the payoffs from a maximin and a minimax mixed strategy (while the other plays a maximin mixed strategy) and postulates that the distance between the two payoffs should be taken to be the same for both men. There is absolutely no reason for thinking that this distance would have any constant relation to interpersonally comparable utilities, if we actually had access to them. In the end, I think we have to say that Braithwaite says one thing and does another. He produces a solution whose rationale ought to be on Nash's lines while defending it on lines that are like Raiffa's.

If solutions based on equal normalized utility gain are put forward as practical ways of accommodating the difficulty of obtaining estimates of interpersonally comparable utility, then they are open to two opposite objections. They are not in fact a lot easier to operate or a lot less open to dispute than a direct attempt to find an outcome that gives an equal interpersonally comparable utility gain. At the same time, the proposed methods of normalization are exceedingly implausible, regarded as ways of approximating what one might get by comparing utility gain directly.

This suggests that normalized utility gain is a precarious criterion of fairness. If we are prepared to accept problems of implementation in pursuit of equal gain in interpersonally comparable utilities, it makes little sense to stop at such a manifestly imperfect (and indeed arbitrary) method of approximating the thing we would like to measure. If, on the other hand, we are worried about problems of implementation, we should not stop there either but should (as I argued at the end of section 12) go on to a criterion based on the division of the resource in question.

UTILITARIANISM

I have not so far said anything in this chapter about the implications that arise for the utilitarian criterion from the facts that utility information is hard to obtain, subject to strategic manipulation, and never decisive. I should like to say a bit about it here, since the discussion will enable me to fill out further the argument in favor of resource-based criteria for particular decisions, even where the rationale is utility-based.

To illustrate this, I shall take an example often analyzed in the literature on bargaining under the title "Battle of the Sexes." The idea, as usually presented, is that a man and a woman prefer going out together to going out separately but have different preferences about where to go. This situation is then analyzed as a game in which the nonagreement point is that each goes to his or her favored entertainment alone and going together to the two alternative entertainments constitutes two Pareto optima. The Nash solution will obviously turn on the parties' relative preferences for going together to their own most preferred entertainment, going together to the other party's most preferred entertainment, and going alone to their most preferred one.

I am going to take this story and assume that to solve the problem about where to go the parties agree that they will try to follow the principle of maximizing their joint utility. And let us say, to simplify matters, that the question is the same each week, namely, which of the films showing in the area to attend. Given the preference orderings we have attributed to them, it is apparent that utility will be maximized when they both go to the same one. The only question is which one they should choose, and the answer requires a comparison of strengths of preference for various alternatives.

In theory, it would be necessary for them to assign each film a number such that the distances between the numbers reflected the same differences in utility for both. The two numbers for each film would then be added and the film selected that had the highest aggregate score. One could imagine that two people might do this, but it seems more likely that two people seeking to apply the utilitarian criterion would use qualitative indicators—"very keen" or "couldn't stand it"—and would evolve fairly simple rules of thumb for moving to decisions from expressed strengths of preference. For example, they might decide that they will go to whichever film arouses the most enthusiasm in either unless the other is strongly against it.*

The details are of no importance for the present purpose. What is of interest is to speculate about the way in which the parties might check the calibration of relative strengths of preference. Suppose that one of them almost always succeeds in getting the decision to come out in favor of his or her first preference by expressing immense enthusiasm for it and vetoing most of the others. They might conclude that they simply do differ enormously in the degree to which they care about going to one film rather than another, or indeed that one experiences just about everything a lot more intensely than the other. But the loser

---

* It has been suggested that in group decisions about the choice of a film to see, negative votes are often decisive: that is to say, films are eliminated if anybody objects to them, even if others in the group would like them a lot. The blandness of television programming is even better accounted for as an effect of group choice (see Peter Bowbrick, "The Economics of Superstars: Comment," *American Economic Review* 73 (1983): 459–60.

under this arrangement might instead conclude that there was something wrong with the calibration, and that consciously or unconsciously the other was manipulating the process to gain an unfair advantage. And an outside observer might reach the same judgment. (In this context "gaining an unfair advantage" means "getting more than is provided for in the rules defining the procedure.")

The obvious remedy would be to adopt the working hypothesis that on the average each has a roughly equal intensity of preference over the whole range of films. And the only way of implementing that notion would be to see to it that, taking one week with another, both are roughly equally successful in getting what they want. The most straightforward method would be for them to alternate strictly in picking a film, but this would have the disadvantage that it might be very clear sometimes that the person other than the one whose turn it is to make the choice actually cares more than usual (for him or her) which film they go to.

A natural relaxation of strict alternation would be in effect to allow trading from a base of the right to select a film on alternate weeks, but this would introduce the possibility of gaming since someone indifferent who knows the other party cares a lot to get the right to choose in a certain week might hold out for two choices later. To get around that, one could say that the number of weeks each chooses should in the long run be approximately equal and that whichever expresses the strongest interest should choose in a given week, subject, of course, to the constraint of not building up too big a debt. This, however, suffers from the difficulty that some weeks both will think there is more at stake than other weeks, so a qualification needs to be added that both should have an approximately equal amount of choice, where "amount" is understood as frequency weighted by importance.

Even this, however, is still open to the objection that it is too rigid. For if the whole thing is pitched in terms of the number and importance of the occasions on which each chooses, only films that are somebody's first preference will ever emerge from the process. But it could easily be that in the long run both parties would prefer it if they go to some films that both expect to like fairly well rather than to films that top one person's list but are negatively rated by the other. Ideally, therefore, what is wanted can be expressed vaguely by saying that each should have an equally weighted input into the choice of films. This obviously must not be construed as the Benthamite slogan "everybody to count for one and nobody for more than one." For that simply says that a unit of utility is to have the same effect on the calculation regardless of the identity of its possessor. What is to be counted is not utility but influence on the outcome. Each has the same right to determine the joint choice. We could if we like think of each as having ten points per week to spend on bidding for outcomes. As an actual procedure, anything on these lines would be extremely liable to strategic manipulation. It would be better for the parties simply to employ a general sense of what constitutes equal concessions. But it may be helpful to think about such a formal scheme to illustrate the idea.

It is plain that there is a trade-off to be made. The system of strict alternation of choices will very likely produce a sequence of outcomes such that there are alternative sequences that both parties would have preferred as a whole. Against that, it is very easy to implement and it guarantees a simple form of equal input into the decisions. (It is possible of course that by sheer bad luck one party may more often finish up choosing in weeks when the right to choose is worth less. But this is still equality *ex ante*.) At the other extreme, the most flexible scheme, which simply specifies the ideal of equal input and leaves the implementation of it open to discussion, is relatively time-consuming and open to abuse from strategy, but it does in principle permit the parties to reach a sequence of outcomes that is not dominated by any alternative sequence, that is to say, a Pareto-optimal set of choices.

Leaving aside the practical problems of implementation, we can define the ideal as follows: the outcome (defined over a large enough sequence of choices) should be that point on the Pareto frontier that gives both parties an equal amount of control over the choice of outcomes. Thus, we have arrived at a generalization of the resourcist solution put forward in section 10. If we ask what is the scarce resource to be divided in the present instance, the answer must be that it is the right to decide what films the couple go to see. The practical difficulty is, as we have seen, to define that equal right in a way flexible enough to be compatible with the achievement of Pareto optimality.

There are two challenges that could be mounted to my claim of having got, by invoking problems of information and strategy, from the utilitarian principle to that of equal division of the resource in question. One would be that what I have actually come up with is an argument for moving from utilitarianism to equal normalized utility gain. This is not so, however. For it should be observed that the nonagreement baseline (each going to his or her most preferred film separately) played no part in the specification of the principle of equal control over the

outcome. It might be suggested that we could meet this reply by refor-
mulating the equal-gain criterion so that the utilities were defined in the
way proposed by Raiffa. Under this system, each person's most-liked
film would score 1 and his or her most disliked film would score 0. The
"equal gain" would then be established at a point where each had the
same utility score. However, the objection what I made to Raiffa's normalization seems to me equally valid here. I do not see any reason for
letting what is to count as equal input into the decision depend on how
much each party hates some film each week, if the other would not wish
to go to it anyway. What we should be concerned with is concessions
made to the other. Although much more might be said, I want to suggest that the logic of control and the logic of utility really are different
and that it would be a mistake to try to reduce one to the other.

A second challenge, which I think has to be taken seriously, runs as
follows. I have been suggesting that the hypothesis of equal overall intensity of preference is simply a device adopted to deal with the empirical problem of calibrating the intensities of preference of different
people. But is it really only that? The alternative way in which it could
be conceived of is as a stipulation—a regulative principle for the interpretation of utilitarianism—designed to avoid excessive inequality in
the division of resources. On the second view, it should actually be built
into the interpretation of the principle of utility that overall intensity of
preference is to be taken to be the same in everyone.

The idea has its attractions but I think it is worth emphasizing that
some people who propose to treat overall preference intensity as equal
are quite clear that the only reason for doing so is the lack of information good enough to enable us to do anything else. An example is
provided by Philip Pettit's discussion of utilitarianism in his *Judging Justice*. He suggests that the principle of maximizing aggregate
utility might be made operational by working with von Neumann/
Morgenstern utilities. (This, of course, presupposes that there is no
problem in arriving at them.) We have to bring these individual utility
ratios into relation with one another, Pettit says, and he suggests that
"the reasonable line would seem to be that we scale the preferences of
the individuals between the same mathematical limits, say between 0
and 1." That this is purely a concession to our lack of good information
is made clear when he goes on to say: "We cannot hope to determine
that one or another individual has a particularly passionate disposition,
deserving of a scale with a larger mathematical spread, and in ignorance
of such variation we may well treat all as equal."[28]

RESOURCISM

The theme of this section has been the importance of having criteria of fair division that do not require utility information to be fed into them, because this is hard to obtain, often subject to strategic misrepresentation by the parties, and never decisive. The argument can be carried further by a reanalysis of the resourcist solution put forward in section 10.

It might at first be thought that there is nothing to be said here. Since fair division is defined in terms of the resources to be divided, why does this create any problems of the kind we have been discussing up to now? Isn't one of the charms of the solution precisely that it eschews utility information? The answer is: yes and no. In the rest of this section I shall expand on that answer. I shall also try to draw some general lessons about when relatively sophisticated solutions are appropriate and when it is more sensible to settle for crude but undemanding solutions.

To begin with the "yes" part of the answer, it is true (as I mentioned above at the end of section 12) that so long as Matthew and Luke actually have the utilities ascribed to them by Braithwaite, there is no incentive, if it is settled that the strict solution is to be applied, for either to misrepresent his preferences. There is in this case a precise coincidence between Matthew's preference ordering and Luke's preference ordering over the alternatives satisfying the equal-time constraint. Both rank three nights of playing apiece top, followed by two, one, and none, in that order. So there is no advantage to either Matthew or Luke in misrepresenting his preference ordering, whether the context is face-to-face negotiation or submissions to an arbitrator. The bargaining game created by the initial statement of the problem is reduced by the equal-time requirement to a simple coordination game.

It makes no difference what equal-time distribution of resources constitutes the nonagreement baseline. Since there is in this case an equal-time outcome that is preferred by both parties to any departure from it, any misrepresentation of preferences either makes no difference to the outcome or makes things worse for both parties. There is no possible way in which either can hope to do better than play half the time without going outside the requirement that playing time is to be divided equally.

With the two variations on Braithwaite's payoffs that I introduced, it is no longer true that there is a single equal-time outcome that comes top in both men's preference orderings. In the first variant, Luke's highest preference among equal-time outcomes is for silence, whereas Matthew's is for each playing three evenings per week. In the second variant, Luke would most like to have each play twice a week, while Matthew would still most like to have each play three times per week. Because of this additional complexity, I shall from now on pursue the analysis in terms of the nonagreement baseline that received the most attention in section 10, namely, that in which neither party plays any of the time.

With a baseline of silence, then, we can say that there is no advantage to either man in misrepresenting his preferences in the first variant on Braithwaite's payoffs, so long as we confine the outcomes to those generated by the strict solution. The reason for this is not, as it was with Braithwaite's payoffs, that there is (within the constraints on possible outcomes imposed by the strict solution) a coincidence of interest on one outcome. As I have just said, that is not so in this case. The point is, rather, that Luke prefers silence to any equal amounts of playing and listening—and equal amounts are the only ratio permitted by the strict solution. Whatever Matthew may say about his own preferences, therefore, Luke has no incentive to misrepresent his own, which are for silence. Of the available alternatives, Luke most prefers silence and it is in his interest to say so and insist that silence be the outcome. In this second example, however, it has to be observed that the denial of any incentive for dissimulation is bought at a heavy price in that there are combinations of playing time violating the equal-time constraint that would be preferred by both Matthew and Luke to no playing. But, as we shall see in a little while, opening up the possibility of moving from the strict solution to the extended solution has its costs too.

The second variant on Braithwaite's utilities involved a departure from the assumption that utility was linear with frequency of playing. It had the feature that the strict solution generated two alternative outcomes and did not contain any way of picking one over the other. I suggested several ways in which, once these two alternative fair outcomes had been identified, the choice between them might be made. There might be a toss-up between them, or a solution halfway between the two might be created. I also said that the parties could bargain over it or invite an arbitrator to come up with a choice between the two alternatives by applying a solution designed to simulate the result of rational bargaining. If the parties actually bargain, this presumably means that the threat of the nonagreement point is used to induce compliance with the demand for one's preferred equal-time outcome, and they may finish up at the nonagreement point. A bargaining solution will avoid this danger and ensure that one or the other of the two solutions picked out will be chosen. The worst that can happen is that the "wrong" one is selected as a result of misrepresentation of preferences, and that may not worry us too much.

However, all this presupposes that the two alternative equal-time outcomes picked out as fair by the strict solution have already been identified. The real problem about the incentive to misrepresent one's preferences is that there is no guarantee that the application of the strict solution to strategically misrepresented preferences will arrive at either of the alternatives that would be fair. It may in fact result in an outcome that neither party likes, namely, the nonagreement point of silence. I should emphasize that the argument here does not turn in any way on the method used to decide between alternative outcomes that satisfy the strict solution. Rather, it shows what happens when each party attempts to make it appear that the strict solution has only one outcome, namely, the one more favorable to itself.

Both Matthew and Luke prefer playing either two or three evenings a week to not playing at all, but Luke prefers the first of these and Matthew the second. Now suppose that Luke misrepresents his preference ordering by saying that he rates playing three evenings apiece below silence. (He will have to pretend that the utility to him of playing drops off faster than it really does.) Given this preference information, plus the true information about Matthew's preference order, the strict solution produces as the unique outcome the one where each plays twice a week. For, since silence is the nonagreement baseline, Luke cannot be expected to accept any outcome that is worse for him than that. Thus, by strategic misrepresentation of his preferences Luke has succeeded in pre-empting the choice between playing twice apiece and playing three times apiece per week, constraining the strict solution to his preferred alternative.

The trouble is, of course, that misrepresenting one's preferences is a game that two can play, with a risk of mutual frustration. Suppose Matthew maintains that of equal-time solutions only the one that has each playing three times per week is preferable to silence. If Luke stated his preferences truly, this would eliminate playing two evenings a week as a possible outcome under the strict situation, leaving only Matthew's more preferred alternative of playing three times a week. But if Luke also misrepresents his preferences in the way we just envisaged, the outcome must be that nobody plays. For there is no outcome satisfying the requirement of equal time that is better for both (as they have stated their preferences) than silence.

The most important upshot of this analysis is that in many cases the strict solution will create no incentives for misrepresentation of preferences. This is so for two of the three versions of the Braithwaite problem, and it is also true for the problem of dividing up the legacy and all others with the same structure. For the constraint of equal division ensures that neither party can obtain more than half, and if both say they prefer more to less they will get half each. Departing from the truth about one's preferences, if they are really for more rather than less (as with the money left to the legatees), will either have no effect on the outcome or, if it does have one, must result in both getting less than half the total.

But the price that the strict solution carries with it is that it rules out mutually advantageous alternatives to the outcome that it selects. In other words, it may fail to get the parties to the Pareto frontier. But the strict solution looks better when we take account of the problem of strategic manipulation of preferences than it did in section 10.

Let us look at the case that presented no difficulties at all for the strict solution: the one with Braithwaite's original payoffs. The strict solution allowed no advantage from misrepresentation of preferences and got to the Pareto frontier. This was because, within the alternatives permitted as possible solutions, there was no conflict of interest. The same outcome—playing three evenings each—was best for both. Now let us see what happens if they agree to include outcomes that are preferred by both to equal-time outcomes. Each now has an incentive to misreport his preferences.

Suppose, for example, that Luke were to say that his preferences were those of the first variation on Braithwaite's payoffs. He would then be maintaining that he would prefer silence all the time to any equal-time combination of playing and listening but that he would prefer four evenings of playing and two of listening to silence all the time. Given those preferences on the part of Luke and a nonagreement baseline of silence, the strict solution will mandate that nobody plays. Matthew then has to choose between silence and an unequal division of playing time that favors Luke. But we know that Matthew prefers any unequal division (even the one that has Luke playing every evening) to silence. So he will do better to accept an unequal division if he believes what Luke says or—it is worth observing—if he thinks Luke is lying but is sure that he will not admit it and would accept an outcome of silence rather than lose face. An arbitrator who managed to divine Luke's true preferences would award each man three evenings of playing. But, as Luce and Raiffa put it, "ferreting out" the truth is no easy matter. So, even with an arbitrator pledged to apply the extended resourcist solution, Luke's ploy might succeed.

The situation is, however, completely symmetrical: both men have in actual fact exactly the same preference ordering. So everything we just said of Luke could have been equally well said of Matthew. But if both simultaneously try to play the same game, then unless one or the other backs off (or is seen through by an arbitrator) the outcome must be silence. Each is asserting that the only outcomes he prefers to silence are those more favorable to him than any equal split. Since there is no way of satisfying them both at once, they have ruled out all outcomes other than the baseline of silence.

The analysis of strategic possibilities opened up by the extended solution could be elaborated further, but I think this example is striking enough. It shows how the availability of the extended solution may actually *prevent* negotiation or arbitration from reaching a Pareto-optimal outcome that, under the strict solution, should have been easily attainable. Leaving aside any question of fairness, the efficiency loss that is clearly associated with the strict solution must be set against the less immediately apparent efficiency loss associated with the extended solution. Because in analyzing the working of alternative schemes we tend to write down utilities that in the real world would be a matter of conjecture and dispute, we tend to be much more sensitive to the first source of inefficiency than the second. Yet the second may actually be more important.

We can thus see that the issue between the strict and extended solutions is not clear-cut even when we confine ourselves to the question of which is likely to produce the most outcomes on (or near) the Pareto-optimal frontier. But that is not, of course, the only consideration. Another is that, with the strict solution, whatever outcomes are arrived at, whether they are Pareto-optimal or not, are at least fair in the basic sense that they divide whatever is to be divided equally. We can have no similar assurance with the extended solution. If Luke successfully maintains that his preferences are as in the second example when they are really as in the first, while Matthew is honest about his, Luke is able to get an outcome from the application of the extended solution that is genuinely unfair.

But that is not all. There is also a "welfare loss" to many people from *being in* a situation where it is known that one can gain substantially by lying, and where one may feel that it is necessary to lie in self-defense against the possibility of the other's lying. My impression is that, partly as a matter of basic personality and partly as a matter of training, economists and game theorists tend to be far more tolerant of this kind of "gaming" than the average of the population as a whole. (Conjecture: they have an above-average predilection for playing poker.) They therefore, I believe, systematically underestimate the importance most people attach to not being in such situations. If we put all this together with the sheer additional time and effort that the extended solution is liable to require for its application, it would be easy to conclude that it would always be better to do without its potential benefits. Yet that might in some cases entail giving up very large mutual gains over what any equal division could provide. Can we say anything further?

As a no doubt rough-and-ready guide, let me suggest that there are three relevant questions to ask. First, how important are the personal relations of the parties to them? Second, how far do the parties believe that the other(s) can be depended on to tell the truth? (As a variant on this which will often have much the same implications, we may ask: do they at any rate believe that they will be able to see through one another's attempts to bluff?) And, third, how important is it to the parties to get one division rather than another? Does it make a big difference where the outcome falls? I shall call the three variables that are generated by the answers to these questions the degree of friendship, the degree of trust, and the size of the stakes. To simplify matters, I shall consider only two values of each variable: high and low. Putting the three variables together, we get a matrix with eight cells (Figure 3.1). I shall carry out my analysis by asking what can be said about the conduct appropriate to each of the cells.

Consider the case of people who are not friends and therefore have less objection to engaging in bargaining than they would if they were friends, but nevertheless know enough about one another (perhaps from regular dealings in the past) to trust each other, so they do not have to fear misrepresentation of preferences. In such a case, the extended solution would seem suitable both where the stakes are trivial and where they are substantial. Switching our attention from the top right quarter to the bottom left quarter of the matrix, we get the case of friends who mistrust one another—not, I think, a psychological impossibility. Here the strict solution is definitely indicated, because it is

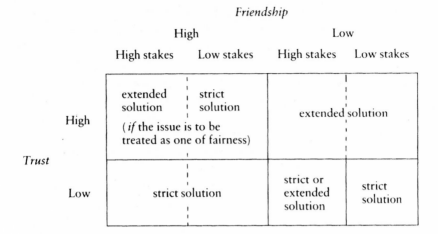

Figure 3.1. Choice of Solutions according to Parties' Relations

especially awkward to have to accuse a friend of misrepresenting his preferences for strategic advantage. (As I said before, this may have to be waived for economists and game theorists, who seem to take this kind of thing in their stride.)

Among people who are not friends and who mistrust one another, there is, I would suggest, a strong but defeasible presumption in favor of the strict solution because of the way in which it limits the scope of misrepresentation. But the bigger the stake, the more the extra psychic and time costs generated by the extended solution become worth paying in order to leave open the possibility of getting to a Pareto-optimal outcome which the application of the strict solution might rule out. The more experienced and flexible the negotiators, the more willing they should be to move to the extended solution, since they have less likelihood of locking themselves into positions, taken up for bargaining advantage, that turn out to preclude any Pareto-optimal agreement. The recommendation in the lower right-hand quarter is thus divided according to the size of the stakes.

Finally, we have the case of friends who can trust one another not to misrepresent their preferences. The two factors work here in opposite directions: the extended solution is applicable because the requisite information will be volunteered truthfully, but the process of bargaining involved in moving to the extended solution is itself inimical to friendship. Perhaps we can at least say this: the more the friendship is in itself of value compared to whatever is at stake in the problem of division at hand, the more sensible it is to forget about Pareto-optimality and settle for the ground rule that whatever division is chosen shall be equal.

But among friends it may be considered inappropriate to pose the question as one of fairness in the first place. In the words of Montaigne, "If, in the friendship I speak of, one could give to the other, it would be the one who received the benefit who would oblige his friend. For, each of them seeking above all things to benefit the other, the one who provides the matter and the occasion is the liberal one, giving his friend the satisfaction of doing for him what he most wants to do."[29]

Richard Flathman has approached what is essentially the same point in his discussion of rights. He says that "rights involve a certain holding back, a certain reserve . . . [so that] shared concerns remain within definite limits" and suggests that "asserting and respecting rights against one another is surely not, as such, a feature of relationships among or between friends."[30] Although I do not understand the force of "as such" here or the distinction between "among" and "between" in this context, I think the drift is plain enough: that what Hume called the "cautious, jealous virtue of justice" would be out of place where people cared enough about one another's welfare. I shall discuss this in relation to Hume's theory of justice in the next chapter. (See especially section 18 under "The Moderate Scarcity Condition.")

14. SOCIAL RULES AND FAIR DIVISION

In this section I want to make the move from looking at problems of fair division in an *ad hoc* manner after they have arisen to talking about social rules for dealing with them—or preventing them from arising. The ground has been prepared by the discussion so far, since this has illustrated the way in which practical considerations heavily constrain the choice of a decision rule in an individual case. The extension here consists in saying that the same point applies even more when we think of general rules drawn up to cover all the specific cases that fall under them. No system of rules—whether those of a legal system or of an organization or other collectivity—could possibly fulfill its function unless in the vast majority of the cases covered by it the parties affected were able to apply the rules themselves. It is absolutely essential that only the exceptional case should need authoritative adjudication. Otherwise the system will inevitably break down.

What implications does this have for Braithwaite's case of the pianist and the trumpeter? Suppose, for example, that we accept the utilitarian criterion but are looking for a set of general rules to cover noise made by musical instruments, record players, and so on. What we want is a set of rules that are simple enough to be imposed on all cases but, as far as is consistent with that, will maximize the aggregate utility brought about by adherence to them. (We could complicate the formulation to allow for a possibility of balancing off greater utility of adherence against greater cost of enforcement. But the simpler formula will suffice for the present purpose.)

In thinking about this, it is useful to throw a glance in the direction of the "economic analysis of law" as it has been developed by Richard Posner.[31] Posner's concern is with efficiency. Given frictionless bargaining, parties can always (as we have seen in Chapter 1) reach the Pareto frontier, and that constitutes a kind of efficiency. Therefore, it does not matter, from an efficiency point of view, what baseline is established by law in matters that lend themselves easily to being resolved by contract. But where the parties are liable to finish up with whatever rights they are initially allocated by the law, it does make a difference from the point of efficiency who gets what rights. Posner's proposal is that the law should as far as possible simulate the effects of perfect bargaining, and allocate a right to the party that would have finished up with it as a result of bargaining. One way of putting the rule is to say that a right should be allocated to the party that would have paid most for it.

An obvious utilitarian adaptation of this would be to say that a right should go to the party that stands to garner the most want-satisfaction from its exercise. Modifying this general formula to the kind of problem we are discussing here, we must allow not only for the satisfaction of the person who is allowed to play but also for the frustration of his neighbor who might prefer silence. And we must make room for the idea that the right to play a musical instrument is not just something one has or does not have but something that can be limited by duration or time of day.

We can put forward the following formal condition for a utilitarian rule specifying the amounts and occasions of playing that the parties should be able to engage in without securing one another's agreement: it should be a rule that, when applied to all cases, comes as close as possible to ensuring that at any given moment in the day or night, the use made of the time will be whatever maximizes aggregate utility. This is not of course much use as it stands. All it does is to gesture toward the questions that have to be asked. Since we do not want the application of the rule to turn on the psychological peculiarities of each pair (or larger number) of neighbors, filling in the abstract formula will require that we furnish some generalizations about people's attitudes, on the average, toward the playing of, and involuntarily listening to the playing of, musical instruments.

Some plausible generalizations might, I suggest, be the following. (1) Most people, unlike Braithwaite's Matthew and Luke, dislike hearing others practice musical instruments. We should not assume a general preference for an hour of solo playing and an hour of listening over an hour of simultaneous playing. (2) Most people particularly dislike it when they are trying to sleep, and there is a certain range of hours that covers most people's sleeping periods. (3) Among those who like to play, the frustration of the desire to do so is greater than the frustration of the desire for silence. (4) Playing is subject for most people to diminishing marginal utility; conversely, irritation at listening is probably cumulative.

Putting this together, we arrive at the unsurprising conclusion that the kind of rules that can be expected to maximize utility when applied generally would prohibit the playing of musical instruments during normal sleeping hours and would set some reasonable limit to the amount allowed the rest of the time, where "reasonableness" is based on an estimation of the point at which, on the average, the marginal utility of playing more falls below the marginal utility of listening more: the figure of an hour has the obvious merit of being round.

It should be borne in mind that this is proposed only as a rule enforceable at the behest of either party. It would be open to modification by the parties in either direction—to permit more, or less, playing of musical instruments. All that can be said for it is that, compared to other sets of rules that abstract from the preferences of the parties in the particular case, this set will produce tolerable results on the whole if all else fails. It may be noticed, incidentally, that for the case of Matthew and Luke (as it was presented originally by Braithwaite) the implication is that both would be permitted to play during the same hour every evening, on the assumption that an hour per day is a permitted length of practice. Thus, at any rate for the one hour that is all they have, Braithwaite's stipulation that there is nothing to prevent them from playing as much as they like would be satisfied. The scene would still be set for negotiation or arbitration to share out solo playing time. But many other disputes would be settled.

The discussion so far has been deficient in that it leaves out one of the most important advantages of general rules over one-off adjudications, namely, that when people know in advance what the rule is they can adapt their behavior to avoid or reduce conflicts. We cannot take it for granted that the best general rule is to be arrived at simply by universalizing the best adjudication in a single case. For it is of the nature of an individual adjudication that it has to take the situation as it finds it. And, unless there is some reason for expecting the decision to be taken as a precedent by people in similar situations in the future, there is no advantage to be gained by asking how a rule embodying it would affect people in the long run when they had had time to adapt to it.

Exactly what are the implications of this general point for our problem still remains to be seen, however. It seems reasonable to suggest that, once we allow for dynamic considerations, the efficiency loss from imposing a rule mandating a low level of noise-pollution will be diminished. Soundproofing can be incorporated at the stage of design and construction, and people can take up quieter musical instruments right from the start, or change to them. There might also be an incentive for the invention and mass production of quieter alternatives to noisy instruments: something as sturdy as a piano but as quiet as a clavichord, for example.

It is true that *any* set of rules will operate more efficiently the longer people have to adapt to them. However, there are more things that can be done to adapt to a rule restricting the transmission of sound than to one that permits the making of noise. An obligation not to create noise that reaches neighbors can be met by making less noise as well as by installing better soundproofing, whereas the only way of defending oneself against unwanted noise is soundproofing. We should also bear in mind a second dynamic factor. In drawing up a standard, we should not simply take as given the adaptations people could make, and at what cost, under existing technology. The technology may improve and—this is critical—a stringent standard may stimulate it to improve.

The discussion so far has been predicated on the assumption that there had to be a single set of rules about noisemaking. This assumption can, however, be relaxed. And when it is, we open up a whole new way of gaining fairness without having to sacrifice a lot of efficiency. Suppose we say that apartment buildings or neighborhoods may be designated as either permitting no noise or as permitting some specified amount of noise. Then people can choose which they prefer. When people have sorted themselves, the heterogeneity of rules will have brought about homogeneity or complementarity in the tastes of those living under each rule.

For the sake of simplicity, let us dichotomize dwellings into (1) those that are sufficiently far from neighbors or sufficiently well soundproofed that normal levels of noise will not travel from one to another and (2) those that are not. And let us imagine that there is only one kind of rule for the first category. This is a rule prohibiting amounts of noise beyond the normal: amounts so great that the sound-separation between these well-insulated dwellings would break down. Buildings in the second category are, let us suppose, covered by one of just two kinds of rule. One is a rule that prohibits making any noise that will carry from one residence to another, and the other is a rule that permits some moderate level for a certain part of the day.

How may we expect people to sort themselves into these three kinds of housing according to their preferences? To discuss this question we need a taxonomy of preferences. I will put it in terms of playing and listening to music, but it can obviously be generalized. We can distinguish four categories: first, those who want to play and don't want to hear others; second, those who want to play and also want to hear others; third, those who don't want to play and also don't want to hear others; and, fourth, those who don't want to play but want to hear others.

If there were no drawbacks to living in soundproofed housing, one would expect all those in the first category to live in it. Moreover, those in the third category would have nothing to lose from it. However, good-quality soundproofing in high-density housing is expensive; and low-density housing uses more land, so it will be either expensive or poorly located. We would therefore expect soundproofed housing to be occupied (holding income constant) by those with particularly strong preferences for the combination of playing themselves and not hearing others play, since they should be prepared to sacrifice other things to satisfy those preferences. Those with similar preferences but less strongly held we would expect to go into the unsoundproofed housing, picking their rule according to the relative strength of their preferences for playing and for listening: those who wanted to play and didn't too much mind listening would go for one rule and those with the reverse order of preferences would go for the other.

What can we say about unsoundproofed housing? On the assumption that it is cheaper than well-soundproofed housing, we can predict that the kind with an anti-noise rule will attract those who want neither to play nor to listen. Unsoundproofed housing with no anti-noise rule would be a positive attraction to those (if they exist) who like to listen indiscriminately, whether or not they like playing themselves as well. (It may be recalled that in Braithwaite's original statement of his problem, Matthew liked, next only after improvising jazz on the trumpet, to listen to Luke playing classical piano music, and that Luke returned the compliment. But such omnivorous tastes are, I suspect, rare enough to remind us again how unwise it would be to take our guide to the general run of similar cases from that example.) A less eccentric class of client for such housing would be made up of those who like to play and do not object to listening enough to be willing to pay the cost of sound-proofed housing.

I shall not elaborate any further on the example. I hope that what has been said here is enough to illustrate the point that the processes of self-selection and adaptation described earlier in the section can be given even greater scope if there is a choice of rules for the handling of micro-level conflicts.

15. SMOKING AND CONTEMPORARY MORES

I carried on the discussion in the previous section in terms of the problem of Matthew and Luke, or modest extensions of it. This was done to ensure continuity and to realize the intellectual investment made in the rest of Part I in analyzing such cases. However, I am sure it will not have escaped notice that another somewhat parallel example is currently a more live public-policy issue, especially in the United States. I have in mind, of course, the regulation of smoking in public transport, in restaurants and places of entertainment, and in the workplace. (As an aside, I may say that I regard the imposition of noise pollution, in the form of piped music, in the same places as an almost equally serious problem. But this is apparently an idea whose time has not yet come.) It would be tedious to go through all the same points and apply them to smoking. But it is, I think, illuminating to see how the terms of debate are set by the interaction of technical factors, relative strengths of preference, and issues about the legitimacy of satisfying different preferences.

Starting with the first two, the following facts about tobacco smoke are important. The first is that, whereas sound insulation is difficult and expensive, preventing the flow of smoke from one area to another can be achieved with complete success by the use of even the thinnest glass or plywood partition. With a well-designed ventilation system much can be achieved by mere physical separation. A second fact which is also technical in nature is that taking evasive action against tobacco smoke is difficult and inconvenient. It is easy to travel with a pair of earplugs, but carrying around, and wearing, a portable respirator is a good deal more cumbersome. The third fact is one about preferences. As the example of Matthew and Luke illustrates, those who make noise are not necessarily tolerant of noise made by others, and may well prefer restrictions on themselves as the price of restrictions on others. But the vast majority of smokers are not much troubled by smoke from others. The U.S. Surgeon General's report *Smoking and Health* reported that only 5 percent of smokers "found others' smoke to be objectionable."[32] (By contrast, 80 percent of those who have never smoked—44 percent of the U.S. population—said it was "annoying to be near a person who is smoking cigarettes."[33])

The net effect of the three facts I have adduced is that it is both a necessary and sufficient condition for solving the problem of tobacco smoke to the satisfaction of all parties to segregate smokers and non-smokers. The provision of "separate but equal" facilities for smokers and nonsmokers originated, as far as I can tell, with trains. Curiously, the original legislation in Britain that led to the creation of designated smoking and nonsmoking compartments took the form of a demand that there be a certain proportion of *smoking* compartments on all trains. The background to this was that before 1868 the official rule was that there was no smoking anywhere on trains. The rationale for the legislation in that year was that the rule was being widely violated by smokers with impunity. According to Hansard, "Mr J. Stuart Mill [who was a Liberal Member of Parliament at this time] said, public opinion in this instance was swayed by a majority of smokers. It was a case of oppression by a majority of a minority."[34] Now, of course, legislation normally takes the form of requiring the provision of nonsmoking areas, while leaving the provision of facilities for smokers at the discretion of the management.

Given the relative cheapness, ease, and effectiveness of providing separate areas for smokers and nonsmokers, what is most striking about the history of the past century is the failure of segregation between smokers and nonsmokers to spread on any scale beyond public transport—even to the nonmoving elements in public transport such as waiting rooms. If we ask for an explanation of this, and an explanation for the way in which things have recently started to change, I think we should look at two things: the proportion of the population constituted by smokers, and the social acceptability of smoking. There is probably some causal interaction between the two in both directions: decreased social acceptability leads to less smoking, and, as smoking becomes a minority phenomenon, its social acceptability decreases. But the two also work together in the following way. In 1966, about the high point of smoking in the United States, "52 percent of men and 34 percent of women smoked cigarettes."[35] The implication of this is that in any group associated for purposes of work or conviviality there would be likely to be at least one smoker, and the prevailing social norms of the time would have suggested that, if there were a choice of smoking or nonsmoking areas, the smoker(s) would be accommodated by the rest of the group. This would imply a relatively small demand for segregated nonsmoking facilities.

What has happened since then is that there have been dramatic changes in both factors. Especially among the professional classes, the incidence of smoking has greatly decreased (and it should be borne in mind that both work and leisure tend to be shared with members of the same social class). At the same time the assumption that in a mixed group of smokers and nonsmokers the smokers should be accommodated has come under increasing challenge. The two factors together obviously make for an increased demand for nonsmoking facilities.

How can we account for the shift in attitudes toward smoking in groups of mixed smokers and nonsmokers? It seems plausible that a part of the explanation stems from the reduction in the incidence of smoking itself. Although a minority of nonsmokers (about 4 percent) experience acute physical symptoms from exposure to tobacco smoke,[36] the objections of most people to the immediate effects are more esthetic than physical, and it seems likely that this kind of objection can be dulled by habituation. The less tobacco smoke there is around, therefore, the more likely nonsmokers are to notice it and find it strongly objectionable.

The main reason for the change is no doubt the one everyone would give, namely, the increased awareness of the health hazards associated with smoking. However, this is not as straightforwardly connected with the decline in the social acceptability of smoking in public as might appear. The information about the enhanced risks of lung cancer, heart disease, emphysema, and a variety of other ills is after all fairly well spread through Western and Eastern Europe, but anyone going from the United States to any of these countries will become suddenly aware of the prevalence of tobacco smoke in public places.

What has to be added in order to make an explanation is the special status health has acquired recently in the United States, especially among the middle class. The same people who have given up, or not taken up, smoking, can also be seen jogging, cutting down on dairy products and red meat, and losing weight. Michael Walzer has suggested that in modern societies health has assumed the position that salvation held in earlier times.[37] As with much of Walzer's work, this is a highly culture-bound remark, but I do think that within the group I have indicated it is true that much of the earnestness that in other times would have gone into worrying about the state of one's soul has been translated into a concern for the condition of one's body.

The point here is the simple one that facts by themselves do not provide reasons for action. A soldier in a foxhole may refrain from lighting a cigarette because he fears that he will attract a sniper's bullet. But he is not likely to be too concerned about what he is doing to his chances of getting lung cancer in forty years' time. The relative importance given to health is a cultural variable and it is only against the background of the distinctive attitude of the contemporary American middle class that we can locate the true significance of the damning evidence against tobacco products.

The most obvious way in which the health issue can be brought in to establish a nonagreement point of nonsmoking wherever segregation is not a feasible solution is to say that "passive smoking"—the exposure of nonsmokers to others' smoke—is not merely a nuisance but also a harm. Thus, after a study published in 1980 claimed that "long-term exposure to indoor tobacco smoke in the workplace was deleterious to the healthy normal nonsmoker and significantly reduced small airways function to the same extent as smoking one to ten cigarettes a day," the *New York Times* editorialized to the effect that this "is another reason, on top of earlier reasons, to prohibit smoking in indoor public places unless the smokers can be segregated so that they cannot jeopardize their neighbors."[38]

However, such research is quite recent and still a matter of some scientific controversy.[39] The move I am trying to account for antedates it and is still quite largely independent of reliance on it. What is mainly important is not, I suggest, this research but the whole body of evidence showing smoking to be a hazard to the health of the smoker. Now it might at first blush seem odd that (leaving aside a paternalistic desire to prevent people from smoking by reducing the range of situations in which they can do so) a shift in the nonagreement point should be stimulated by an increasing awareness of the danger of smoking to the health of the smoker himself. But this is to overlook the significance of the evangelistic attitude to health I have mentioned, which is often shared by smokers. From being a habit, smoking has become widely regarded as a vice. And such a large proportion of all smokers claim to have tried to give it up that anyone who still smokes is seen by many as a *prima facie* sufferer from terminal weakness of will. The result of this is, in effect, to delegitimize smoking. The smoker's claim that his enjoyment of smoking should stand on a par with the nonsmoker's dislike of it is therefore undermined.

A utilitarian approach would not be affected by this. The long-term health risks should, needless to say, be factored in. But, so long as that is done properly, the rule defining the nonagreement point should, according to the utilitarian principle, be drawn up in a way that offers the optimum balance between the pleasures and pains of smokers and nonsmokers. Segregation will no doubt score very high on the utilitarian calculus, as a solution to be pressed wherever feasible, but beyond that it is hard to say how the rule should come out. Perhaps we might go back to the assumption that, at any rate as a first approximation, intensities of preference should be assumed to be equal. (See section 13 above, under "Utilitarianism.") This would imply that *prima facie* a group with a majority of smokers should permit smoking and a group with a majority of nonsmokers should not. This rule of thumb could then be modified to take account of well-established peculiarities. Somebody with a respiratory ailment should be able to veto smoking; someone who is notoriously so addicted that he gets jumpy and irritable if he has to go without smoking for long should be indulged; and so on.

In contrast, a resourcist solution can start from the question: what is the fair way to divide up the scarce resource? In this case, the scarce resource is air, which can either be kept free of tobacco smoke (which is good for nonsmokers and bad for smokers) or used as a repository for used smoke (which is bad for nonsmokers but good for smokers). Here, too, it seems evident that the solution of giving each group what it wants without stint—which means segregation—is the ideal. But how should we proceed where this is not feasible? Within a resourcist framework we are not bound by the requirement that long-run utility must be maximized. We can ask who has the strongest claim to the resource, which means that, in the terminology introduced by Thomas Scanlon, we can take account of "urgency" rather than simply "preference."[40] Alternative uses of the resource can, in other words, be compared according to some shared conception of their value or importance, where these notions are not reducible to some function of preference-satisfaction.

The answer that emerges when the question is posed in this way will, obviously, depend upon the currently prevailing ideas about the value or importance of various activities or states of affairs. Given what I have said about the current sentiment in the United States, it is easy to see that a nonsmoking nonagreement point, or a nonagreement point with very few concessions to smokers built into it, would seem appropriate. But we cannot expect this to be a universal answer. In a society where the claims of smokers and nonsmokers are seen as equally legitimate, for example, it would be the most natural application of the resourcist approach to look for a solution that shares the resource equally between smokers and nonsmokers. Smoking might be allowed on alternate days, or it in the afternoon but not in the morning, and so on.

It might be thought that, since this resolution rests on the equal legitimacy of the desires of smokers and nonsmokers, it is very similar to what would be arrived at by starting from the utilitarian principle and adding the assumption (either as a stipulation or as an empirical approximation) of equal preference intensity. If we add the fairly plausible idea that the intensity of the desire to smoke on the part of the smokers declines (at any rate over periods of a few hours) with the amount smoked and that the intensity of the desire to avoid smoke on the part of the nonsmokers increases with the amount smoked (again, over the short term if not the long), we can indeed get the answer that time should be equally divided between smoking and nonsmoking periods— provided the number of smokers and nonsmokers is approximately equal. (It may be noted that our filmgoing example [in section 13 above] did not introduce the problem of unequal numbers on different sides because it was worked out for two people throughout.)

Suppose, however, that we have two smokers and one nonsmoker, or one smoker and two nonsmokers, who have to work together in a single office. Utilitarianism is sensitive to numbers, so the outcome must shift away from an equal division of time under these conditions. How far it should shift depends on the shape of the marginal utility functions we are imputing to the people involved. The simplest rule, and one with a good deal of *prima facie* plausibility, would be to reckon that with two smokers utility is maximized with no restrictions on smoking, and with two nonsmokers it is maximized with no smoking. Any concession to the minority would have to depend on the claim that the marginal utility of smoking declines very rapidly, that the marginal disutility of breathing smoke rises very rapidly, or both.

By contrast, the resourcist solution would not turn on such questions. It would ask what is a fair way of dividing up the time, and in the light of what has been said the answer is to think of control over the time as being divided up so that each person controls an equal share. The implication of this would be that smoking time should be proportioned to the number of smokers. For my present purpose it is not necessary to pursue further the rival claims of alternative baselines. It is enough if I have shown that, even with neutrality between preferences, resourcism still operates differently from utilitarianism and will in general reach different practical conclusions.

16. CONCLUSION TO PART I

The work of the game theorists discussed in Part I of this book is, on the whole, more sophisticated technically than philosophically. This is not to say that it is necessarily mistaken from the philosophical point of view, merely that it tends to pass very quickly over the philosophically important questions, insofar as it notices them at all. Thus, the Nash solution seems to me one of the most fruitful contributions that have been made to the theory of games. But Nash's explanation (which I mentioned in section 4) of the fairness of his solution to the bargaining problem is remarkably perfunctory. As we saw in section 6, a good deal of excavation is required even to reveal the premises that are needed to give any plausibility to the claim that a bargaining solution is fair if it gives the parties what they could reasonably expect to get out of an actual process of bargaining.

Similarly, I raise my hat to Harsanyi's proof that rational maximizers operating behind a thin veil of ignorance that concealed from them only their own identities would opt for the principle of maximizing utility. But neither Harsanyi nor Sen (who, as we saw, commended Harsanyi as an improvement on Nash and Braithwaite) offered any serious reason for thinking that we should find morally compelling the choices of poorly informed egoists. I have not in Part I pursued that line of discussion because my main focus has been on baseline-dependent solutions. But I shall take it up in Part III, first presenting and then criticizing what appears to be the best available rationale. (See especially section 41.)

Not too surprisingly, given that his intellectual background lay in decision theory rather than in moral philosophy, Braithwaite has the characteristics typical of a game theorist rather than a moral philosopher. The largest part of his lecture is concerned with the geometry of parabolas. As we have seen, his attempt to show that his proposed solution should be denominated fair is at best obscure and at worst confused. The remaining professional philosophers whose work we have examined in Part I tend to suffer from the opposite failings. Thus, Gauthier and Lucas are pretty clear about the rationale for their baseline as one where the parties are doing as well for themselves as possible. But they are, I think, far too quick to assume that a maximin mixed strategy is really "prudential." Moreover, neither seems to me to deal adequately with the move from the nonagreement point to the Pareto frontier. Lucas takes over Braithwaite's method, but when he has thrown out the rest of Braithwaite's solution it is hard to see how this can make any sense. And Gauthier, who wants a bargaining simulation, offers arguments against the Nash solution that are (as I point out in Appendix B) plainly fallacious.

Finally, what can be said about Rawls? I have suggested that he (along with others) has allowed himself to be misled by the claim of Luce and Raiffa that Matthew's getting the lion's share of the time under Braithwaite's solution is due to his "threat advantage." This is in fact true for Braithwaite's own solution but, as I pointed out, almost any bargaining solution or equal-gain solution (where equal gain is measured in terms of von Neumann/Morgenstern utilities normalized in some way) will award Matthew over half the solo playing time. There is, indeed, a line of complaint that can be made against allowing threats to determine the noncooperative baseline, and that is the line taken by Gauthier and Lucas. But Rawls himself clearly wishes to expand the category of "threats" so that any kind of advantage in bargaining—not simply in the establishing of a nonagreement point—is to be counted as morally illegitimate insofar as it plays any role in bringing about an allocation.

Rawls believes that bargaining is relevant to justice, but only when it is carried out under conditions that embody what he called "the constraints of having a morality" (see the epigraph to this volume for Rawls's exposition of this idea in "Justice as Fairness"). Since these conditions, formalized in *A Theory of Justice* as the "original position," create the same decision problem for everyone, it is clear that there is no room for bargaining in the ordinary sense of the term.

As we shall see in Part II, however, there is another strand in Rawls's theory of justice, which ties in far more closely with two-stage thinking. According to this, justice has a place only where the "circumstances of justice" obtain, and these are circumstances such that everyone stands to gain from adherence to principles restraining the untrammelled pursuit of self-interest, when the point of comparison is the results of "general egoism." This clearly envisages a structure containing a nonagreement point and a possibility of mutual gain by moving away from it. One of the central questions to be asked in Part II is whether there is any way in which Rawls's two apparently quite different ideas about justice can be fitted together.

It is of some curiosity value in the present context to observe that at some point during the years following the publication of his discussion of Braithwaite, "Moralists and Gamesmen," Lucas appears to have undergone some kind of Damascene experience. With all the enthusiasm of a convert denouncing his former heresies, Lucas wrote in an article entitled "Justice" that "I am not being fair if I merely maximise my own relative advantage, even if I also collaborate with you in maximising our joint advantage. I am fair only if I am prepared, at least to some extent, to see things from your point of view, and to give some weight to your desire to serve your interests as well as to my desire to serve mine."[41] Those who held the position now rejected were said to be offering "a rational reconstruction not of justice but of something more like prudence."[42] And the two people identified with it by Lucas were Braithwaite and Rawls.

It is, I think, broadly correct to say that Braithwaite turns the search for a fair division into the search for a division that corresponds to the demands of rational prudence. But his own failure to offer a good justification for doing so does not mean that none exists. Perhaps if behaving justly is assumed to be something we must have reason to do, the only conception of justice that is tenable will turn out to be rational prudence. That will have to be discussed later. (See especially section 35.) As far as Rawls is concerned, truth and error are closely intertwined in what Lucas says. Rawls would fully endorse the conception of fairness that Lucas himself puts forward here in the last sentence of the quotation. But he would then argue that asking what would be a prudential choice in certain conditions, drawn up to represent central features of morality, is a way of asking what fairness actually requires. In section 41 I shall ask how plausible this is.

I have had fairly modest aims in Part I. My main object has been to lay out as perspicuously as possible various theories of fair division and to analyze what might be said for or against them. Two-person problems, which have been the staple of Part I, have many obvious limitations. At the same time they have the advantage that their analysis can be carried on in some depth without becoming so complex as to overwhelm the critical faculty. I have tried as best I can to get the advantages without the disadvantages by eschewing premature generalization from the micro level to the macro level and by pointing explicitly to the way in which micro-level problems cannot really be treated independently from the macro-level institutional framework.

In the present chapter I have also tried to take advantage of the simplicity of small-scale problems of resource allocation to work out some ideas about information and strategy that I believe have some general applicability. This will make the exposition in Part II, where I shall be discussing the same problems in whole societies, a good deal easier than it would otherwise have been.

It is my hope that Part I will prove to be of interest in its own right, as a critical exposition of a body of recent work at the intersection of game theory and normative philosophy. But it also plays a part in the larger design of this volume, as will, if all goes well, become clear in Part III. In Part II, I shall offer a critical-*cum*-expository review of the theories of justice in society put forward by David Hume and John Rawls. Then, in Part III, I shall put the results of that together with what has been done in Part I and try to arrive at an integrated view of justice in both small-scale and large-scale contexts.

Hume and Rawls on Justice in Society

CHAPTER IV

Hume on Justice

17. INTRODUCTION

FROM FAIRNESS TO JUSTICE

With this chapter we move on from fair division to social justice. By "fair division" I mean to refer to proposed solutions to conflicts among small numbers of people (typically two) in situations marked by the existence of a nonagreement point and a cooperative surplus. By "social justice" I intend to refer to criteria for appraising social institutions—including those that define the situations within which problems of fair division occur.

The two words "just" and "fair" have many more specialized uses, some of which we shall have to take account of later. One distinction, which has been seized on by Rawls in his notion of "justice as fairness," is that in some contexts fairness is attributed to procedures and justice to outcomes. It is a cardinal error, however, to suppose that merely because there are two words there must be two well-differentiated concepts. (The same error is often made about the words "freedom" and "liberty.") In fact, each of the terms has a whole mass of special uses, where it would be unidiomatic to use one and not the other; and, where both terms may be used, there are usually nuances of meaning distinguishing them—but different nuances in different settings. Since this is a book about the ethics of distribution and not about the peculiar historical development of the English language, I shall not seek to derive any conclusions from fine points of usage.

Following Rawls, I shall say that social justice is predicated primarily of the basic structure of a society. This structure is made up of the institutions that together determine the access (or chances of access) of the members of a society to resources that are the means to the satisfaction of a wide variety of desires. These resources can be grouped under three headings: power, status, and money. Examples—this is not an exhaustive list—of institutions that fall under the basic structure of the society are the following: the rules that allocate fundamental legal rights and privileges (equal or unequal) to members of the society; the rules that specify how access is gained to political decision-making power; the rules that permit concentrations of private decision-making power, such as that exercised by business corporations, real-estate developers, and so on, in market societies; the institutions (including the educational system and rules of apprenticeship or licensure) that determine access to professions, crafts, or other sought-after occupational positions; and the whole complex of institutions (including some already mentioned but also including rules for the acquisition and inheritance of property and the system of taxation and transfers) that determine the distribution of income and wealth in a society.

HUME AND RAWLS

Part II is devoted to a critical examination of certain arguments to be found in the work of David Hume and John Rawls—primarily, though not exclusively, those in *A Treatise of Human Nature* and *A Theory of Justice*,[1] respectively. My reason for devoting this amount of space to an examination of these two men's writings is primarily neither antiquarian nor exegetical. I do believe that I have cleared up some knotty passages in *A Theory of Justice*, but this is incidental to my main purpose, which is to develop further the analysis of the two theories of justice sketched in section 1 of this book.

The choice of Hume and Rawls is dictated by my view that there is most to be learned from them. Hume stated with unsurpassed clarity the view of justice as mutual gain over a nonagreement baseline. In addition, however, he has a fair claim to be counted as at least the intellectual godfather of Benthamite utilitarianism. Thus the baseline-independent solutions analyzed in chapter 2 can also be traced back to him. Moreover, the method by which he arrived at his proto-utilitarianism—his claim that we should ask what can be approved of impartially—is a fruitful and significant contribution in its own right.

Rawls, to whom I give more attention, is in my judgment the most original and interesting political philosopher of this century. I cannot do better than extend Jonathan Harrison's words from Hume to Rawls:

> I have sometimes been accused of treating him unsympathetically in my [previous] book [on him]. I do not know whether any of my readers will feel I have made the same mistake again. If so, I am disinclined to apologize for it. Pointing out his merits sounds patronizing, and is in any case superfluous. Hume was a great enough man to be capable of surviving the most rigorous criticism. Indeed I think his stature is more apparent as his work is studied in greater detail, and, like a musical instrument which improves the more it is played, the more intensively he is studied, the more rewarding his work becomes.[2]

A Theory of Justice and the major articles written before and since then by Rawls constitute an inexhaustibly rich source of ideas. Rawls is, like Hume, a protean figure. We can find in his writings not one theory of justice but several, of different levels of abstraction and different degrees of articulation. The driving forces behind his work are a striving toward synthesis and systematization on one side and, on the other side, an equally strong desire to get everything in—to keep hold of a mass of disparate insights without sacrificing any of them. It is in the tension between these two driving forces that much of the value of his work lies.

Some thinkers have one or two central ideas and everything else is a matter of working through their implications. The value of the whole theory depends on the validity of these ideas. Thus, for example, a theory that deduces a regime of property rights from some corresponding set of presocial "rights" is worthless if there are no such rights. It is tempting to treat Rawls as a theorist of this kind, with the notion of justice as fairness—that the principles of justice are those that would arise from a fair procedure—playing the role of the central idea from which everything else flows. This, however, would be a mistake.

Although justice as fairness does act as something of an organizing principle, it would be quite wrong to think that the value of everything Rawls has to say depends on the acceptability of his claims for justice as fairness. Rawls has a tolerably clear overall strategy for proving (or at any rate making plausible) his conclusions by giving structure to the notion of a fair procedure, hence creating an "original position" in which choices of principles are to be made. He also has a number of definite substantive positions that he wants to maintain. But in spite of a strong systematizing urge, he never succumbs to the temptation to trim these views so that they fit neatly together or follow in a simple and straightforward way from a few higher-level ideas.

This may sound like a backhanded compliment to pay to the constructor of a philosophical system, but in my view it is a great strength in Rawls that he has struggled to order the complexity he sees rather than make things easy for himself by slapping down a few principles and then simply declaring that whatever follows from them must be the right answer. In any case, the result is that Rawls's work contains many subsidiary discussions that to a large degree stand on their own and deserve to be taken seriously in their own right. To push the matter to the edges of paradox, one might say that in his heroic efforts to bring his insights into a single system Rawls runs the risk that his sheer fertility as a political philosopher will be underestimated.

My claims about the relation between Hume and Rawls do not stop at my saying that both have written about justice in ways that are full of originality and interest, or that both advance a variety of ideas about it that are on the face of it of very different kinds. The most important claim I want to make is that both men have two theories of justice, and that these are the same two theories of justice. Since Hume is (quite rightly) regarded as a closet Hobbesian and a proto-utilitarian, while Rawls is a self-proclaimed follower of Kant, my claim that they both have the same two theories of justice may be surprising. I shall nevertheless hope to make it good in the balance of Part II.

TWO THEORIES OF JUSTICE

I shall be drawing on Hume and Rawls in developing my own analysis of the two theories of justice outlined at the beginning of chapter 1. But I should like first to say a little about the role each of the two theories plays in the work of Hume and Rawls.

The first theory of justice is to be found in Hume's discussion of the origins of justice in the *Treatise of Human Nature*. According to Hume, rules of justice arise out of a sense of the general advantage to be obtained, provided certain conditions hold, from a system of mutual constraints on the pursuit of self-interest. These conditions were called the circumstances of justice by Rawls, who says that those choosing principles of justice in an original position must be informed that these circumstances exist in their society. I therefore attribute to Rawls as well as Hume the idea that justice represents the terms of rational cooperation for mutual advantage under the circumstances of justice. And I shall show

how this idea works itself out at critical points in *A Theory of Justice*.

Hume's second theory of justice is contained in his account in the *Treatise* of how justice comes to be a virtue, and is based on the notion that moral judgments (of which the judgment that justice is a virtue is one) require a common standard if they are to be uniform and that that standard can only be an impartial sympathy with the interests of all those affected. Although Rawls rejects the formulation in terms of an impartial spectator, the other theory that I attribute to him shares with it the fundamental idea of a link between impartiality and justice. But he substitutes for impartiality as an attribute of an observer the idea that impartiality should be guaranteed by the appropriate specification of a situation within which choices are to be made. Impartiality is thus, for Rawls, something to be ascribed to a choice situation rather than to a person.

That Hume and Rawls operate along parallel tracks should not be too surprising when one bears in mind that they are united on an initial negative point: the rejection of any external and independent criterion of justice. Neither thinks that it makes any sense to ask at the outset what is people's "due" and then to say that justice consists in their getting it. Rather, what is due to people is to be determined from within the theory. Thus, Hume takes as his starting point an attack on the venerable tag (from the *Institutes* of Justinian) that justice is "the constant perpetual will of giving everyone his due." This presupposes that it makes sense to ask what somebody's "due" is in the abstract. But, Hume argues, this is a fallacy. Justice is, he says, an "artificial virtue." One can be just (or unjust) only against the background of some pre-existing social convention that itself defines the content of justice.

We can tell that justice is an artificial virtue because a single act of justice would have no point unless it formed part of a general practice in which others by and large acted on the same rules.

> The only difference betwixt the natural virtues and justice lies in this, that the good, which results from the former, arises from every single act, and is the object of some natural passion: Whereas a single act of justice, consider'd in itself, may often be contrary to the public good; and 'tis only the concurrence of mankind, in a general scheme or system of action, which is advantageous. When I relieve persons in distress, my natural humanity is my motive; and so far as my succor extends, so far have I promoted the happiness of my fellow-creatures. But if we examine all the questions, that come before any tribunal of justice, we shall find, that, considering each case apart, it wou'd as often be an instance of humanity to decide contrary to the laws of justice as conformable to them.[3]

In an attractive metaphor, Hume likens the product of benevolence to "a wall, built by many hands, which still rises by each stone that is heaped upon it, and receives increase proportional to the diligence and care of each workman."[4] Justice, by contrast, produces its effects in the manner of "a vault, where each individual stone would, of itself, fall to the ground; nor is the whole fabric supported but by the mutual assistance and combination of its corresponding parts. . . . Whatever is advantageous to two or more persons, if all perform their part; but what loses all advantage if only one perform, can arise from no other principle."[5]

Harrison, in *Hume's Theory of Justice*, has objected that there could be cases where one person acting benevolently will be able to do no good but several people acting benevolently would do some good, yet the action of the one person still constitutes benevolence: for example, there might be a man in a poor community so badly off that "no good would come of one man giving him as much as this man could afford, though much good would come of them all giving him as much as they could afford."[6] Three comments are in order. First, if the aid is certain to be useless unless the others contribute as well, Hume would presumably say that there really is no reason for giving anything; for the act is one not of benevolence but of waste of resources. Second, we might indeed still say the act of giving to the man in distress bespeaks a benevolent disposition. The virtue of benevolence is not actually being displayed, but we surmise that someone willing to put himself out when it does no good will presumably be even more willing to do so when it does do some good. We might therefore commend such a person's heart, if not his head. And, third, the issue of knowledge comes in here, as with so many made-up philosophers' examples. Harrison says that the help given by this one person does no good in this case. But how can we be sure in advance that it will do no good—and, more to the point, how can the person who has to decide whether to help be sure it will do no good? (A case in which an individual contribution does *no* good to someone desperately poor is farfetched, even though not inconceivable.) Provided there is any uncertainty, there need be no question that the motive is benevolent.

Much of Harrison's discussion of this issue is vitiated by the failure to grasp the distinction between acts that naturally do good (even if it takes more than one of them to do it) and acts that do good only in virtue of some convention or rule—"artifice," in Hume's vocabulary.

According to Harrison, Hume cannot think that individual acts of justice always tend to the public good, even when their part in maintaining the convention or rule is allowed for in calculating that good, because then public benevolence would be an adequate motive and justice would not be an artificial virtue.[7] But this is a fallacy. Justice remains an artificial virtue, because the individual act of justice tends to the public good only in the context of the "artificial" institution of justice. The distinction here is not that individual acts of benevolence tend to the public good whereas individual acts of justice do not. Rather, the point is that individual acts of benevolence tend to the public good naturally whereas individual acts of justice tend to the public good only in virtue of artifice.

Because justice is conventional (that is, a virtue only in the context of general observation of a practice), Hume maintains that there is no external standard of justice against which the content of the practice can be assessed. The rules define what is just; it is nonsense to suppose that they could be defined by it. The "vulgar definition of justice" is thus mistaken in talking about a "due" that is "independent of justice and antecedent to it."[8]

Notice that this negative claim is compatible with both mutual self-protection and impartiality (taken by Hume to imply general utility) as the bases of justice. Both would fit the claim that justice is useful, and only for that reason a virtue. On the first interpretation of the "usefulness" of justice, the conventions are useful to each of us only insofar as other people are restrained by them, and the price we pay for the restraint of others is having to observe the conventions ourselves. (Recall Glaucon's account of the common view of justice.) On the second interpretation, justice is conventional in that it is a contingent matter what rules of justice are in fact useful to society—that is to say, conducive to general utility.

Hume himself was not, I fear, above muddling together these two different claims about the usefulness of justice: that it is advantageous to each person compared with the absence of mutual constraint, and that it is socially beneficial. The problem is particularly acute in the *Enquiry Concerning the Principles of Morals*, where Hume's account of the circumstances of justice absolutely requires at crucial points that "usefulness" be construed as meaning "useful to each of the people covered by the rules of justice," whereas his subsequent discussion of the content of the rules of justice often seems to lend itself to a more utilitarian interpretation. The *Treatise of Human Nature* is less trouble-some, with its sharp distinction between the origins of justice and the reason why justice is a virtue. But even here, I shall sometimes be pressing Hume, for the sake of exposition, further than he might have wanted to go in separating the two strands.

Now, for comparison with Hume's attack on "independent" and "antecedent" principles of justice, here is a quotation from Rawls: "The parties in the original position do not recognize any principles of justice as true or correct and so as antecedently given; their aim is simply to select the conception most rational for them, given their circumstances. This conception is not regarded as a workable approximation to the moral facts: there are no such moral facts to which the principles adopted could approximate."[9] Rawls thus joins Hume in rejecting the notion that there are any eternal fitnesses of things to be discovered. (For further discussion see section 33.) Justice is, for both, a human creation—which is not inconsistent with saying it may be created well or ill. But Rawls also, I suggest, offers the same two alternative bases of justice: mutual advantage and impartiality.

I shall maintain that neither Hume nor Rawls succeeds in reconciling the two approaches. Hume, as we shall see later in this chapter, skirts the difficulty by assuming with little argument that an impartial sympathetic spectator would endorse existing property rules. Rawls, having specified the parties by their potential for mutually beneficial co-operation, moves from there to specifying the terms of cooperation in accordance with the requirements of impartiality. But, as we shall see, the two approaches do not have the same practical implications. (See especially section 30.)

18. THE CIRCUMSTANCES OF JUSTICE

I have said that Rawls's conception of social justice is that social justice is predicated of the basic structure of a society. This is to be contrasted with Hume's usage. Hume, who is here following an ancient tradition of writing about justice, predicates justice primarily of people rather than institutions. Justice is a virtue, a disposition to behave in certain ways. Specifically, according to Hume, justice is the disposition to respect the rules governing property in one's society. But it is noteworthy that in the course of explicating the content of the virtue of justice—what it specifically calls for—Hume refers to "rules of equity or justice."[10] These are the rules in a society that establish how property is acquired and transmitted. We are thus scarcely distorting Hume by talking about his theory of justice as his theory of the rules of justice.*

As I have said, one of Hume's central ideas is that rules defining property (rules of justice) come about because everyone finds that a free-for-all is less advantageous than a regime of mutual forbearance. I shall explain in the rest of this section why Hume believes that rules of justice could arise only out of mutual self-interest. Hume adds that once rules of justice are in existence, respecting the rules comes to be seen as a virtue. When we adopt an impartial standpoint we can all approve of justice, because we all see how conducive it is to general utility. Hume's argument for this will be taken up in the next section. In section 20 I shall discuss the implications of Hume's two theories of justice for the rules of property that can be justified. Hume convinced himself rather easily that inflexible rules of property would make for the most utility in the long run—a position espoused in our own time notably by F. A. Hayek—but this can be questioned, and there is a distinguished tradition of utilitarian speculation on the matter, running from Bentham to A. C. Pigou and recently revived by Richard Brandt. I shall say a little about Hume's divided legacy in section 21 to close the chapter.

In this section, then, I shall focus on Hume's first theory of justice.

---

*A more tricky definitional problem is what the concept of justice is supposed by Hume to cover. Hume himself was not altogether consistent in his usage when discussing the artificial virtues. I am reading him as distinguishing justice, as the observance of property rules, from other artificial virtues, namely, promise-keeping ("fidelity"), obeying the law ("allegiance"), adhering to the rules regulating the conduct between the sexes ("chastity") and, for states, observing the "laws of nations." This is the usage he most commonly adopts, and in the *Enquiry Concerning the Principles of Morals* he is pretty consistent in it, even speaking flatly of that "property which is the object of justice" (*Enquiries Concerning Human Understanding and Concerning The Principles of Morals*, ed. L. A. Selby-Bigge, 3d ed., ed. P. H. Nidditch [Oxford: Clarendon Press, 1975], p. 201). On the other hand, the part of the *Treatise* (Book 3, Part 2) that deals with all the artificial virtues is entitled "Of Justice and Injustice." And Hume does occasionally employ the term "justice" outside the context of property.

Not a great deal turns on this, and perhaps Hume never considered it worth making a big issue of the question of whether "justice" is a generic name for all the artificial virtues or whether it is the name for one of them. The most plausible interpretation is, I suggest, that he wanted primarily to use "justice" in a narrow sense to refer to observance of property rules because there was no other convenient word (corresponding to "fidelity" or "allegiance") for this, but that he occasionally also found convenient a wider use of the word to refer to all the artificial virtues.

I shall confine myself to the narrow usage because in practice much of what Hume says about justice applies directly to property rules, and only to them. It can be extended with some effort to fidelity, allegiance, and observance of the laws of nations, insofar as Hume apparently believes that all of them arise mainly as a result of the potentiality for disputes over material possessions, and what he says about justice would require quite substantial modification before it would apply to chastity. Rather than try to work all this through, I shall take the case that Hume himself worked through, that of property rules.

Hume argues that if certain conditions—the circumstances of justice—
did not obtain, justice would not be advantageous and the convention
of separate property would never have been developed. In both the
Treatise and the *Enquiry* Hume holds "that 'tis only from the selfishness and confin'd generosity of men, along with the scanty provision
nature has made for his wants, that justice derives its origin."[11] That
these are necessary conditions will be shown by supposing them not to
obtain: "Reverse, in any considerable circumstance, the condition of
men: Produce extreme abundance or extreme necessity: Implant in the
human breast perfect moderation and humanity, or perfect rapacious-
ness and malice: by rendering justice totally *useless*, you thereby totally
destroy its essence, and suspend its obligation upon mankind."[12] A
third condition, approximate equality of strength, is introduced explicitly only in the *Enquiry*, though it is implicit in the *Treatise*. I shall
take up each of these three circumstances of justice in turn.

THE MODERATE SCARCITY CONDITION

The condition described as moderate scarcity is analyzed by Hume in
terms of an upper and a lower bound on the generosity of nature in
supplying human wants. The upper bound is that, if everything human
beings wanted were as freely available as air normally is (the mythical
Golden Age of the classical poets), the "cautious, jealous virtue of justice" would never have become established. "Justice, in that case, being
totally useless, would be an idle ceremonial, and could never possibly
have place in the catalogue of virtues."[13]

Since the subject matter of justice is the distribution of things that are
in short supply, it follows that if nothing were in short supply (relative
to the total demand) the concept of justice would have no application.
This entails, as the classical poets recognized, not only that nature
should be abundant but also that wants should be limited.[14] Once
people come to want things the demand for which has no natural limit
(such as gold) or come to be concerned not simply with what they have
themselves but with having more than others have, then farewell primitive bliss. (Marx's communist utopia, envy-free and committed to use
value rather than commodity value, is the poets' Golden Age with
machinery standing in for the bounty of nature.)*

---

* "Marx appears to have believed that technical progress already made under capital-
ism had fundamentally *solved* the problem of production, but that the shackles imposed
on the forces of production by the capitalist system prevented this from being realised in

We can accept Hume's claim that justice would be "useless" in a Golden Age without accepting the corollary that in real life, where resources are scarce in relation to demands, what makes justice a virtue is its usefulness. That justice comes into play where there is a conflict does not tell us anything about the way in which it should operate when it does come into play.

Hume's assertion of a lower bound to the generosity of nature as a circumstance of justice seems to me to be without foundation.

> Suppose a society to fall into such want of all common necessaries, that the utmost frugality and industry cannot preserve the greater number from perishing, and the whole from extreme misery; it will readily, I believe, be admitted, that the strict laws of justice are suspended, in such a pressing emergence, and give place to the stronger motives of necessity and self-preservation. . . . The public, even in less urgent necessities, opens granaries, without the consent of proprietors; as justly supposing, that the authority of magistracy may, consistent with equity, extend so far: but were any number of men to assemble, without the tie of laws or civil jurisdiction; would an equal partition of bread in a famine, though effected by power and even violence, be regarded as criminal or injurious?[15]

Hume might, if he had stopped at the first sentence, have been taken as saying that under conditions of real extremity human beings are driven to pursue self-preservation at all costs, as a sort of Hobbesian psychological necessity. In that case not only justice but any other basis for appraising a person's conduct except conduciveness to that individual's survival would be strictly beside the point. But the continuation makes it clear that Hume's real point is that the existing property rules (in his

---

practice. There are passages in which he speaks of 'the unlimited growth of production', 'the absolute development of social productivity of labor', such as would in fact make possible 'continual relative production'. . . . Let us define abundance as a sufficiency to meet requirements at zero price, leaving no reasonable person dissatisfied or seeking more of anything (or at least of anything reproducible). This concept plays a crucial role in Marx's vision of socialism/communism. . . . Abundance removes conflict over resource allocation, since by definition there is enough for everyone, and so there are no mutually exclusive choices, no opportunity is forgone and therefore there is no opportunity-cost. The golden age, a communist steady-state equilibrium, will have been reached. Gradual change, growth, will be simple and painless. The task of planning becomes one of simple routine; the role of economics is virtually eliminated. There is then no reason for various individuals and groups to compete, to take possession for their own use of what is freely available to all. . . . If other goods were as easily and freely available as water is in Scotland, then new human attitudes would develop: acquisitiveness would wither away; property rights, and crimes related to property, would also vanish, not because the citizens would have become 'good' by reading Marxist books but because acquisitiveness would have lost all purpose." (Alec Nove, *The Politics of Feasible Socialism* [London: George Allen & Unwin, 1983], pp.15–16.)

property rules

terminology, the rules of justice) would be inappropriate, so that it would not in the circumstances be "criminal or injurious" to breach them. But this, it seems to me, may be conceded without generating the conclusion that Hume wants to draw, namely, that justice applies only in situations where it is mutually advantageous. We can talk about justice where the question is simply one of the right way to distribute a fixed stock. This is a case where the only issue is who gains and who loses, but it is, I suggest, actually a paradigm of a circumstance in which questions of justice are pressed. (I shall take this up in relation to Rawls in section 29.)

Hume himself, be it noted, speaks of "an *equal* partition of bread in a famine."[16] Might not an unequal partition (or, more precisely, an unequal partition in which the departures from equality were not based on conditions such as pregnancy, sickness, heavy manual labor, and so forth) be criticized as unjust? It seems to me that the justice of a rationing scheme can always be intelligibly queried. Perhaps even more plainly, the application of the scheme can be brought before the bar of fair procedure: Is it being administered impartially, or are some people getting specially favorable treatment? Experience suggests, indeed, that any system of rationing automatically produces public controversy, in which the concepts of justice and fairness come naturally into play. The wartime food rationing scheme in England is a case in point; and in the postwar period the allocation of council housing to applicants (which is usually done by a system of "points") has similarly attracted much controversy conducted largely in terms of fairness.

Even in a wealthy country such as the United States, there are limits to the expensive medical treatment that can be carried out. Hospitals with a certain number of beds in intensive care units have to decide, in effect, whose life to attempt to save. The existence of a *de facto* rationing system has led inevitably to questions about the fair way to select people for treatment.*[17] This shows that the criteria of justice extend

---

* To illustrate the kinds of problems that immediately present themselves, consider the criteria used by the selection committee in the early days of the Seattle Artificial Kidney Center: "A person 'worthy' of having his life preserved by a scarce, expensive treatment like chronic dialysis was judged to have qualities such as decency and responsibility. Any history of social deviance, such as a prison record, any suggestion that a person's married life was not intact and scandal-free, were strong contraindications to selection. The preferred candidate was a person who had demonstrated achievement through hard work and success in his job, who went to church, joined groups, and was actively involved in community affairs" (Renée C. Fox and Judith P. Swazey, *The Courage to Fail: A Social View of Organ Transplants and Dialysis* [Chicago: University of Chicago Press, 1974], p. 246). This state of affairs induced the caustic remark that "the Pacific Northwest is no

even to cases in which "the utmost frugality and industry cannot prevent the greater number from perishing."[18] For as the pioneer of chronic hemodialysis has said, scarcity and the selection it makes necessary entail "the decision by somebody on some grounds that somebody will not be permitted dialysis or transplant, which says, in effect, he must now die."[19] The question "Who is to be saved?" is one within the scope of justice.

THE MODERATE SELFISHNESS CONDITION

The second circumstance of justice is moderate selfishness. Again, Hume suggests that the virtue of justice can arise only if the extremes are absent: "if men pursu'd the publick interest naturally, and with a hearty affection, they wou'd never have dream'd of restraining each other by these rules [of justice]; and if they pursu'd their own interest, without any precaution, they wou'd run head-long into every kind of injustice and violence."[20]

It should be noticed at once that, although Hume wishes, for the sake of symmetry, to extend the "not too much, not too little" formula from scarcity to selfishness, the two extremes that he presents are not really two extremes of selfishness. Hume does, indeed, deny that, as a matter of fact, people are totally selfish. He suggests that "tho' it be rare to meet with one, who loves any single person better than himself; yet 'tis as rare to meet with one, in whom all the kind affections, taken together, do not over-balance all the selfish."[21] But this does not help much in securing social union, because "in the original frame of our mind, our strongest attention is confin'd to ourselves; our next is extended to our relations and acquaintance; and 'tis only the weakest which reaches to strangers and indifferent persons."[22] "Benevolence to strangers" is therefore "too weak" to render men fit members of society, by making them "abstain from the possessions of others."[23]

The point is not, therefore, that justice would be impossible under conditions of universal selfishness. The benevolent sentiments people actually have are confined to too narrow a circle to reduce the level of

---

place for a Henry David Thoreau with bad kidneys." The authors of this comment, a psychiatrist and a lawyer, went on to say, in terms highly relevant to the present discussion, that "justice requires that selection be made by a fairer method than the unbridled consciences, the built-in biases, and the fantasies of omnipotence of a secret committee" (D. Sanders and J. Dukeminier, "Medical Advance and Legal Lag: Hemodialysis and Kidney Transplantation," UCLA Law Review 15 [1968]: 377–78).

conflict in society, so as far as that goes it would make no difference as far as justice is concerned if people were totally selfish. The circumstances of justice would still obtain. Justice, Hume says, is founded on self-interest: "itself alone restrains it." The question is not one of the "wickedness or goodness of human nature" but of "the degrees of men's sagacity or folly."[24] The rhetorical "not too much, not too little" device is thus misleading here. The opposite extreme to total benevolence, which makes the virtue of justice inapplicable, is not total self-interest but *unintelligent* self-interest.

In the formulation (which pays acknowledgment to Hobbes and Hume) of H. L. A. Hart in chapter 9 of *The Concept of Law*, the intermediate position of human nature is expressed by saying that men are neither angels nor devils. "With angels, never tempted to harm others, rules requiring forbearances would not be necessary. With devils prepared to destroy, reckless of the cost to themselves, they would be impossible." But that men are not "devils" in this sense does not entail, as Hart implies, that "human altruism is limited in range and intermittent."[25] All that it entails is that, in the conception of self-interest, human beings give higher priority to the prospect of gaining personal security (which carries with it the cost of restraints on their ability to attack others) than to the prospect of being able to attack others at will (which carries with it the cost of a constant danger of being attacked by them). In other words, what is necessary is that the great majority of people should have in these matters the kind of preference-ordering Hobbes attributed to them.

To show that total benevolence makes justice redundant, Hume asks us to imagine a society each of whose members "feels no more concern for his own interest than for that of his fellows." Then, he says, somebody would always perform a service for me "except the hurt, he thereby receives, be greater than the benefit accruing to me."[26] There is some question about the interpretation of this statement. When Hume says, just after this passage, that my heart "shares all [my neighbour's] joys and sorrows with the same force and vivacity as if originally my own," this might make it appear that Hume is positing a psychological mechanism ("sympathy") that literally makes my happiness a function of the sum total of the happiness of the human race. Philip Mercer has argued, persuasively to my mind, that at the time he wrote the *Treatise* Hume regarded "sympathy" as the literal reconstitution in ourselves (in a faint form) of the feelings of another, somewhat as one of the "sympathetic" strings of an instrument is excited when the same note is played with the bow on another string.[27] Sympathy was seen here as the psychological foundation of fellow feeling. We desire to ease the pain of others to lessen the "uneasiness" that the contemplation of their suffering evokes in us.*

By the time he came to write the *Enquiry*, however, Hume had repudiated this, saying, "it is needless to push our researches so far as to ask, why we have humanity or a fellow-feeling with others. It is sufficient, that this is experienced to be a principle in human nature."[28] And in Appendix II of the *Enquiry* he expanded on this. Here he decried attempts to reduce all wants to the more or less subtle pursuit of personal gratification and said that "the hypothesis. . . of a disinterested benevolence"—that "from the original frame of our temper, we may feel a desire of another's happiness or good"[29]—has the merit of simplicity and intrinsic plausibility. This seems to me an unquestionable improvement, and I think we would do well to restate the passage from the *Treatise* without the psychological baggage of sympathy as a cause of fellow feeling.

Let us therefore simply say that we are to imagine a society in which, for whatever reason, everyone desires and pursues the general interest. The only qualification that has to be made is that this must come about through natural sentiment and not as a result of people acting on moral conviction. In such a society each person would act as if he were pursuing the greatest total happiness, counting everyone for one in the calculation. But there would be no self-conscious utilitarians, if we understand utilitarianism as a prescriptive system that tells people what they ought morally to do. In the society we are envisaging people pursue the general interest because they want to do it. If we assume (as Hume appears to) that there is a utility-maximizing calculus capable of yield-

---

* Fans of Stanislaw Lem may be reminded of his tale of the drug Altruizine and its effects when introduced experimentally into the water supply of first a small hamlet and then a city. Lem describes the drug as follows: "ALTRUIZINE. A metapsychotropic transmitting agent effective for all sentient homoproteinates. The drug duplicates into others, within a radius of fifty yards, whatever sensations, emotions, and mental states one may experience. . . . According to its discoverer, ALTRUIZINE will ensure the untrammeled reign of Brotherhood, Cooperation and Compassion in any society, since the neighbors of a happy man must share his happiness, and the happier he, the happier perforce they, so it is entirely in their own interest that they wish him nothing but the best. Should he suffer any hurt, they will rush to help at once, so as to spare themselves the pain induced by his. Neither walls, fences, hedges, nor any other obstacle will weaken the altruizing influence. . . . We assume no responsibility for results at variance with the discoverer's claims." ("Altruizine, or A True Account of How Bonhomius the Hermetic Hermit Tried to Bring About Universal Happiness and What Came of It," in *The Cyberiad: Fables for the Cybernetic Age*, trans. Michael Kandel [New York: Avon Boosk, 1976], p. 218.)

ing determinate conclusions on every occasion, we must expect that in such a society there will be universal agreement about what each person should do in order best to carry out the purpose that he or she shares with all the other members of the society.

Clearly, if questions of justice arise only in situations of conflict, there can be no questions of justice here. But all this means is that we extend the conclusion we reached about the first circumstance of justice. We agreed that justice has no application in matters where there is no conflict of interest arising from competition for scarce resources. We now add that where everyone has the same end (e.g., maximizing total utility) there is no application for justice. But we may again say that this tells us nothing about cases where there actually are conflicts.

THE EQUALITY CONDITION

The third "circumstance of justice" makes an explicit appearance only in the *Enquiry*, though it is implied by the account of the origins of justice in the *Treatise*. It differs from those so far discussed in two ways. First, it does not even nominally fit the "not too much, not too little" formula around which Hume organized his treatment of the circumstances of justice in the *Treatise*. There is no extreme of equality in power under which justice would be impossible. On the contrary, the more equal the power of the parties, the greater the incentive to arrive at rules of justice and adhere to them. We are thus left only with the other pole. Under circumstances of extreme inequality in power, Hume claims, justice becomes redundant. But that brings us to the other way in which the third circumstance of justice is distinctive. The sense in which justice is redundant in the first two instances is very different from—and far more benign than—the sense in which it is redundant here.

In the Golden Age of the classical poets, the bounty of nature and the paucity of human wants jointly bring about the result that there is no conflict over scarce resources. Everyone can get as much as he wants just by reaching out for it. In the case where everyone is naturally moved to pursue the greatest total utility, there is no conflict of wants because everyone wants the same thing. The sense in which justice is redundant is clear: in neither the Golden Age nor the society of perfect fellow feeling is there any conflict of wants to be adjudicated. In the third case, however, this is not so. Where there is extreme inequality of power, there may well still be a conflict of wants between the parties.

The sense in which justice is "useless" here is not (as before) that it is pointless, but that it is not advantageous to all the parties. There is no point in it, from a self-interested angle, for the powerful actors. As Hobbes put it, a being of infinite power would have no need of covenants because it could hope to gain nothing from them: it could get anything it wanted without having to give anything up in return. Hume's conventions of justice are his version of Hobbes's covenants and the same restriction applies to them. Conventions to restrain the pursuit of self-interest cannot be advantageous unless all the parties can plausibly threaten to damage one another in the absence of a convention.

It may be illuminating to glance back for a moment to Matthew and Luke and trace out the parallels. Corresponding to the Golden Age of the poets we have Matthew and Luke living in perfectly soundproofed apartments and wishing for nothing in the world except to play their instruments undisturbed. The society of perfect fellow feeling would be constituted for our two-person society if Matthew and Luke, though living in rooms that were inadequately soundproofed, were both quite spontaneously driven by a desire to maximize their joint utility. Assuming that they could agree on what that called for, they would both want it, and no question of fair division would arise.

What, then, does the third case, of extreme inequality of power, correspond to? It has in fact already been discussed. (See section 8.) It is the case where Matthew is indifferent between Luke's playing and not playing. Since he cannot be hurt or helped by Luke, he has no self-interested reason for restraint in the pursuit of his own interest. The nonagreement point is already at the Pareto frontier, so the setting is not one in which a problem of fair division, as envisaged by the two-stage theorists, can occur. Fair division is a matter of mutual advantage, and there is no mutual advantage here in moving from the nonagreement baseline. Matthew would have to give up something without getting anything in return, and the two-stage theory of fair division has no provision for unilateral transfers of utility like that.

Hume's notion of extreme inequality of power is simply a generalization of that specific relation between Matthew and Luke.

Were there a species of creatures intermingled with men, which, though rational, were possessed of such inferior strength, both of body and mind, that they were incapable of all resistance, and could never, upon the highest provocation, make us feel the effects of their resentment; the necessary consequence, I think, is that we should be bound by the laws of humanity to give gentle usage to these creatures, but should not, properly speaking, lie under any restraint of justice with regard to them, nor could they possess any right or property, exclusive of such arbitrary lords. Our intercourse with them could not be called society, which supposes a degree of equality; but absolute command on the one side, and servile obedience on the other. Whatever we covet, they must instantly resign: Our permission is the only tenure, by which they hold their possessions: Our compassion and kindness the only check, by which they curb our lawless will: And as no inconvenience ever results from the exercise of a power, so firmly established in nature, the restraints of justice and property, being totally *useless*, would never have place in so unequal a confederacy.[30]

Here is an immediate consequence of Hume's position. Suppose that beings from another world arrived on earth, with some combination of personal characteristics and technology that made them collectively as superior to us as we are to animals. We could appeal to them to give us "gentle usage" but could make no complaint of injustice, *even among ourselves*, if they declared the whole of the earth to be their property and proceeded to exploit it (and us) for their own purposes.

But there is no need to resort to science fiction. Hume himself, in the paragraph following the one quoted above, observes that "the great superiority of civilized Europeans above barbarous Indians, tempted us to imagine ourselves on the same footing with regard to them [as men are in regard to animals], and made us throw off all restraints of justice, and even of humanity, in our treatment of them."[31]

Here, I think, Hume must be accused of drawing back from the full implications of his doctrine. Why does he say that the European settlers were only "tempted to imagine" themselves above justice? Surely, on his theory, they *were* above justice in relation to the Indians. Right from the start, the European settlers were able to impose their "lawless will" on the Indians; and, although the Indians were not, of course, as help-less as Hume's hypothetical "species of creatures" to cause trouble, they could not (as events proved) long resist any course of action that the Europeans determined on.[32] Red Cloud, the Sioux Chief, said in a speech in New York in 1870: "All I want is right and just."[33] A follow-er of Hume would have to say that he was mistaken in thinking that right and just had any place in relations between Indians and whites, given the superiority of the rifle to the bow and arrow and (eventually) the superiority of the U.S. Army's organization to that of the Indian bands.

Hume's case of the "race of creatures" and reflection on its historical analogues (all too easy to find) force upon us in a way that can no longer be evaded the question: Is the theory of justice as mutual advantage really a theory of justice at all? It is surely normally regarded as a paradigm of injustice to kill some innocent person simply because that person is in the way of your getting something you want, or to take what you want from someone under threat of death. To say that this killing or taking is rendered just by the inability of the victims to organize an effective resistance would surely be a hollow mockery of the idea of justice—adding insult to injury. Justice is normally thought of not as ceasing to be relevant in conditions of extreme inequality in power but, rather, as being especially relevant to such conditions.

The only counterargument that seems possible is that we are mistaken in thinking that practical reason can conceivably recommend anything except the sophisticated pursuit of self-interest. Justice as commonly understood is therefore an illusion and should be redefined so as to form part of a reconstructed moral vocabulary consistent with the claims of practical reason.[34] Justice as mutual advantage will coincide with common views over a large core area (namely, where the circumstances of justice do obtain), so it is the obvious candidate for the job of replacing the notion of justice in the new streamlined moral system.

But why should practical reason be so limited in what is encompassed? Why should it not be reasonable to be moved by considerations of justice, even if they run counter to one's long-term self-interest? To make the positive answer plausible we must seek out an alternative rationale for justice to the one that roots it in mutual advantage. We can take the first steps along that road by turning from Hume's first theory of justice to his second theory of justice. This we shall now do.

19. JUSTICE AND IMPARTIALITY

Hume's first theory of justice is a theory about the origins of rules that define private property. According to Hume, the only possible foundation upon which the institution of property could have developed is mutual advantage. We cannot, he believes, imagine a convention growing up in any way other than the gradual realization, on the basis of sad experience, that it is more advantageous for each of us to respect the possessions of others than to persist in a "war of all against all." But once the convention has developed, he argues, other sentiments come into play to support it and to give respect for the possessions of others the quality of virtue. Thus what makes justice a virtue is not that it is mutually advantageous but something else about it. What this other thing is and what is its motivational basis now falls to be considered.

The relation between Hume's two theories of justice is summarized by him in the following passage in the *Treatise*, which is worth quoting at length:

> Upon the whole, then, we are to consider this distinction betwixt justice and injustice, as having two different foundations, *viz.* that of *self-interest*, when men observe, that 'tis impossible to live in society without restraining themselves by certain rules; and that of *morality*, when this interest is once observ'd to be common to all mankind, and men receive a pleasure from the view of such actions as tend to the peace of society, and an uneasiness from such as are contrary to it. 'Tis the voluntary convention and artifice of men, which makes the first interest take place; and therefore those laws of justice are so far to be consider'd as *artificial.* After that interest is once establish'd and acknowledg'd, the sense of morality in the observance of these rules follows *naturally*, and of itself; tho' 'tis certain, that it is also augmented by a new *artifice*, and that the public instructions of politicians, and the private education of parents, contribute to the giving us a sense of honour and duty in the strict regulation of our actions with regard to the properties of others.[35]

There is a parallel account of promise-keeping: here too what forms the "concert or convention" is "but that every one have a sense of interest in the faithful fulfilling of engagements, and express that sense to other members of society. . . . Afterwards a sentiment of morals concurs with interest, and becomes a new obligation upon mankind."[36]

These accounts of the origins of the obligation to respect others' property and to keep promises are not without plausibility; and it seems clear that the sense of mutual interest in those institutions continues to provide a strong motive for adherence to them. I shall, indeed, put forward some speculations of my own later (in section 35) about the part played by approximate equality of power in stimulating the sense of justice. However, even if we concede that institutions such as those regulating property may well have grown up originally in the form that Hume describes, and also that the original motive for conformity with them was self-interest, what we have to recognize is that these institutions can be assessed in terms of the second theory of justice. Thus, institutions that reflect relations of power may be criticized as failing to measure up to the criteria of justice in the sense that detaches it from mutual advantage. That Hume did not acknowledge and investigate the implications of this possibility simply shows that at this point in the development of his theory he proved to be a better conservative than he was a philosopher. (I shall expand on this in the next section.)

We still have not said what the second theory of justice actually is, or what Hume thinks is the reason for acting on it. To pursue this, we should recall that the second theory of justice is a theory of why justice is a virtue. We therefore need to know what, for Hume, makes something a virtue. Virtues and vices are (as we have already seen) the primary objects of moral judgment, according to Hume. And moral judgments are judgments of praise and blame that issue from an impartial point of view.

If we ask why we should adopt an impartial point of view when we engage in praising and blaming, Hume's reply is that moral discourse must arise from a common viewpoint. "Every man's interest is peculiar to himself, and the aversions and desires, which result from it, cannot be supposed to affect others in a like degree. General language, therefore, being formed for general use, must be moulded on some more general views, and must affix the epithets of praise or blame, in conformity to sentiments, which arise from the general interests of the community.[37] Thus, the shift to an impersonal standard occurs because it provides a unique reference point.

> When we form our judgements of persons, merely from the tendency of their characters to our own benefit, or to that of our friends, we find so many contradictions to our sentiments in society and conversation, and such an uncertainty from the incessant changes of our situation, that we may seek some other standard of merit and demerit, which may not admit of so great variation. Being thus loosen'd from our first station, we cannot afterwards fix ourselves so commodiously by any means as by a sympathy with those, who have any commerce with the person we consider. This is far from being as lively as when our own interest is concern'd, or that of our particular friends; nor has it such an influence on our love and hatred: But being equally conformable to our calm and general principles, 'tis said to have an equal authority over our reason, and to command our judgement and opinion.[38]

It is important to see what Hume is *not* saying here. He is not simply extending his analysis of the origins of the institution of property to the institution of morality. His argument is not, in other words, that subscription to a universal standard of moral judgment is a game we all play (like keeping our hands off one another's possessions in a "state of nature") because we recognize the advantages to ourselves of having conduct regulated by a set of universally applicable norms and thus (as Glaucon suggested—see section 1) play our part as the price of having others restrain themselves likewise. Rather, the detachment from our own particular interest is a distinguishing feature of morality: " 'Tis only when a character is considered in general, without reference to our particular interest, that it causes such a feeling or sentiment, as denominates it morally good or evil."[39] This seems to me, as far as it goes, quite correct. Surely, if somebody were to put forward something as a moral judgment, and on being asked to defend it, were to say simply, "It suits me that way," he would be rightly regarded as engaging in irrelevances.

Why, however, should we choose to enter into discourse that gives our own interests the same weight as everyone else's? Hume may indeed say that once we are embarked on the exercise of "forming our judgements of persons" we shall find it "commodious" to adopt an impersonal standpoint. But why should we do that, especially since the results are "said to . . . command our judgement and opinion?"

Hume's official theory is, as I understand it, that the moral sentiment is an extension of our natural sentiment of sympathy. Thus, in Mercer's words, Hume claims in the *Treatise* that "whilst the original motive for [the] formation [of the notion of justice] is interest, it is only by reference to sympathy that we account for the fact that the idea of *virtue* is attached to the observance of the rules of justice."[40] As Hume puts it:

> when the injustice is so distant from us, as no way to affect our interest, it still displeases us; because we consider it as prejudicial to human society, and pernicious to everyone that approaches the person guilty of it. We partake of their uneasiness by *sympathy*; and as every thing, which gives uneasiness in human actions, upon the general survey, is call'd Vice, and whatever produces satisfaction, in the same manner, is denominated Virtue; this is the reason why the sense of moral good and evil follows on justice.[41]

A little later, Hume sums up as follows: "Thus *Self-interest* is the original Motive to the *Establishment* of Justice: but a Sympathy with the *public* Interest is the Source of the *moral* Approbation, which attends that Virtue. This latter Principle of Sympathy is too weak to controul our Passions; but has sufficient Force to influence our Taste, and give us the Sentiments of Approbation or Blame."[42]

This is all expressed within the framework provided by the mechanical conception of the workings of sympathy discussed in the previous section. But we can easily reformulate it without that, so that (as in the *Enquiry*) "sympathy" is a synonym for "humanity" or "fellow feeling" rather than a mechanism to explain how they come about. The question is: why should we want to bring our own sympathetic judgments into line with those of everybody else? And why, even more, should we be prepared to regard these judgments as providing us with reasons for acting? Hume does not seem to have explained why we should not each form our judgments on the basis of our own interests and sympathies. Admittedly this will entail (in the absence of the perfect fellow feeling whose absence constituted the second circumstance of justice) that our judgments will differ, but what of that?

In the end, I think that Hume was forced to abandon his official theory and allow that the desire to behave in a way that can be justified in impersonal terms must be admitted as an irreducible motive. At the end of the *Enquiry*, Hume considered the question raised by a "sensible knave" who "may think that an act of iniquity or infidelity will make a considerable addition to his fortune, without causing any considerable breach in the social union or confederacy."[43]

Hume offers two answers which seem somewhat off the point. One is that the best things in life are free: the "natural pleasures" are incomparably preferable to the "feverish, empty amusements of luxury and expense."[44] But while it is true that health is more important than money, most people may still believe that health plus money is better than health without money. In any case, Hume has built his whole theory on the proposition that the desire for more material possessions is an almost universal feature of human nature, and it is a bit late in the day to go back on that. Another argument is that there is always the risk of overreaching oneself and being found out, but this amounts to a recommendation of cautious knavery rather than a reason for not being a knave.

Hume's only serious argument is that "in all ingenuous natures, the antipathy to treachery and roguery is too strong to be counterbalanced by any views of profit or pecuniary advantage. Inward peace of mind, consciousness of integrity, a satisfactory review of our own conduct; these are circumstances, very requisite to happiness, and will be cherished and cultivated by every honest man, who feels the importance of them."[45] This is of course transparently circular: it says in effect that an honest man is an honest man. If a man is not a knave, he will feel uncomfortable if he behaves in a knavish fashion. But what reason has he for not being a knave, or (if it is too late now to change his character) for not wishing he has been brought up as a knave?

No wonder Hume concedes, in introducing this argument, that "if a man think that this reasoning [that honesty is not invariably the best policy] much requires an answer, it will be a little difficult to find any which will to him appear satisfactory and convincing."[46] But perhaps he *has* given the only answer there is and it is unconvincing only be-

cause Hume gives the impression of thinking that there should be something else, so that he really would have to show that honesty is the best
policy (from the selfish point of view of the agent) before being able to
commend it. Yet, as he says himself in the penultimate paragraph of the
Enquiry, "virtue is an end, and is desirable on its own account, without
fee or reward, merely for the immediate satisfaction which it conveys; it
is requisite that there should be some sentiment which it touches, some
internal taste or feeling, or whatever you please to call it, which distin-
guishes moral good and evil, and which embraces the one and rejects
the other."[47] In Part III (see especially section 35) I shall make an explicit argument for the existence of a distinctively moral motive, and
my account of its nature will build on Hume's idea that it is inherently
related to an impartial viewpoint.

20. IMPLICATIONS OF THE TWO
   THEORIES FOR THE RULES OF JUSTICE

Hume's official theory of morality as extended sympathy plays a crucial
role in establishing what he takes to be the criterion for evaluating character on which impartial judgment will converge. If we were simply to
specify that people should adopt an impartial viewpoint, this might be
compatible with many alternatives. Kant, for example, would certainly
say that one should adopt an impartial viewpoint in thinking morally.
But when we add Hume's notion that impartiality is an extension of
natural sympathy, we are inevitably pushed in one particular direction.
The generalization of sympathy is general benevolence—a concern for
the public good. The implication of impartiality is, therefore, for Hume,
some sort of utilitarianism.

Now when we ask what Hume meant by terms like "public utility"
we should be aware of the dangers of anachronism. We should not
attribute to him a definite view on distinctions that in many cases became salient only in the past fifty years. Nor should we make him into a
Benthamite before Bentham. When he speaks of "public utility" or the
"public interest," the contexts suggest that he is thinking primarily of
the interests people have in common, in public order, the carrying out
of collectively beneficial public works, and so on.[48] (This is, in my view,
the standard use of the term "public interest": it refers to interests that
people have in common *qua* members of the public.)[49] It is, I am inclined
to believe, this that explains why Hume apparently did not consider it a
serious problem that mutual self-interest and public utility might come

apart in practice and lead to the recommendation of different rules of justice. So he says of the system of private property that "comprehending the interest of each individual, [it] is of course advantageous to the public; tho' it be not intended for that purpose by the inventors."[50]

At the same time, though, we should notice this use of the term "public interest": Hume says that "if men pursu'd the publick interest naturally, and with a hearty affection, they wou'd never have dream'd of restraining each other by these rules [of justice]."[51] Now, this state of affairs, the opposite of the "confin'd generosity" which is one of the circumstances of justice, looks like a formula for making everyone a pursuer of Benthamite aggregate utility, as I pointed out in section 18 under "The Moderate Selfishness Condition."

The true answer to the question is that we should not expect to press Hume very hard on it. He simply does not seem to have worried about the possible divergence between public interest (what all gain from) and public utility (a net gain when all are counted), so he was not forced to refine his criterion. I assent to J. L. Mackie's judgment:

> In neither [the *Treatise* nor the *Enquiry*] does Hume have any explicit theory of how to measure utility, how to weigh advantages to some persons against disadvantages to others. Rather he tends to represent whatever he thinks to be in the public interest as being also in the long-term interest of each person on his own. But this is clearly not the case, at least if we take into account a more finely graded range of alternatives than he usually considers.[52]

As we shall see, given the line on property rules Hume takes in the *Treatise*, the potential incompatibility between the two criteria is fairly well submerged; but the additional arguments he produces in the *Enquiry* bring it to the surface.

In the *Treatise*, Hume gives an elaborate speculative reconstruction of the process by which he supposes the institution of property to have originated. He first imagines "possession" to become established on a *de facto* basis, and posits that men then realize the advantage of security and settle on the rule (which creates property out of possession) "that every one continue to enjoy what he is at present master of, and that property or constant possession be conjoin'd to the immediate possession."[53] Hume then adds that this will not be a sufficient rule to govern property after the initial stage and goes on to set out the usual grounds for property claims recognized in legal systems where private property exists: occupation, prescription, accession, and succession, plus, of course, the transference of property by the owner's consent.

Governments, he suggests, become necessary (and therefore come into existence, analogously with property) when property becomes so plentiful that it requires authoritative adjudication and becomes a tempting target for theft. States thus set up judicial systems to interpret the rules of property and settle disputed cases.

We must have a convention, Hume says, to assign property so as to "cut off all occasions of discord and contention." This rule cannot take account of "the fitness or unfitness of objects to particular persons," and its application must be "inflexible either by spite or favour."[54] This requirement entails that the reasons for giving property in a certain thing to a certain person "are not deriv'd from any utility or advantage, which either the *particular* person or the public may reap from his enjoyment of any *particular* goods, beyond what wou'd result from the possession of them by any other person."[55] It is in this context that we must interpret Hume's famous assertion that an individual act of justice "considered apart" is often disadvantageous to the public but that "the whole scheme...is advantageous to the society."[56] The least strained reading is that each individual act of justice, when considered as part of the whole scheme, *is* advantageous to the society, when we consider the feasible alternatives. For it would be less advantageous to apply the rule "differently in every particular case, according to every particular utility, which might be discovered in such an application."[57]

It is typical of Hume's tendency (later regretted by him) to strain after paradox in the *Treatise* that he should express this in the most extravagant terms, by saying that "when a man of merit, of a beneficent disposition, restores a great fortune to a miser, or a seditious bigot, he has acted justly and laudably, but the public is the real sufferer."[58] This passage must be read in context: the act taken alone and detached from the consideration of its being in accordance with a rule of justice would be disadvantageous, but the advantage bestowed by adherence to the rule outweighs that disadvantage. If this were not so, we could obviously have a better rule under which misers and seditious bigots would get less than men of merit and beneficence. But that is precisely the kind of rule that Hume has said would cause more trouble than it is worth, because it would make distribution depend on qualities whose measurement will always leave room for disagreement.*

---

* J. L. Mackie, having put forward as a possible interpretation this view of the matter, goes on to consider an alternative according to which an individual act might really, even with all the effects derived from its being prescribed by the rule, be on balance harmful, yet it might still be in the public interest to stick to the rule. For it might be "necessary, if the general scheme of justice is to flourish, that there should be a fair number of acts of

Because of his drive toward treating dispute resolution, on any terms, as the only function of property rules, Hume emphasizes in the *Treatise* the way in which the particular rules he cites (the usual ones within the legal systems with which he was familiar) have the advantage of appealing to the imagination. The shift from possession (or occupation) to property rights is conducive to conflict resolution because people attach more importance to what they have been used to occupying than to what others occupy, while other people have formed an association of ideas between the person and the possession.[59] And the other modes of appropriation are assimilated to the same pattern with the exertion of more or less ingenuity.

Harrison, in his study of Hume's theory of justice in the *Treatise*, quite reasonably objects to this that these rules can easily be seen to have advantages over at least some alternatives: thus of the rule of accession he says that "it would obviously be very inconvenient not to allow lambs to be the property of the owners of the sheep" and so on.[60] Similarly, he points out, it is not merely imagination that leads legal systems to deny riparians ownership of navigable waters.[61]

In fact, Harrison is here echoing a shift that Hume himself made when he came to write the *Enquiry*. Although in this the imagination still comes in to decide otherwise arbitrary cases,[62] Hume claims for the rules in their main outlines exactly the sorts of advantages that conservatives have been claiming ever since for such rules: that they encourage people to be frugal, to be productive, and so on.[63]

Only two alternatives to standard property rules are canvassed. The first is "to assign the largest possessions to the most extensive virtue, and give everyone the power of doing good, proportioned to his inclination."[64] This fails, like the rule giving everyone what is of most use to him that was briefly considered in the *Treatise*, on lack of determinacy.

---

honesty whose beneficiaries are misers, debauchees, seditious bigots, and the like; but it may be that more such acts are performed than are strictly necessary for this purpose. Then each such act, given its actual setting, really does more harm than good, but the collection of them does more good than harm." He goes on to say, though, that it may not be a "live option" to reorganize the scheme so that just the right number of such acts are performed: "perhaps this right number could not be ascertained, and in any case such a complex practice could not be organized." But then, of course, it follows that "it may be that the only practicable alternatives are either to perform all the component acts of a beneficial general scheme, or to change our practice so radically that these benefits are lost." (All quotations from J. L. Mackie, *Hume's Moral Theory* [London; Routledge & Kegan Paul, 1980], p. 92.) Quite apart from the absence of any textual support for this version, it seems to me not in the end to amount to any real departure from the first one. For if it is not feasible to get the full benefits of the practice except by adhering to it in all cases, any deviation from it *will* be on balance harmful compared to the feasible alternatives. And that is simply a restatement of the first view.

The other is an equal division. Hume concedes "that, wherever we depart from this equality, we rob the poor of more satisfaction than we add to the rich."[65] (This follows from certain assumptions about utility schedules which we shall discuss in the next section.) But, Hume says, if equality is to be maintained, this will check the virtues of "art, care and industry" that would otherwise upset it; and the result will be to "reduce society to the most extreme indigence; and instead of preventing want and beggary in a few, render it unavoidable to the whole community."[66] (Hume also has political objections, though they might appear to cancel one another out. For he first complains that the degree of political authority required "must soon degenerate into tyranny" but then he goes on to say that "perfect equality of possessions, destroying all subordination, weakens extremely the authority of magistracy, and must reduce all power nearly to a level, as well as property."[67])

For the present purpose, the significant point is that Hume's arguments are based entirely on the alleged consequences of alternative rules of distribution. The "state of nature" story functions only to show how a system based on possession could get off the ground. But if he could be persuaded that a superior system was available (and his canvassing of alternatives could hardly be said to be comprehensive), Hume would be committed by his principles to endorsing it. Thus, for example, his account should not be confused with Locke's superficially similar theory according to which acquisition in the "state of nature" gives rise to natural rights in property that are then carried over and made more secure in political society.

Samuel Johnson once said of Hume that he was "a Tory by chance,"[68] meaning that there was nothing in his principles that led inevitably toward Tory political conclusions. For although he rejected the Whig theory that based the right to rule on an "original contract," he equally rejected the characteristic Tory idea of historically based legitimacy. The same may be said of his theory of property: it underwrites the *status quo* only in virtue of the claim, in principle an empirical one, that the maintenance of whatever property system exists will have better consequences than any alternative. Since the rules of justice are founded on nothing but utility, and there is no independent and external criterion of justice, it would clearly be nonsensical to protest against redistribution in the name of justice.

The most plausible interpretation of Hume's conservatism might be to regard it as analogous to that of Hobbes. For Hobbes, it may be recalled, was prepared to say that some forms of sovereignty were better than others—for example, he believed that there were reasons for preferring to place sovereignty in the hands of one man rather than a body of men—but at the same time he did not believe that it could ever be justifiable to attempt to change the system forcibly. For the certain ill effects of the anarchy inseparable from the change (and in Hobbes's theory any time without a sovereign dissolves society) would so outweigh the speculative good effects of the alternative regime as to make any detailed cost-benefit analysis pointless. We may take Hume as claiming that the existing system, whatever it is, will almost certainly be better, once we take account of the value of widespread acceptance, than any alternative. But this, again, turns on an empirical claim, which can be questioned.

21. HUME'S LEGACY AS A PROBLEM OF FAIR DIVISION

THE FIRST THEORY OF JUSTICE

It is interesting to observe the divergent schools of thought in political philosophy that all lay claim to being the heirs of Hume. The account given here of Hume's theory enables us to say that all of them have some legitimate claim, because all of them can quite correctly find something in Hume that corresponds more or less to what they want to maintain. Thus, Hume's theory of the origin of justice has, not surprisingly, led to his being claimed as a predecessor by David Gauthier.[69] And there is no question that this aspect of Hume's theory brings him close to Hobbes.[70] A more precise correspondence between Hume's theory of the origins of property and more recent work is to be found in the writings of James Buchanan, winner of the Nobel Prize in Economics in 1986, who is the best known and most sophisticated of a group of conservatives (mostly economists) based in Virginia. The account of the origins of property put forward by members of this group follows Hume closely in making it depend on a sense of mutual advantage in comparison with universal predation.[71] Similarly, the state is invoked to provide an assurance of stability. At this point, however, Buchanan takes a different tack from Hume. In effect he abandons the argument from utility in favor of one to which he is, I think, led by the desire to guarantee conservative conclusions.

Once Hume has his system of property in being and underwritten by the state, the justification for not disturbing it is self-contained. The argument rests on the utility—the social advantage—of leaving property alone. The only purpose of introducing the prepolitical stage is, for Hume, to explain how, by convention, some particular distribution of property could come into existence. Buchanan, in contrast, tries to derive a defense of the *status quo* that will not require contingent claims about the superiority of its consequences over those of alternative schemes. Having moved from primitive possession based on physical strength to security of possession based on mutual advantage (relative to a free-for-all), he simply freezes the process at that point. Any further changes in property rules must come about by unanimous consent. This is as if Hume had put forward only the part of his theory concerned with the origins of justice and had not gone on to ask what makes justice a virtue.

Hume recognized unflinchingly that contemporary property titles would not stand up to close examination and could be traced back to force or fraud at some point. But since his defense of the *status quo* was purely that it provided a conventional basis of distribution, this was not a matter of great concern for him. He did not require that titles be traced back through a clear line to some act of aboriginal appropriation. Buchanan presumably no more than Hume believes that the history of all property transfers is one of consent. But he nevertheless apparently wishes to give the *status quo* a privileged status, since he maintains that nobody can rightfully be deprived (even by legislation) of what he now has.

Hume's conservative conclusions, whether plausible or not, are at any rate derived from an intelligible principle, namely, general utility, via an argument about the nonexistence of any external and independent standard of justice to which an appeal might be made. Buchanan's skepticism is far more extreme: he professes to think that all moral principles are merely expressions of personal preference.

> How can we derive a criterion for determining whether or not a change in law, or, if you will, a change in the assignment of rights, is or is not justified? To most social scientists change becomes desirable if "I like it," even though many prefer to dress this reason up in fanciful "social welfare function" or "public interest" semantics. To me, this stance seems to be pure escapism; it represents retreat into empty arguments about personal values which spells the end of rational discourse.[72]

It is rather strange that "rational discourse," for Buchanan, entails jettisoning everything that might normally be thought of as constituting rational discourse (such as arguments about the justice or injustice of

alternative arrangements) in favor of the comparison of brute preferences, however prejudiced or misguided, whether based on true or false
ideas about the world.

From this thoroughgoing skepticism Buchanan arrives at the conclusion that the only possible test is agreement. But that argument obviously undercuts itself, since many people would surely disagree with the
view that no redistribution is legitimate that does not attract universal
consent. In seeking to come up with an impregnable case for conservatism—one that appeals to no principles whatsoever—Buchanan actually comes up with nothing. His theory explodes itself.

THE SECOND THEORY OF JUSTICE

I have shown how Hume's first theory can be adapted to produce an
unconditional endorsement of the *status quo*. I now want to discuss the
way in which Hume's second theory can be employed to generate conclusions far less conservative than the ones he reached. It will be recalled that Hume's argument against modifications in existing property
relations turned on the supreme importance of avoiding disputes. But
the standard of public utility can be used to assess the claim that any
status quo is better than any alternative. Hume, it will be recalled,
rested his case heavily on the disadvantage of trying to decide on a
case-by-case basis who should have what (a point made here in section
14). But this does not entail that the rules themselves might not be
changed with generally advantageous results.

Within the utilitarian tradition, this radical potential took a long
time to be developed. Bentham and his immediate disciples followed the
Humean line in favor of leaving private property undisturbed. Bentham
repeated Hume's concession that, considered in itself, an equal distribution of income would generate the maximum amount of utility. But,
like Hume, he held that this advantage of equality was overwhelmed by
the advantages of stability in possession.

The radical potential of the utilitarian criterion thus lay dormant
until John Stuart Mill, in the *Principles of Political Economy*, laid down
the premise that, whereas production was controlled by natural laws
that specified what inputs had to be used to obtain certain outputs,
distribution was a matter open to social determination.[73] In theory,
the product of an economy could be distributed in any way, once it
was produced. In practice, however, there is a link via the problem of
incentives.

In his *Autobiography*, Mill looked forward to a time in which material incentives would not be needed to get people to work: if a man will fight for his country, he asked, why should he not dig or weave for his country?[74] But in his economic analysis he proceeded on the assumption that people would work to just the degree that, taking the rewards into account, made working worth their while from a self-interested point of view. And in this he was followed by later utilitarian economists. Utilitarian economists thus continued to make use of Bentham's idea that individual self-interest had to be reconciled with aggregate utility via incentives even during a period when utilitarian philosophers were asking what people who were themselves motivated by the principle of utility should do.

The framework was now in place for the development of welfare economics along utilitarian lines which culminates in A. C. Pigou's *The Economics of Welfare*.[75] If we simply took the product at one time and distributed it in whatever way would maximize the aggregate utility derivable from that amount, we would completely sever the connection between production and distribution. What each person received would be related to his or her capacity for turning it into utility and not at all to the contribution that person had made to producing it. Pigou followed the utilitarian tradition and held that an equal distribution of income would have the best chance of maximizing utility. In the face of skepticism about interpersonal comparisons of utility (see above, section 12), later utilitarians have formulated the argument carefully to make it clear that it requires only very general information about the characteristic form of utility functions.

Suppose we look for a policy for the distribution of a certain amount of money that has the best chance of maximizing total utility, subject to the constraint that we will not make the amount that any given individual gets depend upon an estimate of the idiosyncrasies of that person's utility function. We might make the not unreasonable supposition that money has diminishing marginal utility for everybody. This would mean that, however much utility a given person got from the first thousand dollars, that person would get less from a second thousand, and so on—though it is quite consistent with this supposition that one person might get more utility from a third thousand than another would get from the first thousand. With just the assumption of diminishing marginal utility we can derive the conclusion that utility is most likely to be maximized if income is divided equally.[76]

Think of a case involving just two people and a fixed sum of money divided equally between them. It is possible that we could increase aggregate utility by moving away from equality in the right direction. But it is also possible that we might move in the wrong direction and decrease aggregate utility. In the absence of definite individual information we must regard these fortunate and unfortunate consequences of moving away from an equal division of the money as equiprobable.

It might at first sight appear that, since there is an equal chance of increasing or decreasing aggregate utility by moving away from equality, there is no utilitarian reason for preferring an equal division to any other. This would be correct if we had no utility information at all. But recall that we are now supposing that we know one general fact about utilities: that money has decreasing marginal utility for everybody. This enables us to assert that the utility gain from moving a given distance away from an equal distribution of income (say, shifting ten dollars) in the right direction will always be less than the utility loss from moving the same distance away in the wrong direction. Therefore, the expected increase in aggregate utility from moving away from an equal distribution of money in the right direction does not cancel out the expected decrease from moving in the wrong direction. Given that increases and decreases are equiprobable, there is an overall decrease in expected utility from moving away from an equal distribution.

Generalizing this result across a whole society, "we obtain our conclusion that if it is desired to maximize the total satisfaction in a society, the rational procedure is to divide income on an equalitarian basis."[77] Thus, from fairly exiguous assumptions about utility functions, we can derive the result believed in by both Hume and Bentham, as we saw in the previous section, namely, that if we ignore any question of incentives and simply ask what is the best way of dividing a fixed sum in order to maximize aggregate happiness, the answer must be an equal distribution.

Hume and Bentham both rejected an equal distribution, however, on the ground that, although it is best from a static viewpoint, it would be bad when viewed dynamically. And their economist successors have almost without exception shared their assumption that, as soon as we take account of the need to stimulate production, we must underwrite inequality. If we build in considerations involving incentives, we have to say that economic distribution has to serve two purposes: it is itself part of the production process as a motivating factor and at the same time it is the source of utility from consumption. The utilitarian problem is therefore to juggle the maximization of utility from consumption with the need for incentives to maintain production so that, over all, the economy maximizes utility.

A third set of inheritors are those (including the present author) who have taken the most important part of Hume's legacy to be not the substantive content of his second theory of justice but the premises from which those substantive conclusions were derived. On this view, what matters most is the idea of a link between morality and impartiality, and the idea that the moral motive is the desire to be able to defend one's actions before the tribunal of impartial appraisal. This will be developed further in Part III.

CHAPTER V

Rawls on Justice (1): International and Intergenerational Justice

22. THE CIRCUMSTANCES OF JUSTICE

I have tried to show that Hume has two theories of justice. One, involving the notion of the circumstances of justice, rests justice on the advantage to all of having settled rules rather than a free-for-all. The other presents justice as the subject of judgment from an impartial perspective. I claim that the same two theories of justice can be found in John Rawls's *A Theory of Justice.*

Although in Hume's hands the two theories are made to yield the same practical implications, this comes about only because of his claim that established property institutions, whatever form they take in detail, are best left alone. But the two theories have an obvious potential for coming apart in their prescriptions, and I think that this can be seen happening in Rawls's work. In this chapter and the next my main objective is to exhibit the tension between Rawls's two theories of justice by examining three applications of it.

It will help to make my points most clear if I take up last, in the next chapter, the application to which Rawls devotes by far the most of his attention: relations among contemporaries in a single society. For although the tensions exist there, they can be more easily seen in two other cases: relations between different societies, and relations between different generations of members of a society. The discussion of applications begins in the next section with an analysis of relations between societies. Intergenerational justice will then be taken up in section 24.

This chapter will conclude with a discussion (in section 25) of the rather recondite problems raised for a theory such as that of Rawls by non-human animals. Although Rawls disclaims any application of his theory to creatures other than human beings, this disclaimer itself raises questions of great interest and significance.

In the remainder of this section I want to say something about Rawls's version of the Humean doctrine of the circumstances of justice. When we ask about the role played by this in Rawls's theory we must first understand that in *A Theory of Justice* the central expository device is that of the original position. Our question therefore becomes: How are the circumstances of justice linked to the original position?

I shall have a good deal to say in chapter 9 about original position theories in general. For the present purpose, however, all that need be said is that at its core the idea is the same as that of Harsanyi which we discussed in section 9: that we can guarantee an impartial choice of principles if we ask what people would choose if they were denied knowledge of a kind that would enable them to rig the principles in their own favor. Just principles are those emerging from a fair choosing situation: hence the slogan "justice as fairness."

The constitution of the original position thus reflects basic ideas about what is relevant to justice and what is not. These ideas are fed into the construction as stipulations about what the people doing the choosing are to be told and what information should be blocked off from them. To ensure an impartial choice, the people in the original position are to be denied all knowledge of their personal attributes. They do, however, have some general information about the characteristics of human beings and human societies. Since they are to make use of this information in drawing up principles of justice, it is apparent that the principles will be valid only if the data on which their decision is based are correct. Translating this out of the language of the original position, we can put the point by saying that Rawls's principles of justice are claimed to hold only in the conditions that Rawls specifies.

These conditions are, according to Rawls, the Humean circumstances of justice, and he commends Hume's account of them as "especially perspicuous."[1]

> First, there are the objective circumstances which make human cooperation both possible and necessary. Thus, many individuals coexist together at the same time on a definite geographical territory. These individuals are roughly similar in physical and mental powers; or at any rate, their capacities are comparable in that no one among them can dominate the rest. They are

vulnerable to attack, and all are subject to having their plans blocked by the united force of others. Finally, there is the condition of moderate scarcity understood to cover a wide range of situations. Natural and other resources are not so abundant that schemes of cooperation become superfluous, nor are conditions so harsh that fruitful ventures must inevitably break down. While mutually advantageous arrangements are feasible, the benefits they yield fall short of the demands men put forward.[2]

What Rawls describes as the "subjective circumstances" depart in detail from Hume's formulation. In place of Hume's emphasis on "confin'd generosity" we find in Rawls talk of different "plans of life" and "conceptions of the good." However, Rawls still emerges with Hume's conclusion that principles will be required to adjudicate between conflicting interests. These will not necessarily be "interests of the self." People's interests are given by whatever aims they have, and these aims need not be self-interested. But the people in the original position are to be told that "the parties take no interest in one another's interests."[3]

It is important to realize that the "parties" being referred to here are not the people in the original position, who are simply constructs of the theory. The parties referred to here are people in real life with full information about themselves and their society. This must be so, as we can see if we think about the specification of the circumstances of justice. These obviously do not hold in the original position. The parties in the original position do not have productive relations, worry about defending themselves from attack, and so on. The point is, rather, that these conditions are known by the people in the original position to hold in real life.

What is the relation between the people in the original position and the members of the society for which they are choosing regulative principles? In *A Theory of Justice* they *are* the members of that society and are simply suffering from comprehensive amnesia. In later writings Rawls has tended to adopt the formulation that they are representatives of the members of the society charged with advancing their interests subject to the limitation that they do not know the specific identities of their clients or various other things about the society in which they live. As far as I can see, nothing much turns on the distinction between the two ways of conceiving the relation, although the notion that the people in the original position are representatives has the advantage of explaining more easily how infants or those suffering from grave mental incapacity fit into the choice made in the original position.

Given that the circumstances of justice are supposed to hold in the society for which principles of justice are being chosen, it must be seen as on the face of it odd that Rawls should "assume" total "mutual disinterest" among those conditions.[4] For it is manifestly the case that any such assumption is false for any society we know of. Some people some of the time (to put it at its lowest) do regard the fulfillment of others' aims as an adequate motive for doing something they would not themselves otherwise do. We do not in fact live in a world where people take account of others' ends only out of a sense of duty. By suggesting that we do Rawls lays himself open to gratuitous trouble. He becomes vulnerable to a variant of the complaint often made against Kant that doing somebody a good turn would be meritorious on his views only if one didn't like the person. This can be reformulated against Rawls by saying that, as he presents it, justice can be exercised only by people who are totally indifferent to one another's interests. And in fact a small but active branch of the Rawls industry has sprung up around the exploitation of precisely this line.[5]

However, the only thing that Rawls apparently wants to maintain here, like Hume before him, is that there would be no need for justice— it would be, in Hume's terms, "useless"—unless there were conflicts that had somehow to be resolved. "The circumstances of justice may be described as the normal conditions under which human cooperation is both possible and necessary. Thus, . . . although a society is a cooperative venture for mutual advantage, it is typically marked by a conflict as well as an identity of interests."[6] If this is the point, then what Rawls needs to say is simply that principles of justice would not be required if people's identification with one another's interests were so complete as to obviate all conflicts of interest.

Only if all plans were integrated so tightly that they formed a single plan, in which everyone accepted his own part, would justice be unnecessary. "In an association of saints agreeing on a common ideal, if such a community could exist, disputes about justice could not occur. Each would work selflessly for one end as determined by their common religion, and reference to this end (assuming it to be clearly defined) would settle every question of right."[7] But as long as the full realization of some people's plans is not compossible with the full realization of everybody else's plans (after each person has modified his original plan to take whatever account he wants to of all other plans), we have a Rawlsian equivalent of Hume's "confin'd generosity."

Now I have already in Part I discussed Rawls's long footnote about

Braithwaite's problem of Matthew and Luke (section 8). What I said
there about Rawls's objection to Braithwaite's solution, and by implication all other two-stage solutions (he actually mentions Nash's solution
as another defective one) may well make his invocation of the Humean
circumstances of justice here seem rather puzzling. As may be recalled,
Rawls's objection to the solution proposed by Braithwaite was that
it enabled Matthew to exploit his "threat advantage."[8] And, as we
saw, the real force of Rawls's objection was not simply that the nonagreement baseline was established by the strategic pursuit of relative
advantage. Rather, he objected to bargaining power playing any role in
determining the adjudicated outcome. And it is precisely in order to
achieve this elimination of power relations that the original position is
introduced.

Rawls concluded his footnote on Matthew and Luke with the following remark: "What is lacking is a suitable definition of a status quo that
is acceptable from a moral point of view. We cannot take various contingencies as known and individual preferences as given and expect to
elucidate the concept of justice (or fairness) by theories of bargaining.
The conception of the original position is designed to meet the problem
of the appropriate status quo."[9] But it seems hard to see what is the use
of eliminating the actual strategic advantages and disadvantages of the
actors in drawing up principles of justice that are supposed to regulate
their interaction if we are also told that justice applies only in the Humean circumstances of justice. For that is to introduce through the back
door the strategic relations that have just been expelled through the
front door. And I shall in fact try to show that it was indeed an error on
Rawls's part to bring in the circumstances of justice.

23. INTERNATIONAL JUSTICE

Both relations between countries and relations between generations
pose acute challenges to the Rawlsian project of reconciling mutual
advantage and impartiality as bases of justice. I shall take them up in
turn now. International justice is a good deal less exotic than intergenerational justice, so I will begin with it. I have already sketched
the way in which Rawls presents his arguments about the content of
justice within a society. We are to imagine the members of the society
(or their representatives) meeting to choose principles to govern their
life together under conditions that guarantee the exclusion of morally

irrelevant factors. Although Rawls never makes use of the expression, we might draw a parallel to the Humean circumstances of justice by calling these conditions the circumstances of impartiality.

The conditions include a "veil of ignorance" that prevents the members of the society or their representatives from having access to various kinds of information that might bias their decisions about what principles to support. This entails, as I mentioned earlier, that the members of the society lack information about their distinctive personal characteristics—or, if we conceive of the choice as made by representatives, information about the distinctive personal characteristics of their clients. Thus, the members of the society do not know about either their natural or their social advantages—native intelligence or physical prowess, privileged or deprived upbringing, good or bad educational experience, occupation and income, inheritance of wealth or membership in a hereditary group of high or low status, and so on. If the parties are representatives, they do not know any of these things about their clients. Subject to these limitations on information, and others that we need not here enter into, the parties (whether they are the members of the society or their representatives) are to pursue their own or their clients' interests. As we saw in the previous section, mutual disinterest in the achievement of each others' ends is to be assumed.

Under these conditions, the parties would, according to Rawls, agree on two principles of justice. The first would provide everyone in the society with equal civil and political rights: nobody would have any reason for settling for anything less. The second specifies open competition for advantageous occupational positions and says that economic inequalities must be so arranged that there is no way in which the least advantaged stratum in the society could as a whole do any better. I shall devote the whole of the next chapter to an analysis of Rawls's arguments in favor of this second principle of justice, and in particular to the component that regulates inequalities, the so-called difference principle. I shall not therefore attempt to sketch here the way in which Rawls supports it. I shall simply observe that his argument is a good deal more subtle—and a good deal better logically—than has generally been recognized.

Rawls's way of approaching international justice is to make further use of the notion of an original position embodying what I have called the circumstances of impartiality. We are therefore to imagine that, after the principles of justice for societies have been drawn up, representatives of societies ("society" here means "state") meet behind a veil of ignorance that conceals from them "the particular circumstances of their own society [and] its power and strength in comparison with other nations." Thus, the parties have

> only enough knowledge to make a rational choice to protect their interests but not so much that the more fortunate among them can take advantage of their special situation. This original position is fair between nations; it nullifies the contingencies and biases of historical fate. Justice between states is determined by the principles that would be chosen in the original position so interpreted. These principles are political principles, for they govern public policies toward other nations.[10]

The principles that, according to Rawls, would be chosen behind this veil of ignorance would be those of liberal nationalism. Woodrow Wilson would recognize and applaud them.

> The basic principle of the law of nations is a principle of equality. Independent peoples organized as states have certain fundamental equal rights. This principle is analogous to the equal rights of citizens in a constitutional regime. One consequence of this equality of nations is the principle of self-determination, the right of a people to settle its own affairs without the intervention of foreign powers. Another consequence is the right of self-defense against attack, including the right to form defensive alliances to protect this right. A further principle is that treaties are to be kept, provided they are consistent with the other principles governing the relations of states.[11]

The national interest of a state, "as seen from the original position," is, Rawls says, "defined by the principles of justice that have already been acknowledged. . . . It is not moved by the desire for world power or national glory; nor does it wage war for purposes of economic gain or the acquisition of territory. These ends are contrary to the conception of justice that defines a country's legitimate interest, however prevalent they have been in the actual conduct of states."[12]

If we take seriously the doctrine of the circumstances of justice, then these conclusions about the constraints of justice on the conduct of states seem a good deal too stringent. At the very least, one would have to say that they are far from evident. Surely, the reason for the "prevalence," commented on by Rawls, of warfare for "economic gain or the acquisition of territory," or of other deviations from the principles he lays down, is precisely that the rough equality of power which was one of the circumstances of justice obtains only to an extremely attenuated degree in the international arena. Strong states have always been able to colonize, control, or exploit weak ones and they still can, as the recent records of the Soviet Union and the United States abundantly attest.

Such activities may not nowadays be entirely without adverse repercussions. (By contrast, in the nineteenth century the only political cost to be anticipated by European countries and those of European settlement in colonizing or manipulating other areas of the world was the risk of conflict with some rival for the control of the same territory.) But powerful states may not unreasonably take the view that on balance it is still advantageous to breach the formally egalitarian (in political, not economic, terms) principles laid down by Rawls.

The normative equality of states enunciated in Rawls's statement of those principles is not underwritten by the *de facto* equality of states. Even if one takes the view (and most people who have thought about it do) that the circumstances of justice obtain internationally in a minimal sense, all this entails is that no state is in the position of Hobbes's God—so utterly invulnerable as to have nothing to gain from a system of mutual restraint. But if the requirement of mutual advantage is that every state must stand to gain (not from behind a veil of ignorance, but really) from the set of rules defining the rights and duties of states, then we cannot expect that set of rules to have an egalitarian structure. It can be in the interests of the most powerful states only if it concedes a great deal more to them than to weaker states. The actual system we have approximates this by combining egalitarian rhetoric with a good deal of humbug: all states are equal in theory but in practice powerful states can flout the rules without attracting sanctions. (This is formalized within the structure of the United Nations through the system of vetoes in the Security Council.) The circumstance of justice that most effectively drives the Soviet Union and the United States into observing limitations is the fear of mutual annihilation.

It is important to realize that the choice cannot be confined to one between a "state of nature" and a particular set of proposed principles of justice. If the "state of nature" is sufficiently grisly, there may be very many sets of principles of justice that would make everyone better off than it. But not all of these are equally stable. The logic of the circumstances of justice is the logic of the two-stage solutions analyzed in Part I. We saw there that it was not enough for a solution to make both parties better off than they were at the nonagreement point. If the reason for adhering to the solution is self-interest, as the doctrine of the circumstances of justice implies, the solution must first give the parties what they could get at the nonagreement point; but it must then divide the gains that are to be made by moving away from the nonagreement point in a way that leaves them equally satisfied, in a sense of "equally satisfied" that takes account of bargaining strength. The same analysis applies here to principles of international justice.

Thus, suppose that the "state of nature," the unbridled pursuit of national interest unconstrained by rational long-term prudence, would lead to a massive nuclear exchange between the United States and the Soviet Union. Then it seems plausible that almost *any* set of principles that included a constraint on this kind of mutually destructive behavior would be better for both superpowers than the "state of nature." No doubt among the sets of principles capable of passing this test would be the principles of international morality proposed by Rawls. But his principles have to compete with all the others that are capable of passing the same test.

When we subject all the principles that pass this test to the more stringent one, where the criterion is the faithful reflection of bargaining power, Rawls's principles do not look like a strong contender against the available alternatives. It seems evident that the superpowers could come up with alternatives to Rawls's principles that would give them advantages corresponding to their power. The principles that would be to their mutual advantage would commit them to avoiding direct attacks on one another but would allow them to meddle in the affairs of small countries in order to install friendly regimes. They might find it mutually advantageous to have some understanding about the rules for playing this game. But this would still not get us back to Rawls's principles of international political equality.

The implication of the doctrine of the circumstances of justice is, then, that the nonagreement point cannot simply be regarded as providing us with a threshold value which the payoff from adherence to principles of justice must exceed. If the idea is that there should be a sense of common advantage from adherence to principles of justice, the implication must be that the principles of justice should reflect the bargaining strengths of the parties.

Thus, we can say that, from the point of view of mutual advantage, Rawls's principles of international morality go too far in what they demand of rich and powerful states. At the same time, it can be argued strongly that, from the standpoint of justice as impartial agreement, they do not go far enough. As we have seen, Rawls tells us to imagine the representatives of different countries meeting behind a veil of ignorance that conceals from them all information about, for example, the wealth and power of their own countries. They are, as we have seen, supposed to advance the interests of their own countries by the choice of principles of international morality to the greatest extent that they can. Now these interests are defined, according to Rawls, in terms of certain "primary goods" such as basic liberties and access to goods and services. We can therefore say that the representatives of different countries are to choose principles that will do as well as possible for their countries in terms of such things as basic liberties and income.

We should pause here for a moment to notice a complication. Primary goods are conceived of by Rawls as valuable to individuals in the pursuit of their life plans, whereas we are here talking about principles to govern the relations of countries. The problem is that liberties and income for countries do not translate in any predetermined way into liberties and incomes for the residents in those countries. However, this much can be said. Although a country may be independent of foreign control while being internally unfree, it cannot, if we follow Rawls in including democratic government among the basic liberties, be internally free while being under foreign control. In a somewhat similar way, a rich country may have poor people in it if it has an unequal income distribution; but a poor country cannot by any means avoid having many poor people in it. So favorable conditions at the level of the country make possible, and are necessary conditions of, favorable conditions for all those within it, even though they do not guarantee it.

In order to avoid turning this into a book on international justice, I shall take a shortcut that is also taken by Rawls. Although it will greatly limit the applicability of the discussion, it will not, I think, get in the way of the general points that I seek to draw from this excursion into the sphere of international morality. Let us therefore say that the representatives of countries in the original position are to choose principles on the assumption that each country is in any case going to be just internally. Again, to advance the discussion I shall take as given for now Rawls's own conclusions as to what that entails. This means, then, that equal basic liberties are secured to all, there is equal opportunity in the competition for advantageous positions, and inequalities of income are arranged so as to make a representative occupant of the worst-off social position as well off as possible.

Now it is, I think, pretty clear that the first principle of domestic justice—equal liberties for all—underwrites the principles of liberal international morality that Rawls says would be subscribed to by the representatives of states in an original position. For domination of weak countries by strong ones is incompatible with the participation in democratic self-government that forms part of Rawls's conception of the basic liberties that should be everyone's birthright.

The difficulty arises when we come to the second principle, which deals with economic inequalities. Let us focus here on the provision mandating that within each country the worst-off representative person should be made as well off as possible. Let us for the sake of argument take it as given that individual members of a single society would indeed choose this difference principle from behind a Rawlsian veil of ignorance. Then, the question for Rawls is why the representatives of different countries should be so strangely silent on the issue of international redistribution of income.

These representatives know neither to which country they belong nor in what social position within that country they find themselves when the veil is lifted. But they have access to general facts about the world, so they can know that, in the absence of any redistribution, they could be the worst off in a country that, even if it religiously adheres to the difference principle in its internal affairs, will be so poor that the worst off will be at best barely above the subsistence level and at worst lacking some basic essentials. If Rawls's arguments are valid for domestic justice, why would not the same arguments compel the representatives of countries to choose a global difference principle to govern the relations between countries? I must confess that I can see no reason.

The principles that Rawls proposes as principles of international justice are an uneasy compromise between justice as mutual advantage, which requires the principles to be equally to the advantage of all parties under actual conditions of international relations, and justice as impartial agreement, which looks only to the advantage of parties in an original position constructed so as to deny them knowledge of their actual prospective advantages and disadvantages under alternative principles. Justice as mutual advantage would be less egalitarian than Rawls proposes, justice as impartial agreement more so.

24. INTERGENERATIONAL JUSTICE

Whether or not the circumstances of justice obtain among nations is an empirical matter. They may or they may not. Whether or not they obtain between the generation of those currently alive at one time and their successors is a logical matter. They cannot. The directionality of time guarantees that, while those now alive can make their successors better or worse off, those successors cannot do anything to help or harm the current generation. "I would fain ask what posterity has ever done for us," as the wag put it: if justice equals mutual advantage then there can be no justice between generations.

Rawls is alert to the problem that this raises for him if he wants to subscribe to the doctrine of the circumstances of justice and at the same time wants to be able to say (as he does) that it is possible for one generation to behave unjustly toward later ones. Striking evidence that Rawls sees the problem of intergenerational justice as being set by his adherence to the doctrine of the circumstances of justice is that he actually incorporates his initial discussion of it in the section on "The Circumstances of Justice."

Immediately after introducing the Humean circumstances of justice, along the lines I have quoted earlier in this chapter, Rawls goes on to raise the question of whether the people in the original position, who are contemporaries and know that they are, "have obligations and duties to third parties, for example, to their immediate descendants. To say that they do would be one way of handling questions of justice between generations." He rejects this, saying that "the aim of justice as fairness is to derive all duties and obligations from other conditions."[13] The alternative he puts forward is to make a "motivational assumption." This is that the "goodwill" of the parties "stretches over at least two generations. . . . For example, we may think of the parties as heads of families, and therefore as having a desire to further the welfare of their nearest descendants."[14] This is an ingenious attempt to retain the framework and adapt it to give some weight to the claims of later generations. I shall begin my discussion of intergenerational justice by examining this motivational assumption and pointing out its limitations.

THE MOTIVATIONS OF THE PARTIES

The purport of Rawls's motivational assumption is that the people in the original position still pursue their own ends but those ends are now defined so as to include their caring for at least two generations of descendants. They are doing as well as they can for themselves (subject to the constraint that they don't know their own identities) on the basis of the information that one of the things they want is to promote the interests of descendants. This is still "confin'd generosity" in that people are said only to care for their own descendants. But since they have no way of knowing in the original position who they are themselves (and *a fortiori* who their own descendants are) the mechanism of the veil of ignorance transmutes that limited concern into concern for later generations at large.

But where does this motivational assumption come from? One possible answer is that it is entirely *ad hoc*. Rawls sometimes appears to say that the precise specification of the original position should be adjusted until it generates the right answers.[15] I shall discuss Rawls's methodological views in chapter 7; I shall simply say here that Rawls clearly intends his theory to be more than a way of systematizing existing beliefs. The original position is best thought of as a device for representing in an ideal choosing situation the constraints that impartiality imposes on justice. There are, however, independent arguments to the effect that these constraints really are justified, and it is these arguments that ultimately carry the burden of establishing the principles of justice.

It would not, therefore, be an adequate justification of the "motivation assumption" that it enabled us to derive intuitively appealing conclusions about justice between generations—even if it did. The specification of the motives of the people in the original position must be intrinsically reasonable. The motivating force must be provided by their knowing that when they emerge from behind the veil of ignorance they will discover that they actually do care about the welfare of their descendants.

This interpretation of what is going on in Rawls's theory is supported by his remark that if we think of the parties as heads or representatives of families with "a desire to further the welfare of their nearest descendants" then we can say that "their interests are opposed as the circumstances of justice imply."[16] Given that the circumstances of justice apply (or fail to apply) in real life rather than in the original position, this seems to imply that their interests are opposed in real life, because each person in the original position knows that he is (in real life) concerned for the welfare of a different subset of the future generations from that for whose welfare others are concerned. "Confin'd generosity" still therefore obtains but it is, as it were, spread out over time.

If people trying to pursue their interests from behind a veil of ignorance would choose principles designed to protect those interests, whatever they turn out to be, we can presumably say that the result of the "motivational assumption" is to extend those interests. Whoever they may turn out to be, they will also care about their descendants, and from behind a veil of ignorance they must choose principles that will take account of that. We have already said that the interests of the parties do not have to be confined to states of themselves. This is simply one example of that. What makes principles of justice necessary is that people have divergent ends. All we are saying now is that these divergent ends extend into the future as far at any rate as the next two generations.

It is, of course, a striking (but inevitable) implication of thinking about the question in this way that the relation of justice holds only among contemporaries. It is not a matter of justice *between* generations. (Other generations are not, after all, parties to the agreement.) It is, rather, a matter of justice *with respect to* future generations. In exactly the same way, if I promise Alice to do something for Bertha, I have an obligation to Alice with respect to Bertha, but no obligation to Bertha.

This, however, exposes the limitations of any attempt to square intergenerational justice with the doctrine of the circumstances of justice. For it makes the obligations of the present generation toward future generations dependent purely upon the actual goodwill of contemporaries toward their descendants. If they care a lot, it will be a demand of justice that the present generation should do a lot to protect and enhance the interests of its successors; if not, then not. The information supplied to the contracting parties in the original position must in this respect be true. Otherwise the decisions they make behind their veil of ignorance can be of no relevance.

The demands of justice thus depend on the contingent facts about the extent to which people care about the welfare of (at least some) future people. If they care little, there is no basis for saying that they ought to care more, or at any rate no basis in justice. (We might, for example, still say that they would be finer human beings if they cared more, but this would have the same status as the proposition that they would be finer human beings if they cared—spontaneously and naturally, not out of considerations of justice—more about the well-being of their contemporaries.)

As a contingent fact, then, I fear that Rawls is probably right in saying that the information available to the people in the original position should tell them that their concern for the welfare of their descendants extends only to two generations or so, and starts running out pretty fast after that. It seems to me that if we care about the prospects of people in the remote future very much it is not on the basis of a natural sentiment but out of considerations of justice—but of course this must be justice in some form unaccounted for by the present analysis.

Rawls has the comforting belief that the interests of more remote generations will be taken care of so long as there are "ties of sentiment between successive generations."[17] For then it can be said that "representatives from periods adjacent in time have overlapping interests."[18] And, the argument goes, we can, by invoking this chain of concern for successor generations, explain why each generation should care about the welfare of its remote descendants even though it has no *direct* concern for the interests of people in the distant future. Unfortunately, however, this argument is valid only if the empirical relations between generations have a certain form, which I shall explain.

Rawls makes the optimistic assumption that the only interesting question of intergenerational justice is that of the "just savings rate." (It is well to remind ourselves that Rawls's theory was worked out in the 1950s and 1960s.) In other words, the only question that Rawls ever considers the people in the original position asking is: How much better off than we are must we make our successors? The basic idea is that each generation will be better off than its predecessors, until finally a stage is reached at which no further material advance is called for.[19] We are thus talking about a "process of accumulation" of capital, which, Rawls says, includes "not only factories and machines, and so on, but also the knowledge and culture, as well as the techniques and skills, that make possible just institutions and the fair value of liberty."[20]

Now it is a characteristic of this kind of accumulation that the only way in which it can operate is by passing things on to the immediately following generation. There is not much a given generation would do differently if it cared either a lot or a little about the welfare of generations after the next one. Provided it cares enough about the next one, it has an adequate motive for engaging in accumulation whether it cares about subsequent generations or not.

If we adopt a less benign perspective, however, and focus not so much on the just rate of capital accumulation as on the just rate of air and water pollution, degradation of the landscape, depletion of natural resources, destruction of species, creation of radiation hazards, or initiation of potentially disastrous modifications to the world's climate, we find that the same convenient relationship no longer holds. There is, in general, no way of making the next one or two generations materially better off that does not at least leave it open (depending on the decisions of those later generations) that more distant generations will be better off. But it is quite possible, when we turn to environmental issues, to find examples of actions now that will probably on balance be advantageous over the next generation and advantageous or neutral over the next after that, but then increasingly bad for later generations. If people cared only about the welfare of their immediate descendants there would be no injustice about their choosing such a path.

WHO IS TO CHOOSE?

If we are unsatisfied by the solution that the interests of future generations are to be taken account of simply to the degree that the members of the present generation care about the interests of members of future generations, what alternatives have we? One obvious alternative is to follow the same line here as in the case of relations between countries: we imagine that the people in the original position include members of different generations. The veil of ignorance will, as before, operate to conceal from the representatives which generation each of them belongs to, thus ensuring the requisite impartiality.

Rawls himself does actually mention this possibility in his section on intergenerational justice. "If we imagine that the original position contains representatives from all actual generations, the veil of ignorance would make it unnecessary to change the motivation assumption. But as we noted earlier . . . , it is best to take the present time of entry interpretation [according to which] those in the original position know . . . that they are contemporaries."[21] The reference back is not to the section on the circumstances of justice (section 22 of *A Theory of Justice*) on which I based my earlier discussion, but one a little later (section 24 of the book) on the specification of the veil of ignorance. The relevant passage says that "the original position is not to be thought of as a general assembly which includes at one moment everyone who will live at some time; or, much less, as an assembly of everyone who could live at some time. It is not a gathering of all actual or possible persons."[22]

Why not? Rawls makes it sound as if the objection to a multigenerational original position is purely to the tractability of such a conception. He says that "to conceive of the original position in either of these ways [i.e., as a gathering of all actual people or of all possible people] is to stretch fantasy too far; the conception would cease to be a natural guide to intuition."[23] There are indeed difficulties in making precise the notion of a gathering of everyone who ever lives or everyone who could live. On the one hand, if we say that it is everyone who ever does live, that raises the problem that different people will live if different principles are chosen, so if we know who the people at the gathering are, the choice of principles must already have somehow been made. (Even if we retreat to the position that there should be a representative of each generation, we still have the difficulty that there may be different numbers of generations under alternative arrangements.) On the other hand, if we deal with this problem by saying that all the people who *might* live under all alternative arrangements should be present, we not only (as Rawls says) run into problems in imagining the choice situation, but we are bound to worry about the good sense of choosing principles to advance the interests of potential people most of whom will never exist.[24]

However, I think that, in making it sound as if the reason for making the parties to the original position contemporaries is one of convenience, Rawls is being rather misleading. The implication seems to be that if we could crack these problems there would be no objection to putting different generations together. But I believe that there is an underlying objection of principle that is animating Rawls here, namely, that principles of justice should be capable of being presented as mutually advantageous in the real world. This is precisely the significance of the doctrine of the circumstances of justice. If we put people from different generations (among whom the circumstances of justice cannot possibly hold) in the original position together, we lose any reason for believing that their deliberations can have anything to do with mutual advantage.

If we want to see how a pure development along the lines of impartial agreement might go, we may turn to a book developed from a Ph.D. dissertation supervised by Rawls, David Richard's *A Theory of Reasons for Action*. Richards follows Rawls in equating justice (or, more generally, morality) with what would be chosen by rational contractors behind a veil of ignorance. But he departs from Rawls in stipulating that "the class of members of the original position includes, in a hypothetical sense, *all* persons, who have lived, live now, or will live. . . . On this account, not only actual age is irrelevant to the moral point of view . . . ; but also, one's membership of a historic age is irrelevant. Thus, . . . this account provides, in its basic structure, for the moral relations of older generations to children and infants, as well as different historical generations to one another."[25]

In the same passage, Richards contrasts this approach with "G. R. Grice's use of a similar contract conception" in his book *The Grounds of Moral Judgment*.[26] Richards says Grice "limits the contractors only to living adults" and he notes that "Grice claims" that "moral facts" about relations of adults to children or different generations to one another "can be established and justified by 'no remotely respectable argument.' "[27] But the reason why Grice makes this claim is that he

stays close to the idea of moral principles as the content of a contract
drawn up with an eye to the requirements of mutual self-protection. As
Richards himself says, "Grice maintains that basic moral obligations
are explicable in terms of the applicability of his contract ground: 'It is
in everyone's interest to make a contract with everyone else to do x.' "[28]

However, the obvious question that occurs at this point is how
Richards can distance himself from Grice in this way when he also says
that "Hume's general account of the circumstances of justice seems to
me correct; and it is by reference to his account that the problem of
justice will be introduced to the rational contractors."[29] For clearly, as
we have seen, the circumstances of justice do not apply among noncon-
temporaries; nor, indeed, do they apply between adults and at any rate
young children. (Rawls's way of dealing with duties to future generations is in fact best seen as an extension of the way that, from within a
theory bounded by the circumstances of justice, one deals with duties
owed as a matter of justice by adults to children.) I can see no answer to
this, and conclude that Richards is stuck with a flat contradiction.

UNIVERSALIZABILITY

All the commentators on Rawls have seen that it is of no significance
how many people there are in the original position as Rawls constructs
it. However many there are, they all have the same information about
things in general and about themselves in particular and thus face exactly the same decision-making problem. It therefore, of course, follows
that we need focus only on the question of what principles one person
in the original position will choose. This is because all the other people
in the original position, who are going through the same calculations
with the same objectives and the same information, will presumably
make the same choices. It is for this reason that I have assimilated
choice by a single person (as envisaged, for example, by Harsanyi) to
agreement in an original position (as specified by Rawls) without even
bothering to mention that I was doing so.[30]

This observation has an interesting implication for the analysis of
relations between generations. Suppose that the people in the original
position know that they are contemporaries but do not know where
they come in time. (Both features are specified by Rawls.) Then surely
the ignorance of their identity as a generation prevents them from
favoring themselves as a generation in just the same way as ignorance
of their personal identities prevents them from favoring themselves

as individuals. They must presumably draw up principles to govern intergenerational relationships with an eye to the possibility that they might themselves come anywhere in time. So if they make very stringent demands on early generations to make sacrifices for their successors they will regret it if they turn out to come early on, while if they are too lax in their demands on early generations they will regret it if they turn out to come later along in the sequence.

In his section on "Justice between Generations," Rawls makes some use of this idea, suggesting that

> the persons in the original position are to ask themselves how much they would be willing to save at each stage of advance on the assumption that all other generations are to save at the same rates. That is, they are to consider their willingness to save at any given phase of civilization with the understanding that the rates they propose are to regulate the whole span of accumulation. In effect, then, they must choose a just savings principle that assigns an appropriate rate of accumulation to each level of advance.[31]

We might think of this as an amalgamation of the categorical imperative and the veil of ignorance: the people in the original position are being asked to choose a principle to govern their savings for future generations that they can will as a universal law. In terms made familiar in contemporary philosophy by R. M. Hare, they have to choose a principle that satisfies the condition of universalizability.[32] That is to say, they must be prepared for everyone who is situated similarly (where the criteria of similarity are given by the principle itself) to act in the same way. To prevent people from fudging up principles that are designed, though universal in form, to benefit them personally, Hare requires that they should be prepared to accept the principle even if by some chance they turn into somebody else. (An Afrikaner, for example, would have to say that he would still support apartheid if he were a victim of the South African racial laws rather than a beneficiary.)[33] This requirement is met automatically by the Rawlsian veil of ignorance, since it obviously forces people who are choosing principles from behind it to take into account the possibility that they may be in any of the positions underwritten by whatever principles are chosen.

As Rawls envisages it, the relevant principle for savings will have to be a quite complicated one to formulate. We might ask why an intergenerational version of the difference principle would not do. The snag with this is that under it there should never be any net savings, because if there is to be any saving there has to be a first generation which makes itself worse off than any generation would need to be if no generation saved. Now Rawls believes that this would be an absurd result and that any adequate theory must entail that each generation saves, at any rate until a certain level of affluence has been achieved. But this inevitably means that poor people must make themselves poorer to make others richer—something that Rawls prohibits among contemporaries. The rationale can only be some kind of idea that the losses of the earlier and poorer generation are more than outweighed by the benefits to the later and richer generation. Thus, the treatment of the just savings rate by Rawls is significant not only methodologically but substantively: it represents a large concession of principle to an approach to moral decision-making that everywhere else in A Theory of Justice Rawls loses no opportunity to denounce.

If we once think of the question of the just savings rate as one of balancing the losses of the earlier generations against the gains of the later ones (not necessarily, of course, in exactly the way prescribed by utilitarianism), we will have to recognize that there are two considerations at work which tend in opposite directions. A poor society, as Rawls recognizes, undergoes more hardship than a wealthier one in producing any given level of net savings—the forgone consumption is worth more. But by the same token, the net savings are worth more too because economic growth is more important to a poor society than to one that is already rich. Rawls does not tell us how these considerations should be balanced. They perhaps suggest a rate of accumulation starting low to reflect the great sacrifice represented by net savings, then rising as affluence increases, and finally falling again asymptotically to zero as the importance of increased consumption to the good life becomes less and less.

All that Rawls himself says is that the "appropriate rate of accumulation . . . changes depending on the state of the society."[34] The point that matters here, however, is simply that, whatever the right principle may be, the way to arrive at it is for the people in the original position to say what at each stage they would be willing to save, on the assumption that all other generations will at each stage save at the rate prescribed for their own stage. (This formulation, though clumsy, is a more accurate rendition of what Rawls means by "the assumption that all other generations are to save at the same rates," which suggests that there can be only one rate prescribed for all generations.)

Notice that this really is a quite different line of analysis, though Rawls does not seem to see it, from the one that relies on natural sentiment to escape from the problem that the circumstances of justice do not obtain between one generation and its successors. On that other line of analysis, the point is that "those in the original position know . . . that they are contemporaries, so unless they care at least for their immediate successors, there is no reason for them to agree to undertake any saving whatever. To be sure, they do not know to which generation they belong, but this does not matter. Either earlier generations have saved or they have not; there is nothing the parties can do to affect it."[35]

On the line of analysis pursued here, however, it is irrelevant that the parties in the original position cannot by their choice affect what their predecessors did. The assumption that other generations will have lived by the principles that are chosen is not, surely, supposed to be a false assumption about the ability of one generation to alter the past. It is a way of framing the choice that forces it to be an impartial one: the people in the original position are to choose a principle that they could live with, wherever they come in the sequence, on condition that all others have played their part by the same rules.*

Rawls's account of how this is to be done departs from the maximizing motives that he elsewhere imputes to the people in the original position. They are not exactly to ask what, at any stage, would be most advantageous to them, on the assumption that those at all other stages have followed their prescriptions. He recognizes, I suppose, that that would make for an ill-formed choice problem, when the question is how much earlier generations should sacrifice to make later ones better off. He therefore poses the question in terms of what it is "reasonable for members of adjacent generations to expect of one another at each level of advance."[36]

---

* In "The Basic Structure as Subject" (in Alvin I. Goldman and Jaegwon Kim, eds., *Values and Morals: Essays in Honor of William Frankena, Charles Stevenson and Richard B. Brandt* [Dordrecht: Reidel, 1978], pp. 47–71), a paper published subsequently to *A Theory of Justice*, Rawls explicitly commits himself to the idea that "the parties can be required to agree to a savings principle subject to the further condition that they must want all *previous* generations to have followed it. Thus the correct principle is that which the members of any generation (and so all generations) would adopt as the one their generation is to follow and as the principle they would want preceding generations to have followed (and later generations to follow), no matter how far back (or forward) in time" (pp. 58–59 [italics in original]). In a footnote to this passage, Rawls says that it "differs from [the formulation] in *A Theory of Justice*, [where] it is not required that the parties must want the previous generations to have followed the principle they adopt as contemporaries" (ibid., p. 70 n. 11). (Hence the assumption, as Rawls explains, that they care for their successors, since otherwise they would have no reason to save.) This is of some interest biographically as telling us what Rawls himself later thought he had been up to in *A Theory of Justice* and what he later decided to make the theory into. But for my purposes what matters is working out the alternative interpretations that are possible and analyzing their merits rather than trying to pin one rather than another on Rawls.

Now, it must be admitted that this may compromise Rawls's wish to exclude moral considerations from the deliberations in the original position. For what is the criterion of the reasonableness of an expectation? That we have irreducible moral terms entering in seems clear from Rawls's continuation, in which "entitled" and "fair" appear as part of the conceptual apparatus of the people in the original position rather than (as they are supposed to on Rawls's program) as words that we as moral philosophers use to talk about the nature of their situation and the status of their conclusions. Thus, he says that the people in the original position

> try to piece together a just savings schedule by balancing how much at each stage they would be willing to save for their immediate descendants against what they would feel entitled to claim of their immediate predecessors. Thus imagining themselves to be fathers, say, they are to ascertain how much they should set aside for their sons by noting what they would believe themselves entitled to claim of their fathers. When they arrive at an estimate that seems fair from both sides, with due allowance made for the improvement in their circumstances, then the fair rate (or range of rates) for that stage is specified. Now once this is done for all stages, we have defined the just saving principle. When this principle is followed, adjacent generations cannot complain of one another; and in fact no generation can find fault with any other no matter how far removed in time.[37]

I am inclined to think that Rawls gets closer here to setting out his fundamental idea of justice as fairness than he does anywhere else. Because of the peculiarities of the relation between generations, Rawls is forced away from his usual presentation of the choice problem which, however much he may wriggle, amounts to one of maximization under uncertainty. Instead, we get the valuable idea that the key to justice is a willingness to claim and be claimed on in virtue of a given principle. Justice must be "fair from both sides." (I shall follow up this idea in chapter 9.)

Oddly enough, after he has developed this way of dealing with intergenerational justice, Rawls reverts to the claim that we need a "motivational assumption." Past generations, he says, have either saved or not saved, and nothing can be done to change that now by choosing one principle or another. Since nothing can be done to change the past, there is no advantage to the people in the original position in choosing a principle that requires any net saving (or indeed, one might add, prevents them from running things down) unless they actually care about the welfare of the next generation. As it stands, this seems to me no argument at all: to say that the people in the original position are to choose principles for saving on the assumption that other generations will have acted on those principles is a way of stating the decision problem, not an invitation to believe that one's decisions can alter the past.

FAIR PLAY

If Rawls's objection is misplaced, can we conclude that the right thing for any given generation to do does not depend on what others have done in the past? Can we safely affirm that the just savings rate for any generation is that rate that would fall to it under a multigenerational plan that its members would wish all generations before it to have followed? Is it really irrelevant what the predecessor generations actually did? Rawls has, I think, a deeper reason than the one just mentioned for giving a negative answer, though I do not think he ever succeeds in articulating its force very clearly.

The point here is that we should think not of a choice made by a particular generation at a single point in time but of a pattern of collaboration across many generations in a common scheme of justice. Although, in the nature of the case, successive generations cannot take part in any system of mutual benefit, they can all play their part in a system accepted by all as just. The principle of fair play, which says that there is an obligation to do one's bit to sustain just institutions, thus operates here even in the absence of any possibility of mutual benefit. As Rawls put it:

> The just savings principle can be regarded as an understanding between generations to carry their fair share of the burden of realizing and preserving a just society. . . . [I]t represents an interpretation, arrived at in the original position, of the previously accepted natural duty to uphold and to further just institutions. In this case the ethical problem is that of agreeing on a path over time which treats all generations justly during the whole course of a society's history.[38]

And again: "The life of a people is conceived as a scheme of cooperation spread out in historical time. It is to be governed by the same conception of justice that regulates the cooperation of contemporaries."[39] The conception is the one quoted above: that the generation in the original position should ask what it is reasonable for different generations to ask of one another.

On this view of things, it obviously does make a difference whether it turns out that there really has been a common understanding on the principles of saving chosen in the original position or whether earlier generations have acted quite differently. We might say that there are circumstances of justice in a sense different from the Humean one, namely, the actual existence of just institutions. In the same way that an individual is not obliged to do what would be required by just institutions in the absence of such institutions, so, if we think with Rawls of just institutions spread out over time, we can say that there is no obligation on a given generation to uphold an intergenerational scheme of just savings if its predecessors have not done so. This does not of course tell us what it *should* do; and I do not take it to entail that it can justly do anything it likes. Once again the point is purely negative.

The upshot is, then, that Rawls is right to claim relevance for the point that previous generations have either saved or not. But the relevance is not that therefore the present generation has no self-interested reason for saving unless it cares about the welfare of its successors. Rather, it is that what has happened in the past determines whether or not it makes any sense to talk of a scheme of just institutions extending over time.

It is worth noting, however, that, so long as we stick to talking about just institutions, we do not run into any similar problem among contemporaries. If we want to talk about what a society with just institutions would look like, we obviously mean a society in which just institutions were established. We are thus talking about practices that are generally adhered to. (Rawls describes this feature by saying he is putting forward a "full compliance" theory.)

It is Rawls's assumption, which I share, that we can conclude that a just society would be different from any that now exists or ever has existed. We may believe that a just society is very unlikely ever to come into existence. But that does not prevent our talking about what it would look like. It is only in relation to intergenerational justice that what has happened in the past actually enters into the criterion of justice.

I hope that the discussion in this section of alternative ways of dealing with intergenerational justice will have been of some interest in its own right. For the purpose of this book, the point that is central is that the doctrine of the circumstances of justice cannot be squared with the notion that future generations are owed obligations of justice. Rawls's heroic attempt to get around the problem by a "motivational assumption" fails, I have suggested, because it makes justice depend on the actual sentiments of natural concern that people have for their successors. A claim of justice should, rather, be one that can be made by (or in this case on behalf of) certain persons on others as having force even if those on whom the claim is pressed have no sentiments of natural concern for the claimants. All the other three approaches discussed violated the doctrine of the circumstances of justice, and this was unavoidable. In chapter 9 I shall draw on the discussion of these ways of handling intergenerational justice when I offer a general analysis of justice as impartiality.

25. WHY NOT NOAH'S ARK?

If for a moment we take Hume's theory of the circumstances of justice not as a theory of justice but as a theory of the conditions under which moral constraints will in fact be effective, we will, I think, conclude that it has impressive explanatory power. It will account for the traditional killing, raping, enslaving, and pillaging of the vanquished by the victors in battle. It will account for the virtual extermination of native peoples by European settlers in, for example, North America and Australia. And it will account for the record that the human race has set in its relations with the other animals with which it shares the planet.

As unflattering as the facts are, what is if anything even more discreditable to human nature is the seemingly inexhaustible capacity human beings have for inventing justifications for cruelty to one another and to nonhuman animals. From the doctrines of Genesis and Exodus to those of "scientific" racism and the survival of the fittest, intellectual history parallels the history of events as a record of the crimes and follies of mankind.

No doubt against a background that includes the notion that it doesn't matter what you do to animals because they are unconscious mechanisms, or because they do not have souls, theories of morality as mutual advantage may appear to be scarcely worth picking on. But it is worth observing, I think, that no theory that makes morality out to be a practice of mutually advantageous forbearances can have any implication that human beings have direct moral obligations not to cause suffering to animals. (I shall explain what I mean by "direct" below.) For although it is of course possible to train some animals to observe constraints, and human beings undoubtedly can benefit from this, it would, I take it, be an indulgence in anthropomorphism to regard this as amounting to reciprocal engagement in a shared moral practice that has as its *quid pro quo* good treatment of animals by human beings.

Here, as elsewhere, we ought to make a sharp distinction between a rational contract for mutual advantage and what can withstand impartial appraisal. As Peter Singer puts it in *Animal Liberation*, the point "is not that animals are capable of acting morally, but that the moral principle of equal consideration of interests applies to them as it applies to humans. That it is often right to include within the sphere of equal consideration beings that are not themselves capable of making moral choices is implied by our treatment of young children and other humans who, for one reason or another, do not have the mental capacity to understand the nature of moral choice."[40]

There is no reason in principle why we could not derive protection for the interests of nonhuman animals by using the machinery of the original position. All we have to do is to extend its scope to include representatives of all sentient beings. It may seem a little bizarre to imagine the negotiations taking place aboard Noah's Ark, with the species of the participants concealed from them, but is it really much more farfetched than imagining that the parties are (as Richards proposes) all people who have ever lived or ever will live or (as others have suggested) all people who might live?

It is true that it is hard to think about the question: what rules would you draw up for the treatment of other animals by human beings on the assumption that you might turn out to be either a human being or some other animal? I think, however, that the difficulty of thinking about the question posed in those terms reflects the perfectly genuine difficulty that is faced by those who wish to claim that human and nonhuman interests should be weighed in the same scales—in other words, that species as such should not enter into the determination.

It is allowed by those who say this that, whatever the relevant scales may be, the interests of different species will not come out as being of equal weight. Whatever we say is relevant (unless we simply say existence, which would not distinguish sensitive, or even living, things from everything else), some species will have more of it than others. Even the capacity for suffering, which is the nearest thing to a common feature across species, we presume to differ from one to another.[41]

Nothing whatever is gained by saying things like "If I were turned into an animal, I should stop having any desire for political liberty, and therefore the lack of it would be no hardship to me," or "If we were bears we should suffer horribly if [baited]; therefore we cannot accept any maxim which permits bears to be treated thus; therefore we cannot say that it is all right to treat bears thus."[42] In fact, the conclusion seems to me firmer than the supporting reasoning. Once we concede that bears suffer from bear-baiting we have the basis for condemning the practice. To say that if I were a bear I would suffer is to say *no more* than that bears suffer, but it weakens the force of that assertion about bears by obtruding puzzles about cross-species identity. To see that the hypothesis about what we would think or feel if we were to change species is doing no work in the argument, it is only necessary to ask what one's reaction would be to someone who said, "I admit that actual [nonhuman] animals have no desire for political liberty but if I were turned into one I'm pretty sure I still would." The obvious retort is that if you were turned into an animal you would have exactly the same desires as an animal. But it might also be said that what matters here is the desires of actual animals, and it is quite irrelevant what your desires would be if you were turned into one.*

I doubt, too, that it is helpful, in asking about the comparative "value" of the lives of different species, to ask, "given the choice of life as a horse or a human being" which would I choose, if I had had both experiences and could "remember exactly what it was like to be a horse and exactly what it was like to be a human being."[43] So, in rather the same way, I suspect that not much is gained by asking "What moral constraints would I choose to have placed on human beings if I didn't know if I were a human being, a cat, or a flea?"

I believe, however, that Singer is right in saying that our inability to make precise comparisons between the sufferings of different species is not a crippling blow, because we do not have to do any fine balancing of interest to arrive at far-reaching conclusions.

Even if we were to prevent the infliction of suffering on animals only when it is quite certain that the interests of humans will not be affected to anything like the extent that animals are affected, we would be forced to make radical

---

* This kind of reasoning is liable to bring on a throbbing of the temples akin to that produced in Bertie Wooster by Gussie Fink-Nottle's wish that he were a male newt:

"Do you know how a male newt proposes, Bertie? He just stands in front of the female newt vibrating his tail and bending his body in a semicircle. I could do that on my head. No, you wouldn't find me grousing if I were a male newt."

"But if you were a male newt, Madeline Bassett wouldn't look at you. Not with the eye of love, I mean."

"She would, if she were a female newt."

"But she isn't a female newt."

"No, but suppose she was."

"Well, if she was, you wouldn't be in love with her."

"Yes, I would, if I were a male newt."

A slight throbbing about the temples told me that this discussion had reached saturation point. (P. G. Wodehouse, *Right Ho, Jeeves* [Harmondsworth: Penguin, 1953], p. 22.)

changes in our treatment of animals that would involve our diet, the farming methods we use, experimental procedures in many fields of science, our approach to wildlife and to hunting, trapping and the wearing of furs, and areas of entertainment like circuses, rodeos, and zoos. As a result, a vast amount of suffering would be avoided.[44]

This introduces a methodological principle that is quite often useful, namely, to start from the conclusions and work back to the premises rather than the other way round. Instead of asking, "What conclusions follow from these premises?" we can ask, "What are the weakest premises from which we can derive these conclusions?" Singer's *Animal Liberation* is a particularly good illustration because it would be hard to read it without being convinced of the evil of many of the practices described in the use of animals for experimental purposes and in raising them for food. The effect is in this respect quite like that of reading a dispassionate account of everyday life on a slave plantation or in a Nazi concentration camp. Moreover, Singer's book is one of the very few that have led people to change their lives in a fundamental way, by becoming vegetarians. (I know several philosophers of whom this is true.)

But Singer's apparatus of equal consideration of interests is so strong in the form in which he espouses it, amounting as it does to a universal obligation to pursue the maximum aggregate utility, that it is (to say the least) highly controversial when its scope is taken to be the human race, let alone the whole of sentient creation. Yet, nothing like this sort of commitment to our being our brothers' keepers—whether our brothers are all human beings or all animals—is required in order to agree with Singer that a lot of cruelty to animals is going on and ought to be stopped. As Singer himself says, it is enough to give virtually any weight to the interests of nonhuman animals against those of human beings to arrive at that conclusion.

We may naturally wonder how Rawls and Richards will deal with the question. Richards is in practice much less sensitive than Rawls to the constraints of mutual advantage, as we have seen. We might therefore expect him to incorporate animals into his scheme, as he did future generations, by including them among his rational contractors. To the objection that animals cannot actually negotiate it could be replied that nor can people who are defined as not being contemporaries. If it is said, "Well, they could negotiate if they were contemporaries," then it should be noted that Richards allows imbeciles and insane people to be among those in his original position, and they are presumably in no position to negotiate.[45] And if we say, "They could negotiate if they were intelligent or grown up, and anyway someone could represent their interests," then the same could be said of nonhuman animals.

The objection surely smacks of the fallacy of misplaced concreteness. There never was and never will be any original position. Talking about what would go on in it is supposed to be a way of doing moral philosophy, not a branch of imaginative literature. If we start with the presupposition that the whole of morality is going to be yielded by the derivation of principles from an original position (as Richards does, though Rawls, as we shall see, does not), and if we assume (as Rawls and Richards both do) that the rational contractors are to pursue their own ends from within the original position, then it must follow that the only way of guaranteeing that the interests of animals will be protected is to include them among the parties whose assent is required.

Richards accepts that this is so but nevertheless confines his *dramatis personae* to human beings. Where, then, does this leave animals? The answer is: in exactly the same position as future generations are put in by Rawls. That is to say, Richards makes a motivational assumption akin to Rawls's: his rational contractors are to know "that persons generally have certain basic sympathies with animals and animal life," and they "will understand cruelty to animals as an extension of a personality orientation which is prone to cruelty to persons."[46]

However, the rational contractors should not be supposed to "know" what is not in fact the case. They should therefore be aware that sympathy for animals varies a great deal from one time and place to another and is at best concentrated mainly on pets and petlike animals rather than on those defined as food, game, or pests. They should also recognize that the vast mass of suffering inflicted on animals in modern societies is not gratuitous but is incidental to the pursuit of profit or publication. If a guard at Auschwitz could regard his job as a distasteful but necessary one of dealing with subhuman species, it is much more likely that a broiler house attendant or a technician in a biology laboratory can avoid being an across-the-board sadist. I do not therefore think that much regard for the interests of nonhuman animals would emerge from the protection of strictly human interests and, to be fair to Richards, he does not do much to suggest so.

For our present purpose, however, Richards's conclusions matter less than the way in which he gets to them. Why does Richards rule out the idea that the interests of animals should be protected directly (rather than as a by-product of the pursuit of human interests) by including them among the parties in the original position? His answer is at first sight strange, but it gets us to the heart of a central problem in the interpretation of the hypothetical contractarian method.

Richards in fact says two things and, though he treats them as one, they come out of opposite schools of contractarian thinking. The first is that animals "lack the capacities of choice and control" that would "entitle" them to be members of the original position.[47] This clearly harks back to the notion of justice as mutual forbearance: justice is owed only to those who are capable of being just in return. However, this is a view that Richards does not really hold, in spite of the lip service he pays to the doctrine of the circumstances of justice.

We need not, indeed, refer back to the discussion of future generations to see this, because Richards immediately qualifies what he has said by adding that "the original position includes mental deficients and the insane because it is quite possible that a contractor may be so embodied."[48] Animals, it seems, "lack the causal possibility of having the capacities of choice and control of members of the original position,"[49] but the mentally defective and insane do not.

Now a natural response to this might be that since Richards is making up the rules around here we had better take his word for it that one thing is possible and another not. But this would be to miss the point that a crucial shift in ground has taken place with the second move. For if we say that there are direct moral duties (not via an appropriate motivational assumption) to those who are incapable of adhering on the basis of their own judgment and decision to the usual run of moral constraints, we are thinking of membership of the original position as a way of protecting interests. But then why not include animals, since they seem to be in this respect in much the same position?

This brings us to Richards's second argument, which directs attention to one way of thinking about the foundations of the theory of justice as impartiality. He says, in support of the distinction between the proposed treatment of animals and that of the mentally deficient or insane, that "the notion of moral fortuitousness . . . can be pressed only so far and no further: that a person is American or British, Negro or Caucasian, atheist or Anglican, etc., is fortuitous from the point of view of the original position, but that a creature is an animal or a human is not fortuitous in the same way."[50]

To say that something is fortuitous is to say that it comes about by chance (Latin *fors*); the idea of good or ill fortune (*fortuna*) comes from the same root. Now, there may be some very deep (or perhaps it is very shallow) sense in which it is an accident, lucky or unlucky, that I am who I am and not, say, a slave girl in the court of Rameses II. But to the extent that that is an intelligible remark, it seems to me no less so to suggest that it is an accident, lucky or unlucky, that I am not a corgi in the court of Elizabeth II. Construed as serious hypotheses, they are equally subject to Leibnitz's reply to a man who said he wished he were king of China: that what his wish amounted to was, first, that he should not exist and, second, that there should be a king in China.

What, then, is the meaning of fortuitousness in the context of the basic facts about people that constitute their personal identities? We can gain some understanding of this by looking at Richards's more extended discussion of the notion of fortuitousness, which occurs in his specification and defense of the original position. The list of things that the contractors do not know about themselves (on which I drew for my example) includes "sex, age, native talents, particular degree of his capacity for self-control, race, religion, social or economic class and position, the age in which he lives, or the particular form of his desires (e.g. whether he likes asparagus or spinach; or is homosexual or heterosexual in his sexual aims)."[51]

Now it is plain that, if we start from the idea that moral principles are self-interested choices in a suitably specified original position, we are going to have to deny knowledge to the contractors of these things if we are to get impartiality. As Richards puts it, "the choice of *moral* principles by definition implies that the choice is made without favouritism to one's class or race, clan or caste, talent or nationality. Such favouritism is here made impossible by the ignorance of the contractors."[52]

However, it is important to recognize that nothing we have said so far sets any limits on the kinds of principles the contractors will draw up. We know, for example, that they will legislate for relations between the sexes along lines that they would regard *ex ante* as protecting their interests—whether they turn out to be men or women. But that obviously does not entail that they will choose not to differentiate the rights and duties of men and women or the expectations about their characters and concerns. They might decide that an ideal society would be one in which a person's sex had no more significance as such than the color of his or her eyes. But there is absolutely nothing in the construction of the original position so far that inevitably drives the parties toward such a decision.

Similarly, the people in Richards's original position might decide on

perfect cosmopolitanism, decreeing that, morally speaking, membership in a particular society should make no difference to anybody's
obligations. But there is nothing in the construction to prevent them
from declaring that each person should have stronger and more extensive obligations to fellow-citizens than to people in the rest of the world.
This is not favoritism in the choice of moral principles. The hypothesis
is that everyone, without knowing his own country or how he personally will be affected by the alternative possible arrangements, would on
balance prefer a world with moral communities to a world without
them. This would be a choice, made in the circumstances of impartiality, of principles that allow, in real life, for partiality. (I shall return to
this in Volume II.)

Richards, however, having given the defense of his veil of ignorance
that I just quoted, goes on to offer a gloss on it that introduces a very
different notion of the significance of the ignorance of the contractors
from this:

> Put differently, the idea may be expressed thus: from the point of view of
> morality, it is utterly and at bottom fortuitous that a person is born in one
> social class rather than another, or in one racial or ethnic group rather than
> another, or in one body (with associated endowments of physical beauty,
> intelligence, perception, talent, etc.) rather than another, and the like. Since
> these differences between persons are fortuitous, they cannot be of fun-
> damental weight in deciding what count as moral principles. The ignorance
> requirement gives expression to this idea by depriving the contractors, who
> are deciding on moral principles, of the knowledge of their fortuitous posi-
> tion in the natural and cultural lottery.[53]

The point is driven home even more sharply a few pages later, where
Richards writes that, on the ideal contract view, "various particular
facts about onself are irrelevant, by definition, to the moral point of
view, a conception which, I think, gives expression to the intuitive view
that morality involves treating persons as persons, apart from the
irrelevancies of class or colour, clan or caste, talent or nationality."[54]

Fortuitousness here, then, appears as an overtly moral notion: what
is fortuitous is everything about people that should not play any role in
determining the way in which they should be treated. And if all the
features of people that they do not know about in the original position
are "irrelevancies," it is pretty obvious that only one thing is left, namely, the bare fact of belonging to the human race. This is "treating
persons as persons" with a vengeance! Small wonder that Hegel's
complaint about the excessive "abstraction" from the complexities of

real relationships that he found in Kant has been echoed by contemporary Hegelians or fellow-travelers in criticism of contemporary neo-Kantians!

We can now see that Richards is obliged to exclude nonhuman animals from the original position because of the significance he attaches to being included. Moral principles, on his view, apply to all human beings without differentiation. They cannot prescribe differently for the intelligent or unintelligent, for fellow citizens and noncitizens, and so on. It is hard enough to give credence to this. But if we had to go further and say that moral principles must apply to all sentient creatures without differentiation, we would plainly be deep into absurdity.

Let us now turn to Rawls. Clearly, in his Humean persona, Rawls should be able to deal briskly with nonhuman animals. Since the circumstances of justice do not obtain between human beings and animals, they are automatically outside the scope of justice. That he does not dispatch them this fast illustrates once again his less than total commitment to justice as mutual advantage.

The discussion of duties to animals comes at the end of a section on "The Basis of Equality."[55] In this, Rawls enunciates the principle that "those who can give justice are owed justice."[56] But this has to be interpreted with caution: "the capacity for moral personality is a sufficient condition for being entitled to equal justice."[57] This leaves it open whether or not it is also a necessary condition. When he does discuss animals, Rawls notes that he has "not maintained that the capacity for a sense of justice is necessary in order to be owed the duties of justice."[58] However, he continues by saying that "it does seem that we are not required to give strict justice anyway to creatures lacking this capacity."[59]

The greater hesitation about the second step can, I think, be explained by Rawls's including within the scope of justice human beings who are lacking in moral personality either because they have not yet developed it or because they have temporarily lost it. Capacity rather than actuality is what counts.[60] Rawls says that this "seems necessary to match our considered judgments" about the rights of infants and children, and also that "regarding the potentiality as sufficient accords with the hypothetical nature of the original position, and with the idea that as far as possible the choice of principles should not be influenced by arbitrary contingencies. Therefore it is reasonable to say that those who could take part in the initial agreement, were it not for fortuitous circumstances, are assured equal justice."[61] This, however, marks a slide from the position that playing one's part in common institutions is what entitles one to justice. Rather, we are getting (as with Richards) parties included in order to avoid their "fortuitous" disadvantages from being built into the original position. But if a day-old infant can be represented in the original position, why not a monkey or a dog?

Be that as it may, Rawls's discussion of animals is interesting for the questions it raises. Having said that we are not required to give strict justice to animals, he goes on:

> But it does not follow that there are no requirements at all in regard to them, nor in our relations with the natural order. Certainly it is wrong to be cruel to animals and the destruction of a whole species can be a great evil. The capacity for feelings of pleasure and pain and for the forms of life of which animals are capable clearly impose duties of compassion and humanity in their case. I shall not attempt to explain these considered beliefs. They are outside the scope of the theory of justice, and it does not seem possible to extend the contract doctrine so as to include them in a natural way.[62]

This is perhaps not an unreasonable place to come out, and it seems to me clearly preferable to Rawls's proposal to make duties to future generations parasitic on justice among contemporaries. It is curious to notice that the effect of combining the two positions is that the interests of nonhuman animals are better secured than those of future human beings. If the current generation is quite indifferent to the fate of its remote successors, it would seem that the only reason for not polluting the planet in a way that will cause them suffering is that it would be hard to do this in a way that would not also cause suffering to future nonhuman animals.

CHAPTER VI

Rawls on Justice (2): The Difference Principle

26. INTRODUCTION

In this chapter I shall focus on Rawls's principle for the legitimacy of social and economic inequalities within a society, the difference principle. My theme will be, once again, that there is a conflict between justice as impartiality and justice as mutual advantage. The difference principle flows from justice as impartiality. As soon as we try to bring it into line with justice as mutual advantage it collapses, or so I shall maintain.

In the two sections following this one I shall lay out what I take to be Rawls's fundamental argument for the difference principle. I shall do this without at any point invoking any notion of justice as mutual advantage. Only then will I bring up the questions that arise from any attempt to incorporate the requirements of mutual advantage. I must preface this exposition of Rawls's argument by warning that I shall go into only as much complexity as seems necessary for the present purpose. This will mean that I shall pass over many problems that would have to be aired if my object were a full-scale evaluation of the difference principle.

The first point to be made is that in putting forward what I take to be Rawls's fundamental argument for the difference principle I shall not be discussing, except incidentally, the argument that most people would regard as central. That argument, which has also been the one most intensively discussed by his critics, attempts a derivation of the difference principle from the original position: the difference principle is said to be what mutually disinterested people choosing principles to advance their own interests from behind a veil of ignorance would agree in choosing. That this argument takes the center of the stage in Rawls's own exposition is a reflection of Rawls's official view, which is that ultimately all arguments about justice are to be made with reference to what principles would be chosen in a suitably constituted original position. No other aspect of Rawls's theory has attracted more commentary than his effort to show that the difference principle can be derived from the original position as he specifies it, and it is, I think, safe to say that no other aspect of the theory has met with such uniform rejection.[1]

However, Rawls does not in fact rest everything on the derivation from the original position. His full-scale presentation of the original position, and his attempt to get the difference principle out of it, occur in the third of the nine chapters into which *A Theory of Justice* is divided. But in the second chapter, "The Principles of Justice," Rawls constructs an argument for the difference principle that is quite independent of any support from the original position. It runs from equal opportunity to equality of income and from there to the difference principle via the notion of a Pareto improvement on equality. This is the line of argument that I shall try to trace through in the present chapter. It is quite hard to follow and, perhaps in consequence, has frequently been misunderstood. (Thus, for example, Rawls does not, as is often supposed, make the case for equality turn on the impossibility of equalizing environments.) I shall try to show that the difference principle does, as Rawls maintains, pick out a unique Pareto-optimal point that is a Pareto improvement on an equal distribution. His argument is, thus, when stated carefully and with all due qualifications, a valid one.

It might reasonably be asked how Rawls can have two separate and self-contained arguments for the difference principle in successive chapters of his book. The question is, however, misleadingly posed. There are not supposed to be two different arguments but, rather, the same argument presented in two different ways. We should here recall what was said earlier, in section 24, about the status of the original position. It is merely a device for representing in a dramatic form the constraints that impartial appraisal imposes on anything that can count as a principle of justice. Although, therefore, Rawls's official position is, as we have seen, that all arguments should ultimately run in terms of choice in the original position, what enables us to assert that the principles chosen in it are principles of *justice* is that the original position has been appropriately characterized. And in arguing for the appropriate characterization of the original position, it is necessary to develop definite ideas about the general characteristics of justice. But it should then be possible to get from these to principles of justice without ever going through the business of choice in the original position. And that is exactly what Rawls does in chapter 2 of *A Theory of Justice*.

None of this would matter if the direct argument in chapter 2 of *A Theory of Justice* and the indirect one via the original position were really simply alternative ways of putting forward the same moral argument. But although Rawls believes that they are, they are not. The notion of a self-interested choice under conditions of censored information is attractive because it enables the resources of rational-choice theory for prudential choices to be harnessed to moral philosophy. But unfortunately it does not capture adequately the moral insights that underlie Rawls's fundamental egalitarianism and drive his advocacy of the difference principle. Self-interested choice under uncertainty leads naturally, not to equality, but to some sort of maximization of average expectations. Harsanyi's derivation of utilitarianism from such a construction is far more plausible than Rawls's derivation of his two principles of justice.

This does not mean that some rather different kind of original position might not play a useful part in the development of a theory of justice as impartiality. And I shall in chapter 9 present and defend such an alternative. The basic idea of principles of justice as those that would be agreed on in what I have called the circumstances of impartiality is sound enough. But the Rawlsian specification has to go. We have to get rid of the stipulation that the parties are motivated by the pursuit of their own interests, and instead say that they wish to reach agreement on reasonable terms. And the role played by information restriction has to be much more limited and incidental than that which it plays in Rawls's original position. (See especially sections 41 and 42, below.)

In the present chapter, however, I shall not anticipate the development of a new original position. I shall instead present the case for the difference principle directly, following the general lines of Rawls's statement of it in chapter 2 of *A Theory of Justice*. What, then, is the difference principle? Rawls's final statement of it, omitting a clause to deal with the "just savings rate" already discussed in section 24, runs as follows: "social and economic inequalities are to be arranged so that they are . . . to the greatest benefit of the least advantaged."[2] Although much might be said in supplementation of this succinct statement, the only point that needs to be emphasized here is that "the least advantaged" are to be conceived of as a group—an income stratum or social class. From what Rawls says about the possible ways in which groups might be defined, it would appear that he has in mind a number of groups no smaller than four and no larger than six.* The least advantaged are not, for example, to be conceived of as a collection of terminally ill individuals.

Social justice is predicated of the basic structure of a society, and the basic structure is the set of institutions that create, transmit, and reinforce the advantages and disadvantages—in educational qualifications, savoir faire, knowing the right people, or whatever it takes—that lead to economic and social success or the lack of it. (Rawls assumes, not too unrealistically for a society such as that of the United States, that the correlation between economic and social success is high enough that money can be used as a reliable index of overall standing in the hierarchy of positions.) The worst off are those who, given the way in which the major institutions of the society work, face the poorest prospects of gaining the rewards that the society has to dispense.

The proposition to be defended, then, is that, when we assess the justice of a society's institutions, there is one simple and sufficient test we should apply. We should ask: Does this set of institutions operate in such a way that the worst-off group—those who do least well out of them—could not do any better under any alternative set of arrangements? We must, of course, interpret this question in a way that does not ascribe a fixed identity to the worst-off group. That is to say, the question is not: Could some (or even all) of these people who do least well under the present arrangements do better under an alternative set? It may be that these particular people (call them the As) could

* Rawls offers two possible ways of defining the worst-off group: "One possibility is to choose a particular social position, say that of the unskilled worker, and then to count as the least advantaged all those with the average income and wealth of this group, or less. The expectation of the lowest representative man is defined as the average taken over this whole class. Another alternative is a definition solely in terms of relative income and wealth with no reference to social position. Thus all persons with less than half of the median income and wealth may be taken as the least advantaged segment." (*A Theory of Justice* [Cambridge, Mass.: Harvard University Press, 1971], p. 98.) The first formula tells us to take the set of unskilled workers. Then we collect all those below the average in this set and call them the "least advantaged." We then arrive at the "average over this whole class" (the context makes it clear that this refers to those picked out in the second stage) and call that the expectation of the representative worst-off man. In summary, we want the average income of all those below the average unskilled worker. The second formula may be set out in a parallel way. We take all those below the median income of the society. ("This definition depends only upon the lower half of the distribution" [ibid.].) Then we collect all those with less than half the median income and call this "the least

be made better off than they are now, but only by making some other people (call them the Bs) even worse off than the As are now. This is not incompatible with the claim that the present society satisfies the difference principle. In the alternative society, those who were least advantaged (the Bs) would be at a lower level than those (the As) who are least advantaged in the present society. The difference principle then tells us that the society we have now is to be preferred to the alternative society. For what we must do is to see in each society how the least advantaged fare. The most just society is the one in which the least-advantaged group, whatever its composition, is at the highest level.

Now that I have explained what the difference principle is, I have to lay out Rawls's argument in its favor. I shall do this in two stages. In section 27 I shall lay the foundation by showing how Rawls establishes equality as the only *prima facie* just basis of distribution. Then in section 28 I shall follow Rawls's argument for a move from an equal distribution to a distribution governed by the difference principle.

27. FROM EQUAL OPPORTUNITY TO EQUALITY

Rawls's strategy in chapter 2 of *A Theory of Justice* is to move from a very broad and general statement of the conditions under which economic inequality is justified to one particular interpretation of that statement, one that makes equality of incomes the only *prima facie* just distribution. The broad and general statement runs as follows: "social and economic inequalities are to be arranged so that they are both (a) reasonably expected to be to everyone's advantage, and (b) attached to

---

advantaged segment." And third—what? Rawls does not tell us how to get from here to a single expectation but it would seem to be in accordance with his intentions to suppose that we are again to average the incomes of the set of people identified at the second stage (this time all those with less than half the median income), for he goes on to say that "in any case we are to aggregate to some degree over the expectations of the worst off." On this reading, the second formula tells us to compute the average income of all those whose incomes are less than half the median income in the society. This will define the income of a representative member of the worst-off group. If this amount of aggregation goes into the computation of the least-advantaged position there will be only a small number of positions. In fact, this second proposal would seem best fitted to produce four groups: those below half the median, those between half and the median, those between median and twice the median, and those above twice the median. The first proposal, which divides the unskilled workers into two groups (those above and those below the average for unskilled workers) would seem to suggest rather more—maybe five or six groups.

positions and offices open to all."[3] Rawls considers three different interpretations that might be offered of the formula for justifying inequality.
These alternative interpretations embody increasingly stringent notions
of the requirements of equal opportunity.

If opportunities for people to become unequal are to count as equal
opportunities, the parties must obviously be equal in some respect or
other (if only in legal standing to enter the competition). But as we
progress through Rawls's three alternative interpretations, increasingly
more must be equalized for equal opportunity to obtain. More and
more factors that make for a better or worse chance of success are ruled
out until, by the third interpretation, all inequalities, however they
come about, are treated as morally arbitrary. The alternatives are
named by Rawls (i) the system of natural liberty, (ii) liberal equality,
and (iii) democratic equality. I shall present in this section the progression that Rawls traces from one to the next.

THE SYSTEM OF NATURAL LIBERTY

The conception with which Rawls begins corresponds closely to that
which one finds in Adam Smith's *The Wealth of Nations*. According to
this, any distributive outcome is just if it is arrived at by exchange on a
free market. Each person owns his own labor power (there can be no
slavery or serfdom) and there are no arbitrary barriers to advancement:
there is "a formal equality of opportunity in that all have at least the
same legal right of access to all advantaged social positions."[4]

Rawls is vague about how the initial allocation of property rights is
to be made in the system, though in this he does no more than echo
advocates of the system themselves. (From Locke to Nozick there is a
long and disreputable tradition of using a fairy story about the way in
which acquisition might have occurred as the basis for a defense of the
status quo.) However, the important point for Rawls here is that, once
the system has been in operation for some time, the distributive outcomes in any given period will depend on the "initial distribution of
assets" at the beginning of the period, and this will be "strongly influenced by natural and social contingencies."[5] As Rawls explains:

> The existing distribution of income and wealth, say, is the cumulative effect
> of prior distributions of natural assets—that is, natural talents and
> abilities—as these have been developed or left unrealized, and their use
> favored or disfavored over time by social circumstances and such chance

contingencies as accident and good fortune. Intuitively, the most obvious injustice of the system of natural liberty is that it permits distributive shares to be improperly influenced by these factors so arbitrary from a moral point of view.[6]

Rawls in this passage mentions three factors that influence "distributive shares." These are "natural talents and abilities," "social circumstances," and "such chance contingencies as accident and good fortune." The distinction that Rawls makes here between "accident and good fortune" and other determinants of outcomes is in accordance with ordinary usage. We commonly ascribe some things that work out to people's advantage to "accident and good fortune" but not everything. To say that something is accidental or fortunate is normally to suggest that almost exactly the same causal sequence might have produced a much better or much worse outcome. A close shave is lucky; the less close the shave the less we are inclined to talk of luck. Thus, if a plate glass window fell into the street from the top of a tall building just seconds after you passed the spot where it landed, you would no doubt count yourself extremely lucky; but you would feel far less impressed with your good luck if you had passed the same spot an hour before. Yet it is surely just as "arbitrary from a moral point of view" to escape by seconds as by hours. Either way it is not a matter of personal merit to escape, nor would it have been a reflection of any personal failing to be hit.

It is important to recognize that for Rawls all three factors—natural talents and abilities, social circumstances, and accident and good fortune—are equally within the realm of the morally arbitrary. Although he follows common usage in distinguishing "accident and good fortune" from other sources of high social and economic standing, Rawls's deeper claim is that all three sources are equally matters of "accident and good fortune."

LIBERAL EQUALITY

An alternative conception that closes some of the loopholes in the system of natural liberty is described by Rawls as a system of "liberal equality."[7] This adds to the lack of formal barriers to entrance encompassed in the system of natural liberty "the further condition of the principle of fair equality of opportunity."[8] Thus,

assuming that there is a distribution of natural assets, those who are at the
same level of talent and ability, and have the same willingness to use them,
should have the same prospects of success regardless of their initial place in
the social system, that is, irrespective of the income class into which they are
born. In all sectors of society there should be roughly equal prospects of
culture and achievement for everyone similarly motivated and endowed. The
expectations of those with the same abilities and aspirations should not be
affected by their social class.[9]

I believe that Rawls is here tracing out a quite genuine progression of
ideas that is both logical and chronological.[10] The idea of equal opportunity begins, as he says, with the slogan of "careers open to talents."[11]
This calls for the abolition of formal barriers to entry: for example, the
opening up of positions in the civil service to all who qualify on the
basis of competitive examinations, instead of their reservation to members of an hereditary aristocracy and, perhaps, their protégés. But it
does not include the notion of an equal opportunity to acquire those
qualifications.

At the next stage, formal educational barriers are attacked: limitations of elite education to members of a certain religious denomination,
for example. At this point the focus shifts to the inability of many parents to pay for education for their children, so first schooling becomes
free and then there is at any rate some pressure for it to be equally good
in all parts of a country without regard to the wealth of the catchment
area of any school. Economic limitations on the ability of those who
qualify to go on to higher education will also come under fire at this
stage. The ideal of equal opportunity at this point is accurately described by Rawls as follows: "Chances to acquire cultural knowledge
and skills should not depend on one's class position, and so the school
system, whether public or private, should be designed to even out class
barriers."[12]

Now in practice there is probably no country that has completely
equalized the quality of schooling, measured in terms of the physical
facilities and the quality of the instructors, but some have got close
enough to make it apparent that educational attainment would not be
equalized by equalizing the quality of the schooling. Nor, after all, is
this surprising since children spend only a fraction of their time in school
and are already highly differentiated in relevant ways by the time they
start attending school. Moreover, at a cost of some millions of dollars
sociologists discovered the rather obvious fact that a large part of the
educational environment of a child consists of the other children in the

school. Given the tendency of people in a neighborhood within any city to have similar education and cultural backgrounds, this entails that (at any rate in urban areas) the effects of individual parents on their children's prospects will be multiplied by the likelihood that the other children will have similar parents. Nothing short of scattering children at random over an entire metropolitan area could avoid this.

The ideal of equal opportunity began by being related in a rather obvious way to that of fairness: given two people one of whom is more qualified for a job than the other, it is unfair that the more qualified should be ruled out in virtue of, say, parentage. We can here talk of the "accident of birth" because we are, in the context, treating the relative qualifications as nonaccidental features of the candidates. We can say that parentage is a "morally arbitrary" fact about them because we have a firm grip on the contrast we want to make with what is "morally relevant," namely, their qualifications.

The same distinction between what is morally relevant and morally arbitrary can be traced, though it of course falls in a different place, as we take equally able students at some point in their careers and ask whether they have equally good opportunities to go further. The ability is the "morally relevant" factor and such things as the parents' income or the location of the school are by contrast "morally arbitrary." However, if we push this idea further and further back, we finish up by saying that everything (except genetic endowment) that makes for greater or less success is a denial of equal opportunity. Everything that happens to people during their lifetimes that can affect their subsequent success goes into the "morally arbitrary" side and the only thing that is left as "morally relevant" is the physical human being at the moment of birth—or, one should say, at conception, since such things as the mother's diet during pregnancy can make a difference. By the age of a few weeks, the more or less stimulating nature of the infant's environment will (according to what I take to be the current thinking) have made more or less of a contribution to the development of its neural processes and it will be well along the path of the differentiated development that is "morally arbitrary."

Rawls recognizes and draws attention to this implication. His initial statement of the conception of justice as liberal equality, which I quoted above, is not completely explicit. He says that there should be "the same prospects of success" for those who are "at the same level of talent and ability and have the same willingness to use them," and he also uses (apparently as alternative expressions of the same ideas) the phrases

"similarly motivated and endowed," and "same abilities and aspirations." One might read this as allowing for parental or, more generally,
social influence on at any rate part of what is to go on the "morally
relevant" side, since it seems hard to imagine that motivation, aspiration, or willingness to use one's talents is (entirely) genetically determined.

This would, however, be to misconstrue Rawls's intentions. The passage I quoted began with the words: "assuming that there is a distribution of natural assets." This is crucial. For, on the basis of what he
goes on to say a little later, we should recognize that Rawls wants to
draw a distinction along the line of "natural assets" versus environmental effects, and to identify equality of opportunity with the complete
absence of differential environmental effects. We should thus read
Rawls as referring to the (assumed) genetic component in motivation,
aspiration, and willingness to use one's talents when he says there
should be equal prospects of success for those who are equal in these
respects.

This becomes clear when Rawls says that

> the principle of fair opportunity can be only imperfectly carried out, at least
> as long as the institution of the family exists. The extent to which natural
> capacities develop and reach fruition is affected by all kinds of social condi-
> tions and class attitudes. Even the willingness to make an effort, to try, and
> so to be deserving in the ordinary sense is itself dependent upon happy family
> and social circumstances. It is impossible in practice to secure equal chances
> of achievement and culture for those similarly endowed, and therefore we
> may want to adopt a principle which recognizes this fact and also mitigates
> the arbitrary effects of the natural lottery itself.[13]

DEMOCRATIC EQUALITY

Once one has identified equal opportunity with the elimination of all
factors except that of genetic endowment, it is fairly easy to see the
attraction of the final move, which is to ask why we should regard
equality of opportunity so conceived as fair. As Rawls puts it, "even if
[the liberal conception] works to perfection in eliminating the influence
of social contingencies, it still permits the distribution of wealth and
income to be determined by the natural distribution of abilities and
talents . . . and this outcome is arbitrary from a moral perspective."[14]

Equality of opportunity for zygotes that have the capacity (with identical environments pre- and post-natally) to become identically successful within the educational system and then in achieving lucrative and

rewarding careers is, after all, a pretty bizarre notion of equal opportunity, even though we seem to be driven to it by a series of inexorable steps.

 . At about the time Rawls was writing *A Theory of Justice* Christopher Jencks expressed much the same idea in *Inequality*, in relation to education attainment. I quote him because he brings out more clearly than does Rawls the underlying idea of equal opportunity that is operative here and points out how strange it begins to seem once one reflects on it:

> One inevitable result of eliminating environmental inequality would be to increase the correlation between IQ genotype and IQ scores. Indeed, this is often a conscious objective of educational policy. Most schools try to help students with high "native ability" realize their "potential." In effect, this also means eliminating the unfair advantage of students who have unpromising genes but come from stimulating homes. The idea seems to be that inequality based on genetic advantage is morally acceptable, but that inequality based on other accidents of birth is not. Most educators and laymen evidently feel that an individual's genes are his, and that they entitle him to whatever advantages he can get from them. His parents, in contrast, are not "his" in the same sense, and ought not to entitle him to special favors. For a thoroughgoing egalitarian, however, inequality that derives from biology ought to be as repulsive as inequality that derives from early socialization.[15]

Since we are already at this stage dealing heavily in counterfactuals to define equal opportunity, there is an obvious final step: we go to equal opportunity for zygotes irrespective of their genetic potential. But equal opportunity so conceived is, in effect, equal opportunity for beings behind a veil of ignorance with Rawls's specifications: equal opportunity for human beings stripped of all identifying characteristics, either genetic or environmental. As Rawls explains his strategy, his object in going through the alternative conceptions was "to prepare the way for the favored interpretation of the two principles so that these criteria, especially the second one, will not strike the reader as too eccentric or bizarre."[16] (The second principle, in its most general formulation, we may recall, was that "social and economic inequalities are to be arranged so that they are both (a) reasonably expected to be to everyone's advantage, and (b) attached to positions and offices open to all.")[17] Democratic equality is the only interpretation of this principle "which does not weight men's share in the benefits and burdens of social cooperation according to their social fortune or their luck in the natural lottery."[18]

What exactly does the conception of "democratic equality" come to?

What can be meant on the present understanding by the slogan "Equal opportunity for all"? We are to rule out, as lying in the realm of the morally arbitrary, all advantages or disadvantages, whether genetic or environmental.

It is surely plain then that equal opportunity for entities that are not in any way distinguishable from one another can be nothing other than equal prospects of success for all. The third conception of equal opportunity thus amounts to equality of outcomes.

There is, indeed, an obvious sense in which, from behind a veil of ignorance, everyone has an equal opportunity (that is, an equal probability) of being anything, however the unequal outcomes actually come about in real life. But since these inequalities of outcomes are all, on the "democratic" conception, morally arbitrary, we should plainly be misrepresenting Rawls's whole idea by calling this equality of opportunity.* Rawls tries to guard against the interpretation of equal opportunity as equal chances in a lottery by insisting that people in the original position are not disembodied choosers awaiting embodiment but real people (or representatives of real people) denied certain information. He tries to argue that because of this the choice of principles in the original position is not to be construed as a simple maximizing choice under uncertainty. But the consensus of critics has been that the logic of choice in the original position exerts an inexorable pressure for modeling the choice in exactly that way. Hence my suggestion that we would do better to go straight to Rawls's underlying moral intuitions and scrap their formulation in terms of choice in an original position.

---

* One way of putting the essential point is that a "natural lottery" is not somehow made fair by our presenting it in a light in which it might be thought of as a real lottery. An inadvertent *reductio* was provided by James S. Fishkin in his *Justice, Equal Opportunity, and the Family* (New Haven, Conn.: Yale University Press, 1983). He imagined "a lottery system at birth that randomly assigned babies to families" and suggested that "equal life chances, in a quite precise sense, would result from the arrangement. For the random assignment of newborn babies to families would serve to equalize life chances when judged from the perspective of newborns before the lottery. Any newborn infant's chance of reaching any highly valued position would be precisely equal to that of any other newborn infant" (p. 57). Fishkin's only objection to this is the severe impairment of family autonomy that it would entail. But surely there is something very weird about a notion of equal opportunity such that a system of unequal opportunity (e.g., massive differences in life chances depending on one's parentage) could be magically transformed into one of equal opportunity simply by switching babies in their cradles and leaving everything else the same. Suppose it turned out that this kind of switching had in fact been carried out secretly in some country marked by great inequalities of opportunity in the ordinary sense. Once we found out about the random switching of babies would we be in the least inclined to say, "So there was really equal opportunity all along but we didn't know it"?

CONCLUDING COMMENT

Rawls, it is worth noting, has two partly different routes from equal opportunity to equality. The primary way, which is the first he puts forward and the more watertight, runs as follows: (1) the (liberal) ideal of equal opportunity is that all environmental differences that affect occupational achievement should be eliminated; (2) this will entail that all remaining differences are of genetic origin; but (3) if (as is assumed) the case for eliminating environmental differences is that they are morally arbitrary, all we should be doing is making occupational achievement rest on genetic factors which are (in exactly the same sense) morally arbitrary; therefore (4), since what is morally arbitrary should not affect what people get, differences in occupational achievement should not affect incomes.

This is the argument that has been discussed so far. The second, which is by way of being an afterthought in Rawls's sequence of presentation, runs as follows. Point (1) is as before: the ideal is to eliminate all environmental differences that affect occupational differences in achievement. The new premise is (2) that this ideal cannot be realized, or at any rate cannot be realized without unacceptable inroads into personal liberty. The conclusion (3) is that as a second-best solution occupational achievement should not affect incomes.

The two lines are not of course incompatible and it is perfectly reasonable for Rawls to put both forward. But discussions of Rawls often proceed as if he had only the second line of argument,[19] and it is, I think, worth making clear that Rawls is not in fact saying that if we could only achieve equality of opportunity (in the very strong sense put forward) all would be well. He is saying that *everything* about the sources of differential occupational achievement is contingent and morally arbitrary.

Fishkin is, in the passage I quoted, assuming equal genetic endowment, so that at birth it will be true (in the sense that each faces the same gamble) that each has an identical prospect of success in life. For each has the same chance of being assigned to any of the environmental conditions available and these (by hypothesis) will make all the difference to the level of achievement reached. But if that is to count as satisfying (totally, in Fishkin's view) the requirements of equal opportunity, my question is: Why shouldn't we say that, from an original position, where both genetic endowments *and* environments are still to be assigned randomly to, as it were, proto-zygotes, *any* actual distribution will be compatible with equal opportunity? For, from the original position, every proto-zygote faces the same gamble in life chances where life chances depend on the interaction of genetic endowment and environment. The answer is, of course, negative; but what that answer shows is that the underlying notion of equal opportunity on which the question is based is misconceived.

28. FROM EQUALITY TO
THE DIFFERENCE PRINCIPLE

Fundamental to the case for the difference principle is the case for the *prima facie* justice of equality. On Rawls's conception of the morally arbitrary, all differences in achievement are based on morally arbitrary factors. Perhaps the most plausible presentation would be to talk of three lotteries: there is the natural lottery, which distributes genetic endowments; there is the social lottery, which distributes more or less favorable home and school environments; and then there is what Hobbes called "the secret working of God, which men call Good Luck"[20]— the lottery that distributes illnesses, accidents, and the chance of being in the right place at the right time. Let us now add the principle that what is morally arbitrary should make no difference to how well people do in terms of primary goods. Then there is no case at the most basic level of justification for anything except equality in the distribution of primary goods.

How, within Rawls's theory, do we get a move away from equality of incomes to the difference principle? The usual analysis invokes the original position. The choice of the difference principle is then presented as the result of applying the maximin criterion for choice under conditions of uncertainty.[21] This undoubtedly has solid textual support, and chapter 3 of *A Theory of Justice*, "The Original Position," is largely devoted to setting out the argument. The section of the book entitled "The Reasoning Leading to the Two Principles of Justice" is particularly explicit in presenting the difference principle in this way. In the course of it Rawls says that "the original position has been defined so that it is a situation in which the maximin rule applies."[22] I have already said that I do not think this argument gets anywhere, and I shall expand on the point later, in section 41. What I am concerned with here, however, is to draw attention to an alternative line of argument, which can be found in chapter 2 immediately following the analysis of equal opportunity discussed in the previous section.

Very roughly, the argument runs like this. Let us start from a position of equality. Now imagine a series of successively more unequal societies. Everyone stands to gain from at any rate some degree of inequality, because production will increase (presumably due to incentive effects and so forth) and the increased product can be distributed in a way that improves everyone's prospects. But the limits of permissible inequality are reached when the prospects of the worst off reach their highest point. Any greater inequality than that does not meet the requirement that everyone gains.

Now it is plain that, if the criterion of everyone gaining from inequality is to generate the difference principle, some special sense of the words is going to be required. For if we were to stipulate only that everyone must be better off with inequality than equality, this condition might well be met by a whole variety of economic arrangements. Thus, the requirement might be met by a society that was more unequal than is called for by the difference principle: one where the worst off were less well off than they might be but still better off than with equal incomes. The difference principle picks out the most egalitarian of all the Pareto-optimal arrangements satisfying the requirement that everyone should gain from inequality. The question is whether there is any plausible way of showing that this particular distribution is the one required by justice.

I want to begin by looking more closely at the first element in Rawls's move from equality to the difference principle, namely, the notion that if everyone gains from an inequality it is irrational not to prefer the situation with the inequality in it to the one without it. It will not, I hope, have escaped notice that the move envisaged by Rawls—from an equal distribution of income to an unequal one from which everyone gains—corresponds to the move from the strict solution to the extended solution in the analysis of the resourcist solution put forward in section 10. We can, I believe, learn a good deal about the problems that Rawls faces in developing the difference principle by reflecting on the move from the strict to the extended solution. It will, therefore, be worth taking a little time to recapitulate the rationale and definition of the extended solution.

It may be recalled, then, that our initial resourcist solution to the problem of Matthew and Luke entailed that any allocation of playing time should give an equal amount of time to each man. With the structure of preferences given by Braithwaite, this solution got to the Pareto frontier with no difficulty: all the available playing time was simply divided equally between Matthew and Luke. But I then changed Luke's preferences so that he preferred silence to any equal distribution of playing time. With silence as the nonagreement baseline, this meant that our solution would produce an outcome of silence. But the preferences attributed to Luke also had the implication that there were unequal combinations of playing and listening (weighted in his favor, of course) that he would have preferred to silence. Matthew's preferences, as given by Braithwaite and left unchanged in this modification of the case, made any combination of playing and listening—including listening on every evening—preferable to silence. The Pareto frontier lying to the northeast of the nonagreement point therefore consisted of all those (unequal) combinations of playing and listening preferred by Luke to silence.

Thus, the nonagreement point, which was the outcome picked by our solution, lay within the Pareto frontier. To deal with this I dubbed the initial solution—equal amounts of playing time or no playing at all—the "strict solution." And I proposed that we should allow the possibility of an "extended solution" taking off from it. The extended solution should consist, I stipulated, of any Pareto-optimal outcome preferred by both parties to the strict solution.

Now let us turn to Rawls. Rawls has two principles of justice, whose initial (and most general) statement runs as follows: "First: each person is to have an equal right to the most extensive basic liberty compatible with a similar liberty for others. Second: social and economic inequalities are to be arranged so that they are both (a) reasonably expected to be to everyone's advantage, and (b) attached to positions and offices open to all."[23] These two principles of justice can be subsumed, Rawls says, under one master principle of justice. This "more general principle" can, he tells us, "be expressed as follows":

> All social values—liberty and opportunity, income and wealth, and the bases of self-respect—are to be distributed equally unless an unequal distribution of any, or all, of these values is to everyone's advantage.[24]

And he adds the telling assertion: "Injustice, then, is simply inequalities that are not to the benefit of all."[25]

The parallel to the move from the strict to the extended solution comes out especially clearly when, just after this, Rawls says:

> Imagine, then, a hypothetical initial arrangement in which all the social primary goods are equally distributed: everyone has similar rights and duties, and income and wealth are evenly shared. This state of affairs provides a benchmark for judging improvements. If certain inequalities of wealth and organizational powers would make everyone better off than in this hypothetical starting situation, then they accord with the general conception.[26]

This is, I think, as clear as statement as one could hope for of the general idea underlying the move from the strict to the extended solution. We take an equal distribution as being a just one in the first instance: it provides a "benchmark." Nobody can be asked to accept a less preferred outcome to the one defined by this benchmark, however much others might gain from such a move. But if it is possible to "make everyone better off" then it is legitimate to make a move from the benchmark. The only remaining question is how to pick a unique outcome from those that make everyone better off than an equal distribution, and the difference principle is, as we know, supposed to provide the answer to this question.

In the rest of this section I shall trace through two alternative ways of getting from the general idea that inequalities from which everyone gains are justifiable to the conclusion that the worst off are to be made as well off as possible. For the present purpose I shall take for granted that "better off" means the same as "having more income." Questioning that assumption would take us into issues of great complexity. I shall postpone their analysis until I offer a full-dress discussion of income distribution in Volume III of this *Treatise*.

FIRST ARGUMENT

Suppose there are only two groups in a society, defined by their higher and lower productive capacities. We may now imagine that each group has a representative whose job it is to advance the collective interests of that group. The representatives are to negotiate an agreement on a principle that is to govern inequalities in their society. The rule under which they are to work is as follows. They are to start from the benchmark of equal incomes. They are then to pass in review societies marked by gradually increasing departures from equality. At each stage, either of the representatives can veto a move to a further stage of inequality. The degree of inequality that will arise from this procedure will then be the largest amount that neither of the representatives objects to.

As we have seen, Rawls assumes that a move away from equality will result in an increase in total production and that at any rate some degree of inequality will increase the incomes of both the better-off and the worse-off group. In the initial stages of increasing inequality, therefore, we are to suppose that the representatives of both groups will agree in moving ahead. At a certain point, however, the prospects of the worse-off group will decline as inequality increases, although the prospects of the better-off group continue to improve. (Notice that if the prospects of the better-off group declined while those of the worse-off group improved, this could not be an increase in inequality.) At the point where the prospects of the worse-off group decline, there is a conflict of interest between the two groups, but the worse-off group prevails by virtue of the decision-procedure, which gives the representative of each group a veto over shifts to greater inequality.

Now it is apparent that what we have just done is to derive the difference principle for our two-group society. For the degree of inequality picked out by the procedure is precisely the one that maximizes the prospects of the worse-off group. At the same time we have given a specific sense to the notion that "everyone must gain" from an inequality such that it generates a unique solution. Up to the point where the prospects of the worse-off group decline from a further increase in inequality, everyone is gaining in the sense that both groups are gaining. Beyond that point it would no longer be true to say this. The better off would be gaining but the worse off would be losing from a further dose of inequality.

Now it may, of course, be asked what is the rationale for setting up the whole procedure in this way. There is, I think, no suggestion that the procedure is not loaded. But the bias toward equality stems from the *prima facie* justice of equality. In other words, if the argument presented in the previous section is accepted, so that any inequality is automatically suspect, it does seem reasonable to say that each step away from equality must be freely authorized by every section of the society, and that is what the procedure in effect guarantees.

There is, however, a snag. I have presented the argument for two groups but, as we saw in section 26, Rawls envisages some number of groups like four, five, or six. Now as soon as we get more than two groups, it is possible that the same procedure will generate a result that is not the difference principle. Imagine that there are three groups in the society. As inequality increases, it could be that the expectations of the middle group turn down before those of the worst-off group. The procedure described before fails to produce the difference principle in this case. If we give the representatives of each group a veto on increasing inequality, the middle group's representative will use it to stop the move to more inequality at the point where the expectations of the middle group turn down, and this will be a point at which the expectations of the worst-off group are still rising. Thus, the outcome will be a more egalitarian society than that which would be recommended by the difference principle.

Rawls notices this possibility and says, correctly, that the problem would not arise if a condition he defines as "chain connection" holds.

This is the condition that the expectations of all groups move up with increasing inequality to the point at which those of the worst-off group turn down. The argument is now back to where it was before, but only for societies that are in fact characterized by chain connection. I believe that in modern societies chain connection probably does hold, and that even if in some particular case it does not hold we should find it well-nigh impossible ever to show that it does not. But it would take me too far out of my way to argue this here. Rawls himself does not offer an opinion about the likelihood that chain connection will be violated by modern societies. He leaves open the possibility that it never holds, in which case the derivation of the difference principle we have just presented would never have any application. But he says that even where chain connection does not hold, the difference principle should still be applied: "those who are better off should not have a veto over the benefits available for the least favored. We are still to maximize the expectations of those most disadvantaged."[27] This obviously suggests that Rawls has an argument for the difference principle that does not depend on chain connection. The problem is to figure out what it is.

The reason why this is a problem is that almost all the arguments put forward in chapter 2 of A Theory of Justice to establish the difference principle do in fact depend on the assumption of chain connection for their persuasiveness. Thus, there is a section on "The Tendency to Equality" which consists almost entirely of subsidiary arguments for the difference principle; but nearly all of them suffer from the weakness that they presuppose chain connection.[28] Nevertheless, I believe that Rawls has one argument here that does not depend on chain connection for its general validity. This presents the difference principle as an embodiment of the idea of fraternity.[29] It can be supplemented by extracting from other of Rawls's arguments elements that survive the withdrawal of the assumption that chain connection holds.

SECOND ARGUMENT

Without making any claim that I am following Rawls in detail, let me simply put this second argument as persuasively as I can. Suppose, then, that chain connection does not hold and we are at the degree of inequality where the expectations of some group above the bottom turn down although the worst off would still benefit from more inequality. We have to keep in mind all the time that the whole analysis is founded on the moral arbitrariness of any departure from equality: inequality can be justified only on the ground that it is rational for representatives of all social positions to accept a certain amount. Now, as we have seen, the scenario so far followed permits any representative to veto an increase in inequality if his group stands to lose from it. The question that has to be raised here is whether the representative of the worst-off group has a legitimate argument against a setup in which another group's representative can frustrate the maximization of the worst-off group's expectations.

What might the argument look like? I suggest that the representative of the worst-off group might try this: "You all accept the moral primacy of equality. You agree that nobody has a ground-floor claim of justice to finish up with a higher income than anybody else. But then there can surely be no morally well-founded claim to check the increase in inequality at a point where the expectations of a group above us reach a maximum. For the extra amount that those people are getting at that point over what we are getting derives from morally arbitrary advantages. They cannot therefore reasonably keep all of those gains if by giving up some of them we could be made better off. Since all inequalities are morally arbitrary, it should be the worst off who determine how great they should be. For at the level of inequality where the worst off are doing as well as they can, the rest of you will still be doing better, so you can have nothing to complain of. That some of you might have done better still at a point of greater equality than that which maximizes our expectations is neither here nor there. It is just as irrelevant as is the fact that most of you would do better at a point of still greater *inequality* than that which maximizes our expectations."

This is, it seems to me, an argument of the right general shape. That is to say, it does not employ (and indeed explicitly repudiates) the criterion that "everyone must gain from an inequality" in the sense given by the notion of successive Pareto improvements; but at the same time it drives toward the difference principle uniquely rather than simply requiring that "everyone must gain" in the loose sense that everyone must get more with inequality than without it. What it turns on is, in effect, the claim of the worst-off to paramount importance in determining the justice of alternative departures from equality.* The question is where that claim comes from.

---

* The idea that the worst-off should have a paramount claim in determining the just set of arrangements appeared in two articles by Steven Strasnick, who coined the term "the dictatorship of the worst off" ("Social Choice and the Derivation of Rawls' Difference Principle," *Journal of Philosophy* 73 [1976]: 85–99; and "The Problem of Social Choice:

To answer that question I must revert to the crucial role that is played by the idea that what is fundamentally just is equality and that departures from it reward features that are morally arbitrary. Critics of that idea will, of course, go on to criticize the difference principle. But if one accepts the premise (at least for the sake of argument) then it seems to me quite reasonable to say that in justifying inequality all that matters is to justify it to the worst off. And the best justification is that they could not be any better off. (Recall that "the worst off" are a large group with a single representative.) Those who are better off than the worst-off group have no moral standing for any complaint on the ground that they might under alternative arrangements be even better off. For the only reason for their being permitted to be better off than some others at all is that this is necessary in order to benefit the worst off.

It may be recalled that the difference principle was to satisfy the criterion that "everyone must gain" from an inequality in some sense beyond that of creating a Pareto improvement on equality. We have seen how the argument from successively more unequal Pareto improvement works. It can, I think, reasonably be said to meet the demand. Can this second line of argument for the difference principle meet the same demand? I think it has to be confessed that the sense in which the criterion that "everyone must gain" gives rise uniquely to the difference principle is a bit strained. What can be said is simply this. The worst off gain as much as they possibly can gain from inequality, so they have no reasonable complaint; and the rest gain even more than the worst off, so *they* have no reasonable complaint. Thus, all groups gain as much as they can reasonably demand.

If the argument so stated is not regarded as compelling, I do not know how to make it more so. It seems to me that, where chain connec-

---

Arrow to Rawls," *Philosophy and Public Affairs* 5 [1976]: 241–73). Once we have the premise that the worst off should determine (in a self-interested way) the outcome, the difference principle emerges immediately (provided we define expectations purely in terms of income), and I do not think that Strasnick's social-choice framework does anything to illuminate this point. Rawls himself, in an article subsequent to *A Theory of Justice*, explicitly introduced the idea of the worst off having a veto on any move away from equality. "Because they start from equal shares, those who benefit least (taking equal division as the benchmark) have, so to speak, a veto. And thus the parties arrive at the difference principle. . . . Among [free and equal moral] persons, those who have gained more than others are to do so on terms that improve the situation of those who have gained less" ("The Basic Structure as Subject," in Alvin I. Goldman and Jaegwon Kim, eds., *Values and Morals: Essays in Honor of William Frankena, Charles Stevenson and Richard B. Brandt* [Dordrecht: Reidel, 1978], p. 64).

tion holds, the argument in favor of moving from equality to the different principle is a good deal stronger, because each group really does gain continuously as we proceed through successively more unequal hypothetical societies to the one picked out by the difference principle. Nevertheless, the idea that any move away from equality must be justified by what it does for the worst off seems to me an appealing one, if one accepts the premise that inequality is at best a necessary evil.

We must be careful, however, not to misunderstand the sense in which inequality is a necessary evil for Rawls. The point is that it is permissible only insofar as it makes the worst off as well off as they can be made. But to that extent it really is permissible: it is not a second-best form of justice. The acceptance of inequality is not a concession to the "strains of commitment," for example. Now, several critics have urged that Rawls cannot coherently take this position. They say that if everyone accepted the argument for the *prima facie* justice of equality that we looked at in section 27, incentives would not be needed because everyone would agree that it is just to work for the same income as everyone else. There would therefore be no room for a move from equality to inequality; and the final word on justice would be that it mandates an equal distribution of income. Conversely, if the legitimacy of inequality is accepted, this, the critics suggest, contradicts the premises on which the argument for the *prima facie* justice of equality is based. The case for the difference principle, which depends on the *prima facie* justice of equality, thus collapses. Rawls has never, it seems to me, addressed himself to this line of attack. I believe that a satisfactory defense of Rawls's consistency can be given, and that therefore the exposition in this section can stand as it is. Rather than hold up the discussion at this point in order to substantiate my claim, however, I have decided to put my defense of Rawls in Appendix C, on "Economic Motivation in a Rawlsian Society."

29. WHY A COOPERATIVE VENTURE?

According to Rawls, "a society is a cooperative venture for mutual advantage. . . . Principles of social justice . . . provide a way of assigning rights and duties in the basic institutions of society and they define the appropriate distribution of the benefits and burdens of social cooperation."[30] The argument for the difference principle analyzed so far in this chapter has not, however, made any mention of this restriction on its scope, and it is hard on the face of it to see how any such restriction can fit in with the notions about the moral arbitrariness of natural and social advantages on which that argument relied. Indeed, Rawls himself, in explaining why we need distinctive principles for the justice of the basic structure, might be thought to have made the case for extending the application of the principles beyond the internal affairs of societies.

Thus, in his Dewey lectures, Rawls stipulated that the theory of justice is a theory for what he calls "a well-ordered society." This is a "closed system," which means that "there are no significant relations to other societies" and that "all are born into it to lead a complete life."[31] The main implications that Rawls draws are as follows. First, since a society is a natural association (as against a voluntary, purposive one), which recruits its members typically by birth, it has no defining needs of its own: its only common aim—not a substantive one—is to put into effect a public conception of justice.[32] And, second, since people normally live in one society for their whole lives, it is the basic structure of that society that determines their life prospects. People's prospects depend on their social origins, their realized natural endowments, and the chance opportunities and accidents that have shaped their personal history.[33] "The primary subject of justice . . . is the basic structure of society. The reason for this is that its effects are so profound and pervasive, and present from birth."[34]

In "The Basic Structure as Subject" Rawls adds, presumably as a comment on Robert Nozick's so-called utopia, that the basic structure should not "permit arrangements that would be just only if emigration were allowed" since "this structure is to be viewed as a scheme into which people are born and expected to lead a complete life."[35] The import of this is perhaps obscure but I believe the thought underlying it is something like this. Suppose we had a whole lot of societies which one could apply to join at (say) the age of majority, and that movement were without personal, social or financial cost. And suppose that some of these societies allowed great inequalities, rewarding success hugely and letting the unsuccessful starve to death, while others were more equal. This set of arrangements would eliminate one objection that can legitimately be made against existing societies that are more unequal than would be endorsed by the difference principle. For it would now be possible to say with a straight face to those who did very poorly in a society whose inequalities violated the difference principle that they had taken their chances voluntarily. But this arrangement would be objectionable for a different reason. The more unequal societies would presumably attract disproportionate numbers of the talented and would obviously be unattractive to the permanently sick or disabled. There would thus be a typical problem of adverse selection familiar to all insurance schemes that allow people to opt in on the basis of known characteristics.* We can, indeed, see the phenomenon at work in the United States, where those states with relatively generous levels of welfare provision find welfare recipients from the rest of the country migrating to them.

Now it seems to me that everything Rawls says about people being born into and living in particular societies points toward making the application of the difference principle universal. People are, after all, born into the world and almost everybody up till now has died on it. Moreover, it is surely far more plain that there is no substantive end uniting the world than that there is no substantive end uniting any particular society. Rawls could of course say that this is true but that his theory is intended to hold only for those societies (contemporary liberal ones, I suppose) for which the description might be thought to hold true. But the world as a whole is surely, on this criterion, the most uncontroversial field of application for the principles of justice.

Rawls is quite right to emphasize that we need distinctive principles of justice to take account of the unique features of a basic structure. And he is in particular absolutely right to insist that we cannot hope to get anywhere by asking what would be a fair way of dividing up the proceeds of some small-scale cooperative enterprise and employing the answers as a yardstick for social justice. To suppose that justice in societies must be small-scale justice writ large is to commit an elementary fallacy. We need principles for the basic structure that make due allowance for the way in which people are born into certain positions that carry with them a certain range of prospects for living a healthy, prosperous, and satisfying life. But it is precisely because of

---

*A simple illustration of adverse selection at work is provided by the medical insurance system at the California Institute of Technology, which could be matched at many other places in the United States. The employees are offered a choice of three schemes. One service is so overextended and inconvenient that it is attractive only to the young and healthy, which enables it to be very cheap. At the other end is the kind of insurance scheme that allows choice of physicians, surgeons, and so on. It is subscribed to only by those who have well-founded expectations of needing a lot of high-quality medical care. Being "experience rated," it has premiums of horrendous proportions. The other scheme falls in between, in coverage and accessibility and in cost. Thus, the effect of offering a choice of policies is to undermine the principle of insurance itself, which is to spread risks over a large group. Essentially, Caltech employees are divided into three groups, differentiated by health status, whose members form separate insurance pools.

this that there is no reason for restricting the sphere of distributive justice to "societies." The basic structure of the world—the institutions that (by omission and commission) define differential life chances—is no less open to criticism on the basis of the principles of justice than is that of any single country. It is surely obvious that among the most important things that determine people's prospects—including the elementary one of their chance of surviving to celebrate their first birthday—is the country in which they are born.

The background condition for the application of the difference principle would thus seem to be the existence of institutions that determine life chances. However, Rawls has continually insisted on more. Thus, in the Dewey lectures he wrote: "We assume that, as an on-going society, the scheme of social and economic activities set up and framed by the basic structure is productive and fruitful. This implies, for example, that a well-ordered society does not have a manna economy, nor are its economic arrangements a zero-sum game in which none can gain unless others lose."[36] Now, in the general sense that there can be no gain for anyone unless someone else loses, it would be true of any economy that was on the Pareto frontier that it was zero-sum. But such an economy could of course be the kind of productive one that Rawls wishes to apply the difference principle to—indeed, the difference principle is precisely a principle for picking out one point on the Pareto frontier. In the strict sense of "zero-sum," that there is a fixed amount going, it is hard to see how it can refer to any economy other than a manna economy (that is, less poetically, one in which all the goods are supplied from outside), since there seems to be no reason why, if goods are produced by the people themselves, they should not be able to produce more or less depending on what they choose to do.

Suppose, anyway, that we have for some reason a fixed amount available for consumption. What is the rationale for saying that this is not a kind of situation to which the principles of justice apply? I can find none, and, oddly enough, Rawls at one place in A Theory of Justice seems to concede that there is none. Buried in the middle of a discussion of envy we find the remark that if people viewed "the aggregate of social wealth" as "more or less fixed" so that "the social system" was regarded as a "zero-sum game," then "it would be correct to think that justice requires equal shares. Social wealth is not viewed as the outcome of mutually advantageous cooperation and so there is no fair basis for an unequal division of advantages."[37] Quite so. It is not that the principles of justice have no application in a zero-sum economy but simply that the difference principle does not separate out from a criterion of equality in such an economy.

The point is simply that the strict solution lies on the Pareto frontier so there is no room for a move to the extended solution. As Rawls put it, "The two principles [of justice] express the idea that no one should have less than they would receive in an equal division of primary goods, and that when the fruitfulness of social cooperation allows for a general improvement, then the existing inequalities are to work to the benefit of those whose position has improved the least, taking equal division as the benchmark."[38] Thus, in comparison with an equal distribution we can indeed say that "the difference principle is. . .a principle of mutual benefit."[39] The more productive do better than the less productive but their gains are justified because part of their production is siphoned off for the benefit of the less productive.

What must be stressed here is that, if we look at it this way, mutual advantage is to be reckoned from the initially just solution of an equal distribution. There is simply no need to refer to what people could obtain independently. To see the irrelevance of this, we have only to think of a society in which there were no "gains from cooperation," in the sense that no more was produced by working together than by working separately. The case for the *prima facie* justice of an equal division of the total product would be unaffected, and the argument for moving from there to the difference principle would likewise still take exactly the same form.

Suppose that on the island inhabited by Crusoe and Friday the only economic activity is picking coconuts, and that there is no more efficient organization than for each to work on his own. Suppose also that, because he damaged a leg in the shipwreck, Crusoe is far less productive than Friday. The case for an equal distribution as the benchmark would still operate, and so would the possibility that Crusoe might do better by letting the more productive Friday get more than an equal share of the total. Obviously, nothing turns here on the possibility of interaction that living together affords to Crusoe and Friday: the only contact they have to make is whatever is necessary for organizing the optimal redistribution. So long as goods could be shipped, it would make no odds if they were on different islands. Indeed, this would enable us to make the case even clearer.

Those who wish to discredit the notion of distributive justice often argue from the supposedly axiomatic premise that if there were two self-sufficient islands with no relations between them we could not pos-

sibly say that there was any injustice in the situation, even if all the
people on one were much richer than all those on the other. Suppose
that Crusoe and Friday, now on two desert islands, work equally hard
and equally skillfully, but that there is a great difference in their production entirely due to one island's being fertile while the other is barren.
Plainly, if anything can be called morally arbitrary—not reflecting any
credit or discredit on the people concerned—it is this difference in the
bounty of nature. If we accept Rawls's argument for "democratic equality" (as against "natural liberty" and the "liberal conception") that I
presented in section 27, we shall extend the reasoning and say that, even
if the differences in prosperity flow from differences in the quality of
what economists call "human capital," the greater prosperity of one
than the other still derives from a morally arbitrary advantage. But the
essential point is that if we agree in rejecting the justice of inequalities
based on morally arbitrary advantages, we cannot combine it with the
proviso that redistribution can occur only among those engaged in
fruitful cooperation.

Although I hesitate to call it an argument, Rawls suggests at one
point in *A Theory of Justice* that the limitation of the difference principle to those who stand in cooperative relations with one another is
somehow tied up with the claim that justice is predicated of institutions
rather than particular allocations. This means, he says, that "the correctness of the distribution is founded on the justice of the scheme of
cooperation from which it arises and on answering the claims of individuals engaged in it."[40] The implication is that we can judge a distribution only by seeing how it came about: did it arise from the operation of
the rules defining a just basic structure? We cannot simply ask what
would be the just distribution of "a given stock of things to definite
individuals with known desires and preferences."[41]

In saying this Rawls is pretty obviously here striking at the way in
which philosophers frequently discuss the problem of dividing up a
cake (or, if they are of a classical bent, allocating a flute to one of several
claimants) without asking elementary questions such as: Who supplied
the materials, who made it, and what gives this philosopher the authority to decide who should get it anyway? This is made explicit when he
contrasts his kind of distributive justice, which is defined in terms of the
basic structure, with what he calls "allocative justice." This, he says,

> seems naturally to apply when a given collection of goods is to be divided
> among definite individuals with known desires and needs. The goods to be
> allotted are not produced by these individuals, nor do these individuals stand

in any existing cooperative relations. Since there are no prior claims on the things to be distributed, it is natural to share them out according to desires and needs, or even to maximize the net balance of satisfaction. Justice becomes a kind of efficiency, unless equality is preferred.[42]

The claim that justice is institutional is put together with the claim that its scope is delimited by the extent of "existing cooperative relations" in the following passage:

> In justice as fairness society is interpreted as a cooperative venture for mutual advantage. The basic structure is a public system of rules defining a scheme of activities that leads men to act together so as to produce a greater sum of benefits and assigns to each certain recognized claims to a share in the proceeds. What a person does depends upon what the public rules say he will be entitled to, and what a person is entitled to depends on what he does. The distribution which results is arrived at by honoring the claims determined by what persons undertake to do in the light of these legitimate expectations.[43]

It seems to me, however, that we could agree to conceive of distributive justice as institutional without having to draw the conclusion that its scope should be confined to cooperative ventures for mutual advantage. The invocation of a "greater sum of benefits" (presumably from cooperating rather than going it alone) is quite gratuitous. There is no reason for saying that people can be covered by common institutions only when these yield a "greater sum of benefits." An institution can operate perfectly well in the absence of any cooperative relations. All that is required here is a system for transferring income.

We can see this by thinking again about Crusoe and Friday. Suppose they are engaged in entirely independent production, and that each begins by keeping what he produces. The difference principle, introduced here, will almost certainly not bring about "a greater sum of benefits" measured in aggregate production. In general we may expect that total production will decline with its introduction. The justification for making the change is, of course, nothing to do with any of this but derives from the comparison with an equal distribution. (As Rawls himself says, just distribution is to take priority over the maximization of total production.) Now, as far as I can see, the point that just distribution is to operate through general institutions has no bearing on this, because the difference principle would, obviously, operate by means of a set tax and transfer scheme to which the members of this small society would adapt their behavior. Exactly as Rawls says, they would develop legitimate expectations about what they were entitled to under the prevailing set of rules.

We can apply this to international distribution. A global difference principle would not, any more than a national one, entail taking a stock of existing goods and making specific allocations to individuals. It would operate, just as a national one would, through a set of general rules establishing property rights, tax rates, criteria for transfers, and so on. Yet it could perfectly well work out, as with Crusoe and Friday, that total world production would be greater if, instead of being taxed at high rates to provide transfers to the majority of poor people in the world, the rich countries kept the whole of their national incomes, as (with trifling exceptions) is the case now. Once again, this would not invalidate the moral case for international redistribution based on the kinds of arguments discussed in section 23. And I do not see that the procedural/allocative distinction does anything to impugn that conclusion.

30. WHY MUTUAL ADVANTAGE?

If we press the question of why justice has to be confined to those who are engaged in cooperative relations we cannot long escape the conclusion that the driving force behind it is the idea that everyone must gain from justice. A zero-sum relation is one in which whatever one party gains the other loses, so if justice mandates a transfer from one to the other it cannot be advantageous to both. Justice must be productive if it is to be mutually beneficial.

That Rawls holds such a view should already be clear from the discussion in chapter 5 of his adhesion to the doctrine of the circumstances of justice. And I think that the arguments in that chapter about international and intergenerational justice should suffice to show the problems that it gives the principles of justice when they are extended beyond contemporaries who belong to the same society. I want now, however, to redeem the pledge I made in chapter 5 of showing how the requirement that all should stand to gain from justice undermines the difference principle even in the favored case of fellow-citizens. The reason why Rawls does not see the problem is that he believes it is enough to salvage the difference principle to show that everyone stands to gain from it, in comparison with some relevant alternative. I shall suggest that, even if they do, this is not enough.

Rawls's general statement of the context within which principles of justice are developed is an exposition of what I have called a two-stage theory of justice.

> There is an identity of interests since social cooperation makes possible a
> better life for all than any would have if each were to live solely by his own
> efforts. There is a conflict of interests since persons are not indifferent as to
> how the greater benefits produced by their collaboration are distributed, for
> in order to pursue their ends they each prefer a larger to a lesser share. A set
> of principles is required for choosing among the various social arrangements
> which determine this division of advantages and for underwriting an agree-
> ment on the proper distributive shares.[44]

Putting this into the terminology of Part I, Rawls tells us to pick the
noncooperative baseline defined by what each party can obtain independently. ("Social cooperation" is contrasted with what "any would
have if each were to live solely by his own efforts.") And we are told
that a theory of justice is a solution concept that specifies how the gains
that are to be made by moving from the baseline to the Pareto frontier
are to be divided. (Justice is concerned with the way in which the
"greater benefits produced are distributed," where "greater" here must
mean "greater than each could obtain working alone.")

The use that Rawls proposes to make of all this comes out very well
when he asks what could be said to defend the difference principle, first
to someone who does badly under it, and second to someone who does
well under it. The reply to one who does badly is, as we saw in section
28, that if others did not do better he would be even worse off.[45] It is the
reply to one who does well that is of interest here. This goes as follows:

> The difficulty is to show that A [the well-off representative person] has no
> grounds for complaint. Perhaps he is required to have less than he might
> since his having more would result in some loss to B [the less-well-off repre-
> sentative person]. Now what can be said to the more favored man? To begin
> with, it is clear that the well-being of each depends on a scheme of social
> cooperation without which no one could have a satisfactory life. Secondly,
> we can ask for the willing cooperation of everyone only if the terms of the
> scheme are reasonable. The difference principle, then, seems to be a fair basis
> on which those better endowed, or more fortunate in their social circum-
> stances, could expect others to collaborate with them when some work-
> able arrangement is a necessary condition of the good of all.[46]

Clearly, all of this invokes a baseline of noncooperation in comparison with which all are to gain. But what exactly is this baseline? One
suggestion opened up by this reply is that the class of those with talent
gains from the cooperation of the class of those who lack talent. In the
context this is most naturally read as calling for a comparison between
what the better off get under the difference principle and what they
could get if the less well off withdrew their cooperation—that is, if they

simply did not form part of the economy. Now it is of course possible that the better off under the difference principle would be worse off if the less-well-off section of the community withdrew their labor. Clearly, in the short run this would be true, as the crippling effects of strikes by manual workers attest. But if we allow enough time for adjustments it seems quite reasonable to suppose that, with the difference principle in operation in both situations, the representatives of the three upper quartiles could all be made better off if they could expel those making up the bottom quartile of the income distribution. For it is surely plausible to suppose that, if the difference principle is being rigorously applied in the complete society, the bottom group will be receiving more in income than they add to total production.

Whether or not this is so (and I am aware that I am bypassing all kinds of problems of measuring what an individual or group adds to the total social product) is not of any great importance in the present context. What really matters is that, if once we start to think that it is relevant even to ask what is the contribution of different social groups to the national income and how it compares with what they get out of it, we are bound to wonder why we are still applying the difference principle as our distributive criterion. The underlying idea on which we are building is clearly no longer that of neutralizing morally arbitrary natural and social advantages. Rather, it would seem to be that justice is done when the distribution of income is such that there is no coalition that could do better for itself economically by withdrawing with a per-capita equal share of the society's nonhuman productive assets—capital goods, natural resources, etc. *

It is fairly clear that allowing the withdrawal of whole blocs from the society to define alternative nonagreement points would pose severe dangers to the claim that the difference principle is better for (almost) everyone than they could do in the absence of cooperation. It might therefore reasonably be thought that this interpretation of the test cannot be one that Rawls will have anything to do with. But there is actual-

---

* If we follow John E. Roemer (*A General Theory of Exploitation and Class* [Cambridge, Mass.: Harvard University Press, 1982], esp. chap. 7) in defining different conceptions of exploitation according to the way in which they characterize the assets that coalitions are permitted to take with them when they withdraw, we can say that a society that is just on the criterion I put forward avoids capitalist exploitation because it does not let any group benefit from differential access to nonhuman resources. But it does not transcend what Marx called the "narrow horizon of bourgeois right" ("Critique of the Gotha Programme," in Karl Marx and Friedrich Engels, *Selected Works in Two Volumes* [Moscow: Foreign Languages Publishing House, 1951], vol. 2, pp. 13–45). Its slogan is "To each according to his contribution."

ly some evidence to suggest that he has it in the back of his mind even though he never, as far as I know, sets it out openly.

I have argued that we cannot be sure that the most talented sector of the population might not be better off withdrawing from the rest and taking in one another's washing. This could be doubted, I admit. Perhaps they would do better to stay in, and live under the economic institutions called for by the difference principle. But what if all the members of a society were to withdraw except those who suffered from congenital disabilities severe enough to ensure that they would never be productive members of society? Such people can clearly only be a net drain on the society's resources throughout their lives. It can hardly be doubted that the rest of the society could do better by withdrawing and leaving them behind.

Now although Rawls does not discuss precisely this case he does say in the Dewey lectures that we are to assume "that all citizens are fully cooperating members of society over the course of a complete life. This means that everyone has sufficient intellectual powers to play a normal part in society, and no one suffers from unusual needs that are especially difficult to fulfill, for example, unusual and costly medical requirements."[47] It should be said that Rawls goes on to admit that "care for those with such requirements is a pressing practical question." But his theoretical commitments come out when he remarks that "at this initial stage, the fundamental problem of social justice arises between those who are full and active and morally conscientious participants in society, and directly or indirectly associated together throughout a complete life."[48]

If we start from the basic ideas that were used in section 27 as the underpinnings of the difference principle, it must seem quite bizarre to claim that people who enjoy less than rude health (mental and physical), and especially those afflicted with a disease that gives rise to "unusual and costly medical requirements," create peculiar difficulties for a theory of justice. Such conditions are, we might think, the paradigm of the kind of undeserved misfortune whose translation into actual disadvantage Rawls describes as arbitrary from the moral point of view. From the perspective of justice as impartiality, it would seem that the issues raised by incapacity and disease are clear and central. We might be inclined to reverse everything Rawls says and suggest that what is obscure and difficult, best left aside for later treatment, is the question raised (and answered in a highly controversial way) by the difference principle, namely: To what extent are differences in productivity among people not suffering from some manifest mental or physical disability to be properly regarded as their own responsibility?

If we ask how Rawls could ever have come to believe that the theory of justice should first be worked out for relations among the healthy and able-bodied, and only then extended, if possible, to those left out of this treatment, I suggest that broadly the same answer should be given as that given to the question of why he wants to work out the theory of justice in the first instance for members of a single society who are contemporaries. Here, too, Rawls says that we should start from the clearest and most central case, and only later try to extend it. And, as we saw in chapter 5, what he does have to say about the extensions shows how much trouble they give him. In the case of justice between societies, he comes up with a set of rules that do not speak to the issue of economic distribution at all. And in the case of future generations his favored approach is to make their claims parasitic upon whatever good feelings toward them the body of those currently alive happen to have.

Curiously, Rawls does not even vouchsafe a hint of what he has in mind when he says of the restriction of justice within a society to the healthy and able-bodied that "if we can work out a theory that covers the fundamental case, we can try to extend it to other cases later."[49] However, I imagine that when I suggested that all the members of a society except the congenitally disabled would find it advantageous to withdraw, leaving them behind, most people's immediate reaction will have been to say, "But what about their families?" And this obviously suggests a possible line of extension. In exactly the same way as future generations were brought in via a "motivational assumption," so might be the congenitally disabled or the medically expensive people mentioned by Rawls. This would, of course, mean that they would not have any just claims in their own right, but would simply have indirect claims by virtue of the sentiments of the principal parties to the social contract.

The only alternative that I can see to this is to abandon the contractarian approach and deal with these cases in the same way as Rawls proposed to do with nonhuman animals. It may be recalled that Rawls (unlike Richards) did not think that animals should be squeezed into the contract in the same way as he (but not Richards) thought future generations could be. Rather, "they are outside the scope of justice" but should nevertheless be treated with "compassion and humanity." (However, Rawls said that he would "not attempt to explain these considered beliefs.")[50] Clearly, it would be possible to say the same about those members of a society who fall outside the core of social justice.

It will immediately be seen that none of the three cases that Rawls identifies as troublesome for a theory of justice would present any difficulties of principle if we said that the enemy is moral arbitrariness. For a person's country, generation, and state of health (especially whether or not he suffers from congenital disability) are all bound to be high up on anyone's list of things that are relatively beyond individual control. What makes them all problematic is the doctrine of the circumstances of justice, with its underlying idea that all must stand to gain from justice.

There are, however, distinctions to be drawn between the intergenerational case, the international case, and the intrasocietal case. In the intergenerational case it is a matter of pure logic that, because future generations have no bargaining power, the nonagreement point will have to be simply the outcome of the present generation pursuing its own interests in a completely unbridled way: there is no room for gains from cooperation. In the international case, two alternative conceptions of the relevant nonagreement point suggest themselves. One is the method of selective withdrawal of countries from an international redistributive order, such as that which would be called for by a global difference principle. Rawls may have this in mind when (by his conspicuous silence on the subject) he appears to deny that international justice calls for any institutions for transferring income from rich countries to poor ones. But in international relations there is something obviously incomplete about the conception of a nonagreement point which consists of a country's withdrawing from international institutions. The nonagreement point of a Hobbesian "war of all against all" must also be acknowledged, and one might regard Rawls's endorsement of rules about nonaggression, nonexploitation, and so on as a way of proposing arrangements that all countries stand to benefit from compared to this.

I argued in section 23 that Rawls was too sanguine in thinking that the principles of international morality that he proposes would really be found mutually advantageous by all countries irrespective of power. I argued that we must take the relevant criterion to be equal gain over the nonagreement baseline, in the sense in which the Nash solution, for example, may be said to provide equal gain. Because the circumstances of justice do hold to a certain limited extent, rational prudence would support some principles of international morality—some constraints on the untrammelled pursuit of national interest. Thus, we can extract some principles of justice, with applicability to all states, from the requirement of mutual advantage in comparison with the baseline of a free-for-all. But they will reflect the underlying inequality of power relationships.

What about the intrasociety case? We have seen that the method of selective withdrawal leaves the weakest members of a society with no claims of justice. What about the alternative baseline of a free-for-all? The obvious difficulty in answering this stems from the imprecision of the alternative "possible world." However, if what we are looking for is a bargaining solution it seems hard to imagine that the congenitally disabled or the expensively sick could expect to be cut in on the deal. What would they be able to threaten to do if they were left out?

This conclusion, however, should give us pause for thought. Can the retreat be stopped there, or is it liable to turn into a rout? To see both what the danger is and why Rawls does not acknowledge its seriousness, we need to observe two points about Rawls. The first is that he does acknowledge the relevance of a nonagreement point of general egoism. The second is that he does not see the need, as a matter of consistency, to employ it in the way I have just done for the international and intrasocietal cases. His most extended discussion comes in his article "The Basic Structure as Subject," where he writes that

> we can, if we like, in setting up the argument from the original position, introduce the state of nature in relation to the so-called non-agreement point. This point can be defined as general egoism and its consequences, and this can serve as the state of nature. But these conditions do not identify a definite state. All that is known in the original position is that each of the conceptions of justice available to the parties have consequences superior to general egoism.[51]

There is a somewhat similar remark in *A Theory of Justice*:

> From the standpoint of the original position principles of justice are collectively rational; everyone may expect to improve his situation if all comply with these principles, at least in comparison with what his prospects would be in the absence of any agreement. General egoism represents this no-agreement point.[52]

What we immediately notice here is that Rawls has a conception of the nonagreement point as a threshold. In order to satisfy the demand that everyone should stand to gain from justice all we have to do is to show that abiding by principles of justice is better for everyone than a condition of "general egoism."

Now if this is all that Rawls wants to get out of the idea of justice as mutual advantage it is puzzling why he should have the qualms he expressed about the inclusiveness of the principles of justice within a society. Whatever "general egoism" may be like, Rawls apparently assumes it would be pretty awful. Yet if the only test that principles of justice have to pass is that of a two-point comparison—principles of justice versus "general egoism"—it is hard to imagine that simply including everyone in the society would push the healthy able-bodied members down to the level at which they would prefer "general egoism."

If it were simply a matter of seeing what principles could be approved of impartially and then checking to see that they are better for everyone than "general egoism" we would surely come up with principles (for example, Rawls's principles of justice) that were stipulated to apply to all the members of a society—we might even add, *especially* the disabled and those with expensive medical problems. It is because this seems so clear that I have spent some time exploring the alternative nonagreement baseline given by selective withdrawal. If we suppose that Rawls somehow wants to use both, we might be able to explain what he says.

It is worth noticing, however, that if we treat the nonagreement point of "general egoism" as a threshold that must be passed by any principles of justice, but as no more than that, we have to reopen the discussion that took place in chapter 5 on international justice. I said there (in section 23) that Rawls's principles of international morality, with their demand for the political equality and independence of all states, were too egalitarian to satisfy the requirements of mutual advantage. But I based that on the idea that, if the doctrine of the circumstances of justice is to be taken seriously, it should be construed as underwriting a bargaining solution of the kind analyzed in Part I. My complaint against Rawls's principles from this point of view was, then, that they failed to correspond closely enough to the international balance of power.

It may be recalled, however, that I also considered what would be the implications of regarding the nonagreement point of a "state of nature" as setting a threshold value which must simply be exceeded by the workings of institutions satisfying the principles of justice. I suggested that, if the consequences of unrestrained pursuit of national interest were horrendous enough (as they almost certainly would be) we could quite easily reinstate Rawls's principles of international morality. But there would be no reason for stopping there. We could no doubt go on to add large elements of international redistribution. If the only criterion is that the principles of justice have to do better than the unleashing of the superpowers' nuclear arsenals, virtually any principles, however stringent, would pass.

I argued, however, that it would violate the logic of mutual advantage to treat the nonagreement point merely as a threshold. If we are going to insist that everyone must stand to gain from justice, then this should mean that the solution will be seen as equally advantageous, compared to the nonagreement point, by all parties. So if the nonagreement point is a state of unequal benefits, this should be reflected in the solution. To be stable, in other words, the solution should reflect the bargaining power of the parties. It is not enough that they all prefer the principles of justice to the nonagreement outcome; they should prefer it to the same degree—in the appropriate sense of "same degree."

Perhaps the most forceful way of pressing the point that introducing the requirement of mutual advantage threatens to unravel Rawls's theory is to observe that it gives him the same premises as Gauthier has. And it is hard to imagine that from Gauthier's premises he can avoid deriving something like Gauthier's conclusions. Now Gauthier does not draw back from the implications of his theory of justice as mutual advantage. "Animals, the unborn, the congenitally handicapped and defective, fall beyond the pale of a morality tied to mutuality. The disposition to comply with moral constraints...may be rationally defended only within the scope of expected benefit."[53]

As Gauthier points out, his theory has nothing to say about "equalizing" or "meeting needs." As far as it is concerned "the rich man may feast on caviare and champagne, while the poor woman starves at his gate. And she may not even take the crumbs from his table, if that would deprive him of his pleasure in feeding them to his birds."[54] All that is necessary is that the poverty of the one should not have been brought about by impermissible activities on the part of the other. Poverty due to incapacity will never violate this condition, so long as the incapacity is not brought about by the rich person in pursuit of a more advantageous market position. For example, by blinding a competing artist he may be able to sell his own work for more, and that would be wrong. But if the competitor goes blind as the result of disease or accident and is unable to provide for himself, he can be left to starve to death.

Even leaving aside these extreme cases, we may well suspect that letting in the principle of mutual advantage will systematically undermine the difference principle. Gauthier himself has made this argument explicitly in an article entitled "Justice and Natural Endowment" and I shall explore that discussion here.[55] Gauthier argues that Rawls's idea of society as a "cooperative venture for mutual advantage" naturally leads, not to the third of the conceptions of equal opportunity, "democratic equality," canvassed by him, but to the second. (See section 27.) It does not, Gauthier says, lead to the first conception, the "system of natural liberty," because that would make the outcome too dependent on social contingencies such as inherited wealth, which should not go into the nonagreement baseline. It is also inconsistent with the third conception, which Rawls himself favors, because that would nullify natural advantages from which people should be allowed to reap the benefits. However, the second conception of equal opportunity, the so-called liberal interpretation is, Gauthier claims, just right. It is, in effect, the system of natural liberty modified by the elimination of gains from social but not natural advantages. It thus, according to Gauthier, responds in the way required to the differential natural endowments of people.

In making his argument, Gauthier shrewdly seizes on Rawls's assertion that the nonagreement point, defined as what everyone could get independently, is relevant because justice is about the distribution of gains from cooperation. He then observes: "This distribution cannot be expected to be equal. The persons who make up society differ in their natural endowment, and differences in natural endowment will affect differentially men's ability to secure economic goods for themselves in the condition of general egoism. Hence the 'no agreement point' will provide a different level of well-being for different persons, albeit a low level for everyone."[56]

Gauthier's next move is to draw on Rawls's concessions to the doctrine of the circumstances of justice.

> The rationale for agreement is provided by the circumstances of justice. Men "view society as a cooperative venture for mutual advantage." Through cooperation they are able to produce more of the primary goods which each wants. I shall term those primary goods produced through cooperation, the *social surplus*; it is that portion of the total quantity of primary social goods which would not be produced without cooperation. The content of the agreement men make must ensure the production and provide for the distribution of this social surplus.[57]

I think that Gauthier is correct in suggesting that the logic of what Rawls says about the nonagreement point is that only the surplus due to cooperation is open for redistribution. The next question is how this surplus should be distributed. The difference principle might still be able to make a comeback here, albeit compromised by its restriction to the distribution of the cooperative surplus. Gauthier considers this possibility and rejects it, but in a way that I think represents a falling-off from the form with which he started.

As we know, Rawls's argument for the difference principle is founded on the idea that advantages arising from natural and social contingencies are morally arbitrary and that therefore we should start from an equal distribution and then look for Pareto improvements. Gauthier simply denies this, at any rate for natural contingencies. He says that "natural inequalities are undeserved. They do not accord with desert, but equally they are not undeserved, they are not contrary to desert."[58] Applying the difference principle to the cooperative surplus would, he says, "nullify the effects of natural abilities, treating them as undeserved."[59] People should therefore, he claims, get whatever they would have at the nonagreement point. They should then share the cooperative surplus according to the criterion of splitting the difference that we saw Gauthier arguing for in chapter 1. What this comes to is that the gains over the nonagreement point should be equal in utility terms, but only when utilities are normalized so that zero is "general egoism" and unity is the "optimum social arrangement" that "each representative person can expect" with the utmost help of the rest (subject to their not themselves falling below the level of "general egoism").[60] The effect is, then, that each person gets the same relative distance from what he or she would get under a condition of "general egoism" to the most he or she could aspire to.

However, Gauthier does not make any serious effort to explain why the technique of splitting the difference gives exactly the right weight to natural inequalities, and I must confess that I find it hard to imagine how an explanation could be supplied. I believe that he would have done better to make an argument that I have already anticipated earlier in this section. This would go as follows. Once we have conceded that only the cooperative surplus is up for redistribution according to principles of justice, we have already breached the principle that gains from natural advantages should be nullified. For the inequalities at the nonagreement point are obviously derived from natural advantages. If we ask why the nonagreement point matters at all, the answer is presumably that justice must be shown to be in everyone's interest. But the implication of this is that the cooperative surplus should be divided in a way that simulates the results of rational bargaining. We can then say that the criterion of splitting the difference is the best bargaining solution. This gives us the answer Gauthier wants to reach.

Obviously, somebody who is not persuaded that splitting the difference is indeed the best bargaining solution can substitute some other according to taste. The basic line of argument would be unaffected. The essential point is that once we depart from justice as impartiality there is no way of stopping short of justice as mutual advantage, and this entails a bargaining solution. All we have to add is the scarcely deniable point that the difference principle is not by any stretch of the imagination a plausible candidate for a bargaining solution.

Gauthier's own attempt to suggest the implications for a society of his favored solution is not of any significance to this discussion of objections to the difference principle. But it is relevant to the larger themes of this book, as will become clear in chapter 9. I shall therefore conclude the present section by looking at what he says on this score.

Plainly, we need to establish three things: the nonagreement payoff for each person, the maximum that each person could hope to achieve with the maximum cooperation of all the others (consistent with nobody falling below the nonagreement payoff), and a way of scaling the distance between the two so that each person is the same proportional distance between the first and the second. Remarkably enough, in "Justice as Natural Endowment" Gauthier makes absolutely no attempt to discuss how any of these might be estimated. This is no doubt prudent since I do not think that there is the faintest chance of establishing any of them. How could we conceivably hope to find out how each person would fare in the absence of any social cooperation? And how could we establish the maximum amount that any given person could expect to get, if everybody else were maximally cooperative? In a large society it would presumably be an enormous amount—surely billions of dollars in the United States, for example. But how could we begin to set about putting a number on it for each person? Finally, we would need for each person elaborate information, based on choices among hypothetical lotteries, to say what would constitute an equal normalized utility gain for each.

Gauthier rises above all these difficulties and simply asserts flatly that "it is precisely a competitive market society . . . which is characterized by the proportionate difference principle" (Gauthier's name here for splitting the difference). And, in line with the annotation allegedly found on the briefs of courtroom advocates, "Case weak here—speak louder," he says that "the answer is clear."[61] It seems that the "competitive market is the mechanism by which an optimal social surplus is produced and distributed in accordance with the contribution which each person makes" so long as there is no inheritance of wealth.[62]

Now the first and obvious objection to this is precisely the one that Gauthier deployed against Rawls, namely, that the principle which is supposed to deal with the distribution of the surplus due to cooperation is in fact operative over the whole of the product. It is surely clear that there is nothing in the way a market works to reflect what people might have got independently. A brilliant but severely handicapped person may do very well in a market society but would starve to death if he had to fend for himself. Pretty farfetched claims for the virtues of markets have been made over the years but I do not believe that anybody has ever had the effrontery to make this one.

Suppose, however, that we waive this objection. And suppose we even grant Gauthier the highly ideological claim that a market gives people an income that is in accordance with "the contribution that each person makes" in some sense other than the tautologous one that the market gives people something and we can if we like call it the contribution that each makes. We still have, as far as I can see, no grounds for establishing any connection between Gauthier's idea that each person should get the same proportion (measured in utility terms) of his maximum possible gain from social cooperation and what people get from the workings of a competitive market. There is simply nothing in the way that a market works that relates what people get to the most that they might conceivably get from the maximum cooperation of others.

In work subsequent to the article that I have been discussing, Gauthier has kept the conclusion—that a competitive market satisfies the requirements of justice—but has changed the premises from which it is derived. (Given the giant leap of faith that was needed to get from the earlier premises to the conclusion one might, indeed, reasonably deduce that Gauthier is a good deal more attached to the conclusion than to any particular premises.) His later view is like his earlier one in that it says that distributive justice is concerned only with the division of gains above a noncooperative baseline. But whereas before he envisaged, it would seem, a state of noncooperation in which the "level of well being" would be "a low level for everyone"—thus permitting a move to a cooperative, Pareto-optimal outcome from which everyone could benefit—he now envisages the noncooperative baseline as constituted by "a Lockean state of nature."[63] This is one in which there is already an entire set of institutions that create a market economy.

Since it is a theorem of neoclassical economics that (under a number of strong conditions) a competitive market is capable of reaching a Pareto optimum, it follows that no issue about the justice of the outcome of a competitive market can arise.[64] Obviously, if all of this is achieved in the absence of cooperation, and justice is concerned only with the distribution of the cooperative surplus, justice will have very little scope. In fact, its only role is to deal with externalities and public goods—with the proviso that people should not be taxed to pay for the provision of public goods more than the amount they would be willing to pay for them.

This is a nice illustration of the truth of the dictum that one person's proof is another's *reductio ad absurdum*. A market, according to Gauthier, is not "a *cooperative* venture,"[65] because it does not require any constraint on individual maximization. It is therefore "a morally free zone, a context within which the constraints of morality would have no place."[66] All this is based simply on the idea that, starting from given factor endowments, in a perfect market individuals can trade to a Pareto optimum. But the notion that this generates the conclusion that market outcomes are beyond moral criticism seems to me quite bizarre.

Justice as impartiality will provide a basis on which to say that a distribution can be unjust even if if is a Pareto optimum and arises from trading with given factor endowments. All we need to be able to claim is that the distribution would not withstand the test of impartial scrutiny. When we recall that a market distribution leaves those who lack productive capacity to starve, it is not very difficult to believe that an unmodified market distribution will stand condemned, quite apart from any objections arising from so-called market failure.

In the rest of this volume, I shall make a systematic comparison of the two approaches to justice—as mutual advantage and as impartiality—that have been identified in Parts I and II. This will try to show in detail how they work and what presuppositions they rest on.

Justice as Mutual Advantage versus Justice as Impartiality

CHAPTER VII

Some Questions
of Method

31. INTRODUCTION

Part III is partly backward-looking and partly forward-looking. It is intended to take stock of Parts I and II, pulling together in a systematic analysis a number of points that have emerged. But it is also intended to arrive at some definite conclusions about justice and to defend them. These will provide the foundation for the rest of this *Treatise*.

I shall begin in this chapter with an exploration of certain fundamental questions of method in moral philosophy. It might perhaps be thought that it is a little late in the day to be raising such issues. Would it not have been more logical to start by settling the deep issues of philosophical method at the beginning, rather than slipping in a discussion of them after a hundred and twenty thousand words have already elapsed? It should be said at once that, posed in this form, the question somewhat exaggerates the innocence of the preceding pages. A large part of what I shall be doing here is making explicit what has hitherto been implicit. But I should still like to meet the question head on. Both common experience of actual moral arguments and the record of Anglo-American moral philosophy in the past couple of decades strongly suggest that it is neither necessary nor even desirable to precede the doing of something—in this case, arguing about justice—by trying to establish general prescriptions telling one how to do it. The point is of broad applicability. Artists who derive their practice from a philosophy of art, or scientists who derive theirs from a philosophy of science, rarely come to much good. Normally the practice comes first and the philosophy attempts to make sense of it after the fact.

We all know how to engage in moral arguments, even if we would be flummoxed by being asked whether or not we subscribe to moral realism, objectivism, subjectivism, prescriptivism, or what have you. It is, moreover, noticeable how little difference is made by people's commitments to such general positions about the nature of morality when it comes down to arguing about some concrete moral question. (I refer here throughout to arguments based on secular rather than theological considerations.) Thus, everyone proposes general principles, derives more specific principles from them, tests them by examples, argues from case to case by analogy, and so on.

The accounts of what is going on here will differ, of course. One person will claim to be getting in touch with a moral reality that inheres in the nature of things; another will say that all there is to do is to attempt to bring our various judgements into a coherent whole. But these rival accounts do not apparently have distinctive implications for the practice of moral argumentation. In the course of a long life, Bertrand Russell embraced successively a number of different theories about the nature of morality but his actual moral views remained quite stable from adolescence until the end of his life. There is, I suggest, no reason for surprise at this. A new theory about something does not have to change our practice of that thing.

There are nevertheless some questions of method that have to be addressed here before I can get on with the substantive business of Part III. I can best explain how these arise by describing the object of the two chapters that come after this one. In chapters 8 and 9, then, I shall be making a systematic study of two approaches to justice. One is the two-stage approach analyzed in Part I, according to which a theory of justice has two parts, one specifying a noncooperative baseline and the other a method of dividing the cooperative surplus. Hume's theory of the origins of property, discussed in Part II, is also a two-stage theory of justice, while Rawls's view that the nonagreement point of "general egoism" should provide a threshold value commits him to what is best thought of as a half-baked two-stage theory.

The other theory of justice is one that has been discussed from time to time in both Part I and Part II but has not yet been elaborated. This is the theory that principles of justice are those principles that would be agreed upon in a certain kind of situation—dubbed by Rawls an "original position"—whose features are such that whatever is agreed upon in it should count as just. Rawls's own version of this is the best known and has been mentioned in Part II. I also, in Part I, presented Harsanyi's derivation of utilitarianism from a choice by people trying to maximize their utility in ignorance of their identities.

What these two approaches have in common is that they follow a roundabout route to specifying the content of justice. Thus, if we think of the Nash solution as an example of a two-stage theory, we can say that the decision produced by the adjudication is intended to model the outcome of two games played by the parties: a "threat game" to establish the nonagreement point, and a "bargaining game" in which the implicit threat (in a broad sense of threat) that failure to agree will result in the nonagreement payoff is supposed to drive rational bargainers to a determinate point on the Pareto frontier. And if we take Harsanyi's "proof" of utilitarianism as an example of an original-position theory, we can say that this too is a roundabout approach, also consisting of two parts. This time the first part is the description of the original position (defined by the motivations of the parties and the information available to them), and then the second part is an argument to the effect that rational actors placed in such an original position would choose a certain principle or set of principles.

Using a term introduced by Rawls, though stretching it beyond his own usage, I shall dub these indirect approaches "constructivist" theories of justice. The obvious alternative is the direct route, which would have us simply say what we think justice requires, either in general or in some particular instance. I shall call this approach "intuitionist," again using the term more broadly than many people would do. In Part I, the resourcist solution to the problem of the two musicians presented in section 10 was derived from premises that were presented intuitionistically, and in Part II I explicitly eschewed any appeal to the Rawlsian original position in working through the argument for the difference principle. Instead, I followed the exposition in chapter 2 of *A Theory of Justice* in which the attempt to derive principles from a choice in the original position played no essential part. As may be recalled, the key move there lay in establishing the initial justice of an equal distribution of income, and this rested on two claims: that natural or social advantages making for greater productivity should not translate into more income if their source lies outside people's control; and that all natural and social advantages making for greater productivity are beyond people's control. We might say that the first claim represented a moral intuition and the second a very broad empirical (or perhaps metaphysical) proposition.

In the next three sections of this chapter I shall first fill in the thumbnail sketches I have just given of the two methods and their subvarieties, and then I shall say something about the relations between the two methods.

32. INTUITIONISM

Intuitionism is often understood, with a good deal of historical justification, as a theory of moral knowledge. According to this, intuition is a mode of apprehending a moral reality. It is akin to sense-perception but its object is a "nonnatural" realm of objects: moral truths. G. E. Moore is, I suppose, the person now most readily identified with this view but, with or without the actual term "intuition," it has been common enough before and after him. As the word "intuition" is commonly used nowadays among moral philosophers, however, it does not necessarily carry any such portentous epistemological baggage along with it. To say that one has an intuition that it would be wrong to do such-and-such in a certain situation seems often to mean no more than that one has a strong conviction to that effect, which one finds it hard to believe that one could be induced to give up by any process of argumentation.

Although some would say that this is a debasement of the idea of a moral intuition, I am bound to say that I can see nothing in talk about the apperception of nonnatural qualities but an elaborate way of thumping on the table. What leads to it is the feeling that unless moral judgments are dignified in this way they will appear to be left as mere whims. I shall try to show in the final section of this chapter that such fears are ungrounded and that moral judgments can have a kind of objectivity appropriate to them—and one that fits in with the function they play in human life. (It is a long-standing puzzle how moral judgments can provide us with reasons for acting if they consist of reports about the existence of a peculiar set of objects.)*

---

* It might, of course, be said that claiming a correspondence with an external reality independent of our thought is no more than a way of thumping on the table in any context. "It is no use being told that truth is 'correspondence to reality'" (Richard Rorty, *Consequences of Pragmatism: Essays 1972–1980* [Minneapolis: University of Minnesota Press, 1982], p. 162). For a pragmatist, Richard Rorty tells us, "there is no epistemological difference between truth about what ought to be and truth about what is, nor any metaphysical difference between facts and values, nor any methodological difference between morality and science" (ibid., p. 163). Morality is no worse off than science because science is no better off than morality: "Pragmatism, by contrast [with positivism], does not erect Science as an idol to fill the place once held by God. It views science as one genre of literature—or, put the other way round, literature and the arts as inquiries, on the same footing as scientific inquiries. Thus it sees ethics as neither more 'relative' or 'subjective'

Rather than attempt a formal definition of intuitionism I shall let it emerge by giving examples from Part I. One form of intuitionism, which makes a brief appearance there, is constituted by the notion that we can give rational assent to propositions setting out formal requirements that must be met by any admissible outcome. This is the typical method of social choice theory, of which the paradigm is Kenneth Arrow's proof (in *Social Choice and Individual Values*) that several apparently innocuous constraints on the aggregation of preferences into a single ordering cannot be met simultaneously.[1] Although this approach retains some popularity among social choice theorists, it is being met with increasing and well-merited skepticism. The more we understand of the way in which seemingly weak stipulations can interact with one another to produce powerful results, the less willing we are likely to be to think that it makes any sense to suppose that we can have any worthwhile *a priori* beliefs about such conditions as anonymity or the independence of irrelevant alternatives. We are more likely to adopt the attitude of the ultracautious disputant who, asked by his adversary to agree that grass is green, replied that before conceding this he wanted to know what use the other was planning to make of the proposition.

In Part I this kind of formal intuitionism was represented by Nash's own principal rationale for his solution to the bargaining problem. This consisted of a proof that it uniquely satisfied a set of formal conditions: Pareto optimality, symmetry, the independence of irrelevant alternatives, and invariance under alternative units of utility measurement. As I pointed out, uniqueness is scarcely enough to induce us to endorse a solution. And the criteria put forward by Nash are not really self-evident, whatever else might be said in their favor. (See above, section 2, under "The Idea of a Bargaining Solution.")

General intuitionism (distinguished here from specific intuitionism, the belief that one intuits moral truths about particular cases) also takes a substantive form. A good illustration is provided by the ethical premises from which I derived the resourcist solution to the problem of the two musicians in section 10. Thus, for example, I suggested that there is

---

than scientific theory, nor as needing to be made 'scientific.' Physics is a way of trying to cope with various bits of the universe; ethics is a matter of trying to cope with other bits" (ibid., p. xliii). Nothing in this book, as far as I can see, turns on the acceptance or rejection of pragmatism à la Rorty. For the present purpose, the point to be made is simply that "intuitionism," as I shall be using the term, is intended to straddle realist and nonrealist views about the status of moral intuitions.

a strong intuitive appeal to the principle that, in the absence of any special claim, the fair division of a scarce resource will be the one that gives equal amounts of it to each of the claimants. The utilitarian principle that aggregate utility should be maximized and its variants (such as maximin utility or a trade-off between equal distribution and amount of utility) are also sometimes put forward as fundamental intuitions. As Harsanyi's work shows, however, they can also be arrived at within a constructivist framework.

In his discussion of intuitionism in *The Methods of Ethics*, Henry Sidgwick said that "in order to settle the doubts arising from the uncertainties and discrepancies that are found when we compare our judgments on particular cases, reflective persons naturally appeal to general rules or formulae: and it is to such general formulae that Intuitional Moralists commonly attribute ultimate certainty and validity."[2] But he also noted a tradition of intuitionist thinking, which he dated back to Socrates, according to which

> just as the generalisations of physical science rest on particular observations, so in ethics general truths can only be reached by induction from judgments or perceptions relating to the rightness or wrongness of particular acts. . . . [Socrates] discovered, as we are told, the latent ignorance of himself and other men: that is, that they used general terms confidently, without being able, when called upon, to explain the meaning of those terms. His plan for remedying this ignorance was to work towards the true definition of each term, by examining and comparing different instances of its application. Thus the definition of Justice would be sought by comparing different actions commonly judged to be just, and framing a general proposition that would harmonise with all these particular judgments.[3]

As a description of Socrates' methods, in the form represented by the Platonic dialogues, this leaves a good deal to be desired. In the *Republic*, for example, Socrates is shown as being more concerned to show that his interlocutors' ideas about justice are confused than to construct a theory that will accommodate the particular judgments that he elicits from them. But this is by the way. What Sidgwick offers as a conception of the intuitionist method is one that seems to have a recurrent appeal. As Ronald Dworkin has described this conception, "concrete intuitions of political morality in particular situations . . . are clues to the nature and existence of more abstract and fundamental moral principles, as physical observations are clues to the existence and nature of fundamental physical laws."[4] As Dworkin notes, this "analogy between moral intuitions and observational data" implies that we might on occasion "suppose that direct observations, made through a moral faculty, have outstripped the explanatory powers of those who observe."[5]

This model seems to me, however, to be one entirely driven by the analogy with a (rather naive) picture of science in which one collects a set of data points and then looks around for some generalization that fits the points—for example, a mathematical function that connects them. I find it hard to believe that anyone really regards principles simply as hypotheses put forward to explain a mass of particular intuitions. It is, all the same, quite true that puzzling over examples forms a large part of the practice of moral philosophy.

What alternative account of what is going on can we offer? I suggest something like this. We start from some principle that is assumed to be correct at any rate over a central range of cases, and then we try it out on other cases that are in some way more problematic. If we do not like the implications of the principle as originally stated when it is extended to these cases, we do not simply abandon it but seek to reformulate it so that it will accommodate the new judgments we are inclined to make.

Principles are given content in the process of applying them to particular cases. Until we see how a principle would work out in a variety of cases, we can hardly be said to know what the principle is, so it does not make a lot of sense to assent to it. In this respect, what I said about formal criteria such as the independence of irrelevant alternatives applies with considerable force to substantive principles as well. That is why in section 10, having put forward the resourcist solution to the problem of the two musicians, I worked through several variants on the original story to show how the solution would come out when it was applied to them.

There is, however, this important difference between formal and substantive principles. Whereas I do not believe that anyone can have worthwhile intuitions about the independence of irrelevant alternatives, we quite reasonably believe that there is a core of cases where it would be wrong, for example, not to tell the truth or return what one had borrowed. It does not matter that we cannot say in advance what the exceptions are. And it does not matter that we are unable to state the more general principle from which it would follow that most of the time we should tell the truth and return what we borrow but occasionally not. It is a profound misunderstanding to suppose that a principle with a core of clear application is somehow compromised or undermined if we cannot set it out in full generality.

If I am right about the way in which principles and examples are related in moral discourse, the scientific model of inductive ethics is quite inappropriate. Normally, it seems to me, even if we cannot state precisely the considerations that move us to reach a certain conclusion in a particular case, we are by no means at a loss to say what is their general nature. To make use of the well-worn Wittgensteinian example of asking someone to show the children a game: when, returning after a time, we find them playing poker and say "I didn't mean that kind of game," we do not have to be able to claim that we had in our minds, when we first spoke, a definition that excluded poker. Nor do we have to be able to come up with one now. But equally we do not have to resort to running through a long list of other games and then hazarding a hypothesis to cover the series of yesses and noes before we can say in general terms why poker was the wrong sort of game.

Unfortunately, the model of moral intuitions as akin to observations has infected some philosophers and fellow-travelers. A good example from Part I is provided by Braithwaite's remark in his discussion of the Nash solution that the division of time between Matthew and Luke that it generates "seems to me clearly unfair to Luke." We would surely like to know why, if a two-to-one split in favor of Matthew (as recommended by Braithwaite's own theory) is fair, a thirteen-to-one split (as recommended by Nash for the same payoffs) is "clearly unfair." As I said in section 4, Braithwaite's remark suggests that he has some sort of direct intuition about what constitutes a fair division of the time, against which he is prepared to test solution concepts such as his own and that of Nash. But then it must be, I believe, the germ of an independent theory of fair division. As a mere data point it seems to me to have no value whatever.

Nash's theory is an example of a constructivist theory, and, as this case illustrates, a constructivist theory may produce answers that fail to accord with our particular intuitions. (The same may be said of Braithwaite's own theory, of course.) I shall want to ask later in this chapter how constructivist and intuitionist approaches are related. Before that I shall present constructivism itself.

33. CONSTRUCTIVISM

The term "constructivism" was first used by Rawls in print, as far as I am aware, in his Dewey lectures on "Kantian Constructivism in Moral

Theory," which were delivered and published in 1980. Curiously, Rawls does not in these lectures acknowledge the innovation. Rather than beginning by explaining what constructivism is in general and then differentiating the Kantian variant, he plunges straight in and talks as if the notion itself were familiar so that all we need to know is what is special about Kantian constructivism.[6] In a way somewhat reminiscent of that in which *A Theory of Justice* unfolds, we have to wait until the middle of the first lecture for a general characterization of constructivism.

The treatment of constructivism in the middle of the first lecture is significant for the connection it makes between the notions of constructivism and of pure procedural justice. Here Rawls explains the sense in which his theory is one of "justice as fairness," by saying that

> justice as fairness begins from the idea that the most appropriate conception of justice for the basic structure of a democratic society is one that its citizens would adopt in a situation that is fair between them and in which they are represented solely as free and equal moral persons. This situation is the original position: we conjecture that the fairness of the circumstances under which agreement is reached transfers to the principles of justice agreed to; since the original position situates free and equal moral persons fairly with respect to one another, any conception of justice they adopt is likewise fair. Thus the name: "justice as fairness."[7]

Although Rawls does not actually use the term "constructivism" here, we can see that a construction is involved in the determination of principles of justice. We are to create (or, more precisely, to imagine the creation of) a certain kind of choice situation—an "original position"— such that whatever principles are chosen in it will be just.

Rawls emphasizes—and this is of cardinal importance for the comprehension of constructivism—that the point is not supposed to be that we already have a substantive conception of justice and are looking around for a way of implementing it. In that case all the work in moral philosophy is done by the time we have the conception of justice. Thus, in dividing a cake, "if equal division is taken as fair, then we simply require the person who cuts it to have the last piece."[8] In fact, there are plenty of ways of getting a cake sliced into equal parts, such as asking a third party to do it or simply having the allocation made by one of the beneficiaries who is not a crook.

Rawls contrasts the choice of institutions to implement "an independent and already given criterion of what is just (or fair),"[9] which he calls perfect or imperfect procedural justice, with "pure procedural justice." The distinctive feature of the latter is that the operation of the institution itself establishes the content of justice.

> Now the original position, as described, incorporates pure procedural justice at the highest level. This means that whatever principles the parties select from the list of alternative conceptions presented to them are just. Put another way, the outcome of the original position defines, let us say, the appropriate principles of justice. . . . The essential feature of pure procedural justice, as opposed to perfect procedural justice, is that there exists no independent criterion of justice; what is just is defined by the outcome of the procedure itself.[10]

Although we still have no reference to constructivism here, Rawls does immediately after this draw an explicit connection between pure procedural justice and construction, telling us that "the use of pure procedural justice implies that the principles of justice themselves are to be constructed by a process of deliberation, a process visualized as being carried out by the parties in the original position."[11]

Since Rawls never, as far as I can see, defines constructivism (as against Kantian constructivism), it is hard to say exactly what he intended to mean by the general term. But for my own purposes I should like to define a constructivist conception of justice in the following way. I shall set two conditions. First, then, I want to keep a link with the notion of pure procedural justice by stipulating that there must be a theory to the effect that what comes out of a certain kind of situation is to count as just. "What comes out" might be a principle, a rule, or a particular outcome. Justice can be predicated of any of these, and the point is that we can derive its justice from its having emerged from the situation. A "situation" is specified by a description of the actors in it (including their knowledge and objectives) and the norms governing their pursuit of their objectives: what moves are to be legitimate. And the "emergence" is to be a particular kind of emergence, namely, the result of the actors in the situation pursuing their given objectives within the given constraints.

That is a necessary condition of a constructivist conception of justice but not a sufficient one. The second requirement is that the constructing is to be done by a theorist and not by the people in the situation themselves. Suppose, in other words, that in some instance a situation of the kind described actually exists and the people in it actually produce a result—a principle, rule, or outcome, as the case may be. Then pure procedural justice is satisfied but there is no construction.

Rawls would, I believe, endorse the idea that not all pure procedural justice is constructivism. In fact, it is, I believe, only with the "Kantian Constructivism" lectures that he has begun to speak of the kind of hypothetical operation represented by "justice as fairness" as an example of pure procedural justice at all. Hitherto he had been more inclined to contrast them. Thus, in "The Basic Structure as Subject," he wrote:

> the agreement in the original position represents the outcome of a rational process of deliberation under ideal and nonhistorical conditions that express certain reasonable constraints. There exists no practicable way actually to carry out this deliberative process and to be sure that it conforms to the conditions imposed. Therefore, the outcome cannot be ascertained by pure procedural justice as realized by deliberations of the parties on some actual occasion. Instead the outcome must be determined by reasoning analytically: that is, the original position is to be characterized with sufficient exactness so that it is possible to work out from the nature of the parties and the situation they confront which conception of justice is favored by the balance of reasons. The content of justice must be discovered by reason: that is, by solving the agreement problem posed by the original position.[12]

I think that the reason why Rawls took this line was that he misled himself by a "one-sided diet of examples," namely, an overattention to the peculiar case of a lottery, where it is of the essence that fairness means randomness. Obviously in the case of a lottery it makes no sense to second-guess the actual procedure. All we can say is that whatever the lottery actually produces is fair, so long as the lottery is conducted fairly. In *A Theory of Justice* we can see Rawls introduce the concept of pure procedural justice, illustrate it with the sole example of gambling, and then generalize the conclusion to all procedures. He concludes his discussion by saying: "What makes the final outcome of betting fair, or not unfair, is that it is one which has arisen after a series of fair gambles. A fair procedure translates its fairness to the outcome only when it is actually carried out."[13]

Obviously, it is true that there is no room for a constructivist theory of the outcome of a lottery. But in other cases we can talk about what rational actors would bring about in the specified conditions, and this is a constructivist solution to a problem of pure procedural justice. It is plain that, since Rawls now does speak all the time of the original position as a setting for pure procedural justice, he has backed off the claim I quoted from *A Theory of Justice*. (It should be noted that Rawls does not refer to justice as fairness as a case of pure procedural justice in *A Theory of Justice*. This strongly supports the contention that he must have changed his mind since.) The upshot is that we should think of two kinds of pure procedural justice, actual and constructivist. Actual procedural justice is inherently *ex post*: we wait for the procedure to be used and dub the actual outcome just. Constructivist procedural justice is a matter of deducing (or speculating about) what rational actors would bring about.

It should be noted that constructivism (as against Rawls's conception of Kantian constructivism) omits a stipulation that Rawls sets great store by, namely, that it must be possible to characterize the situation from which justice emerges as itself fair. (This is, of course, the essence of the slogan "justice as fairness.") I do not want to make this a part of the definition of a constructivist theory. Rather, I shall treat it as defining one large branch of constructivist theories. Constructivism in general is, I shall say, the doctrine that what would be agreed on in some specified kind of situation constitutes justice. Whether the situation itself has to be characterized by fairness for the outcome to be just is left as an open question.

In defense of this wide definition I can offer two arguments. First, if we want to retain the link between constructivism and the tradition of social contract theory, we should certainly not insist that the situation within which agreement defines the content of justice must itself pass some ethical test. Hobbes, to give the obvious example, would have denied vehemently that the justice of keeping covenants reflected any fairness in the situation giving rise to the agreement. Indeed, he emphasized that covenants entered into out of fear are valid—the one setting up the sovereign being an example.

Second, as we have seen in chapters 5 and 6, Rawls himself flirts with the doctrine of the circumstances of justice, and I think that the notion that what would be agreed upon in the circumstances of justice constitutes justice should indeed be included within the scope of constructivism. It clearly fits my own definition of constructivism in that we eschew any independent criterion of justice and say that the agreement itself creates the content of justice. Yet the circumstances of justice are not plausibly represented as satisfying any requirements of fairness. All we can say about the circumstances of justice is that they are circumstances in which it is possible for justice—that is, some rules or principles restraining the direct and uninhibited pursuit of individual self-interest—to be mutually advantageous. Thus, for example, there must be a minimal degree of equality, in the sense that if somebody can get everything he wants without giving up anything in return there is no way in which restraint can be advantageous to all. But this is not saying much, as is evident when we recall that a Hobbesian state of nature is a paradigm of the circumstances of justice in operation.

Constructivist theories of justice, I wish to suggest, fall into two categories, defined by the nature of the situation within which agreement is to be reached. In one category we have those that rest on the circumstances of justice. Here, we have a nonagreement point which is constituted by the interaction of the parties' self-interested endeavors. Each seeks to do as well for himself as he can and the result is a noncooperative payoff. Provided the circumstances of justice hold, the parties can all gain by moving away from the nonagreement point. (This follows directly from the definition of "circumstances of justice.") There is thus a cooperative surplus to be gained, and a constructivist theory of justice must give some account of the way in which it would be divided by ideally rational bargainers.

The other category of constructivist theories is comprised of those that rest on what I shall call (to parallel the circumstances of justice) the circumstances of impartiality. These theories start from the idea that the choosing situation must be characterized by features that somehow ensure that the choices made will (in some sense) take an equal account of the interests of all the parties. Rawls, of course, has his own specific ideas about the requirements that an original position must satisfy if it is to be fair between the parties, and he also has his own proposals about the way in which these requirements of fairness can be built into the specification of an original position. But, as Rawls himself says, one should not identify the general idea of an original position with his own list of requirements or his own specification of the appropriate motives and informational constraints. I shall therefore say only that the second category of theories comprises those that require an original position somehow embodying the circumstances of impartiality.

If it is asked whether these two forms of constructivist theory are united at some deeper level, a positive answer might be given by saying that both are in a broad sense of the term contractualist. What would be meant by this is that in both versions a lot of weight is placed on what the parties would themselves agree on in some hypothetical situation. Thus, we can show some relation between both forms of constructivist theory and the tradition of social contract theory. I throw this idea out for what it is worth, but I should offer the cautionary note that it should not be pressed too far. The theories are what they are, and it would be a mistake to imagine that the notion of contractualism provides a key to understanding them in any terms except their own.

Thus, two-stage theories most obviously fit the ordinary conception of a contract. That is to say, we have a state of affairs that will obtain unless a contract is made, and the parties anticipate some advantage to themselves from the contract. But, as may be recalled from chapter 1, only one strand in two-stage theorizing insists that the way to move to the Pareto frontier is to simulate the outcome of bargaining by rational agents. The other imposes on the move the ethical injunction that the parties should gain equally (according to some metric). The notion here is that the contract must be a fair one, as far as the move from the nonagreement baseline is concerned. (The nonagreement baseline itself is taken as given.) We are still at liberty to say that such a theory is contractualist—it does retain the essential aspect of a contract in that all stand to gain in relation to the nonagreement payoff—but we should be clear that there may be parties who think (perhaps rightly) that they could have done better for themselves through exploiting their bargaining power.

When we come on to original position theories the connection with ordinary contracts is a good deal more attenuated. In all versions, the notion of mutual advantage over a noncooperative baseline—which one might think of as the essence of contract—is missing. And, as we shall see in more detail in chapter 9, the two main types of original position theory in different ways further violate the usual conditions of contract.

In one version, the parties pursue their own advantage (so far as good), but they are deprived of any information that would enable them to individuate their own interests from those of others. The ordinary notion of contract is that the parties have conflicting interests: what would be the ideal outcome for one (such as getting the other's house while keeping his own money) is different from what would be the ideal outcome for the other (such as keeping his house while getting the other's money). The contract represents the terms of a *quid pro quo*. Each gives up something in exchange for something from the other that is deemed to be of greater value. (For example, the house is exchanged for money.) But in an original position defined by—among other things, perhaps—lack of information about personal identity, everyone ranks alternative outcomes in the same order. There is thus agreement, but no bargaining.[14]

In the other main version of original position theory, the parties do know who they are, and have conflicting interests (so far so good), but we now have a different assumption about their motivation. Instead of supposing that each is pursuing his own interest as best he can in the choice of outcomes, rules, or principles, we now attribute to the parties the desire to reach an agreement on reasonable terms. Exactly what "reasonable" means here will have to be explored in some detail in the proper place. But for the present purpose let us simply emphasize that it is to be taken as standing for some criterion other than means-end rationality. Very roughly, we may say that reasonable terms are those that everyone, looking at the matter impartially, can accept. We can if we like say that what comes out of this process (assuming that some consensual decision does come out of it) represents the terms of a contract. But we must then bear in mind that it does not have the usual feature of a contract: that the parties arrive at it by consulting only their own interests.

I do not want to enter into an argument about whether, when we take the points of similarity and dissimilarity into account, we should call all or any types of constructivist theory contractarian. Quite the contrary: the burden of my analysis is that it does not matter what we say on that score. What does matter is that we should understand the theories themselves. We should not start by assuming that constructivist theories must be contractualist and then distort them to fit some preconceived notion of the features a contractarian theory "must" have.

34. IS CONSTRUCTIVISM A FORM OF INTUITIONISM?

In the previous section I tried to get as clear as possible what I was going to mean by constructivism. I did not ask how constructivism as a method might be justified. I also implicitly treated constructivism as an alternative to intuitionism, but I did not ask seriously how they are related. There are, I think, three possible views about the relation between them. The first is that constructivism can be an entirely independent method. The second, at the other extreme, is that constructivism is simply a variety of intuitionism. The third is that constructivism cannot be entirely independent of intuitionism but is not entirely reducible to it either.

I can begin by dismissing the first possibility in a fairly summary way. It is easy enough to see how one might be an intuitionist of some stripe and nothing else. But I do not see how constructivism could ever be a completely self-contained moral theory. For the question that always has to be answered is: Why should I accept that the construction you propose is the right one? You can of course simply stipulate that the word "justice" is to be attached to what comes out of it, but why should I pay any attention to that?

It would seem that at the minimum it is going to be necessary to offer some general arguments to the effect that there is something about justice which enables us to assert that our construction is the right kind of construction to produce it. How to do this is a tricky problem, since we must somehow talk about justice without appealing to any particular intuitions about its content.

The only possible solution that I can see is that we must talk about the function that justice plays and claim that our construction will somehow connect up with that function. Two candidates immediately present themselves. One is that the function of justice is to enable egoists to get along better with one another. The motive for being just on this conception is simply a sophisticated sense of self-interest. In the circumstances of justice, it pays to be just. If it turns out that it does not pay, we shall have to go back to the drawing board. The principles of justice will have to be rejigged so as to make it true that it does pay to be just. The other candidate is that the function of justice is to provide a rational basis for agreement among people who do not simply look at things from the point of view of their own interests but seek to take due account of the interests of all. Justice, on this conception, is what can be justified to everyone, where justifying something to a person means more than showing that, given the way things actually stand, it is the most he can reasonably hope to get from a collection of sophisticated egoists. It is inherent in this conception that there is a distinctively moral motive, namely, the desire to behave in accordance with principles that can be defended to oneself and others in an impartial way.

It will be apparent without any elaborate explanation how these two candidates for the function of justice fit with our two categories of constructivist theory. We represent the first one by asking what would be chosen in the circumstances of justice, and the second by asking what would be chosen in the circumstances of impartiality. But how do we decide which account (if either) of the function of morality is true? At some point, it seems, we cannot press the argument back any further. Sidgwick notoriously concluded that "Prudence" and "Rational Benevolence" appeared to him as alternative conceptions of the "ultimate end of rational action for an individual."[15] He did think that, if an egoist could be persuaded to say that "his own greatest happiness is not merely the rational ultimate end for himself, but a part of Universal Good,"[16] he might be argued into being a utilitarian. But Sidgwick admitted that an egoist need not say anything except that his own good was good for him, and that he would then be immune to any charge of inconsistency in denying the equal importance of the good of others.

It is not, I think, at all surprising that the two intuitions—I think we can legitimately call them that—which are needed to get the two forms of constructivism off the ground are so similar to Sidgwick's two fundamental intuitions about the rational basis of human action. For in the nature of the case, constructivism requires that we have only the most general characterization of morality at the outset. Otherwise the construction will not have the room it needs in which to operate. And surely the two most general starting points—the ones that leave most to fill in—are the pursuit of one's own interests and the pursuit of everybody's interests.

Can we go further than identifying the fundamental intuitions on which the two constructions rest? I think we can, and in the next (and final) section of this chapter I shall seek to do so. As Sidgwick recognized, the real issue is whether or not the bifurcation of practical reason can be defended. For the typical exponents of impartial morality, Kantians and utilitarians, concede the rationality of pursuing one's own interest. Where they differ from an egoist is in saying that this pursuit should be circumscribed by moral constraints derived from reasoning about what can be subscribed to impartially.

Sidgwick was also correct, I believe, in saying that it is not possible to refute egoism in the literal sense of showing it to be logically inconsistent. I shall in the next section discuss a more recent attempt than the one mentioned by Sidgwick to show that egoists must, on pain of self-contradiction, concede the claims of impartial morality. I shall conclude that it is no more successful. But I shall also argue that, while falling short of a proof, the considerations that it calls upon do indeed constitute powerful reasons for accepting the claims of impartial morality.

If we could really get results from nothing but the bare specification of justice as mutual advantage or justice as impartiality, it seems to me that we could confidently say that constructivism, although not independent of intuitions, was nevertheless not simply a form of intuitionism. The construction is really doing work and the way of getting from the broad intuition at the base of it to the particular implications is distinctively different from the method of casuistry. It is, of course, true that once we have the choice situation set up it is purely a matter of calculation to derive the implications. And if someone wants to insist that this makes a constructivist theory simply a way of deriving implications from general intuitions and therefore a form of intuitionism, I do not see any knock-down argument against. But I can see no intellectual advantage in saying it.

The question is, of course, whether it is possible to get constructivism off the ground with nothing more than a bare characterization of the point of morality. I believe it is fairly clear that the answer must be negative for original position theories. Mutual advantage clearly has the better chance of providing a self-sufficient basis for a construction, but I have doubts there too. It is apparent that what is in people's interest depends on what people are like, and the different answers to that question have led social contract theorists to widely differing conclusions. Are the differences between Hobbes, Locke, and Rousseau, say, differences about matters of fact alone? That is obviously a deep problem and one that I do not intend to take up. I simply observe that, to believe in the self-sufficiency of mutual advantage as a basis for a construction, one would have to be prepared to say that they are.

In the case of original position theories, it seems plain that the appeal to further intuitions is unavoidable. I should say that Rawls himself does not speak in this way about the role of intuitions in his own theory. In A Theory of Justice "intuitionism" is identified with the notion of a plurality of principles with trade-offs but no priority rules.[17] And in the third of the Dewey lectures, Rawls contrasts constructivism with "rational intuitionism," which is identified with the notion that intuitions give us news about a moral realm.[18] However, he does talk constantly about "considered judgments" or "considered convictions," which are in my terms intuitions. In an original position theory like Rawls's the specification of the choice situation will have to be justified by some substantive moral claims. In the alternative kind of construction, in which the people who are deliberating are not pursuing their own interests but trying to reach agreement on reasonable terms, I think that the notion of "reasonableness" is going to involve an unavoidable reference to intuitions. This will become clearer when I develop such a theory in chapter 9. But I can make the case about Rawls simply by referring back to Part II.

The point here is simply that Rawls is quite explicit in telling us that specific features of the original position are intended to model specific constraints on principles of justice. For example, Rawls says that it is "one of the fixed points of our considered judgments that no one deserves his place in the distribution of native endowments, any more than one deserves one's initial starting place in society."[19] This "fixed point" is in my terminology an ethical intuition of a rather general substantive kind. It is represented in the original position by denying the parties information about their natural and social advantages. The rationale for this is that the parties should not be able, consistently with justice, to make demands on one another on the strength of their natural and social advantages, and by denying them knowledge of those advantages, we can ensure that they will be unable to do so.

It is precisely Rawls's willingness to set out explicitly the intuitions underlying the construction of the original position that made it feasible to do what I did in chapter 6. There I took the intuitions and derived the difference principle without going through the original position. My reason for extracting the intuitions from the representation in the original position was that I do not believe that the form of original position constructed by Rawls is in fact a good one for his own purposes. (I shall enlarge on this further in section 41.)

Once we admit that substantive intuitions have to go into the specification of the original position if we are to derive definite implications, the case for saying constructivism is something different from intuitionism becomes weaker. But it seems to me that there is still a good case for saying the construction is doing some real work provided what is put in is more general than what comes out. Where I think the claim of constructivism to be distinctive would completely break down would be if it were construed as no more than a method for articulating intuitions about particular cases.

Rawls himself has been regarded as holding to this last view of constructivism by, among others, Ronald Dworkin, who actually introduced the notion that Rawls is a constructivist. Since the point is of some importance it is worth commenting on Dworkin's discussion. In section 32, I cited Dworkin as putting forward for consideration one idea about the relation between particular intuitions and general principles, namely, that they "are clues to the nature and existence of more abstract and fundamental moral principles, as physical observations are clues to the existence and nature of fundamental physical laws."[20] Dworkin calls this the "natural model" and contrasts it with the "constructive model."[21]

It should be noticed that for Dworkin the constructive model is a

rival to the natural model as a method of achieving the same end, namely, the rendering of isolated intuitions into general principles. The difference is that the constructive model "treats intuitions of justice not as
clues to the existence of independent principles, but rather as stipulated
features of a general theory to be constructed."[22] In a rather curious
analogy he suggests that on the natural model reconstructing fundamental principles from intuitions is like "a natural historian reconstruct[ing] the shape of the whole animal from the fragments of its
bones he has found," whereas on the constructive model it is "as if a
sculptor set himself to carve the animal that best fit a pile of bones he
happened to find together."[23]

Those familiar with Dworkin's work in jurisprudence may suspect
on reading this that the notion of constructivism with which he here
saddles Rawls owes more to the Dworkinian theory of legal interpretation than to anything to be found in Rawls. Such a suspicion will be
compounded when it is noted that Dworkin himself points out that the
constructive model is "analogous to one model of common law adjudication" in which judges construct principles as ways of rationaliz-
ing existing cases and extending them in new directions. "The particular precedents are analogous to intuitions; the judge tries to reach an
accommodation between these precedents and a set of principles that
might justify them and also justify further decisions that go beyond
them."[24] This is, of course, an answer to the old question about
whether judges make the law or find it. They make it but (as Marx said
of the way in which men make history) not out of whole cloth. The
judge "does not suppose . . . that the precedents are glimpses into a
moral reality, and therefore clues to objective principles he ends by declaring. . . . Instead, in the spirit of the constructive model, he accepts
these precedents as specifications for a principle that he must construct,
out of a sense of responsibility for consistency with what has gone
before."[25]

I have no wish to enter here into the question of the adequacy or
plausibility of this as a theory of adjudication in law. But I do feel sure
that it is seldom if ever appropriate in moral reasoning. The example
that Dworkin mentions is the famous one of the development of the
notion in American law of a "right of privacy."[26] This originated in a
scholarly article arguing that a number of cases decided on a variety of
different grounds (e.g., breach of contract) could be reconceptualized as
falling under a "right of privacy" and that this right could then be invoked to provide for damages to be paid in new cases (for example,

unwanted publicity) where there had hitherto been no remedy. In the fullness of time the "right of privacy" became so well entrenched that it was used as the basis for the Supreme Court decisions striking down laws against contraception and then abortion. Another, more recent illustration is the way in which, as traditional common-law limitations on the right to sue manufacturers of defective products were relaxed, the conceptual basis for recovery was shifted from contract to tort.

This is a way of proceeding that makes sense only if one attaches a good deal of importance to conserving the decisions in old cases but very little importance to the reasons offered by judges at the time for reaching those decisions. Now if this makes sense at all in the law, it must be, it seems to me, because of the role the law plays in society as a source of stable expectations and, even more, because of the distinctive role of judges compared to that of legislators. But the reason for accepting the new principle must be that it is a good principle—that the development of the law will go better with a right of privacy or with the sale of defective products as a tort. We are not, after all, talking about a more convenient device for getting the same results, like Arabic as against Roman numerals. Conformity with past decisions is a constraint on new principles but not a reason for adopting them.

Now it seems to me that the analogy between legal and moral reasoning does not work very well. As I pointed out in section 32, we do not normally have bare intuitions about particular cases—intuitions for which we could not, at any rate in general terms, give an account of what moves us in the case. And if we did occasionally have one it is hard to see why any significance should be attached to it. So far we are in line with the legal analogue, where judges normally do not (in cases where some point of law is at issue) simply hand down decisions but also offer reasons for deciding the way they did. The difference comes in at the point where someone changes his principles. If I decide that I can no longer accept the rightness of killing under any circumstances, say, this will presumably entail a number of changes in my views about particular cases. But surely the natural reaction to that is that I previously had bad views about particular cases because I had a bad principle about killing. It is hard to see any room for the idea that my views about particular cases should be conserved under a change of principles. It might be said that the situation is different where the principles are principles for the basic institutions of a society. But it seems to me that the relevance of conservatism comes at the stage of implemention, not that of argument about principles. It may be that wise legislation should

take account of existing expectations. But arguments about the principles for just institutions do not have to be constrained in the way that
we should like common-law judges to be constrained by precedent.

If constructivism were what Dworkin says it is, what could we say
about its relation to intuitionism? I think that we should have to write
off constructivism as even a partially independent method. We might
still go through the motions of drawing up the specifications of an
original position and asking what the "agents of construction" would
choose in it, but the results would have no force in themselves. They
would have to be checked against our particular intuitions and accepted
or rejected according to whether or not they corresponded with them.

Pretty clearly the notion of pure procedural justice goes by the board
here. The justification of the original position is that it produces the
right answers. This is, in Rawls's terms, perfect procedural justice
rather than pure procedural justice. As David Lyons put the point: "If
there are grounds external to the contract argument for judging the
justice of social arrangements, then Rawls' 'justice as fairness' notion
would seem to be discredited. . . . But if the notion of pure procedural
justice is to do its job of validating the contract argument, then Rawls
cannot regard the coherence argument as anything like a justification or
defense of moral principles."[27]

For Dworkin, it should be recalled, the "constructive model" was
contrasted with the "natural model." Rawls would in this sense necessarily be a constructivist since his rejection of what he calls "rational
intuitionism" entails the rejection of the "natural model."[28] But in the
broad sense of "intuitionism" that I am employing, it is plain that constructing principles to fit given particular intuitions is a thoroughly intuitionistic enterprise.

Is it Rawls's? If it is then everything he has said about the original
position as the highest level of pure procedural justice must be nonsense. However, it will be recalled that Rawls did not speak in these
terms in A Theory of Justice. Is Dworkin's characterization of Rawls's
method correct for the book? I think that Lyons is right in saying that
Rawls wanted it both ways in A Theory of Justice. On the one hand, he
stresses the ways in which the original position has attractions as a
representation of a fair situation for deciding on principles. But on the
other hand he undoubtedly does also expound what Lyons calls the
"coherence argument": that ultimately the theory is to be tested by its
ability to accommodate our particular intuitions about justice.[29]

As a matter of intellectual biography, A Theory of Justice may be seen as a point of transition between the coherentism of Rawls's early article (based on his Ph.D. dissertation) "Outline of a Decision Procedure for Ethics," dating from twenty years before the book,[30] and the constructivism of the Dewey lectures and subsequent articles. The "Outline" fits Dworkin's notion of the "constructive model" pretty well in that Rawls explicitly tells us that the raw material to be worked up into principles consists of the "considered judgments" made by reasonable, impartial, well-informed people under conditions free from pressure and inducement (ideally they should not stand to gain or lose from the outcome) about actual cases that are "not especially difficult" and are "likely to arise in ordinary life."[31]

That the model is one that takes judgments on particular cases as data is made manifest in Rawls's requirement

> that the judgment be intuitive with respect to ethical principles, that is, that it should not be determined by a conscious application of principles so far as this may be evidenced by introspection. . . . The reason for this restriction will be evident if one keeps in mind the aim of the present inquiry, namely, to describe a decision procedure whereby principles, by means of which we may justify specific moral decisions, may themselves be shown to be justifiable. Now part of this procedure will consist in showing that these principles are implicit in the considered judgments of competent judges."[32]

And, Rawls says, it would obviously pose a threat of circularity if these considered judgments were themselves derived by applying principles.

"Reasonable principles" are marked by four features, and Rawls's description of these further accentuates his allegiance to Dworkin's "constructive model." The first is that they should "explicate" the considered judgments of competent judges—at any rate those held with "certitude," which is simply a strong sense of conviction. "Explication" is explained as follows. "Consider a group of competent judges making considered judgments in review of a set of cases which would be likely to arise in ordinary life. Then an explication of these judgments is defined to be a set of principles, such that, if any competent man were to apply them intelligently and consistently to the same cases under review, his judgments, made systematically nonintuitive by the explicit and conscious use of the principles, would be, nevertheless, identical, case by case, with the considered judgments of the group of competent judges."[33]

So far, what Rawls says might be consistent with Dworkin's "natural model" as well, but the constructive aspect appears in the remaining three conditions. The second condition is that a principle is reasonable insofar as it "shows a capacity to become accepted by competent moral judges after they have freely weighed its merits by criticism and open discussion, and after each has thought it over and compared it with his own considered judgments."[34] The third condition is that a principle, to be reasonable, should be able to "function in existing instances of conflicting opinion, and in new cases causing difficulty, to yield a result which, after criticism and discussion, seems acceptable to all, or nearly all, competent judges, and to conform to their intuitive notion of a reasonable decision."[35] And finally, "the reasonableness of a principle is tested by seeing whether it shows a capacity to hold its own (that is, to continue to be felt reasonable), against a subclass of the considered judgments of competent judges, as this fact may be evidenced by our intuitive conviction that the considered judgments are incorrect rather than the principle, when we confront them with the principle. . . . To the extent that principles exhibit this capacity to alter what we think to be our considered judgments in cases of conflict, they satisfy the fourth test."[36] As it stands, there is obviously something puzzling about the relation of the fourth condition to the first. But it could, I think, be filled out adequately by invoking an analogue to Dworkinian jurisprudence. We might be able to cook up a principle to "explicate" a subclass of cases but feel that it has an *ad hoc* look about it and that some more general principle looks as if it should subsume these cases. This generates a tension which may be resolved by a move to greater generality in our principles.

I have dwelt on this early article for two reasons. One, which will become relevant in section 42, is that if one concludes (as I do) that Rawls's later construction of an original position is an unsatisfactory representation of the circumstances of impartiality, some aspects of the earlier position become quite attractive. The other reason, which is relevant to the present discussion, is that there are unquestionably many traces of the "Outline" in *A Theory of Justice*. The language of "considered judgments" is, of course, taken over wholesale, and there are a number of passages that recall the emphasis on judgments about particular cases as the ultimate touchstone for principles. Thus, in a passage much relied on by those who lay emphasis on the role of low-level intuitions in Rawls's methodology, he writes that we can justify a description of the original position not only by pointing to its formal characteristics but also by seeing "if the principles which would be chosen match our considered convictions of justice or extend them in an acceptable way. We can note whether applying these principles would lead us to make the same judgments about the basic structure of society which we now make intuitively and in which we have the greatest confidence; or whether, in cases where our present judgments are in doubt and given with hesitation, these principles offer a resolution which we can affirm on reflection."[37] We are to go to and fro, sometimes changing the description of the original position until it yields principles we are prepared to accept, and sometimes bringing our particular judgments into line with the principles we have derived, until we reach a state of "reflective equilibrium."[38]

What is striking is that Rawls actually does none of this in *A Theory of Justice*. At no point does Rawls develop minutely described cases and ask us to exercise our intuitions, unguided by any prior commitment to principle, upon them. The examples he gives, in the context of the passage just quoted, of "considered convictions" that may be taken as "provisional fixed points"[39] are "that religious intolerance and racial discrimination are unjust."[40] These are, obviously, quite abstract and high-level principles already. Religious toleration is in fact the core and paradigm of the first principle of justice, maximum equal liberty, while racial discrimination is the most glaring denial of the part of the second principle that mandates fair equality of opportunity. And other "fixed points" are even further away from being intuitions about well-described particular cases. Thus, the considered judgment that nobody deserves his place in the natural or social ordering of advantages[41] is in fact *more* abstract than the principles of justice themselves, and serves as a premise for the difference principle via the principle that benefits from such advantages are *prima facie* morally arbitrary.

A sustained example of Rawls's practice, as against his official theory about how to proceed, is his discussion of commonsense precepts of economic justice.[42] Once again we may note that what are examined are very far from being the deliverances of intuition about concrete cases. What Rawls has in mind here are precepts, or slogans, such as "To each according to his contribution," "To each according to his effort," or "To each according to his training and education." These are, obviously, principles potentially in competition with the difference principle rather than judgments about what would be just in certain particular fully described cases.

Moreover, Rawls certainly does not treat the commonsense precepts with the kind of deference that one might have been led to expect by his methodological pronouncements. On the contrary, his procedure is strikingly reminiscent of that of Sidgwick, who, in a series of swift moves, aimed to demonstrate in *The Methods of Ethics* that "Common Sense morality" is a tissue of confusions and contradictions that can be cleared up only by invoking a higher-level principle.[43] Thus, Rawls claims that the various precepts contradict one another, are indeterminate, and vary in importance according to conditions. The difference principle, Rawls claims, provides a determinate solution to the problem of economic justice in which each of the commonsense precepts can find its appropriate place. Clearly, Rawls is not seeking support here for the difference principle from common sense. Rather, he is trying to show that common sense provides no valid basis from which to mount an objection.

Summing up, it seems to me fair to say that, in spite of recurrent intrusions by the methodological claims first made in the "Outline," Rawls's actual practice in *A Theory of Justice* is best described by the model that I explored earlier in this section. The formal requirements of a fair choosing situation are recognized as insufficient to generate principles of justice. But the additional substantive ethical premises required are of a rather high-level kind, taking the form of principles or even meta-principles. This leaves the construction with a certain degree of autonomy and thus, in my terms, makes constructivism dependent on but not reducible to intuitionism. In this interpretation, what has happened in the years after *A Theory of Justice* is that Rawls has brought his rhetoric in line with his practice.

35. JUSTICE AS IMPARTIALITY

I want to conclude this chapter by returning to a question that I left hanging when describing the two kinds of constructivist theory and explaining how one might regard their forms of construction as relevant to justice. I suggested there that the two-stage construction of a nonagreement point and a mutually advantageous move to the Pareto frontier would be a natural way of representing an egoistic approach to the basis of justice. And I said that the alternative construction of an original position would be the natural way of representing the notion of justice as impartiality. I shall argue here for the superiority of the latter.

An important office of morality, and one which any adequate account must comprehend, is that it should provide prescriptions for dealing with situations where interests conflict. This is not to say that a system of morality has to provide a definite answer to every question of who should get what. It may simply specify the procedure for settling the dispute: that an heirloom with two equally strong claimants should go to the one who calls a coin toss correctly; that of two suitors of the same girl the successful one (if either) should simply be the one that the girl chooses; and so on. But a system of morality should at least provide a framework for dealing with any conflict.

Thus, suppose we have a situation in which two or more parties (individuals, groups, organizations, countries, or whatever you like) are in a state of conflict: they want incompatible outcomes and they do not agree on any procedure for producing an outcome. It seems clear that no progress can be made in settling this dispute if all we can ever say is such things as "From your point of view the best outcome is X; but from his point of view the best outcome is Y." We can pack anything into "best" that we like. However high-minded may be the ideals that go into the determination of the best outcome, the conflict persists. What we have to find is some course of conduct that can be accepted by all parties. Notice that the course of conduct does not have to be the same for different parties, nor do different courses of conduct even have to fit together harmoniously. It would count as a solution that the two parties should fight it out—so long as this proposal could be accepted by both parties.

The question that now arises, and determines the kind of moral system we shall have, is: What is the basis of agreement to be? As we have seen, one answer is that the basis should be the rational pursuit of self-interest. On this view, a moral principle for the settlement of a conflict of interest is one that reflects the balance of forces—the strategic advantages and disadvantages of the parties—so that they all have an equally strong incentive to comply with its requirements on condition that others do so as well.

The motive for acting in accordance with such moral principles can easily enough be seen. There is no need to invoke a distinct moral motive. Practical reason is not bifurcated (as has often been thought) into moral and prudential branches. There is simply rationality, construed as taking the means best adapted to the successful pursuit of one's ends. Under certain conditions (the circumstances of justice) rationality prescribes adherence to the constraints of morality. These are situations where unconstrained maximization leads to a less favorable outcome than constrained maximization. To put it another way, the office of morality is to propose what Hobbes called "convenient articles of peace" in situations where there is a possible Pareto improvement over the result of a free-for-all. On this conception, there can be no competition between the claims of morality and those of self-interest, because morality is simply the form that self-interest takes under certain conditions.

As a conception of morality this has all the attractions of simplicity and tractability. However, simplicity and tractability, although undeniably virtues in a theory, are not the supreme ones. The objections raised in the course of Part II (see especially sections 18, under "The Equality Condition," and 30) seem to me to be formidable. Someone may accept a certain outcome as the best that he or she can reasonably hope to get in a given situation, given a baseline constituted by the results of unconstrained maximization all round, but this may be acceptance only in the sense of resignation to one's fate. Hobbesian peace may simply be that of a bully whom nobody cares to challenge. What is missing in this account of morality is any notion of justification.

There is an alternative view which makes agreement on reasonable terms something of value in itself, rather than a more or less efficient means to the successful pursuit of one's ends. The possibility is thus opened up that the requirements of morality might run counter to those of even the most sophisticated long-run self-interest. As T. M. Scanlon has put this idea, the moral motive is "the desire to be able to justify one's actions to others on grounds they could not reasonably reject," where the basis on which others decide whether or not they can reasonably reject the grounds one offers is given by *their* "desire to find principles which others similarly motivated could not reasonably reject."[44]

The desire to be able to justify our actions to ourselves and others on a basis capable of eliciting free agreement is, as common experience attests, widely shared and deeply grounded. We find the same desire manifesting itself when people defend institutions from which they benefit. It is indeed a curious and striking illustration of the strength of this desire that the beneficiaries of such institutions as slavery and racial discrimination seldom defend their position as a frankly unjustifiable assertion of superior power, with the implication that, if the tables were turned, they would have nothing to say against their new position of inferiority except that they didn't like it and would overthrow it if they could. Rather, we find elaborate defenses in terms suggesting, however implausibly, that even those on the losing end would, if they understood the position aright, find it reasonable to accept their status. Granted that this is a perversion of the intellect, it still seems to me significant that it occurs at all.

So far I have simply drawn attention to the existence of a motive for caring about what can be defended before everyone. It may be said that this is not much. But I think it is enough, in the following limited sense. The argument in favor of egoism as the universal standard of practical reason, as we find it for example in the work of David Gauthier,[45] seems to rest on the idea that, whereas the prudent pursuit of one's own ends is obviously rational, concern for the impartial justifiability of one's actions is not. If it is to be shown to be rational it must be brought into relation with what is unquestionably rational. The implication that morality is rational only insofar as it can be reduced to a sophisticated form of egoism follows trivially, of course.

However, the equation of rationality with the efficient pursuit of self-interest is, as far as I can see, pure assertion. It can therefore fitly be opposed by a counter-assertion, namely, that it is equally rational to care about what can be defended impartially. I do not know how to prove that the term "rationality" is appropriately employed in this way, but I think that the virtually unanimous concurrence of the human race in caring about the defensibility of actions in a way that does not simply appeal to power is a highly relevant supporting consideration. Perhaps almost the whole human race is crazy and only Gauthier and a few others who think like him are sane. But until somebody produces more than an argument by definitional fiat for the equation of rationality and self-interest we can safely continue to deny it.

To say that it is rational to be concerned about the possibility of justifying one's conduct in the manner stipulated is not, however, to say that people in whom such a motive is not present can be given a demonstration that they should. (It is worth noting, though, that just the same can be said of anyone who does not care about his own future well-being.) I do not believe that it is possible to show that people would actually be contradicting themselves if they were to refuse to accept the authority over them of morality, understood in this way. I mentioned in section 34 that I would discuss here an argument to that effect which is somewhat parallel to the one that Sidgwick considered (and reluctantly rejected) for the self-contradictory nature of egoism. This more recent argument was advanced by Alan Gewirth.[46] In finding it wanting, I am following the consensus of philosophers who have discussed it. I know of nobody who has found it convincing. My reason for bringing it up here is that I believe Gewirth's argument, although admittedly not logically watertight, is a good deal deeper than most critics have conceded. Considerations of the kind Gewirth advances are indeed powerful ones that should, I think, lead reasonable people to accept the authority of morality, though not (as Gewirth claims) on pain of self-contradiction.[47]

Gewirth sets up the problem very lucidly:

> The amoralist as I here conceive him . . . professes to be guided by reason in that he is prepared to do that for which (logically) good justifying reasons can be given. He accepts the reasons of deductive and inductive logic, including the evidence of empirical facts. But he denies that these reasons justify or require that he make any moral judgments or accept moral obligations; and he also denies that there is any other "rationality" (including a distinctively moral one) which would rationally justify these things. My question, then, is whether, given the deductive and inductive reasons which the amoralist accepts, he also rationally must, in virtue of accepting these reasons, accept for himself the use of moral language and the corresponding moral obligations.[48]

Although Gewirth has elaborated his line of argument a good deal over the years, there is a basic move common to all versions, and the persuasiveness of Gewirth's theory depends critically on whether or not one accepts this move. I have therefore quoted from and shall discuss below the relatively early and straightforward formulation in "Must One Play the Moral Language Game?"[49] The general conclusion for which Gewirth argues is that I cannot consistently make claims for myself that I deny to others who are similarly placed in the relevant respects. One relevant respect in which we are all similar is that we have desires and we need certain basic conditions in order to satisfy them. Therefore, if I claim the conditions of action for myself I must admit that all others have an equal claim.

What is the nature of the self-contradiction? The essence of Gewirth's answer is that "it is a logical feature of all reasons that they are implicitly general, referring to a general rule or principle that serves to ground the connection asserted in the particular case. Such a connection must hence obtain in all other cases to which the same rule or reason applies."[50] Thus, if I am the rational amoralist depicted by Gewirth at the outset, I must draw the conclusion that I have reasons for wanting those things that are necessary means for my acting; but since reasons are general, I must in doing that admit also that all others have reasons for wanting the necessary means for *their* acting.

Suppose that we accept this. The obvious problem is that so far we do not seem to have got beyond saying that I have reasons for wanting things and other people have reasons for wanting things. My allowing that their reasons for wanting things are of the same kind and the same validity as mine does not, on the face of it, entail that I must, on pain of self-contradiction, concede that their reasons are also reasons for me. The reasons apparently come irreducibly attached to particular people. Gewirth himself puts the point very well as follows:

> It may still be objected, however, that X's reason for doing the act is so irreducibly egocentric that it cannot be expressed without explicit personal reference to him; hence it cannot be generalized so as to be the "same reason" as any other persons may have for performing their respective acts. "*My* reason for doing z is simply that *I* want that *I* have y, and *this* reason is different from any other persons' wanting that *they* have y. I don't care about anyone else's wants but only about my own; and nobody else has *my* wants." What is here claimed is that there is no way, by logic alone, to eliminate indexical expressions like "my" or "I" from the reason X has given for his doing z. If X's reason can be universalized at all, it must be in a way that retains the individualizing reference to his own personal wants: "All persons who have my want that I have y ought to do z."[51]

I do not believe that Gewirth ever succeeds in overcoming the objection that he has so forcefully expressed here. The method that he proposes is to suggest that a rational agent such as his amoralist must be prepared to say such things as "I ought to have x because it is necessary for the achievement of y, which I want." And, because of the generic quality of reasons, this entails that anyone else who wants y ought to have x. Thus, "the 'transition' accompanied by [the] canons [of logic invoked here] is simply from an 'ought'-predication justified by a certain reason in X's own case to its being justified in all other cases to which the same reason applies."[52] Although Gewirth has later introduced more steps into the argument, the key move is that the generalizing force of reason licenses the extension of the "ought" statements that the speaker makes of himself to all others who are relevantly similar in having wants and being in a position where certain means are necessary to their fulfillment.

In spite of Gewirth's disarming remarks, there is unfortunately something wrong with the transition from the kind of "I ought" statement that Gewirth puts into the mouth of a rational amoralist to the full-blown respect for the interests of all that he claims to be able to deduce from that statement. The amoralist's "I ought to have x because it is a means to y" has to be understood as "I ought to have x because it is a means to *my* having y," and this, let us say, gives him a reason for pursuing x. But even if we go along with Gewirth in drawing the conclusion that he is thereby committed to saying that "A ought to have x

because it is a means to *his* having *y*," it does not follow that he is committed to any more than the proposition that it is rational for A to pursue *x*. He can, without self-contradiction, deny that it entails an obligation on him to aid A's pursuit of *x* or even not to hinder it. This, of course, Gewirth vehemently rejects.[53] But I do not believe that there is any way round it.

If that were all there was to be said on the matter, I should not have devoted this amount of space to discussing Gewirth's theory. However, it may be recalled that in introducing the discussion I said that Gewirth's argument cuts deep though falling short of demonstration. What I have in mind is this. Although Gewirth's argument does require additional premises to make it go, these premises are so natural and reasonable that it is easy to take them for granted. But when we trace them we shall see, I think, that they are precisely the (admittedly inconclusive) arguments advanced by David Hume and Adam Smith for an impartial standard of appraisal that I discussed back in section 19. The implication, if I am right, is that the battle between "rationalist" and "moral sense" approaches to morality should be declared a draw: both sides are right in what they deny and wrong in what they affirm. Rational argument cannot prove, in the sense that it is self-contradictory to deny them, the claims of impartial morality; but it is not purely a matter of how one feels, and rational arguments have an important part to play.

The premises that are lacking in Gewirth's argument and supplied by Hume and Smith are, I suggest, the following. First, although there is nothing actually inconsistent in sticking with the claim that my reasons are reasons for me and your reasons are reasons for you, it does seem natural to ask if we cannot get beyond looking at things each from our own perspective and find reasons for acting that are reasons for anyone. The driving force is no longer logical consistency but what we might call human consistency; but it may be no less strong for that. And, second, if we once start looking for a standpoint that will bring our own demands into relation to those of others, it is hard to deny the force of Smith's idea "that we are but one of the multitude, in no respect better than any other in it," so "we dare not, as self-love might suggest to us, prefer the interest of one to that of many." "Dare not" is, of course, to be understood here not as a matter of what we can reasonably hope to get away with but as a matter of what we can decently demand: "The man within immediately calls to us, that we value ourselves too much and other people too little, and that, by doing so, we render ourselves the proper object of the contempt and indignation of our brethren."[54]

Once again, it seems to me that it is not actually a question of logical inconsistency that is at stake, but all the same a question that may be pretty compelling: what one can with any show of plausibility maintain. This sort of fundamental moral egalitarianism is not, as Gewirth suggests, entailed by the canons of logic, but it is still highly persuasive. An argument on the same lines can be made for the priority of the distinctively moral motive over the claims of self-interest. Although we may, of course, in practice fail to do what we recognize it to require of us, it is, again, hard to see how, if we once acknowledge its authority at all, we can treat it simply as one reason for acting to be played off against others.

If it is true that moral motivation cannot be argued into existence from nothing, it is clearly of importance to know what are the conditions that predispose people to acquire moral motivation. I speculate that at any rate a part of the answer is going to be that the experience of dependence on others is an important predisposing factor. Those who are in a position to control the lives of others commonly become tyrannical. They behave in ways that they certainly would not voluntarily put up with if they were on the receiving end. There is nothing like constantly finding oneself in situations where one has to gain the cooperation of others in order to achieve one's own ends for encouraging one to cultivate the habit of looking at things from the other person's viewpoint and asking oneself what kind of conduct the other might reasonably find acceptable.*

I should emphasize that I am here talking about the conditions under which the moral motive may be aroused. As a proposition of speculative moral psychology, the suggestion is that—roughly speaking—equality of power, or at least a not too extreme inequality of power, is what is conducive to the formation and elicitation of moral motivation. It is important to recognize that I am not reinstating the "circumstances of justice" through the back door. In other words, I am not saying that the

---

* This suggestion is, I believe, supported by Piaget's work: see Jean Piaget, *The Moral Judgment of the Child* (New York: Free Press, 1965). Mary Gibson's "impressionistic account" ("Consent and Autonomy," in Mary Gibson, ed., *To Breathe Freely: Risk, Consent, and Air* [Totowa, N. J.: Rowman & Allanheld, 1985], p. 166 n. 6) brings out what I have in mind when she writes that "relations of cooperation give rise to such intellectual norms as logical thought and intersubjective verification, as well as to such moral norms as reciprocity and mutual respect" (ibid., p. 147).

reason for acting morally is that, under conditions of approximately equal power, it is necessary for the pursuit of one's own advantage to cooperate with others on terms that can be mutually accepted as reasonable. The motive for acting morally remains what I said it was: the desire to be able to justify our conduct. My point is simply that the desire is more likely to come to the fore in conditions of approximately equal power than in conditions of radical inequality.

This section is entitled "Justice as Impartiality," yet so far I have talked about morality rather than justice and have touched on impartiality only in passing. I shall conclude by addressing these two points, in reverse order. I suggest, then, that moral principles capable of passing the test proposed must have a certain quality of impartiality. What, after all, is the virtue of impartiality, as we seek it in, paradigmatically, judges and arbitrators or other public officials? An impartial decision-maker is one who acts "without fear or favor." This includes, of course, not taking bribes, anticipating rewards, or succumbing to threats. But it also means the absence of more subtle departures from objectivity: impartiality excludes favoritism based on friendship, similarity of race or class, and so on. (The precept that nobody should be a judge in his own cause embodies the most obvious precaution against partiality.) The reasons for deciding should be general, publicly statable, and publicly defensible. It is the claim that the decision can be defended in ways that can in principle be equally acceptable to everyone that gives us the link between morality and impartiality. It also, incidentally, shows the sense in which morality can be said to be objective.

Someone who was engaged in impartially choosing principles to govern his life with others would not endorse a principle on the basis of its favoring himself, his friends and relations, or those with whom he felt some kind of affinity. But in just the same way someone seriously engaged in the search for principles that could not reasonably be rejected by others engaged in the same search would surely recognize that it would be a waste of time (as well as a breach of good faith) to put forward a principle whose only merit was that it would be favorable to himself, his friends and relations, or those with whom he felt some kind of affinity. For it is obvious that those who were put at a relative disadvantage by such a principle would wish to reject it, and it could not possibly be said that they were being unreasonable in so doing. Thus, just as Hume argued, the quest for a basis of unforced agreement with others necessitates the abandonment of partiality. Common ground can be found, if at all, only when all adopt an impartial perspective.

Before leaving this subject for now, I should like to safeguard against an oversimplification of the relation between morality and impartiality that is easily made. I described above the stern commandments of impartiality. Manifestly, it is a virtue for those in official positions but extended to the whole of life would be a pretty appalling prospect. Does morality, then, require that people must go around all the time scrupulously avoiding any suspicion that they would do something for their friends or families that they would not be prepared to do for a perfect stranger? To suppose this is to overlook the fact that impartiality comes in at the point where the principles are chosen. Whether or not it comes in at the point where they are applied depends on what the principles themselves prescribe. If the principles are agreed upon by normal human beings for normal human conditions we should surely expect them to prescribe impartiality in some contexts and to allow (or even mandate) partiality in others. I shall take all this up at greater length in Volume II, but the misconception is important and pervasive enough to be worth clearing up at the outset.

I have been talking about morality and impartiality. But there is, I think, an especially intimate link between justice and impartiality. Morality includes an impartially defensible core, but it has other aspects too. Justice is, however, wholly contained within that impartial core. Let me explain what I have in mind here. The province of morality is not, I think, very sharply defined. It merges into etiquette in one direction, esthetics in another, and prudence in a third. For most people it would include ideals of personal development and social relationships. But not a lot turns on the choice of a more or less comprehensive conception of morality. If a society of superstitious, ill-fed, mistrustful people living in conditions of squalor is bad, does it make much difference whether or not we say that it is morally bad? There is no difficulty in explaining why those things are bad, and when we have done so, at whatever length seems necessary, there is nothing more to be said. But there are some actions about which we want to say something more: that they are morally wrong. And in saying this we are, I think, saying that they violate the constraints of impartiality. Unextenuated cases of killing or inflicting bodily harm, lying, or promise-breaking run counter to principles that nobody—including the perpetrator—could reasonably reject. We have here, then, the core of morality as impartiality.

That this core is not coextensive with justice may be seen by reflecting on the fact that it would jar our linguistic sensibilities to say that murder was unfair or that a law prohibiting it was a just law (except perhaps as a way of denying that it was unjust). Similarly, it would be linguistically odd to say that what is wrong with lying is that it is unfair. But if we ask how justice or fairness might naturally come in here, we should be able to see what is distinctive about these notions. Suppose a law setting one penalty for blacks who murder and another for whites who murder, and we should have no doubt that this was properly described as an unjust law. (One of the arguments against the death penalty in the United States is that *de facto* it is such a law.) Similarly, lying in a context where it constitutes fraud—for example, as a means of inducing someone to buy something he would not pay for in the absence of misrepresentation—is clearly an unfair practice.

Whether we are dealing with individual acts or whole social institutions, justice is concerned with the way in which benefits and burdens are distributed. The subject of justice is the distribution of rights and privileges, powers and opportunities, and the command over material resources. Taking the term "resources" in a suitably broad sense, we can put this succinctly by saying that justice is concerned with the distribution of scarce resources—resources about whose distribution a potential for conflict of interest arises. And if we ask what we are saying about an action or an institution when we say it is unjust, the general answer is, I suggest, this. We are claiming that it cannot be defended publicly—that the principles of distribution it instantiates could reasonably be rejected by those who do badly under it.

Even if this precise formula would not immediately come to many people's lips, we can show that it is implicit in the argumentative strategies that they use when the justice of an action or institution is at issue. The accusation that someone would not accept something if he were on the losing end is one that, if it can be made to look plausible, is regarded as damaging. This kind of argument suggests a constructivist approach to justice, and I shall develop this when I examine original position theories of justice in chapter 9. Before that, in the next chapter, I shall analyze the other constructivist approach to justice: two-stage theories of justice.

CHAPTER VIII

Constructing Theories of Justice (1): Two-Stage Theories

36. INTRODUCTION

In this chapter and the next I shall be looking at the decisions about key structural variables that create alternative constructivist theories of justice. Explicitly or implicitly, I suggest, every writer has to answer certain questions in creating a constructivist theory, and the answers to these questions taken together define a certain structure. I shall be concerned not with the content of constructivist theories of justice but with their structure. The result will be that theories with very different substantive conclusions will be treated together as having the same structure; at the same time, theories with the same substantive conclusions will on occasion be shown to be structurally dissimilar.

When I say that two theories have the same structure, I should be understood as claiming identity only when structures are categorized in the way that I propose here. Thus, I shall define four types of two-stage structure and four types of original position structure, and I shall say that two theories have the same structure if they are of the same type. It would, however, be possible to analyze structure at a higher level of resolution, and then one could say that theories with different substantive implications also had different structures.

What I am saying should be easier to understand if I explain how the four types of two-stage structure and four types of original position structure are created. There are two key decisions that define a two-stage structure. The first thing that has to be settled is the nature of the nonagreement baseline: Should it depend on the results of strategic play for relative advantage, or should it reflect the best the parties could do for themselves independently? The second thing that is needed is a way of getting from the nonagreement baseline to the Pareto frontier: Should it correspond to the outcome of simulated bargaining, or should it be in accordance with some criterion for equal gain? By putting together the logically possible pairs of decisions, we generate four types of structure. And at this level of resolution, it may be seen that the same structure may be compatible with different outcomes in a given situation. Thus, two theorists might advocate a structure defined by, say, the second of each of the two options but still reach quite divergent substantive conclusions if they had different ideas about the requirements of independent maximization and the appropriate way of measuring gain. But if we were to differentiate structures more finely, we could say that their substantive disagreements flowed from disagreements about the precise specifications of the two structural features.

A similar point may be made in relation to original position structures. I shall define two theories as having the same structure if they give the same answers to two key questions. First, are the parties motivated by the desire to advance their own interests, or are other motivations allowed into the original position? And, second, do the parties know their own identities or are they behind a veil of ignorance that denies them this information? Here again two theories with the same structure as defined in these terms might come out with different substantive conclusions. Thus, Harsanyi and Rawls both have, within this classification, the same structure (self-interested choice without knowledge of personal identity), but one derives utilitarianism and the other the two principles of justice. Again we can explain this difference structurally if we make finer discriminations or if we notice that Rawls has a different notion of what a person's interests are from that assumed by Harsanyi and also that his veil of ignorance denies the parties more information than does Harsanyi's—not only knowledge of their own identities but a variety of other particular facts about their society. I shall, indeed, discuss these differences when I take up original position theories in the next chapter.

I want in the rest of this section to follow up on the sketch I have already given of the structure of two-stage theories. I shall bring together aspects of Parts I and II by pointing out that exactly the same structural issues arise both in theories intended to apply to division between two parties and those intended to tell us about rules of justice for

Division of Gains from Cooperation

	Simulated bargaining	Equal gains
Strategic maximization of advantage	1 Nash (Braithwaite) —————— Hume	2 Braithwaite (Nash) —————— Rawls
Nonstrategic maximization of advantage	3 Gauthier Gauthier	4 Lucas Rawls

Noncooperative Baseline

Figure 8.1.   The Structure of Two-Stage Theories

whole societies. I have indeed made occasional comparisons in passing (as in section 7) but I think it is worth doing systematically. In Figure 8.1, theories in the upper row allow the actors to behave with an eye toward the move to the Pareto frontier by trying to maximize their relative advantage at the first stage, and those in the lower row hold the parties to the more modest (and, if you like, shortsighted) goal of doing as well for themselves as they can in the absence of cooperation, but not concerning themselves with what this will do to their eventual prospects under conditions of cooperation. Those in the left column hold that the move to the Pareto frontier should simulate the outcome of rational bargaining while those in the right column propose to divide the gains from cooperation equally, according to some criterion of equal gain.

The names in each of the four cells are those of writers who, I claim, have supported that structure. The line between the upper and lower entries in each cell is intended to mark the division between Part I and Part II, the upper set of names representing theorists of fair division. I shall discuss these placings, taking one cell at a time. The third cell is the easiest to talk about so I shall start with it. Gauthier's name appears both above and below the line, and I have already discussed his ideas in both micro and macro contexts. It will be recalled that in Part I we looked at Gauthier's proposed solution to Braithwaite's problem of the two musicians: splitting the difference as the method of dividing the cooperative surplus above a baseline of each man's "security level" (sections 5 and 7). And in section 30 we saw that he supports a generalization of that solution as the criterion of justice in a society's economic institutions. We take as a baseline the most that people could guarantee themselves in the absence of cooperation and then divide the cooperative surplus so that each one gets an equal distance from there to the most that would be obtainable with the maximum cooperation of all others, which is the method of splitting the difference.

Gauthier's placement in the third cell reflects his rationale for the choice of a noncooperative baseline and a method of dividing the cooperative surplus. The noncooperative baseline is to be established nonstrategically. That is to say, the parties are to act in the (hypothetical) noncooperative stage without any thought of improving their position vis-à-vis others in preparation for the second stage, at which a move is made to the Pareto frontier. They are thus not to engage in the kind of maneuvering envisaged by Nash and Braithwaite (a "threat game") in order to gain the maximum relative advantage. Of course, it is not easy to give an operational account of what doing the best for oneself nonstrategically in a noncooperative condition actually amounts to. In Part I, I criticized the so-called security level as a contrived nonagreement baseline with no sound connection to the supposed object of representing the results of independent utility maximization. Finding a plausible way of characterizing independent utility maximizing for a whole society is, needless to say, far harder than doing so for Braithwaite's two musicians. Gauthier's most recent line is, as I noted in section 30, that since (under ideal conditions) market exchange can arrive at a Pareto optimum from individual maximizing behavior, a market distribution would (under these ideal conditions) constitute a nonagreement baseline. He has not explained what implications this has for the real world where these ideal conditions do not hold.

So much for Gauthier's location in the second row. As far as his being placed in the first column is concerned, this reflects his claim that the method of splitting the difference is to be seen not primarily as an ethically attractive way of seeing to it that the parties share the cooperative surplus equitably but, rather, as a rival to the Nash solution (especially as presented by Harsanyi), that is to say, as a way of simulating the outcome of bargaining between ideally rational parties. As I pointed out in section 30, Gauthier does have a subsidiary argument for splitting the difference as a way of proportioning rewards to contributions. But this is so much a matter of defining "contribution" to fit the formula that it is hard to take it very seriously as an independent justification.

I have taken exception to the claim that splitting the difference is superior as a bargaining solution to that of Nash. And I try to show (in Appendix B) that Gauthier's attacks on the Nash solution are based on a variety of misunderstandings and confusions. But the larger question that arises here is: How does a "Hobbesian" method (whatever the details) of dividing the cooperative surplus fit together with a "Lockean" way of establishing the nonagreement point? I shall return to this question in the next section, when I shall be asking about the rationale of the structural choices that have been made.

A similar question about coherence may be asked about the diagonally opposite cell, which reverses the "Hobbesian" and "Lockean" elements in the two stages. Thus, according to Braithwaite, the baseline is to be established by a no-holds-barred struggle for relative advantage, including the deliberate infliction of injury on the other party purely in order to lower his baseline payoff. Yet at the same time, Braithwaite's predominant rationale for his proposed method of moving from the nonagreement baseline to the Pareto frontier is, if I interpret him correctly, that it divides the cooperative surplus in a way that gives the two men equal shares in it, measured in terms of utility normalized in accordance with the formula recommended by Braithwaite. (See section 4 and Appendix A.) The obvious question that arises here is: Why should people who are prepared to contemplate mayhem to establish a relatively favorable baseline payoff be willing to accept that the move to the Pareto frontier should be conducted so as to secure equal gains rather than by simulating rational bargaining?

If no good answer is forthcoming—and I certainly do not think Braithwaite offers us one—we may conclude that the theory would be more coherent if we took the alternative interpretation of the method proposed for normalizing utilities, under which it is understood as a way of capturing the relative bargaining strengths of the two men. This interpretation puts Braithwaite into the first cell of Figure 8.1, where his name is shown in parentheses to indicate that this is not the main interpretation. I may add that on neither interpretation does Braithwaite's proposal for dividing the cooperative surplus seem to me to have much to commend it (see Appendix A). But my concern here is primarily with the positions taken on the two dichotomies that define Figure 8.1, and only incidentally with the detailed specifications of the baseline and method of dividing the cooperative surplus.

Since Rawls makes the explicit criticism of Braithwaite that "to each according to his threat advantage is not a principle of justice" (see above, section 8), it may seem strange that his name should appear in the lower half of the second cell, under Braithwaite's name. In fact, his placement in both the second and the fourth cells is designed to represent within the schema Rawls's attempt in *A Theory of Justice* to embrace the Humean idea that "everyone must find himself a gainer" from justice. By attributing to him both a "Hobbesian" and a "Lockean" state of nature as the nonagreement point I intend to signify that he seems to me to have two different forms of the comparison from which justice has to emerge as relatively advantageous.

If we take seriously Rawls's invocation of the Humean circumstances of justice, the baseline of what he describes as "general egoism" would seem to be set by the unconstrained use of whatever power one has to improve one's position. I suggested in section 23 that Rawls's discussion of international justice may have this as its background. But then in section 30 I suggested that in general Rawls seems to envisage a state of "general egoism" as one in which people engage in independent maximization. This, of course, corresponds to the form of nonagreement baseline endorsed by Gauthier and Lucas.

In *A Theory of Justice*, Rawls does not bother to say much about the noncooperative baseline. The reason for this perfunctory treatment of the nonagreement point is, of course, that Rawls maintains that it plays no part in the determination of the principles of justice. People cannot, he says, make any legitimate claim to preserve the relative advantages they would have had under conditions of noncooperation. And clearly there is nothing in the principles of justice—equal civil rights, fair equality of opportunity, and the difference principle to regulate economic inequalities—that makes any reference to what people might be able to obtain in the absence of just institutions.

Rawls's willingness to talk about noncooperative baselines is not enough to make him into a bona fide adherent of two-stage solutions. For the specification of a two-stage solution was not simply that the outcome must make everyone better off (or at least no worse off) than at the nonagreement point. It also includes the stipulation that the nonagreement payoffs should constitute the jumping-off point for the move to the Pareto frontier. This entails that if someone's position at the noncooperative baseline improves relative to that of others, this advantage should be reflected in that person's doing better out of the cooperative outcome. This condition is obviously violated by Rawls's principles of justice.

I have left until the last the first cell in Figure 8.1, which has the name of Hume below the line. The just-concluded discussion of Rawls will enable me to deal expeditiously with the reasons for placing Hume here. Unlike Rawls, Hume can I believe be regarded as a true two-stage theorist. (I am here referring, of course, to his theory of the origin of justice, as against his theory of why justice is a virtue.) It is scarcely necessary, I hope, to offer the caution that there is always an element of anachronism at work when one tries to force on a historical figure distinctions of which he was quite unaware. Nevertheless, it does seem to me that Hume really has the essence of the two-stage approach in his account of the origins of property. There is no need to rehearse the reasons set forth in section 18 for saying that the doctrine of the circumstances of justice puts him in the upper rather than the lower row in Figure 8.1. But if we recall Hume's account (discussed in section 20) of the way in which sheer physical possession gets transformed into assured property, we can surely say that the positions people have at the nonagreement point (possession) form the basis for the move to the Pareto frontier (property). Those with more at the nonagreement point retain their advantage, since Hume tells us that everyone would naturally settle on the rule that people should retain as property what they held before as possessions. Thus, in contrast to Rawls, the determination of justice in Hume's theory requires a reference to what people had at the nonagreement point.

37. TWO-STAGE FOUNDATIONS OF SOCIAL INSTITUTIONS

In the previous section I was engaged primarily in tying up loose ends from Parts I and II by showing how a number of writers fit, more or less comfortably, into the four cells of Figure 8.1. I now want to ask what ideas about the nature of justice would be required to underwrite the choices that define the four structures set out in Figure 8.1.

Let me begin by picking up the discussion of Rawls from the previous section. I said there that Rawls was in an anomalous position in that he appeared to accept the relevance of the nonagreement point as setting a threshold payoff which must be surpassed by the payoff from justice, yet at the same time he did not accept the relevance of the nonagreement baseline beyond that. If we say that everyone should get the nonagreement payoff and then ask how the cooperative surplus is to be divided, it is hard to imagine how we could defend the answer that the cooperative surplus is to be divided unequally in a way that exactly cancels out advantages and disadvantages at the nonagreement point. Yet that is the implication of prescribing that the final distribution should be equal. There is no need to repeat here the discussion in section 30. All we have to observe is that Rawls's attempt to combine a nonagreement point as a threshold value with his two principles of justice is not a success. If we took seriously the logic of the nonagreement point, we would have to shift him into the left-hand column. And if we take seriously the principles of justice we should drop him from Figure 8.1 altogether.

In Figure 8.1, I divided two-stage theorists into those who proposed two-stage solutions for micro-level disputes such as that of Matthew and Luke or the two legatees and those who saw the two-stage technique as a way of providing principles on the basis of which a society's major institutions could be founded. If I have succeeded in expelling Rawls from the upper and lower cells in the right-hand column of Figure 8.1, the only remaining macro-level theorists of two-stage justice are Hume and Gauthier, occupying respectively the upper and lower cells in the left-hand column. My discussion of Rawls should have prepared the way for what I now want to argue: first, that there are good reasons for the surviving macro-level entries being in the left-hand column only; and second, that Hume's place is more secure than Gauthier's.

Both points arise from what I said in section 30 about the assumptions that might lead a philosopher to think it relevant to be able to assure people that justice will pay better than a free-for-all, and thus to embrace a two-stage theory of justice. I said that the assumption that would naturally lead to such a concern was that justice must be a matter of mutual advantage. But I then went on to argue that stability based on self-interest dictates the rationale of the division of the cooperative surplus. It must rest on relative bargaining strength. This leads us to the left-hand rather than the right-hand column in Figure 8.1.

As I pointed out in section 5, a bargaining solution is, indeed, an equal-gain solution in a certain sense. But what divides the left-hand and right-hand columns is not the formula itself (the Nash solution, splitting the difference, and Braithwaite's solution could appear in either column) but what is claimed as the merit of the formula. If its merit is claimed to be that it is fair because it provides equal gains, that puts it in the right-hand column. If it is claimed to be stable because it corresponds to relative bargaining strength, that puts it in the left-hand column.

Both Gauthier and Hume (in his theory of the origins of property) appeal only to self-interest, and I think it is clear that they are properly situated in the left-hand column. Gauthier, as we have seen, is quite explicit that the division of the cooperative surplus should simulate the outcome of rational bargaining. Hume's answer has to be inferred, but there are two strong grounds for putting him in the left-hand column. The first is that, if I am correct, the logic of his position commits him to that. The other is that his proposal about the convention establishing property—that everyone should keep what he already possesses—is plausibly seen as a way of ensuring that the relative bargaining power of the parties will be reflected in the cooperative solution.

The second point is that Hume's position is more secure than Gauthier's. If we are to depend on nothing but self-interest for our derivation of the principles of justice, how can we postulate that the parties will forgo the helps and advantages of force and fraud that Hobbes allowed them in the state of nature? Why would they be constrained by a rule that tells them to ignore strategic advantage and behave as if they were independent unstrategic maximizers of utility? Locke's fanciful state of nature, in which the institutions of a market society were established without any need for political arrangements, depended on an equally fantastic "law of nature" which most people supposedly knew and respected, that told them about rules for the acquisition of property and such. Gauthier tries to get the same results without the Lockean baggage, but this makes his theory even more fantastic. Without taking the space to argue it here, let me just say that Gauthier seems to me to have got himself into a hopeless position. If he wants to stick with all the implications of denying the bifurcation of practical reason, he must admit that a stable outcome has to reflect bargaining power, without picking and choosing among its sources. But if he wants to say that people ought to respect the alleged rights of others even if this means voluntarily accepting an outcome that could be improved on by making someone else worse off, then he requires some constraints on the maximizing of utility other than those derivable from considerations of mutual advantage. Why should anyone who is pursuing his own advantage accept a nonagreement point that is hugely contrary to his own interests if this nonagreement point rests on nothing stronger than Gauthier's fiat?

Let me make this more concrete. As we saw in section 7, Gauthier claims that it is legitimate to make others worse off than they would otherwise be so long as this is the by-product of making oneself better off, but not if it comes about as the result of a deliberate attempt to improve one's relative advantage. This gives rise to a "proviso" that "prohibits bettering one's situation through interaction that worsens the situation of another."[1] To see how this works, consider the following example:

> Suppose that we live as fisherfolk along the banks of a river. If you compel me to fish for you then you violate the proviso in preventing me from exercising my powers as I see fit. If you seize the fish I catch then you violate the proviso unless you compensate me for my labour and my intended use of the fish. But if you, living upstream from me, merely use the river for the disposal of your wastes, then even though you thereby kill many of the fish in my part of the stream, you do not violate the proviso. For although you worsen my situation in relation to what I should expect in your absence, you do not better your own situation through interaction with me. You are no better off than you would be were no one to live downstream from you. The cost you impose on me is not necessary to the benefit you receive; it is not a *displaced cost*. Rather, the cost is occasioned solely by my presence, which from your point of view may be simply unwanted.[2]

According to Gauthier, all this changes as soon as the upstream and downstream people enter into trading relations. But if the price of trading to the upstreamers is that they have to clean up the pollution it may well not be advantageous to them to initiate trading. The question is: Why should the downstream people put up with the pollution of the river in the absence of trading relations? If they have the ability to threaten the upstream people with unpleasant consequences unless they stop polluting, why should they not do so? It is hard to see why they should be deterred by the thought that all they are doing is bringing about an "unproductive" transfer by shifting the outcome along the Pareto frontier.

I have taken the story about pollution as the most simple and egregious illustration of Gauthier's "proviso" at work. He also has a fairy story about the individual appropriation of land from a common which follows Locke without invoking a "law of nature" to regulate appropriation. I find this obscure in detail, but the upshot is at any rate clear enough: that so long as nobody is worse off than under a regime of common ownership, the inequality of holdings can be as unequal as you like.[3] Yet here again I see no reason why those who are relatively disadvantaged by this unequal system of ownership should not, if they can, impose a redistribution that works to their benefit.

Gauthier is clear enough that in a two-stage theory such as his own the notion of mutually advantageous agreement can come in only at the second stage. There must be a first stage, which defines the initial position from which bargaining takes place, and this must rest on something other than agreement.

> Contractarianism offers a secular understanding of rights. But the idea of morals by agreement may mislead, if it is supposed that rights must be the product or outcome of agreement. Were we to adopt this account, we should suppose that rights were determined by the principle of minimax relative concession. But as we have seen, the application of this principle, or more generally, the emergence of either co-operative or market interaction, demands an initial definition of the actors in terms of their factor endowments, and we have identified individual rights with these endowments. Rights provide the starting point for, and not the outcome of, agreement. They are what each person brings to the bargaining table, not what she takes from it.[4]

As I have pointed out (especially in chapter 2), it is quite possible to define the nonagreement point on the basis of ethical considerations. We can simply impose on the parties some nonagreement point—for example, silence in the case of the two musicians—and work out our hypothetical bargains from there. But if the parties are left to themselves (as in the state of nature that Gauthier presupposes) then an ethical baseline can occur only if the parties are moved by ethical considerations. Gauthier denies that there are ethical considerations of this kind: he claims that it is inconsistent with reason for people to hold back from any other motive than that of long-term self-interest. But this entails that the nonagreement point has to be one based on the pursuit of individual interest. Gauthier claims that the rights defining the nonagreement point are "rationally grounded."[5] But I do not think that he gets anywhere with this project.[6] Indeed, one has only to reflect on the examples of pollution and enclosure to realize how hopeless an undertaking this must be.

Gauthier's way of setting up the nonagreement point in a state of nature seems to me singularly unappetizing as a moral principle, in the sense of "moral principle" in which everybody except Gauthier uses the expression. I cannot imagine why people who were seeking terms of agreement that could not reasonably be rejected should accept that the baseline should be defined so that nobody can ever be made worse off than if other people did not exist. (This means, as we saw, that the upstreamers cannot rightly be compelled by the downstreamers to avoid polluting the river, so long as the upstreamers do not actually gain any benefit from the losses inflicted on the downstreamers, that is to say, so long as the damage arises as a by-product of independent maximization.) From a moral point of view, there seems to be no substance in a prohibition on any redistribution that would violate such a baseline. For the criterion of "not taking advantage" which Gauthier uses to define the nonagreement point has no moral appeal once we understand exactly what it means. At the same time, it is abundantly clear that a nonagreement point established by people who were attempting to maximize their own utility would not incorporate any such limitation on the pursuit of relative advantage.

The conclusion that I draw from this discussion is that there is only one way of creating a theory of justice as mutual advantage based entirely on utility-maximizing motivation. That is to define the noncooperative baseline as one arising from a strategic struggle for relative advantage and then move from there to the Pareto frontier via simulated bargaining over the division of the cooperative surplus.

38. FAIR DIVISION AND SOCIAL JUSTICE

I have made my arguments (see especially sections 18, 30, and 35) against the conception of justice as what is to the mutual advantage of people pursuing their own interests. I have nothing to add here. The question I now want to ask is this. Suppose I am right in suggesting that justice as impartially is the superior conception. Could we still treat justice as exclusively a matter of distributing gains from cooperation over a suitably defined nonagreement point? Suppose, in other words, that we took the requirement of impartial approval to give rise to, say, the utilitarian principle or Rawls's principles of justice. Could we then say that such principles are to be used to define a set of nonagreement points and that a just outcome is what arises when people move from these nonagreement points to the Pareto frontier in a permissible way?

It should be noticed that as soon as we look at a two-stage construction in this way it ceases to be a self-contained theory of justice. The nonagreement baseline is now imported from outside the two-stage construction. That is to say, it does not in the version we are now canvassing come about as a result of the actors pursuing their own interests. Rather, it is imposed on the basis of a notion of justice that appeals to the moral motive. I shall devote the next chapter to a discussion of the way in which impartial principles might be derived. For the present, however, let us simply take it that the utilitarian principle and Rawls's principles can be taken as examples of principles that are of the right kind. The real disagreements between them are, from this point of view, family quarrels.

Another way of putting our question is, then, as follows. Let us concede that there can be no macro-level two-stage theory of justice corresponding to justice as impartiality. For we need external criteria in order to establish the nonagreement point. Can we nevertheless rescue the two-stage approach for micro-level justice? Can we, in other words, say that justice is fair division of the cooperative surplus over a non-cooperative baseline derived from impartially approvable principles such as those of the utilitarians or Rawls? I want in the end to reject this suggestion. But I should begin by making it clear that it cannot be rejected out of hand. It has a certain plausibility. Indeed, as we shall see, Rawls himself comes very close to endorsing it, even if he does not endorse it without qualification.

What gives the suggestion some plausibility is this. It is surely undeniable that in any complex society (probably any society at all) people will constantly be faced with micro-level situations in which there is a nonagreement point and a possibility of moving beyond it in a way that produces mutual gain. Whatever its official ideology, no modern society can do without institutions that make room for millions of transactions every day that fall within the two-stage framework.

To take an obvious and important example, no society will try to allocate all consumer goods directly to its members. Whether it is called money, coupons, or (the favorite of science fiction writers) credits, there has to be some resource representing generalized purchasing power. Its possessor then has a choice on any given occasion of keeping it, in which case the shop or commissary (or whatever it is called) keeps the goods, or exchanging some of the generalized resource for some of the goods. This is the simplest case of a two-stage transaction, with a nonagreement point and a move to a (presumably) Pareto-preferred outcome. Similarly, we need not doubt that in, say, the Soviet Union, as in Britain or the United States, problems such as those of Matthew and Luke arise among occupants of adjacent poorly soundproofed apartments, and couples try to reach some joint decision about what film to go to. Throwing out the grand theory of two-stage justice thus leaves us with ubiquitous problems of fair division.

Wherever there are rights we have the potential for a problem of fair division. Some rights are officially inalienable. Except in certain special contexts (such as entering a boxing ring or undergoing surgery) nobody can by consent license another to inflict physical injury, for example. But most rights are available as bargaining chips: we stand ready to give up the discretion they provide us with if we can get something in return (such as a similar waiver of discretion by somebody else) that we value more. Thus, Matthew and Luke had, in Braithwaite's story, the right to play their musical instruments every evening if they chose; they could exercise this right at their own discretion (for example, in order to create an advantageous nonagreement baseline), and they could also give up the right as part of an agreement that gave them larger benefits (the chance to play solo part of the time) than the value of the rights given up.

From an impartial perspective we cannot avoid a choice of principles for the creation of nonagreement points by actors who have certain rights. (For example, should Matthew and Luke establish relative advantage by inflicting the maximum legally permissible damage on one another?) And, similarly, we cannot avoid taking a view about the right way of sharing the cooperative surplus. We may, of course, choose the answer that it shall be considered fair for the parties to do anything within their rights to further their interests. But that is still an answer. If we want a constructivist solution tracking this decision rule, it must be that contained in the upper left-hand cell in Figure 8.1. Suppose someone were to complain that such a solution was unfair to him because it was unreasonably one-sided. The reply that could be made to him would be that the principle of exploiting one's rights to maximum advantage is impartially acceptable, so he cannot properly complain of the workings of the solution modeling the outcomes of such behavior.

The alternative line is, of course, to say that not every use of a right is beyond criticism. Someone who makes use of threats in order to enhance a bargaining position is, it may be said, behaving shabbily even if the threat is legal. "Thus, for example, Steven Pepe of the University of Michigan Law School has studied the responses of hundreds of lawyers to an ethically-charged negotiation problem [where negotiation is the alternative to going to trial]. One side is given information that the adversary's clients are illegal immigrants. Many lawyers use the threat of deportation to force a favorable settlement, despite the fact that this comes very close to extortion."[7] I suspect that the great majority of people who are not lawyers would instinctively regard this as a sleazy way of conducting oneself, which obviously presupposes some notions, however inchoate, about the elements that can properly enter into the establishment of the nonagreement baseline—here, that failure to agree should mean going to trial rather than the deportation of one of the parties.

Again, where the nonagreement baseline is not itself in question, one might well think that the exploitation of an asymmetry in it is not necessarily fair. Thus, to take our cinema example again, suppose we accept that either person has the right to go off without the other if they cannot agree on a film to see together. If one of them attaches more importance than the other to going together (because it makes more difference to the enjoyment of the evening, because the other one has a car, or for whatever other reason), should this result in the one to whom it matters less dictating the choice of film week after week, as the Nash solution would predict? Many people would, I think, regard this as an unfair exploitation of the nonagreement point, while at the same time not wishing to propose as impartially defensible any alternative to the underlying system of rights that generates the nonagreement baseline.

UTILITARIAN FAIR DIVISION

Let us look more systematically at the relation between macro-level principles for institutions and the specification of the appropriate kind of two-stage procedure in various problems of fair division on the small scale. And let us begin by returning to Rawls's distinction (mentioned in section 33) between on one side pure procedural justice and on the other side perfect or imperfect procedural justice. According to Rawls, his own theory about the assessment of outcomes is one of pure procedural justice: once just institutions are in place, their justice carries over to whatever outcomes arise from people acting in the ways that are permitted by the rules defining these institutions. I shall discuss this idea below. What I shall do here is to take up the contrast that Rawls wants to draw between this procedural approach and that to which he says utilitarianism is committed.

Rawls tells us that, unlike his own theory,

> utilitarianism does not interpret the basic structure as a scheme of pure procedural justice. For the utilitarian has, in principle anyway, an independent standard for judging all distributions, namely, whether they produce the greatest net balance of satisfaction. In his theory, institutions are more or less imperfect arrangements for bringing about this end. Thus given existing desires and preferences, and the natural continuations into the future which they allow, the statesman's aim is to set up those social schemes that will best approximate an already specified goal. Since these arrangements are subject to the unavoidable constraints and hindrances of everyday life, the basic structure is a case of imperfect procedural justice.[8]

The notion of imperfect procedural justice is illustrated by the example of a trial. Here, Rawls says,

> the desired outcome is that the defendant should be declared guilty if and only if he has committed the offense with which he is charged. . . . But it seems impossible to design the legal rules so that they always lead to the correct result. . . . A trial, then, is an instance of imperfect procedural justice. Even though the law is carefully followed, and the proceedings fairly and properly conducted, it may reach the wrong outcome. An innocent man may be found guilty, a guilty man may be set free. In such cases we speak of a miscarriage of justice: the injustice springs from no human fault but from a fortuitous combination of circumstances which defeats the purpose of the legal rules. The characteristic mark of imperfect procedural justice is that while there is an independent criterion for the correct outcome, there is no feasible procedure which is sure to lead to it.[9]

I am inclined to think that the notion of imperfect procedural justice is in fact tailor-made to fit the example of a trial and that its extension to such matters as the utilitarian appraisal of institutions is confusing. There are two reasons for this. The first is that not all institutions are well characterized as procedures. A trial is indeed a procedure. But a substantive law addressed to citizens or a rule instructing a civil servant to pay so many dollars a week to anyone meeting certain requirements of eligibility is only quite artificially described as a procedure. To equate institutions with procedures is to load the dice in favor of proceduralism.

The second objection, which explains why utilitarianism does not fit the model well, is that we cannot always separate the "correct outcome" from the performance of the institution. A correct verdict is a target, but the utilitarian criterion is an arrow. That is to say, it does not define a goal in the ordinary sense—something finite that might be reached or missed—but simple gives a direction. All we can say is that more utility is better than less. "The maximum utility" means nothing in itself—it is like "the largest real number." It can be given sense only when interpreted as "the maximum feasible utility." This has significant implications, as I shall try to show.

What makes a trial an example of imperfect procedural justice is, according to Rawls, that we can in principle specify the "right answer" and compare the actual outcome of the trial with it. (This is, of course, not an uncontroversial position itself. It entails denial of the legal-realist view that the outcome is the outcome and to say it is wrong is merely to say one dislikes it or wishes the case had been decided otherwise.) It is important to observe here that a trial is an instrument of imperfect procedural justice even under conditions of ideal theory: there is no appeal here by Rawls to imperfections of the usual kind. What makes the institution of a trial imperfect is that there may be miscarriages of justice even if (a) we have the system of rules best adapted to reach the right results, and (b) everybody follows the rules conscientiously. (The evidence against someone may be sufficient for conviction yet the person may still actually be innocent, for example.)

Now transfer the argument about the imperfection of procedures to utilitarian institutions. We have (a) the set of institutions that produces the most utility attainable in the actual conditions of human life if adhered to, and (b) a situation in which everybody complies with the requirements that these institutions impose on individual conduct. We are now invited to say that, because "these arrangements are subject to the unavoidable constraints and hindrances of everyday life," they can therefore realize only "imperfect procedural justice." But now bear in mind that "maximum utility" defines a direction and not a point to be aimed at. To say that an arrangement fails to maximize utility can only mean that there is some feasible alternative arrangement that would do better on the utilitarian criterion. Rawls tells us, however, that the constraints and hindrances that prevent the set of institutions we have picked out from doing even better on the utilitarian criterion are unavoidable. But if this is so, how can the institutions be said to be defective from a utilitarian standpoint?

Of course, if human beings were capable of making quicker and more accurate calculations, the optimal utilitarian institutions might be different from those optimal in actual conditions. Perhaps the rules could be more flexible, and this would permit the attainment of a greater sum of utility. But this seems beside the point. If the end is to maximize utility and the set of institutions is the one best adapted to achieve that end under conditions of full compliance, it seems to me we have perfect procedural justice as Rawls defines it.

However, the larger conclusion to be drawn is, I suggest, that no gain in understanding is to be secured by deploying Rawls's distinction between perfect and imperfect procedural justice in the present context. In practice, of course, all institutions are imperfect. To begin with, they are rarely if ever the best possible and, even if they were, full compliance with their demands would be far too much to hope for. Whether or not under ideal conditions an institution could be perfect (on Rawls's criteria of perfection) does not seem to be of any great interest. I believe that we should do better to drop any talk of perfect and imperfect procedural justice and instead simply talk about outcome-oriented principles for the assessment of social institutions.

Thus, utilitarianism is an outcome-oriented theory in that it tells us to reach a judgment on a social institution by trying to work out what would actually happen if it were put into operation. We look at outcomes, in other words, and judge them better or worse according to the utilitarian standard by seeing how far wants are satisfied. (We could, alternatively or additionally, look to see how equally utility is distributed, or how much those with the least are getting.) These assessments of outcomes feed back to create our assessments of institutions. If the outcomes arising from the operation of an institution are good, then the institution is good.

The contrast with outcome-based principles is resource-based principles. Thus, Rawls—who here stands for a host of liberal theorists—maintains that we can define just institutions without having to talk about the outcomes that can be anticipated from their operation. All we have to talk about is the distribution of resources, in the broadest sense of the word—that is to say, such things as rights, opportunities, and income. Although, as we shall see, these two kinds of theory need not lead to different cells in Figure 8.1, they must in the nature of the case get to their destinations by different routes.

As a matter of pure logic, it is clear that utilitarianism, as an outcome-oriented criterion for assessing institutions, cannot subscribe to pure procedural justice. The idea of pure procedural justice, which is epitomized by a fairly run lottery, is that if the procedure is fair the outcome, whatever it may turn out to be, is morally acceptable. Even if a utilitarian thought lotteries were defensible (which is possible, for although they only move money around they also generate hope, excitement, and so on), the institution itself would still be judged by its outcomes, namely, its tendency (when fairly run) to produce a net surplus of utility.

Whether a resource-oriented principle for assessing institutions is tied to pure procedural justice is a question that will have to be raised later in this section. I want first to focus on fair division from a utilitarian perspective and ask what can be said about problems such as the legacy case or the case of Matthew and Luke.

It may be recalled from chapter 2 that utilitarianism does not, when applied directly, give rise to baseline-dependent solutions at all (see especially section 9). In theory, we can generate a best set of outcomes directly from the utilitarian principle itself. Thus, in the case of dividing the legacy that we first discussed in chapter 1, the direct application of the utilitarian principle to the legacy case would not give privileged position to a nonagreement point but would simply pick the outcome most conducive to the end of maximizing utility. There would be no requirement that both legatees should gain over the nonagreement point of keeping what they had to begin with. If it would maximize utility for the poor legatee not only to get the whole of the legacy but also to get half of the rich one's bank account, that would be the best outcome.

This, however, was qualified heavily in chapter 3 when we brought in larger questions of adaptation (making choices in anticipation of the effects of rules), coordination, and information. On the basis of such considerations, I reached the conclusion that the direct application of the utilitarian principle to all questions would be disastrous in its own terms. It would be self-defeating (in the sense that it would fail to get close to the achievement of the utilitarian end) to refer all decisions straight back to the utilitarian criterion. There must be institutions that give rights to people, and once we have rights we have the material for nonagreement points. Then the road is open to problems of fair division. For there may always be the possibility of mutual gain by moving away from a nonagreement point in a way that is coordinated with a move away by somebody else, and this naturally invites questions about fairness.

What, then, can be said in general about utilitarian fair division? The answer must be: in general, not much. I shall take it that the arguments in chapter 3 have established adequately the necessity, as a means to the utilitarian end, of establishing systems of rights. But once these rights exist, we have to ask on a case-by-case basis whether the utilitarian end will best be achieved if the parties exploit the rights to the hilt (thus putting the constructivist solution in the upper left-hand cell of Figure 8.1), or if they follow constraints that will put it in some other cell of Figure 8.1, or if they follow some other rule altogether.

The naive approach would, of course, be to say that people should exercise their rights in such a way as to maximize aggregate utility. The obvious objection to this proposal is that it begs the question. It is precisely the difficulty of knowing what actions would be called for by the utilitarian principle that requires even a society of people dedicated to acting as utilitarians to create a system of rights. If such a prescription for deploying rights could be acted on we would not need rights in the first place.

What has just been said presupposes a society of people committed to following unswervingly the path marked out by utilitarian precepts. The other reason why people who subscribe to utilitarianism in general would want to have institutions that give people rights is that they would be unlikely to trust themselves or one another to act unselfishly whenever the utilitarian criterion called for them to do so. The point here is that it is a good deal easier to act (and to get others to act) on some utilitarian-based rule (whether enforceable or not) than to wait until one is engaged in an actual dispute (so that each party knows its own interests) before asking what the utilitarian principle entails.

On the strength of these ideas, it might be argued that even a society of dedicated utilitarians (and *a fortiori* a society mistrustful of its members' fidelity to utilitarianism) would quite possibly find it best to set up economic institutions designed to produce good outcomes when people took economic decisions calculating what would be in their interests. But there would still be questions left about what should count as a legitimate way of pursuing one's interest. We might guess that a utilitarian theory about the legitimate bounds to the pursuit of one's own interest would have to be very complicated. How, for example, should the nonagreement baseline be defined in a labor market: by individual withdrawal of labor only, or by collective withdrawal as well? What about picketing, boycotts, sympathetic strikes, and so on? It seems hard to see why any general answer should be forthcoming to such questions. The best solution (if it includes the market determination of wages at all) will presumably depend on the disposition of relative bargaining power best calculated to produce an optimal level of settlements. Where a small group of workers can by striking hold a country to ransom, perhaps the collective withdrawal of labor should not be allowed. But in many instances workers will be able to get the amount a utilitarian would want them to have only with every possible help. The same form of argument can clearly be applied to economic relationships across the board.

The general point applies to all outcome-oriented criteria. If we start from desired outcomes and work back to institutions, we cannot sensibly talk about the performance of alternative rules unless we at the same time talk about the objectives and capabilities of the people who are to operate within these rules. We can see this from Rawls's own example of a rule for dividing a cake by having the person who does the dividing take the last piece. As I pointed out when I introduced the example in section 33, there are plenty of ways of getting a cake divided equally besides this one. What is distinctive about this way of securing an equal division is that it employs a procedural device to harness self-interest to the achievement of an equitable end. As Rawls himself says of the example, "certain assumptions are made here, such as that the man selected can divide the cake equally, wants as large a piece as he can get, and so on."[10] Clearly, it is correct to say that "there is . . . a procedure guaranteed to lead to" the desired outcome only if the procedure is operated by someone with the capacities and motivations specified here by Rawls.[11]

RESOURCIST FAIR DIVISION

I shall now take up the approach in which institutions are judged not according to the outcomes they are predicted to bring about but by the distribution of resources they create directly. There is no question here that two-stage micro-level problems will arise, because in the nature of the case we will have a system of rights and, as we have seen, rights contain the seeds for problems of fair division. The question is therefore simply what version of two-stage theory is to be relevant.

I have quoted Rawls as saying that "utilitarianism does not interpret the basic structure as a scheme of pure procedural justice,"[12] and I said that this seems clearly true. The context of that statement is the general discussion of pure procedural justice upon which I drew in talking about constructivism in the previous chapter (section 33), where Rawls told us that "the notion of pure procedural justice is best understood by a comparison with perfect and imperfect procedural justice."[13] I argued earlier in this section in favor of dropping the distinction between perfect and imperfect procedural justice, so I need to reformulate the relevant distinction. For the present purpose all we need to have in order to specify the alternative to pure procedural justice is the idea that there is some end-state (such as securing an equal distribution of some given object, maximizing utility, or finding guilty those and only those who are actually guilty) against which the performance of an institution can be measured. In contrast with this, Rawls claims to espouse pure procedural justice, which "obtains when there is no independent criterion for the right result: instead there is a correct or fair procedure such that the outcome is likewise correct or fair, whatever it is, provided the procedure has been properly followed."[14]

This immediately raises the following question. If an outcome-oriented theory of just institutions rules out pure procedural justice, does a resource-oriented theory of just institutions entail pure procedural justice? It is not, I think, easy to say what Rawls himself believes the answer to that question to be. In any case, I shall myself wish to propose a negative answer.

Rawls is, we may observe, a believer in pure procedural justice both for the derivation of principles and for the operation of social institutions. Thus the notion of justice as fairness discussed in section 33 is pure procedural justice at the stage where principles are chosen for the basic structure of a society. It is important to recognize that this does not in itself do anything to create a presumption in favor of pure procedural justice for the relations between institutions and outcomes. As we have seen, it is possible to get from a variant of Rawls's original position to the principle of utility, which we know to be incompatible with pure procedural justice for outcomes. It is a separate step to say that the justice of institutions carries over to ensure the justice of outcomes. That the principles for institutions should be resource-oriented is a necessary condition of being a proceduralist about outcomes, but it is not, as I shall argue, a sufficient one. In other words, it is possible to say that some distribution of rights is just but also to say that only certain deployments of those rights are fair.

Rawls, however, is quite explicit that, if the institutions are just, the outcomes must be accepted as just. Indeed, it is interesting to notice that at one point he actually invokes the slogan of "justice as fairness" in support of this claim. "The main problem of distributive justice is the choice of a social system. The principles of justice apply to the basic structure and regulate how its major institutions are combined into one scheme. Now, as we have seen, the idea of justice as fairness is to use the notion of pure procedural justice to handle the contingencies of particular situations. The social system is to be designed so that the resulting distribution is just however things turn out."[15]

Let us see what Rawls thinks pure procedural justice might be like in a contemporary Western society. He tells us, then, that "to apply the notion of pure procedural justice to distributive shares it is necessary to set up and to administer impartially a just system of institutions."[16] These include competitive markets, wealth "widely distributed," a "reasonable social minimum," "fair equality of opportunity," and "the other equal liberties." These institutions, Rawls says, can be made to satisfy the difference principle, and are therefore just.[17]

Whatever arises from just institutions is itself just, according to Rawls. "The allotment of the items produced takes place in accordance with the public system of rules, and this system determines what is produced, how much is produced, and by what means. . . . Thus in this kind of procedural justice the correctness of the distribution is founded on the justice of the scheme of cooperation from which it arises and on answering the claims of individuals engaged in it."[18] What Rawls means by the last, rather obscure, clause is that any complaints about a particular outcome are to be referred to the basic structure out of which it arose. "It is the arrangement of the basic structure which is to be judged, and judged from a general point of view. . . . Thus the acceptance of the two principles constitutes an understanding to discard as irrelevant as a matter of social justice much of the information and many of the complications of everyday life."[19]

We can see more clearly what animates Rawls if we turn to chapter 5 of *A Theory of Justice*, on "Distributive Shares," where it becomes apparent that he has almost as rosy a view of the market as does Gauthier. I am inclined to think, indeed, that Rawls's idea of pure procedural justice was probably derived from the Smithian "hidden hand" and then generalized. "The ideal scheme" that he will be sketching, Rawls tells us, "makes considerable use of market arrangements. It is only in this way, I believe, that the problem of distribution can be handled as a case of pure procedural justice. Further, we also gain the advantages of efficiency and protect the important liberty of free choice of occupation."[20]

The relation between the state and society here is reminiscent of the deist's idea of the relation between God and the world. Having set the machinery in motion, God will not intervene to respond to prayers for rain or to strike down some spectacular piece of impiety with a bolt of lightning. Similarly, "income and wages will be just once a (workably) competitive price system is properly organized and embedded in a just basic structure. These conditions are sufficient. The distribution that results is a case of background justice on the analogy of the outcome of a fair game."[21]

As in the standard story told in Economics 101, nobody need worry about anything except pursuing his own interest. If the institutions are once set up correctly they can be counted on to do the rest. So long as we have the right "background institutions" (already briefly mentioned), "the resulting distribution is just however things turn out."[22] Now Rawls does not explicitly say, as far as I can see, that within this set of economic arrangements everyone is to maximize utility, profit, or whatever. But everything he says presupposes the usual assumptions made by economists. (In the absence of such maximizing behavior, for example, the assumption on which Rawls depends, that trading in a market will reach a Pareto optimum, will not in general be true.)

Moreover, as we may see in Appendix C, Rawls does explicitly tell us, in the context of paying people unequal amounts to induce them to work, that nobody can be reproached for not working for the sake of others. The idea here is that it is settled in advance that there shall be freedom of occupational choice; and if this results in having to pay some people a lot to do socially necessary jobs requiring rare skills, nobody can complain about the unequal distribution of income that emerges. It is, in other words, for the society to set things up so that people are faced with incentives sufficient to make it attractive to them, when making a self-interested choice, to do what is needed.

Rawls does not have much to say about the exploitation of rights in the noneconomic sphere. But it can at any rate be said that his sections on "principles for individuals," which consider fairness and justice as attributes of individual actions, nowhere express any qualms about the unfair use of rights guaranteed by the basic structure. On the contrary, what is reinforced in this part of *A Theory of Justice* is the idea that people have done all that can be asked of them when they have complied with the demands of just institutions or, where necessary, have helped to set them up.[23]

It might be thought that Rawls's discussion of the case of Matthew and Luke (see above, section 8) would acquit him of the charge of complacency about institutions, at any rate outside the economic sphere. Does it not imply that there must be principles of micro-level fairness? In fact, Rawls's discussion of the case is an elaborate evasion of the point now at issue, namely, whether or not there have to be principles specifying the fair deployment of rights. Rawls, it may be remembered, says that "we cannot take various contingencies as known and individual preferences as given and expect to elucidate the concept of justice (or fairness) by theories of bargaining. The conception of the original position is designed to meet the problem of the appropriate status quo."[24] But from the original position what are chosen are principles for the design of institutions. What then does choice in an original position have to tell us about Braithwaite's problem?

As far as I can see, Rawls must hope that such principles would produce a social rule preventing Matthew from exploiting his "threat advantage." Yet it is entirely plausible that the general rule that could be endorsed impartially would allow two people in adjacent apartments to play for an hour each day. So if, as in Braithwaite's case, they have only the same hour in which to play, we still have Braithwaite's problem of allocating solo playing time fairly. Throwing the question back to the choice of just institutions makes sense only if one supposes that self-interested behavior within the constraints imposed by just institutions cannot be unfair.

Is Rawls on stronger ground in economic matters? I do not think so. To illustrate the point, consider labor markets, which are notorious for their failure to approximate the conditions of the ideal competitive model. There are many reasons, but let me just give one, the existence of what economists call firm-specific human capital. Wherever a worker's experience working for a firm gives him a high value to it, but he would not have the same value to another employer, we have an inherent bargaining situation. Economic theory tells us that his pay can fall anywhere between the most the firm would pay rather than have him leave and the least he would take rather than have to find another job. If we think it would be fair for his pay to correspond to his value to the firm, rather than the value he would have to another firm, we must think the bargain should be at one end of the range. But there is nothing in the functioning of markets that will predict this outcome.

Trade-union insistence on seniority is a way of dealing with this problem of individual equity. But it has to be admitted that trade-union power introduces problems of fairness too. It makes the relative pay of groups of workers depend on their collective bargaining power, which in turn depends ultimately on the threat of a strike. However, it is questionably fair that the position of workers should depend on the degree of disruption they can cause by withdrawing their labor. Altogether, therefore, "the market" is no panacea.[25]

What I have been saying can, of course, he translated into the terms of Figure 8.1. If we regard it as acceptable for people to make use of whatever rights they have in the manner best calculated to further their interests, the corresponding constructivist solution will be found in the upper left-hand cell, where the name of Nash belongs. This corresponds to the optimal self-interested deployment of rights by both parties: if they succeed in reaching an efficient outcome it will be one that reflects first the amount of damage they can inflict on one another in a struggle for relative advantage and then their relative bargaining power in a move from the strategically motivated nonagreement point to the Pareto frontier. It may seem strange to suggest that Rawls should belong above the line in the first cell of Figure 8.1, but it is in my view an unavoidable implication of his espousal of pure procedural justice for outcomes.

If we reject pure procedural justice in this context, what we are saying is that the use of the rights given by just institutions may still be unfair. I should say at once that we may still conclude in *some* cases that any use will be fair, and then the answer in those cases will be the same as Rawls's. But the answer will be based on study of the particular institution. It will not be imagined to be an *a priori* deduction from the justice of the institution. This means that we are back in business with Figure 8.1, and we may find an application for all of the cells in it.

I said at the beginning of this discussion of resourcism that, whereas I held that outcome-oriented justice unquestionably entails the rejection of pure procedural justice, I was going to maintain that the reverse proposition is not true. I hope that what has been said here makes it plausible that resource-oriented justice for institutions does not entail the acceptance of pure procedural justice for outcomes. It is interesting to speculate about Rawls's grounds for moving so dogmatically from resource-oriented principles for institutions to pure procedural justice for outcomes. My conjecture is that he did not see how otherwise the basis for choosing institutions could be anything other than outcome-oriented. But a resource-oriented theory of justice for institutions does not collapse into an outcome-oriented one the moment we refuse to give a blanket endorsement to whatever outcomes emerge from the operation of these institutions. We can quite reasonably say both that some institution is just—that nobody could reasonably refuse to accept the principles on which it is based—and at the same time that not all outcomes arising from its operation are fair.

To see that this is not equivalent to starting from an ideal end-state and working back, all we have to observe is that there need be no nonartificial way of describing in outcome-oriented terms the overall outcome made up of an allocation of rights and a fair deployment of those rights. Thus, suppose we endorse the right of bequest, including bequests of the peculiar kind discussed in chapter 1, where the legatees get the money only if they agree on its division. Rawls would say that if the institution is just any outcome that arises from such bequests is just. But suppose we disagree with this. We might say that the money should be equally divided. Or we might perhaps say that the legatees can bargain about it but only with the *status quo* as the nonagreement point. (Thus, one of them should not take advantage of the other's being an illegal alien to force an advantageous division.) Whatever we say about the criterion for a fair division of the legacy, the outcome that comes about from applying it to the case at hand will hardly be one that we would have derived from some general depiction of a desirable end-state. It will be recognizably the result of two separate processes, both of which can be judged independently from a moral point of view: the institution that creates the problem of fair division, and the method by which the problem of fair division is resolved.

CHAPTER IX

Constructing Theories of Justice (2): Original Position Theories

39. INTRODUCTION

As in the discussion of two-stage theories, I shall claim that original position theories can be defined by the answers they give to two questions. This again gives us two dichotomies, and when these are cross-tabulated we get another table with four cells. This is Figure 9.1. As may be seen, the first question takes the following form: Is the choice of principles to be made by people who are aware of their personal identities, or is it to be made from behind a veil of ignorance that denies the parties knowledge of at least that? (It may, as in Rawls's theory, exclude much more as well, but I put the dividing line at knowledge of personal identity.) The answer to this question locates a theory in either the upper or lower row of Figure 9.1.

The second question is concerned with the motivations of the actors who are choosing principles. We are to ask whether they are to pursue their own self-interest (perhaps broadly conceived to include whatever ends they may have, including altruistic or public-spirited ones), or whether they are to seek agreement by trying to find principles that represent a reasonable accommodation of their conflicting interests (where again the notion of interest may be construed broadly).

Each cell in Figure 9.1 in effect defines a distinctive theory of justice. Obviously, there are two aspects of any original position theory. To make good the claim that some principle is a principle of justice it is first necessary to give a rationale for the choice of a particular original posi-

Motivation of Parties

		Self-interest	Desire to reach agreement on reasonable terms
	Full	1 Rawls	2 Hume
Information Available to Parties	Excludes personal identity	3 Harsanyi Rawls	4 Rawls

Figure 9.1.   The Structure of Original Position Theories

tion. There must be an answer to the question: Why should I suppose that what would be chosen in that kind of situation ought to count as a principle of justice? Having established that the original position has been appropriately specified, the other part of the exercise consists, of course, in trying to show that certain principles would be chosen by people placed in that situation.

Both parts are equally necessary for the derivation of determinate principles of justice, but the first has logical priority over the second. Unless we have been given some good reason for believing that what would be chosen in a certain kind of situation will constitute a principle of justice, it is a waste of time even to inquire about what might be chosen in it. But if we are persuaded that what would be chosen in a certain kind of situation would indeed be a principle of justice, it is worth persevering with the construction even if it does yield indeterminate results. If we want to know what the temperature is, a thermometer with a certain margin of error is of more use than even the most accurate barometer.

In spite of this rather obvious point, far less effort has been expended on making and criticizing arguments about the specification of original positions than on making and criticizing arguments about attempts to derive principles from original positions. This is probably because the second problem is easier to come to grips with. We know how to argue about decision rules and what follows from them. The first problem is much more diffuse. It is not immediately apparent how we are to set about defending or attacking the proposition that what is chosen in a certain kind of situation ought to be accepted as a principle of justice. It is an advantage of the present framework of discussion that it forces attention to be focused on that second question.

It will be observed that in filling in Figure 9.1 I have not followed the practice of trying to find a micro and a macro example for each cell. The reason for this is that original position theories tend to give rise to baseline-independent solutions. It may be recalled that when I discussed baseline-independent solutions in Part I, I pointed out that such solutions are not very well adapted to small-scale problems when these are considered in isolation from a wider institutional framework. Utilitarianism naturally leads us to look beyond the small-scale case as presented and ask how things might be better arranged so as to avoid such problems in the future. And if we are concerned with equality or maximizing the minimum it is hard to see why we should take the case in isolation, seeking (say) to make two people whose level of welfare is extremely unequal an equal amount better off. Thus, we are once again led to think about institutions whose working will tend over the long run to satisfy the criteria we propose. In what follows, I shall therefore be referring back to points made in both Part I and Part II. But for the reason just given I shall not conduct the discussion in a way parallel to that of two-stage solutions. I shall simply talk about original position theories at large, drawing as necessary on Part I and Part II.

40. JUSTICE AS FAIRNESS

The first cell in Figure 9.1 defines an original position in which people know who they are and are motivated by the desire to advance their own ends. It will be seen that Rawls's name appears here. My reason for attributing to Rawls such a conception of the original position is that I believe it to be the one put forward in his celebrated early article "Justice as Fairness," from which the passage forming the epigraph to this volume was excerpted.

Published thirteen years before the appearance of *A Theory of Justice*, "Justice as Fairness" foreshadowed the major themes of the book (the two principles of justice are in essence the same in both versions) but also differed in some significant respects. The most important of these was the absence in the article of the machinery of the veil of ignorance that is found in *A Theory of Justice*. In "Justice as Fairness" the procedure to be followed is

> to let each person propose the principles upon which he wishes his complaints [about social institutions] to be tried with the understanding that, if acknowledged, the complaints of others will be similarly tried, and that no complaints will be heard at all until everyone is roughly of one mind as to how complaints are to be judged. They each understand further that the principles proposed and acknowledged on this occasion are binding on future occasions. . . . The idea is that everyone should be required to make *in advance* a firm commitment, which others also may reasonably be expected to make, and that no one be given the opportunity to tailor the canons of a legitimate complaint to fit his own special condition, and then to discard them when they no longer suit his purpose. . . . These principles will express the conditions in accordance with which each is the least unwilling to have his interests limited in the design of practices, given the competing interests of the others, on the supposition that the interests of others will be limited likewise.[1]

Rawls tells us that we are to imagine the members of a society to be in the "circumstances of justice." These are essentially the same as those that appear in *A Theory of Justice*. We are, thus, to "suppose that by and large [the members of the society] are mutually self-interested; their allegiance to their established practices is normally founded on the prospect of self-advantage."[2] We "assume that these persons have roughly similar needs and interests, or needs and interests in various ways complementary, so that fruitful cooperation amongst them is possible; and suppose that they are sufficiently equal in power and ability to guarantee that in normal circumstances none is able to dominate the others."[3] Now, when I was discussing the role of the circumstances of justice in *A Theory of Justice* (see above, section 22), I pointed out that it would make no sense to say that the circumstances of justice held in the original position. But in the kind of original position proposed in "Justice as Fairness," it is crucial that the circumstances of justice should actually hold among the people who are to make the choice of principles. The circumstances of justice are, literally, the conditions under which there is reason to suppose that the principles chosen will be principles of justice.

It is tempting but, I want to argue, mistaken to assume that Rawls's invocation of the circumstances of justice puts him in the company of the two-stage theorists. There is, I should confess, some textual support for such an interpretation in the passages that form the first half of the epigraph to this book. What Rawls says about the tradition of Glaucon,

Hobbes, and Hume, in which justice is regarded as a higher-order game, or (more felicitously) a set of rules for playing all future games, might seem to imply that there is no reason for behaving justly where the circumstances of justice do not hold. Where the circumstances of justice obtain, Glaucon, Hobbes, and Hume would concur in maintaining that there are principles of justice which are more advantageous in prospect for everyone than would be the alternative of the absence of any principles of justice. But if there is radical inequality of power—as with the possessor of Gyges' ring, Hobbes's God, or Hume's "race of creatures"—we cannot recommend the principles of justice as rational for everyone to accept.

This interpretation, however, does not seem to me to square with what Rawls says in the last paragraph quoted in the epigraph. A deeper interpretation of what Rawls wants to say about justice must, I suggest, make sense of Rawls's insistence that adherence to the principles of justice "is one of the forms of conduct by which participants in a common practice exhibit their recognition of each other as persons with similar interests and capacities."[4] As Rawls says, revealingly: "one activity in which one can always engage is that of proposing and acknowledging principles to one another supposing each to be similarly circumstanced; and to judge practices by the principles so arrived at is to apply the standard of fairness to them."[5] On the deeper interpretation, we use the thought-experiment of asking what principles would be chosen to govern their life together by people living in the circumstances of justice. These principles are then declared to be the principles of justice. But once we have established these principles of justice by making use of the thought-experiment, we can say that they are valid even where the circumstances of justice do not in fact hold. Thus, we "judge practices by the principles" that are "arrived at" by "*supposing* each to be similarly circumstanced"—whether this is actually the case or not. No doubt the motivation to behave justly is reinforced where the circumstances of justice do hold, because justice is then better for all (on condition that all behave justly) than a free-for-all. But there is an independent motive for behaving justly stemming from the recognition of others as having legitimate claims to have their interests taken into account.

On this view, the claim that rational choice in the circumstances of justice produces principles that are reasonable provides a motive in itself for behaving justly: we want to do what is reasonable in the sense that it balances our own interests against those of others in a way that can be approved of impartially. This, of course, aligns Rawls with the other Hume, the one who tells us that justice is a virtue because it is for the public good and that we adopt the public good as our criterion because it provides an impartial standpoint which all can endorse.

I said in the previous section that original position theories typically produce baseline-independent principles at the macro level. Both the utilitarian principle and Rawls's two principles of justice are illustrations of this, in that we can apply either without ever having to ask how people would have fared at some nonagreement point. I argued in sections 30 and 36 for the thesis that Rawls's principles of justice could not be fitted into a two-stage framework. And I drew from this the implication that, if the principles of justice are to be affirmed, it will be necessary to drop the demand that justice must be capable of being shown to be preferable to "general egoism" from everyone's self-interested point of view. It is an obviously reasonable question whether there is a similar incoherence in "Justice as Fairness" because of its attempt to combine the same two principles of justice with the notion that justice must be better for everyone than the nonagreement point.

The argument I shall make in response to this question is rather complex, but I do not think any simpler one is adequate. It will proceed in two steps. First, I shall try to show that "Justice as Fairness" *embeds* a two-stage construction without *being* one. And then I shall suggest that the solution it arrives at is indeed baseline-dependent but that, for special reasons that would not apply to two-stage constructions in general, this does not undermine the two principles of justice.

If I am right about "Justice as Fairness," the idea is that we discover what justice requires by asking what principles would be chosen to be irrevocably binding in a situation that is fair, where fairness is defined by the presence of the circumstances of justice. This fairness in the relations among the participants in the original position carries over to the principles chosen and makes them just. Hence: justice as fairness. Rawls says that the "typical circumstances of justice" represent "the constraints of having a morality," where "having a morality must at least imply the acknowledgement of principles as impartially applying to one's own conduct as well as to another's, and moreover principles which may constitute a constraint, or limitation, upon the pursuit of one's own interest."[6] Thus, the procedure is, so long as the circumstances of justice obtain, one "whereby rational and mutually self-interested persons are brought to act reasonably." That the people are rational means simply that "they know their own interests more or less accurately; they are capable of tracing out the likely consequences of adopting one practice rather than another; they are capable of adhering to a course of action once they have decided upon it;" and so on.[7] Reasonableness is a richer notion (though defined only by the context in which the word occurs) and should, I think, be taken to mean such things as a willingness to acknowledge that the claims of others are worthy of consideration on the same terms as one's own. The question that will have to be asked later in this chapter is whether rationality plus certain situational constraints on the pursuit of self-interest are really sufficient to generate reasonableness. But for the present purpose all we need do is recognize that Rawls thinks it is.

So far, Rawls sounds like a two-stage theorist. He is telling us that, where the circumstances of justice obtain, principles of justice will be regarded by everyone as advantageous. But my reason for denying that Rawls is a two-stage theorist is that he does not want to maintain that the principles of justice that would be mutually advantageous under the circumstances of justice cease to be morally binding wherever the circumstances of justice do not obtain. Once we have established what principles would be agreed upon in the original position that has been specified, we can say that everyone ought to conform to those principles whether or not doing so is actually more advantageous than a free-for-all. This is what I meant by saying that "Justice as Fairness" embeds a two-stage theory of justice but is not itself a two-stage theory of justice.

Concretely: suppose that in fact the circumstances of justice do not obtain in some society because, say, there is gross inequality of power. Then a two-stage theory, as I define it, would have to say that there is no application for principles of justice drawn up to be mutually advantageous in the counterfactual world in which the circumstances of justice do hold. If the inequality is great enough (as with the Humean "race of creatures"), there may be no room for rules of justice at all: that is to say, there may be no set of restraints on maximization that stand to make everyone better off than they could hope to be in the absence of restraints. (Formally: the nonoperative payoff is on the Pareto frontier.) Even if the inequality of power is less extreme than that (as I suggested in section 23 may be the case in contemporary international relations), we may still expect the terms of mutually advantageous restraint to be far more favorable to the powerful than would be those that would be agreed upon in a situation of approximate equality of power. Thus, we cannot expect that principles of justice which would be appropriate two-stage solutions under conditions of rough equality will be seen as advantageous to all where this rough equality does not obtain. On my interpretation of "Justice as Fairness," however, the members of a society in which the circumstances of justice do not obtain are as much obliged morally to adhere to principles that would be chosen in a fair original position as are the members of a society in which the circumstances of justice do actually obtain.

This is the first leg of my argument. I have tried to show the sense in which "Justice as Fairness" is not a kind of two-stage theory in spite of superficial appearances to the contrary. The second claim I have to substantiate is that the construction used in "Justice as Fairness" could nevertheless give rise to a baseline-dependent solution because the original position that generates the principles of justice is itself a typical two-stage set-up.

Let me explain what I mean by saying this. We have so far defined the original position of "Justice as Fairness" as one characterized by people who are concerned to pursue their own interests under conditions that will make it advantageous to them to accept mutual restraints on the direct pursuit of self-interest. But we have only to think back to the left-hand side of Figure 8.1, where the names of Hume and Gauthier appeared, to realize that bargaining under exactly these conditions is normally thought to lead to a baseline-dependent solution. What happens when we embed a two-stage solution in a theory of justice in the way I have been arguing Rawls does in "Justice as Fairness"? The answer would seem to be that we get a baseline-dependent set of principles out of our original position and we then say that this baseline-dependent set of principles is morally binding on people whether or not they are actually in the circumstances of justice themselves.

It must be admitted that it is not easy to see exactly how a baseline-dependent solution arising in a hypothetical situation is to be transferred to a real situation that (*ex hypothesi*) may be different from it in crucial aspects. I am not sure that this is in fact any more (or any less!) of a problem than the one posed by Gauthier's own theory, which required him to reconstruct what people would have received in a state of nature. (As we saw in section 30, Gauthier simply ignored the problem and proposed a solution that was not really baseline-dependent in this way.) Fortunately, however, it is unnecessary to pursue the practical difficulties of implementing a solution that makes integral use of a baseline existing in a world that may be counterfactual. The only point to be grasped is that one might naturally expect the original position of "Justice as Fairness" to give rise to a baseline-dependent solution. But, as I have already mentioned, the solution actually derived from the original position consists of the two principles of justice, and these are transparently baseline-independent principles.

The question is: How does Rawls steer from the original position as specified to the two principles of justice, and not to a baseline-dependent solution? The answer to this has been foreshadowed in the discussion of the relation between constructivism and contractarianism in chapter 7. Rawls places great emphasis on the point that the agreement on principles is to be irrevocable: once certain principles have been chosen, nobody can ask to have the discussion reopened on the ground that he does not like the way they have worked out in his own case. Although, therefore, everyone has full information, in the sense that there is no artificial limitation of knowledge, the natural uncertainty of the future will mute the conflicts of interest that would ordinarily arise when people seek to pursue their own interests.

For an illustration of this process we can go back to the discussion in section 14 of general rules for regulating small-scale conflicts of interest. If you and I have to argue about a rule to cover the playing of musical instruments in our adjacent apartments over the next twelve months, we may well have conflicting interests, based on our existing tastes. But if we know that whatever rule we settle on will be binding for the rest of our lives, our uncertainty about changing tastes and circumstances in the future may well at any rate reduce the conflict of interest. For both of us must allow that our tastes, and other relevant aspects of our situations, may change drastically in the future. And if the task is to pick not a rule for a specific kind of contingency but a principle to be invoked for the indefinite future to settle all issues of a certain general kind, it seems likely that the uncertainty about the future will be great enough to make agreement far easier to reach.

Rawls takes this idea to the limit. He maintains that where the principles are to be all-embracing criteria for assessing and regulating the basic institutions, the uncertainty of the parties about what the future might have in store would be so great that there would be no conflict of interest remaining at all. Everyone would converge, by making an independent self-interested calculation, on the two principles of justice.

I am concerned here neither with the content of the principles of justice nor with the details of Rawls's attempt to show that they would be chosen in an original position characterized in the way described in "Justice as Fairness." What is important here is to see that Rawls avoids a baseline-dependent solution by making uncertainty about the future so great that the parties' calculations about their advantage coincide. In the original position, defined as one where the circumstances of justice obtain, the parties seek their own advantage; and this presumably means that, if they are to choose principles of justice, they must expect justice to be better for them than a free-for-all. But, because of the radical uncertainty inherent in the original position, they all have identical expectations about any given set of principles—and, presumably, identical expectations about the payoffs from a free-for-all.

The noncooperative baseline is therefore the same for everyone. Because it does not give rise to differential claims, the people in the original position have no reason for putting forward baseline-dependent principles. Each of the parties works out what principles would be most advantageous in prospect, and each arrives at the same answer: the Rawlsian principles of justice. So long as these are more advantageous in prospect than a free-for-all, nobody has any reason for being concerned about what the noncooperative payoff would be. Because of the peculiarities of the choice situation, then, the nonagreement point can here do two things that we have so far denied that it can do: it can function purely as a threshold value that justice must surpass; and it can be combined with a baseline-independent solution such as the Rawlsian principles of justice.

It may be asked whether this conclusion should lead us to reassess the claim made in sections 30 and 37 that the introduction of the nonagreement point makes for incoherence in *A Theory of Justice*. The answer must be that there is no reprieve. What is special about "Justice as Fairness" is that the circumstances of justice are put into the original position. And in this hypothetical choice situation, the degree of uncertainty is so great (according to Rawls) as to turn the circumstances of justice into the circumstances of impartiality. We have no reason for doubting that the circumstances of impartiality can generate baseline-independent solutions, so there is no problem of coherence.

Where the problem arises in *A Theory of Justice* is in shifting the circumstances of justice from the original position into the real-life situation in which principles of justice are to be applied. The contractors are now to be told that the circumstances of justice actually hold in the conditions for which they are drawing up principles. And this, of course, implies that whatever principles they agree on must be found mutually advantageous not only *ex ante* but *ex post*. They must find, when they emerge from behind the veil of ignorance, that justice is the solution to a two-stage game played under conditions of full information.

The upshot of our discussion of "Justice as Fairness" is that its placement in the upper row of Figure 9.1 is misleading. Although it is a "full information" theory, Rawls maintains that the empirical uncertainty of the impact of principles in the future gives everyone the same expectations from any given principle. Thus the theory really belongs in the third cell, defined by self-interested motivation plus ignorance of personal identity, and this is, of course, the theory contained in chapter 3 of *A Theory of Justice*.

The reason for Rawls's move from the one formulation to the other is easy enough to understand. People do, after all, have some high degree of confidence that their race and sex will remain unchanged, and may plausibly have divergent interests even over irrevocable principles based on differing expectations from alternative principles. Those with a high level of mental or physical ability cannot be sure that they will not lose it (due, for example, to catastrophic illness) but they may still believe it advantageous to support economic institutions that would leave them with most of what they make and rely on private insurance to cope with uncertainty, rather than supporting some more egalitarian principle. And it is hard to see how, if it is a matter of playing the odds in the most skillful was possible, the possessors of vast wealth could go wrong in refusing to accept any principle that did not provide safeguards against redistribution or collectivization of private property.

The obvious response to this line of criticism is to retreat from the claim that the uncertainty of the future will render expectations identical, and build it into the theory directly, by stipulating that the parties in the original position are to have identical expectations. This is, of course, achieved by the incorporation of the veil of ignorance into the original position. I shall ask what can be said for such a theory in the next section.

41. CONSTRUCTING AN ORIGINAL POSITION

WHY A VEIL OF IGNORANCE?

Let us focus on the lower half of Figure 9.1. The two theories of justice represented by the third and fourth cells are united in the claim that the original position should be characterized by a veil of ignorance that, at a minimum, denies the parties knowledge of their own identities. Where these two cells differ is over the motivations ascribed to the parties. The left-hand cell corresponds to the claim, common to Harsanyi and Rawls (especially in chapter 3 of *A Theory of Justice*), that the parties are to advance their own ends as best they can within the informational constraints imposed on them. The right-hand cell corresponds to the claim, about which I shall have more to say later in this chapter, that the parties are to be motivated by the desire to reach agreement on reasonable terms.

I want to argue that the role of the veil of ignorance is radically different in original positions defined by the alternative motivations. Where the parties are assumed to be pursuing their own interests, a veil of ignorance is essential. But where they are assumed to be motivated by the desire to reach an agreement on reasonable terms, a veil of ignorance is an optional feature—a heuristic device which can be resorted to on occasion but does not have to be relied on to create solutions. (It should be easy to believe that a veil of ignorance is indispensable with self-interested motivation when we notice that, if the theory of "Justice as Fairness" is dropped down to its proper place in the third cell, the first cell in Figure 9.1 becomes empty.)

Consider an original position in which the actors are motivated by self-interest. If this original position is to represent the circumstances of impartiality, it seems that it must block the ability of the powerful to impose their will on others. Justice as impartiality insists that we should not accept as embodying justice terms of agreement that simply reflect the balance of bargaining power. If we say that we want to eliminate strategic advantages and disadvantages, what we are in effect saying is that the parties should be able to put forward any proposal that is in their interests, without there being any constraint derived from the position they will find themselves in if no agreement is reached. But if we leave it there, we run into the obvious problem that the parties now have no reason for limiting their demands to what others might accept. Once we withdraw the sanction of the nonagreement point, and drive to maximization is not restrained by any pressure to reach agreement.

If we simply ask people, with full information about their own personal characteristics, social position, and so on, what arrangements would best further their ends, it seems inevitable that we will get widely divergent answers from different people. Only if the full realization of each and every one were the condition of the full realization of any could we expect agreement. In this kind of construction, therefore, agreement can be reached only if the parties are denied information about their personal identities. Only by facing them with what is in fact an identical decision-problem can we derive an agreed answer.

Now consider the alternative formulation, in which we think of the parties as being concerned with finding a reasonable basis of agreement. The veil of ignorance may serve a purpose here, but it is no longer essential as a condition of agreement between people with divergent interests. If we ask people to tell us what they think would be reasonable, looking at the matter from all the positions affected by their answer (including the one that they in fact occupy), there is no reason why people in different actual positions must necessarily disagree. No doubt some people are better than others in summoning up the combination of honesty and imagination that is needed to respond adequately. But it would surely be contrary to experience to suggest that people in different positions can never do this and reach agreement.

No doubt people will in practice tend to look at things from their own point of view. Even if they avoid crude self-interest there is the subtler bias of favoring people of one's own personality type or outlook. ("No, I wouldn't mind if I weren't able to do so-and-so"—said of some activity that, even though one can do it, is not very important to oneself though it is to others.) But there is, after all, no veil of ignorance actually available to us. Rawls, in telling us to ask what people behind one would choose, is in fact simply challenging us to put aside, as best we can, the biases that come from our knowing what principles would suit us personally.

There is a common, and quite legitimate, move in moral arguments that goes "You wouldn't be saying that if you weren't an X," where X is anything such that it is in the interest of somebody who is an X to hold that position. The attack is, of course, *ad hominem*: it does not say what is wrong with the position but casts suspicion on the motives of the person putting it forward. But at least in some cases the attack is so obviously well founded that it really does seem a waste of time to discuss the merits of the argument.

The point that is significant here is that "You wouldn't say that if you weren't an X" represents an *attack* only if what is being put forward is claimed to be right, fair, or such. (If the person were claiming that a certain institution or policy was in his interest, one would hardly be *attacking* him by saying that he would not say so unless he were an X. He might well agree, saying "Yes, it's precisely in virtue of my being an X that it's in my interest.") Now, we can think of a veil of ignorance as a formalization of the response that might be made by someone whose *bona fides* are brought into question. Let us imagine someone responding to the charge that he claims something to be right only because it suits him. He might say: "I admit that the principle does work out advantageously for me, because I'm an X. But I'd still say it was right even if I had no idea I was an X."

The veil of ignorance plays an inessential role in this response, which we can see by noticing that it could have been formulated without any mention of what this person would think if he did not know he was an X. All he is really saying is that he would hold the same principle however he was affected by it. The invocation of the veil of ignorance is simply a way of giving the claim some dramatic force. But since there is no practical way of carrying out the test it does not actually add anything to the mere protestation of impartiality.

This is not to say, however, that dramatization can never add anything to arguments. A familiar way of trying to get people to look at things without consulting their own interests is to present them with hypothetical cases (which may or may not be fictitious) involving other people and hoping that they will not see too immediately how the way in which they judge these cases will have implications that affect them. Perhaps the earliest record of this form of moral argument was the prophet Nathan's strategy to make David feel guilty about having Uriah the Hittite killed so that he could marry his wife Bathsheba. Nathan told David of a rich man with "exceedingly many flocks and herds" who took a poor man's "one little ewe lamb." And when David's "anger was greatly kindled against the man . . . Nathan said to David 'Thou art the man.'"[8] This is clearly a version of the nonessential use of a veil of ignorance. That is to say, it presupposes that the king has the capacity to make moral judgments but that where his own interests are at stake he is liable to be blinded by that, with the result that he fails to employ his moral capacity properly.

WHY SELF-INTEREST?

Let us now shift our attention from the division between the upper and lower halves of Figure 9.1 to the division between the left-hand and right-hand sides. Why should we be asked to believe that what emerges when people attempt to pursue their own interests is just—even if their deliberations are carried out behind a veil of ignorance? Let us accept that impartial morality cannot be equated with the outcome of a collective choice made by self-interested people who know everything about themselves. Why should we conclude from that, though, that it can be equated with the outcome of a collective choice made by self-interested people who know nothing about themselves? Perhaps the right conclusion to draw is that impartial morality does not emerge from self-interested choices, however we rig the rest of the specification of the original position.*

I do not think that Harsanyi has addressed himself directly to this problem. Rawls has done so, but he does not seem to me to have bestowed on it the amount of attention that is deserved by such a crucial move in the construction of a theory of justice. As far as I can see, the core of Rawls's defense of the postulate that the people in the original position are to pursue their own interests is that only thus can we get determinate results out of the theory. "To say that a certain conception of justice would be chosen in the original position is equivalent to saying that rational deliberation satisfying certain conditions and restrictions would reach a certain conclusion. If necessary, the argument to this result could be set out more formally."[9] Without the postulate of rational (that is to say, self-interested) motivation "we would not be able to work out any definite theory of justice at all. We would have to be content with a vague formula stating that justice is what would be agreed to without being able to say much, if anything, about the substance of the agreement itself. The formal constraints of the concept of right, those applying to principles directly, are not sufficient for our purpose."[10]

I believe, however, that this case for the postulate of self-interest—that it gets results—confronts a dilemma, one horn of which impales Harsanyi and the other Rawls. Getting results that carry any persuasive force is not just a matter of the conclusions following unambiguously from the premises. It is also a matter of the premises being simple and perspicuous, and here Harsanyi scores. For if we take utility-maximizing motivation plus the simplest specification of a veil of ignorance that will rule out the exploitation of strategic advantage, we get Harsanyi's construction and Harsanyi's result. But the problem here is that simple and perspicuous premises may not be compelling. Suppose I

---

*An analogous point was made with exemplary clarity by C. D. Broad in a comment on R. M. Hare's idea that a moral principle is, roughly speaking, a self-interested choice subject to the constraint of universalizability. "Mr Hare says that A will be inclined to judge it to be *wrong* for him to treat B in a certain way, if, on imagining himself to be in a similar situation as *patient* instead of agent, he finds that he would *dislike* to be treated in that way. . . . It seems to me that all that is *logically* relevant is that A should judge that it would be *wrong* for another to treat him as he is proposing to treat B. Whether or not he would *dislike* or *like* being treated in that way seems logically irrelevant" (*Broad's Critical Essays in Moral Philosophy*, ed. David Cheney [London: George Allen and Unwin, 1971], p. 313).

am initially disinclined to believe that I must always be prepared to sacrifice my own interests whenever by doing so I can provide somebody else with a larger benefit, or whenever I can provide some larger number of people with small benefits that are cumulatively larger. I do not see that I have been given any adequate cause for changing my mind if I am told that, as a utility-maximizer behind a thin veil of ignorance, that is what I would have endorsed as a principle. I may agree that I would indeed have done so but then ask: "So what?"

What I have just been saying should, of course, be music in Rawls's ears. But I now come on to the second horn of the dilemma: to get more acceptable conclusions we have to sacrifice simplicity and perspicuity. Rawls's reaction to the criticism I have just made of Harsanyi would be that his specification of the original position was too simple. Instead of being content with a thin veil of ignorance denying the parties' knowledge of their personal identities, we should have fine-tuned the information available to the parties so as to ensure that a self-interested choice of principles would be constrained to reflect the "constraints of right." But there is an obvious objection to this procedure. If the specification of the original position can be justified only by saying that it is designed to generate certain principles, it may be said, the construction adds nothing to whatever intuitive appeal the principles themselves may happen to have.

It is, I think, fairly clear how Rawls would respond to this charge. I said in section 34 that we should not take too literally Rawls's incautious statement that "we want to define the original position so that we get the desired solution."[11] He should not be read here as saying that we are simply to fudge up the original position to make it come out with the specific answers we want. The idea is supposed to be that the features of the original position can be defended as embodying morally recognizable features of justice: "each aspect of the original position can be given a supporting explanation."[12] But the difficulty that Rawls faces is, I believe, this: there simply is no way in which he can adapt an original position with self-interested choices so as to get it to reflect his basic moral commitments. The foundation is wrong and no amount of work on the detailing can fix the trouble.

I can best explain this by pointing out that a core element in Rawls's theory is his insistence on the so-called separateness of persons. The import of this phrase is obscure, but I think that Rawls intends by it to emphasize that each person has only one life to live. Someone who does very poorly under the existing social arrangements therefore has no reason for putting up with them simply because some other people are doing exceedingly well. The implication is taken to be that we cannot assess states of affairs by aggregating the welfare of different people: one person's woe cannot be compensated by another's weal. But this means that we should reject as morally irrelevant any claim that some state of affairs is justified because someone who does badly in it would have regarded it as a good bet *ex ante* to take his chances on being anyone in this situation. For there never really was an original position with a veil of ignorance and there never really was a gamble. There are only different people with different lots in life. And we cannot defend inequality between those lots by talking about hypothetical gambles.

Rawls periodically asserts, of course, that we should not think of the people in the original position as gamblers trying to make the best bet they can, given that they do not know who they will turn out to be when the veil of ignorance is lifted. But the trouble is that the logic of the construction does not allow any alternative way of approaching the decision problem. All that Rawls can do, short of abandoning the stipulation that the parties in the original position are to be thought of as pursuing their own ends, is to try to make sure that their gamble will not really be a gamble, by adding further features to the original position. But these modifications will never lead in the right direction in a natural way because there is no way in which they can ever overcome the mismatch between the fundamental intuition about the separateness of persons and the machinery of rational choice under uncertainty.

Looking back on Rawls's theoretical development we can, I suggest, discern a constant tendency to react to criticisms of the derivation of the principles of justice (whose basic content has remained unchanged) by building more and more into the specification of the original position. Thus, as we have seen, in "Justice as Fairness" Rawls relied on the uncertainty of the future to discourage people from proposing principles tailored to their own personal attributes and circumstances. In *A Theory of Justice* this natural uncertainty was replaced by a stipulated uncertainty in the form of a thick veil of ignorance. The same trend has continued subsequently to the publication of the book. The logical gap between the premises and the conclusions has narrowed further, so that the conclusions virtually amount to a recapitulation of the premises.

Thus in Rawls's major restatement of the theory, the Dewey lectures, the motivations of the people in the original position remain formally the same as before, but the significance of their maximizing choice is transformed by the information that they are supposed to have about the nature of their desires.[13] They are now to be told that they have three "'higher-order' interests" which they are "moved by." Rawls says that "the motivation of the parties is appropriate to the representation of moral persons,"[14] where this means precisely persons moved by these higher-order interests. According to Rawls, two of the three higher-order interests are "highest-order" interests. These are interests in "realizing and exercising" two "moral powers." The first moral power is "the capacity for an effective sense of justice." The second moral power is "the capacity to form, to revise, and rationally to pursue a conception of the good." There is also a third, but subordinate, higher-order interest. This is the interest that people have "in protecting and advancing their conception of the good as best they can, whatever it may be."[15]

This last interest is straightforward enough and is what Rawls relied on to drive the choice of the two principles of justice in the original position in *A Theory of Justice*. But the two "highest-order interests" in exercising the two "moral powers" build two of Rawls's key conclusions into the premises. The "supremely regulative"[16] status of justice was regarded in *A Theory of Justice* as problematic, and Rawls devoted most of Part III of that book to trying to ground it in considerations derived from social psychology. Now, however, the priority of justice is built in right at the start, by means of the stipulation that the people for whom principles are to be chosen have an overriding desire to be just. And the priority of liberty over the difference principle, which Rawls put forward in *A Theory of Justice* as historically contingent—valid only in a relatively affluent society—is also no longer problematic. For if the ability to form and revise one's ends has a higher priority than more gross desires (such as food and shelter) this would seem to settle the issue between the first and second principles of justice if they come into conflict.

It seems clear that Rawls has hit upon a method whereby you can get anything out of the theory at the end by simply putting it in at the beginning. If the desires of the people in the original position are constrained tightly enough by information about what it is that they want in real life, it can be a trivial matter to derive whatever choices you like.

We might perhaps characterize what Rawls has done subsequently to *A Theory of Justice* by saying that he has taken the approach that he used to get him out of his difficulties with future generations and has extended it massively. As we saw in section 24, under "The Motivations of the Parties," Rawls proposed in *A Theory of Justice* to avoid neglect of the interests of future generations by making what he called a "motivational assumption." This consisted in telling the people behind the veil of ignorance that in real life they cared for the welfare of their descendants. Hence, among the interests they were to pursue in their deliberations was an interest in the well-being of at any rate the next two generations of their descendants. Obviously, having put in this premise, Rawls had no difficulty in getting out the conclusion that the principles of justice should include a concern for the interests of at least the next two generations.

As I pointed out in section 24, if this derivation is to have any appeal to the sense of justice of the members of an actual society, they must in fact care about the welfare of their descendants to the degree attributed to them in the information acted on by the people in the original position. This means that the protection of the interests of future generations is made hostage to the attitudes that people in actual societies have about them. If they do care a lot then justice (among themselves) requires that they do something about it. But if they do not, there is no argument available to say that they should do so. (This follows from the way in which the interests of future generations come into the picture only as an element in the interests of those alive now.) Yet we surely would like to be able to say that it is unjust to neglect the interests of future generations even if people alive now do not happen to find it in their own interests to take account of those interests.

Now all this can be transferred *mutatis mutandis* to the "motivational assumptions" with which Rawls has bedecked his theory in the Dewey lectures. If you do not in fact have the higher-order interests that Rawls attributes to you, then a theory premised on the assumption that you do have them cannot be of any concern to you. However good a job the people in the original position may do in drawing up principles for a society in which everyone has these higher-order interests, the results of their labors are simply irrelevant.

It should be emphasized that if the people he is addressing do not give priority to the concerns postulated by Rawls, he does not have any arguments to put forward to persuade them to change their minds. He acknowledges that "the conception of moral persons as having certain specified highest-order interests selects what is to count as primary goods" and he adds that in saying this he is "revising the suggestions in *A Theory of Justice*, since there it can seem as if the list of primary goods is regarded as the outcome of a purely psychological, statistical, or historical inquiry."[17]

This limitation is particularly serious when we come to talk about the justice of the international basic structure. For it is especially implausible that the kind of psychology to which Rawls appeals is at all widespread in the world. And even a somewhat superficial knowledge of other cultures is enough to make it clear that it would be regarded as quite strange in many places. (Rawls himself speaks of "addressing the public culture of a democratic society.")[18]

Now we could of course deal with this problem by acknowledging its force and simply saying that indeed the implication is that impartial international morality can have application only between countries whose citizens share the kind of psychology stipulated by Rawls. This, however, would be to say that justice runs out exactly when we most need it, namely, in situations of conflict where the parties do not share substantive goals. It seems to me that any theory of justice that is silent about both the internal affairs of societies other than liberal-democratic ones and the relations between societies other than liberal-democratic ones is so deficient that we must of necessity look elsewhere for a foundation of justice.

The upshot of this discussion is, I suggest, that we can eliminate the left-hand side of Figure 9.1, which is marked by the self-interested motivation of the parties in the original position. The theories of Harsanyi and Rawls do not, of course, exhaust the logically possible variants on the information that is postulated to be made available to the parties in the original position. Nevertheless, I think that they illustrate the problems inherent in any construction making use of self-interested motivation in the original position. The form of the decision problem facing the people in the original position is naturally construed as one of maximizing under conditions of uncertainty. And this leads us (as with Harsanyi) to the conclusion that the principle chosen should be one of maximizing the average utility of all the people they might turn out to be. For then each maximizes his expected utility within the constraint on information that denies knowledge of personal identity to the people in the original position.

The objection to this is that we have no reason for accepting the choice as representing the requirements of morality or justice unless we independently accept the legitimacy of averaging over different people's utilities as a way of making judgments. If we do not accept it, the proof of utilitarianism employing the construction does not, it seems to me, have any force. Unless we are already predisposed to agree with averaging, why should we go along with a construction that leads straight to it? The only satisfactory answer would be one that showed us that it is somehow in the nature of morality or justice that it must be what arises from a self-interested choice from behind a veil of ignorance. But I am not aware of any such argument that has ever been put forward, and I cannot imagine the form it might take. As I pointed out above, it is not enough to say that the construction guarantees impartiality. This is a necessary but not a sufficient condition of a satisfactory theory. What we need is some reason for giving this construction a privileged position over rival interpretations.

The rest of the argument does not turn on the details of Rawls's attempts to fix up the information conditions in the original position so as to rule out averaging. For the claim I wish to make is a general one. It is that, because the set-up of a maximizing choice under uncertainty naturally leads to averaging, any additional information conditions strong enough to move the outcome away from averaging will have to be so strong as to amount to putting the conclusions into the premises. The construction will therefore be failing to do any work.

42. ORIGINAL POSITIONS WITHOUT SELF-INTEREST

HUME AND RAWLS

If we eliminate the left-hand side of Figure 9.1 from further consideration, we have remaining two variants (differentiated by the information conditions they stipulate) of an original position in which the parties are themselves imbued with what we have called the moral motive. I shall devote this section, which completes the present chapter, to a discussion of original positions of this kind.

Let me begin with the upper cell in the right-hand column, which allows the parties full information about their own personal characteristics, social positions, and so on. I have put the name of Hume in this cell, but it might reasonably be asked in what sense, if Hume belongs there, the cell represents an original position theory of justice at all. Hume is, of course, assigned to this place on the strength of his analysis of why justice is accounted a virtue. But in developing this he at no point talked about anything that could be construed as an original position. His view was, as we saw in section 19, that we are forced to employ a common standard of judgment in order to ensure that we will use words in consistent ways, and the criterion of the "public good" serves this purpose because it is one that finds a place in it for everyone's interests.

I think it is quite correct to say that in Hume's case the original position is continuous with the situation in actual societies, so that all we really have are people with full information attempting under real-life conditions to reach agreement on impartial premises. However, I believe that reflection on the peculiarities of Hume in this respect will help us to see why the upper right-hand cell ought in fact to be envisaged as something of an abstraction from the conditions of actual societies.

The crucial point about Hume for the present purpose is that he was socially and politically conservative, although intellectually radical. This comes out clearly in the way he develops his theory. Thus, when someone tells us that the basis for a common standard is that the interests of all should be equally represented in it, and proposes the criterion of the public good as satisfying that requirement, we might expect that the criterion will be deployed to attack as unjust gross social, political, legal, and economic inequalities such as those that pervaded eighteenth-century Britain. Yet, as we saw in section 20, Hume calmly concludes that, even if everything is not quite for the best in the best of all possible worlds, the disadvantages of disturbing settled expectations and the practices based on them are so great that the public good dictates leaving things exactly as they are. Thus, the criterion for assessing institutions by asking if they serve everyone's interests equally turns out to lead to the uncritical endorsement of the *status quo*.

Someone less committed than Hume to reaching conservative conclusions might wonder whether it is really plausible to imagine that the institutions of property emerging from the stabilization of possession as described in Hume's account of the origins of property (his two-stage theory of justice) could also be supported unchanged by a criterion that gives all interests equal weight. But then we might turn the inquiry round. We might perhaps start to think that, if it is true that existing moral ideas do not lead to the unequivocal rejection of gross inequalities, this casts doubt on their consistency with the demands of impartiality. If commonly held moral views will underwrite institutions that, on the face of it, are incapable of eliciting free and equal assent, then we should ask if the conditions under which moral ideas arise are really such as to press people so hard toward agreement only on terms that take everyone's interests equally into account.

A possible view is that actual moral systems reflect the interaction of considerations based on impartiality and self-interest. Gilbert Harman, who has proposed this idea, follows Hume in assuming without much discussion that impartiality amounts to taking the common good as a criterion, tightening this up in orthodox post-Humean fashion so that it becomes utilitarianism. Self-interest leaves its mark on popular morality, Harman suggests, in the form of the asymmetrical treatment of helping and harming. The prohibition on harming, he says, is in everyone's interest; but a comparably strong injunction to help others who are in need would entail sacrifices by the strong to aid the weak. Hence, helping is regarded as admirable but not obligatory. The last paragraph of Harman's *The Nature of Morality* summarizes his view of the moral system that these two forces together produce:

> Respect for others involves some concern for them. So there is pressure toward utilitarianism. Self-interest leads us to adopt conventions of respect and concern. Our concern for others will then give us reasons to improve our conventions so as to better promote the general welfare. In this way, we make moral progress, our self-interest giving way to benevolence in the way utilitarianism recommends. Still, we remain self-interested. That keeps a rein on morality and keeps us from going all the way in the direction of unilateral benevolence and altruism.[19]

Harman explicitly recognizes the difference between a two-stage theory and an original position theory. Thus, insofar as moral principles are conventions that are accepted out of a sense of mutual advantage, they must be "seen as deriving from actual, not hypothetical, conventions. . . . We cannot in the same way explain why someone would be motivated to adhere to principles he *would have* agreed to adhere to in a position of equality."[20] He continues:

> Furthermore, the suggested explanation of the moral difference we recognize between harming and not helping depends on the assumption that our morality rests on an actual convention among people of different powers and resources. It is not easy to see how this aspect of our moral views could be explained by assuming that obligations depend on what we *would* agree to in a position of equality. For, in such a position, it seems likely that we would not agree to our present moral principles.[21]

The implication of this is, I take it, that the conditions of actual societies are not conducive to the creation of moral principles on terms that nobody can reasonably reject.* If we want to talk about what such

---

* Harman himself attributes to Hume the theory that moral principles (or at any rate those, like principles of justice, that are "artificial") arise out of a convention that is based on a sense of mutual interest (Gilbert Harman, *The Nature of Morality: An Introduction to Ethics* [New York: Oxford University Press, 1977], chapter 9, "Convention"). He also recognizes that Hume has an "ideal observer" theory of morality according to which moral principles are based on sympathetic identification with the interests of all (see ibid.,

principles might be, we shall have to abstract from the inequalities of power inherent in real-life conditions and postulate a favorable environment for deliberation about principles, one marked by freedom and equality. That is to say, we are to assume that the people who are attempting to reach agreement on reasonable terms are unable to coerce one another, explicitly or implicitly, by the threat that they will be particularly poorly placed if negotiations break down and they are left to fend for themselves. And we should also postulate that the parties are rational: that they have a coherent conception of their ends, that they understand how alternative principles would bear on their prospects of reaching those ends, and that they are either equally skillful in making their cases or, if this seems hard to imagine, are represented by negotiators of equal skill.

The right-hand side of Figure 9.1 thus gives us two kinds of original position, both of which involve enough abstraction from the actual conditions of life to allow for rational deliberation in the absence of coercion. The difference between the two turns on the presence or absence of information about personal identity on the part of the people in the original position. I have put Rawls in the lower cell on the right-hand side of Figure 9.1, which corresponds to a veil of ignorance, in virtue of one element in his discussion of justice between generations. I pointed out in section 24, under "Universalizability," that, for the peculiar case of relations between generations, Rawls conceded that we might imagine the parties asking themselves directly what would be a reasonable savings rate for each generation—one that would equitably balance the interests of different generations. On this line of analysis, the people in the original position

---

chapter 4, "Emotivism as the Ideal Observer Theory"). But he does an even less good job than Hume himself did of explaining how the two theories are to be combined. "Hume says that the original motive to observe conventions is 'natural' rather than moral, by which he means that it is a self-interested motive. . . . According to Hume, these 'natural' obligations will strike us as moral as soon as we reflect sympathetically on the usefulness of the relevent conventions to human society" (ibid., p. 104). But this does not even begin to explain why, when we begin to reflect sympathetically, we should not conclude that the existing conventions, which grew up reflecting mutual advantage, are sadly defective assessed by the standard of general utility. To say that "habits develop" so that "action in accordance with those principles . . . would be hard to change" is scarcely enough (ibid.). Perhaps some habits should be broken even if it does take an effort. Hume at least recognizes that some further argument is needed and offers it in the form of the alleged unsettling effects of reopening distributive questions. But my objection to that is that I can see no reason for accepting it as likely on balance that it will do more harm than good to subject institutions to scrutiny from an impartial standpoint.

try to piece together a just savings schedule by balancing how much at each stage they would be willing to save for their immediate descendants against what they would feel entitled to claim of their immediate predecessors. Thus imagining themselves to be fathers, say, they are to ascertain how much they should set aside for their sons by noting what they would believe themselves entitled to claim of their fathers. When they arrive at an estimate that seems fair from both sides, with due allowance made for the improvement in their circumstances, then the fair rate (or range of rates) for that stage is specified. Now once this is done for all stages, we have defined the just saving principle. When this principle is followed, adjacent generations cannot complain of one another; and in fact no generation can find fault with any other no matter how far removed in time.[22]

Notice that what Rawls is here describing differs from the version of an original position that I propose in that it asks the parties to *imagine* what they would think if they were in various positions. They are actually all members of the same generation (though they don't know which one) but they are to "piece together" a complete specification of just savings rates for all generations by putting themselves in the positions, at each stage, of those who are alive at that point, those who preceded them, and those who are to follow them. What makes this close enough, I believe, to warrant the co-optation of Rawls is that the question the people in the original position are to put to themselves is, in essence: What principles to govern savings would be reasonably acceptable to all generations?

The people in Rawls's original position are, of course, behind a thick veil of ignorance that denies them knowledge of their own identities and much else besides, including the economic condition of their society and their place in the sequence of generations. It is therefore natural to put Rawls's name in the lower half of the right-hand column of Figure 9.1. It is, however, worth noticing that, in the terms introduced in section 41, the veil of ignorance plays an inessential role here. If the parties conscientiously carry out the charge that Rawls lays on them, it can make no difference to the conclusions they will reach whether or not they have full information about their own society vis-à-vis earlier ones. The only role a veil of ignorance could play would be a heuristic one.

If we are concerned that the judgment of the parties will in fact be biased by their knowledge of their own position, we might say that a just savings schedule is one that would be drawn up by people who were not biased in this way—and a crude but effective method of eliminating bias would be to deny them knowledge of their own positions. It should be borne in mind, however, that there is not really any such thing as a veil of ignorance. It exists only as an element in a thought-experiment but in this case it is exactly the same thought-experiment as is called for by specifying lack of bias by parties with full information. Rawls could therefore just as well have dropped the veil of ignorance when he dropped the self-interested motivation of the parties.

Since agreement on reasonable terms does not by its nature require a veil of ignorance, I shall in general assume in what follows that our model is one with full information. Where, on occasion, it seems to me that there is something to be gained by thinking about situations in which information is limited I shall mention this explicitly.

GETTING ANSWERS

As we saw in the previous section, the reason for Rawls's building his theory of justice on self-interested choices (in a suitably defined original position) was the fear that only by doing this could one arrive at determinate answers. Is this a valid fear? To some extent I think the answer must be that it is. We cannot hope for anything like a deductive proof of a set of principles to emerge from a framework in which we ask what people would agree on if they were trying to reach agreement on reasonable terms under conditions that rule out coercion or overpersuasion. But that does not mean, I wish to urge, that the approach is completely toothless. Although it will not normally enable us to say that an institution is the only possible one compatible with justice, we can hope to be able to rule out a variety of institutions as definitely unjust. And if we follow Aristotle's advice and avoid asking for more precision than the subject allows, we may well feel that it is no disadvantage of the approach I advocate that it is not going to produce a detailed blueprint for a just society.

It is, I wish to maintain, a drawback to many theories of justice that they claim a determinacy that is not there and should not be there. Within limits (and it is the job of a theory of justice to state those limits), the arrangements of a society can vary according to the wishes of its members. Thus, it seems to me that it would be just to require a duty of rescue, or to have a compulsory scheme for kidney transplants, but it would also be just not to. The bonds of social solidarity can be drawn more tightly or less tightly in different societies, and it would in my view be sheer parochialism to identify justice with only one point on that spectrum. (These themes will be pursued further in Volume II.)

How much, concretely, can we get from this framework? The basic idea we are pursuing here is that the parties in the original position are themselves actuated by the moral motive. It may be recalled that I quoted in section 35 Scanlon's formulation of the moral motive: that it is the desire to live by principles that could not reasonably be rejected by people motivated by the "desire to find principles which others similarly motivated could not reasonably reject."[23] This may immediately suggest that the problem is to be conceived as one of creating common expectations. On this account of the matter, we are to suppose that the parties are concerned *solely* with reaching some agreement among themselves: they have no preference for agreement on one set of terms rather than another. I believe that this approach is mistaken, but it will advance the discussion to see why.

The branch of formal theory to which we must appeal in order to analyze such a problem is the study pioneered by Thomas Schelling in *The Strategy of Conflict* of pure coordination problems: the sort of problem that arises when two people want to meet in a town without having made prior arrangements about a rendezvous and where each tries to decide where to go with the best chance of meeting the other, given the knowledge that the other is trying to make the same decision.[24] The moral theory that will arise from this is conventionalism: the content of morality is arbitrary but it is still binding because it matters that we all act on the same rules, whatever they may be. Morality, on this view, becomes the search for "prominent solutions" (or "Schelling points," as they have come to be known) in situations where some rule is needed.[25]

The youthful David Hume, ever on the lookout for paradoxes with which to jolt the world of polite learning into paying him some attention, came close to maintaining in the *Treatise* that the rules governing property are conventional in this way. As we saw in section 20, the operations of the "fancy"—the disposition of the human mind to make associations between different ideas where there is no connection in reality—were invoked heavily by Hume to explain why the details of the rules about property took the form they did.[26] But by the time he came to write the *Enquiry* he had modified his position and now maintained only that fanciful analogies or associations of ideas might come in to settle the issue between two or more alternative rules that were equally beneficial. This is surely much more plausible. The rule, for example, that assigns the lambs to the owner of the ewe stems not merely from a tendency of the fancy to run from the one to the other but from the rule's practical advantages and its avoidance of the creation of perverse incentives.[27] The rule of the road—the paradigm of a convention—is scarcely the typical moral rule. Usually it does make a difference what the content of the rule is.

We cannot, therefore, avoid the employment of a concept of reasonableness that has substance to it. But we also want to avoid trivializing the procedure by simply putting in as reasonableness what we take out at the end as justice. This sets the terms of the problem to be faced: without a concept of reasonableness already pregnant with conclusions about what reasonable people would agree on, how are we to proceed? I shall sketch an answer here, leaving a complete account for Volume II. Let me, then, distinguish two methods of trying to determine what could not reasonably be rejected by people in the kind of original position I have depicted. I shall call them the *a priori* method and the empirical method.

The *a priori* method consists of simply asking whether there are things that nobody would reasonably accept in the absence of coercion, including the implicit coercion of a nonagreement outcome. I think that this is not an empty question, and that many kinds of structured inequality fall to the requirement that inequalities must be acceptable to all, including those who do worst under them. (It is this demand that lies at the heart of Rawls's theory of justice, but is not, as I have argued, well served by his invoking the kind of construction he favors.) Examples that spring to mind immediately are slavery, apartheid, and genocide. Less gross cases of inequality can also, I believe, be condemned. But these examples should be enough to illustrate the point that the *a priori* method is not completely toothless.

The empirical method starts from observation rather than pure thought. It is animated by the consideration that actual societies approximate more or less closely the conditions that define the third construction—conditions that I shall refer to for convenience as "the circumstances of impartiality." Thus, a society in which each section of the population has its own organizations and organs of communication to articulate its interests and aspirations is closer to the circumstances of impartiality than one in which, say, business is well organized but labor is not, and in which almost all the organs of mass communication are owned and controlled by the rich. Similarly, a political system in which parties represent the distinctive interests and aspirations of different groups is closer to the circumstances of impartiality than one in which all successful candidates have either to have money or to be acceptable to those who have it. Again, a society in which there is a good deal of fellow feeling for other citizens will be closer to the circumstances of impartiality than one in which many people are unmoved by the lot of sections of the population with which they do not identify. And, finally, a culture in which politics is widely regarded as a matter of debate rather than as a game—where arguments are thought of as more than the window-dressing for self-interest—will obviously be closer to the circumstances of impartiality.

Using criteria such as these, we can roughly rank liberal-democratic societies according to the degree to which they approximate the circumstances of impartiality. I hazard the suggestion that the Scandinavian countries mark out one end of the spectrum and the United States the other. If we then look for characteristic differences in public policy among the countries on our spectrum, we may be able to see that there is a recognizable pattern such that the societies closer to the circumstances of impartiality characteristically have certain kinds of fiscal or social policy that those further away lack. And we can then, of course, carry out the same exercise from the other end. If we look at societies that are the furthest distance away from the circumstances of impartiality, societies in which seething discontent is held down only by brutal force, we may find that there are some institutions that are found only in such societies. By carrying out this kind of investigation we can at the least hope to come up with findings that are highly suggestive as to what can and what cannot reasonably be rejected.

THE ROLE OF INTUITIONS

Before closing this discussion, it may, I think, be of some interest to return to the question raised in section 34 about the relation between constructivism and intuitionism and to ask it in the present context. It will be recalled that I dismissed the possibility of a completely self-sustaining constructivist theory of justice on the ground that we must be given some reason, which cannot be supplied from within the construction itself, for believing that the principles emerging from it should count as principles of justice. In the present case, it is evident that the rationale for the general form of construction is the conception of impartial morality put forward in section 35. Someone who does not accept the ground-floor egalitarianism of that conception will obviously have no reason for taking any interest in the construction. It is hard to imagine Aristotle regarding as a serious objection to his depiction of the good society that the people he called "natural slaves" would be unlikely to accept it voluntarily. And later believers in fundamental biologically based inequalities between races would no doubt be similarly inclined to say that the unwillingness of the inferior races to accept the proper implications of their inferiority without coercion is simply another manifestation of their inferiority.

The other great branch of fundamental anti-egalitarianism is that which attributes to different human groups unequal spiritual value. The best example is, I take it, the Hindu *varna* system, which grounds the unequal worth of castes in an elaborate metaphysic. An orthodox Brahmin would not, presumably, be unduly concerned about the amount of physical violence required in the villages to keep those at the bottom of the status system in the place allotted to them. (This especially applies to those outside the formal caste system altogether, such as the Untouchables.) If the theory represents a deep metaphysical truth about the universe, it is scarcely relevant that it does not look like a promising basis for free agreement.

The notion that inequality must be justified in terms that are potentially acceptable to those at the bottom as well as those who are the chief beneficiaries of it is an essential premise of the present construction. But it is not enough to differentiate our construction from others that lead in a different direction. To see this we have only to bear in mind that Hobbes founded his own political theory on the approximate mental and physical equality of human beings, and accepted the necessity of securing the rational assent of every member of a state to the political arrangements of that state. Yet Hobbes was the first person to put forward a fully elaborated two-stage theory, in which justice is the outcome of a hypothetical rational bargain founded on a sense of mutual advantage.

What makes our construction distinctive is that those who do poorly under a proposed set of principles cannot be coerced into accepting them by fear of the consequences of failure to agree. The argument is the one set out in section 35. I do not pretend that the construction can be defended independently. The case for it is that it instantiates the notion of justice as impartiality. This is not, however, to say that the construction is powerless to advance the underlying conception of justice as impartiality. Someone may be attracted by the general characterization of justice as impartiality but be concerned that it seems too vague to provide a basis for arriving at any definite conclusions. If the construction is helpful in allaying such doubts by making the problem more manageable, then there is obviously more reason for embracing the underlying conception.

I was careful to say that the construction would indirectly support the underlying conception of impartial morality *if* it made the problem of deriving conclusions more manageable. But does it really contribute anything? The challenge is to show that the construction is doing some work. If that challenge can be met we shall be able to say that we have a form of constructivist theory that, while not wholly independent of intuitions, is not simply a mode of presentation for them.

In arguing that the construction has this kind of qualified independence, I must beware of appearing to overstate my case. Let me draw a distinction between hard and soft constructivism. Hard constructivism (which is represented by Rawls in *A Theory of Justice*) makes the claim that, once the original position has been fully specified, no further appeal to morally tinged notions is required. The parties in the original position are not themselves to worry about anything except advancing their own interests.

> If justice as fairness is more convincing than the older presentations of the contract doctrine, I believe that it is because the original position . . . unites in one conception a reasonably clear problem of choice with conditions that are widely recognized as fitting to impose on the adoption of moral principles. . . . It is partly to preserve this clarity that I have avoided attributing to the parties any ethical motivation. They decide solely on the basis of what seems best calculated to further their interests so far as they can ascertain them.[28]

Soft constructivism is distinguished from hard constructivism in imputing to the "agents of construction" in the original position a capacity and preparedness to be moved by moral considerations—by arguments that make an appeal to the equal *prima facie* claim of the interests of all to be taken into account. The form of construction that I am here promoting clearly fits the pattern of soft constructivism. If anyone wishes to insist that only hard constructivism is to count as constructivism, then there is nothing more to be said. But it seems to me that the only reason anyone could have for taking such a line would be a presupposition that hard constructivism is the only form of constructivism with any prospect of constituting a distinctive method. But that is precisely the question that is now at issue.

Rawls himself, it is worth noticing, is prepared to admit that what I am here calling soft constructivism represents a bona fide alternative to his own form of original position. Immediately after the passage I have just quoted he goes on to say that we can "define ethical variations of the initial situation by supposing the parties to be influenced by moral considerations."[29] And he explicitly lists among the possibilities that "some notion of fair and willingly [*sic*] cooperation may limit the conceptions of justice which the parties are prepared to entertain."[30] He adds: "There is no a priori reason for thinking that these variations [of the initial situation] must be less convincing, or the moral constraints they express less widely shared."[31]

Although this testimony is, I think, of some interest coming from the leading exponent of hard constructivism, I do not intend simply to appeal to authority. I believe it is possible to show that the construction makes a difference within a soft-constructivist framework. Imputing to the parties in the original position a sensitivity to moral considerations still leaves us with a type of pure procedural justice. The charge that it reduces to an outcome-oriented approach, where we start from the conclusions and work backward to the specification of the procedure, can be successfully refuted.

The key to this argument is a contrast between the role that personal moral judgments play in intuitionistic accounts and the role they play in the kind of construction we are now discussing. The focus in intuitionism is on the individual, and the typical vocabulary is one of "reflection" or "introspection." There is no built-in requirement that the prospects of reaching agreement with others should be regarded as relevant. As we saw in section 32, classical intuitionism claims that people possess a faculty capable of discerning moral truths. It is, obviously, disconcerting for this theory that the amount of disagreement should be so much greater than it is in the case of, say, perceptual judgments. But it is still possible to claim possession of the moral truth even if few others agree or seem likely to. On the alternative version of intuitionism, where all we can expect to do is to bring our moral convictions into an internally coherent whole, the pressure to be concerned about what others think would appear to be even less.

Where intuitionism is inward-looking, constructivism is outward-looking. Its vocabulary is one in which words such as "agreement," "case," "proposal," and the like are prominent. This really does, I think, change the way we approach things. It is no longer enough to be convinced of something oneself. It is necessary to ask whether other people could (under the favorable conditions defined by the circumstances of impartiality) be convinced as well.

Now it is, of course, true that all of this is simply a form of argument that is, in the end, put forward by one person for consideration by others. How do we know that the construction is really operating to constrain the conclusions advanced? What is to stop someone from simply putting his own views and claiming that they will pass the test? The answer has to be: absolutely nothing. But it is one thing to make a claim and another to make it convincingly. And I believe that the only hope of being convincing is to take seriously the constraints that the construction imposes.

It is a fair question, and one which I have been asked, whether my own views about justice have been affected by putting them through the construction that I recommend. I feel quite confident in answering this affirmatively. The construction encourages—indeed, virtually forces— one to make a distinction between what one would personally support and what one believes could not reasonably be rejected. Unless one has the personality of an Old Testament prophet, it is hard to persuade oneself that the two classes of judgments have the same boundary. There are many social arrangements that I think can be criticized, and which I would prefer not to find in any society of which I was a member, that I am inclined to think could not be reasonably rejected over a strong preference for them by others. I shall explore the tendency toward conventionalism, but also seek to establish its limits, in Volume II. My point here is simply that thinking in the way one is led to by the construction results in definite changes in one's ideas. That is, it seems to me, sufficient to indicate that the construction does do some work, which is what I set out to maintain.

The trick is, I take it, to avoid packing so much substance into the notion of reasonableness as to trivialize the argument. It cannot be stripped down all the way to simple rationality, because then we would open up the possibility of people holding out for a better deal simply in order to exploit the greater need of others for agreement. But the notion of reasonableness should not simply be used to reproduce all the theorist's own views. At the minimum, it constrains the range of reasons that can be given for rejecting a proposal. Flatly asserting "It's contrary to my interest and that's why I oppose it" will be ruled out. It is simply not a valid move in the game. Beyond that, we must invoke a requirement of good faith: that people will not put forward frivolous or tendentious arguments for a position that they actually hold only because it is personally advantageous. There must, in other words, be some shared understanding of what counts as a convincing case, and everyone must be prepared to concede that his position is untenable if a sound argument is made against it.

We are thus, if you like, presupposing that it is possible to define a basic attitude of what you might call human decency, which can be imputed to the people in our original position. They do not have to be completely detached from their own interests—we should, indeed, do better not to attribute that kind of impartiality to the "agents of construction"—but they do have to be prepared to view themselves as one among others, to borrow Adam Smith's formulation.

I emphasize *human* decency. No theory like this can make the claim that its results apply to all rational beings as such. If a group of creatures from outer space arrived, we might conjecture from their apparent capacity to engage in elaborate cooperative enterprises that they must have some capacity to treat one another decently, in their own terms. But their terms might be unimaginably different from ours.

It is not necessary to claim that human decency is a completely universal trait. We can even concede the possibility of a society virtually devoid of it: Colin Turnbull's account of the Ik makes them sound like candidates for such a society.[32] But what should impress us are the extraordinary ecological stresses that the Ik were subjected to before their society fell into such a dismal state. It is no part of the theory that conditions do not exist in which human beings can be got to shed their humanity. All we need is that common decency should be a sufficiently widespread phenomenon to give the construction some real content.

It is here that what I called earlier the empirical approach comes in. If we put agreement under certain conditions at the center, we can make use of information about relative consensus and dissensus in a variety of societies on any number of issues. This is surely another point in favor of the claim that even soft constructivism is a distinctive method. For to anyone wedded to intuitionism it is hard to see how such information can be relevant.

One last point. It is intriguing to observe that what I have been saying here has some echoes of Rawls's early "Outline of a Decision Procedure for Ethics." Although the standard annotated bibliography of Rawlsiana describes it as "Rawls's version of the ideal observer theory,"[33] I pointed in section 34 to the important role played in it by the search for agreement among competent moral judges. It should not be too surprising that the proposed form of soft constructivism should have such parallels. For what in effect happened was that Rawls came to believe he could tighten up the theory to the point at which the conclusions could be derived by strict logical deduction—or at any rate to the point at which that appeared to be a not unreasonable aspiration. If we become convinced (and I have offered my reasons for doing so) that this was a dead end, but still find the underlying ideas attractive, it is quite natural that what we finish up with should bear some resemblance to the earlier form of the theory, before it took the turn to a self-interested choice from behind a veil of ignorance.

CHAPTER X

Conclusion

43. THE SUBJECT OF SOCIAL JUSTICE

In this final chapter I shall draw on what has gone before to offer my answers to three questions about justice. The first is: What is justice? The second is: Why be just? and the third is: How do we go about determining what justice demands? I shall take these questions in turn, devoting this section to the first and taking up the others in the following two sections. I shall not confine myself to recapitulating points that have been made already in this volume. In the course of reordering and synthesizing the material from earlier chapters I have also taken the opportunity on occasion to extend or elaborate what I said the first time round.

To begin, then, let us ask: What is justice? The word "justice" is used in a wide variety of contexts. Perhaps the one that comes to mind most readily is justice as an attribute of individual legal decisions. At any rate as a first move we may say that a verdict in a trial is just if it is in accordance with the law. But suppose that the law on workers' compensation lays down limitations on recovery such that a worker is denied compensation if his disease becomes manifest only some years after he has ceased employment, even though it is not in contention that his disease was incurred in the course of employment. If we feel that the denial of such a worker's claim is unjust, while conceding that it was in accordance with the law, we must be saying that the law itself is unjust.

In this *Treatise on Social Justice* I am concerned with justice in its wholesale rather than its retail form—with institutions rather than individual outcomes. Thus, the provisions of the law on workers' compensation falls within its scope. These provisions can be assessed for their justice or injustice, and my object is to provide a framework within which such judgments can be made. My subject is, then, social justice, or, as it is sometimes called, distributive justice. This kind of justice is in the first instance an attribute of institutions. We can say that an existing institution is just or unjust. We can say that some alternative to what exists would be more just. And we can say that it would be just for a kind of institution that does not now exist (for example, a scheme providing for systematic and nondiscretionary transfers of income from rich countries to poor ones) to be created.

Institutions may be assessed from many points of view. What, then, is the distinctive point of view of justice? When we ask about the justice of an institution we are inquiring into the way in which it distributes benefits and burdens. The currency of social or distributive justice is one of rights and disabilities, privileges and disadvantages, equal or unequal opportunities, power and dependency, wealth (which is a right to control the disposition of certain resources) and poverty. It should be apparent from this that the justice or injustice of an institution is an enormously important fact about it. The judgment that an institution is unjust must tell very strongly against its overall acceptability.

At the same time, however, we should recognize that to ask about the justice of an institution is to look at it in one particular light: it is to look at it as a creator of benefits and burdens. (I shall take "benefits and burdens" as the generic term for those factors listed above.) Thus, aspects of institutions other than the distribution of benefits and burdens that they bring about are left on one side. In cases where the distribution of benefits and burdens is incidental to the rationale of an institution, asking whether the institution is just or unjust may be somewhat beside the point.

An obvious example is that of the public subsidization of grand opera. There is no country in which the highest level of performance can be sustained financially by box office receipts, and the balance is made up out of some mix of private and public support. (In the United States the element of public subsidization comes about mainly through tax relief on charitable contributions and the favorable tax treatment of foundations. The effect on the taxpayer is the same: the instrumentality simply happens to be that taxes which would otherwise have been collected are forgone rather than that taxes are collected and then disbursed.) Now, regarded as a scheme for the distribution of benefits and burdens, the public subsidization of grand opera is bound to seem rather bizarre. For looked at in this light what it amounts to is a scheme for burdening the body of taxpayers and benefiting those who like grand opera and can afford the (often still quite expensive) tickets—and also, of course, benefiting the singers, orchestral players, and others whose salaries are partly paid for by the public subsidy.

The argument against subsidization is, indeed, quite frequently made along these lines. It is an argument that appeals to those on both the philistine left and the philistine right. The former can argue that transfers should not be made to those who have above-average incomes (as most operagoers have), and the latter can argue that grand opera should be treated no differently from any other marketable commodity, so if it cannot be sold at a price that covers its cost it should not be provided at all. But the point of subsidizing grand opera is not to improve the equity of the distribution of benefits and burdens. These arguments do not therefore show that there is anything wrong with subsidization. The most they can show is that it would be crazy to make an argument in favor of subsidization by saying that it is a demand of social justice. But has anyone ever made the argument on these lines? The case must be, rather, that grand opera represents one of the achievements of Western civilization and it is good that some minute fraction of a wealthy country's national income should be devoted to keeping it in being for current and later generations. This is not the place to elaborate or evaluate that case. The point that is relevant here is that it is an example of a public policy issue to which justice is essentially irrelevant.

More common are cases where justice is very important but is not the only consideration that matters. An educational system provides a good example. There are, obviously, many ways in which a society's educational institutions may be evaluated. We may approve or disapprove of the attitude to life that the schools seek to inculcate, for example, and we may assess what is taught according to its truth, its significance for the understanding of the world, its contribution to economic production, and so on. But when we look at educational institutions from the point of view of justice, what we will tend to focus on is the role that they play in the transmission of occupational positions from generation to generation. For when we ask what impact the educational system has on the distribution of benefits and burdens, the feature of it that becomes prominent is the way in which educational qualifications are the key to access to many of the more desirable occupational positions. The educational system is thus seen as a system for the more or less equal distribution of opportunities to acquire these qualifications.

From this point of view, the content of education is of far less significance than the method of allocating the chances to acquire whatever educational qualifications are most valuable. Let me illustrate this. Bureaucratic positions, in societies otherwise as different as ancient China and modern Britain, have been filled on the basis of performance on examinations whose content has little to do with the knowledge required for the carrying out of the duties. Macaulay defended the practice of recruiting to the Indian civil service on the basis of the ability to compose verses in Greek and Latin by arguing that this was as good a test as any of general ability. If it were made known that in future skill in Cherokee would be the criterion, that would do just as well: those who could produce the most mellifluous imitations of the best Cherokee models would undoubtedly be the best-qualified candidates for administrative positions.

One may reasonably question Macaulay's belief that general ability, as manifested in the ability to write elegantly in a foreign (and preferably dead) language, is the ideal basis on which to recruit a civil service. But that is not in itself a question of justice. What makes it a question of justice is that the content of the examinations has a profound influence on the access to the jobs that are filled by them. If (as was the case) Greek and Latin form three-quarters of the curriculum in schools available only to the sons (daughters at that time were not in the running) of the most privileged minority of the population, and are little taught in the rest of the schools, the examination system operates as a method of restricting recruitment to the children of that small stratum.

Thus, we look at the interaction of the educational system and the system of recruitment into desirable positions in the society, and we pass a judgment on the distribution of benefits and burdens that together they bring about. This gives us an assessment in terms of social justice. Clearly, the justice of all the other major social institutions can be appraised in the same way. It will be the task of volumes II and III of this *Treatise* to show how this is to be done.

44. JUSTICE AND MOTIVATION *why be just?*

Our account of the nature of justice cannot be separated from the question of motivation. What is the claim that justice has upon us? Or, as it is often put nowadays: Is it possible to show that it is rational to conform our conduct to the demands of justice? This question must be raised because an inquiry into justice is not a purely theoretical investigation akin to the development of scientific theories about natural phenomena. If we discover something new about muons or gluons this does not lead directly to any implications about what (if anything) we should do about it. But if we reach the conclusion that we are behaving unjustly, it seems that we should somehow be failing to recognize the significance of this if we were to say merely "How interesting!" Unless the acknowledgment of injustice has at any rate some tendency to lead to a determination to do something about it, there seems little point in even talking about justice. We cannot therefore separate the question "What is justice?" from the question "Why be just?"

Before I ask about the motivation for behaving justly, however, I must back up and deal with a prior question. I have claimed that social or distributive justice is a virtue of institutions. But if this is so, how did we somehow start talking about justice as a virtue of people? Presumably there must be some connection, but what is it?

It is extremely hard, in fact, to give a general answer to this question, but I shall offer a partial one that I hope will be adequate for the present purpose. The most straightforward case is one where an existing institution is just. We still, of course, have to say what it is about a distribution of benefits and burdens that makes it just. For now all we need is to take it that justice is a criterion for the assessment of institutions in terms of the distribution of benefits and burdens to which they give rise. Let us say, then, that we have a just institution in some society. Derivatively, we can say some things about just conduct in this instance. The central claim is that it is just to comply voluntarily with the requirements that the institution lays on individuals, at any rate so long as the institution is broadly complied with by those who are covered by it. Sanctions against noncompliance are relevant to justice insofar as they provide assurance that others will comply, so that one will not be put at a relative disadvantage by complying. But justice as a virtue of human beings is not exemplified by compliance that is brought about through fear of sanctions. Rather, justice is a disposition to do what just institutions call for simply on the basis of their being just.

This is all very well as far as it goes, but what does the virtue of justice require in the face of unjust institutions? Since there is a range of reasonable disagreement about what justice requires, no society could subsist for a day if people felt no obligation to comply with institutions that they believed to be unjust. We therefore need some quite robust conditions to be met before justice as a virtue of individuals ceases to commend compliance. We have to look at the overall tendency of the society's institutions and the way in which political decisions get taken in order to form a judgment.

But what if, after we have done that, the injustice appears to be egregious? Should we do what would be required by more just institutions? Should we refuse to obey the existing rules? What means are legitimate in seeking to change them? These are questions of right conduct that are extraordinarily hard to say anything about on anything except a case-by-case basis. And even then I do not believe that political philosophy has a lot to contribute. I shall, however, attempt to address them in Volume III of this *Treatise*.

For the present, let us lay aside these further questions about justice as a virtue of individuals, and take the simplest case, where institutions are just. In this case, as we have seen, justice consists in voluntary compliance with the demands that the institution makes. We can now go back to the question with which we began: Why be just? In the history of Western speculation on this topic (at any rate in its secular forms) there have been two kinds of answer. *Theories of Justice* has been built around the elaboration and comparison of these two kinds of answer.

Because of the practical nature of justice, a theory of the motivation for being just must at the same time be a theory of what justice is. For the content of justice has to be such that people will have a reason for being just. Thus, suppose we say that the motivation for being just is a sense of the long-term advantageousness to oneself of being just. Then justice must consist in what everyone finds advantageous if it is to be something that everyone has a motive for pursuing voluntarily. Alternatively, suppose that the motivation for being just is the desire to act in ways that can be defended to oneself and others without appealing to personal advantage. Then justice will have to be whatever it is that can actually be defended in this way. These are the two approaches that I regard as the main candidates to be considered. Each is, as may be seen, at once a theory of motivation and a theory of what justice is. Let me say a bit more about each in turn.

The first approach to justice can be, and has historically been, arrived at from two directions. Among the ancient Greeks, it was commonly held that every virtue must be advantageous to its possessor. Justice, however, seems on the face of it to be advantageous to others rather than to the person who is just. The thought then arises that under the actual conditions of human life the self-restraint demanded by justice

may be able to be presented as advantageous when viewed as the price
of similar self-restraint by others. A conception of justice on these lines
is mooted in Plato's *Republic*, as I mentioned in section 1, and Socrates
does not in rejecting it question the premise that if justice is to count
among the virtues it must be advantageous to its possessor.

From the seventeenth century on, this first approach has tended to
follow from a theory of human motivation in general. Philosophers
have held either that human beings do in fact ineluctably pursue their
own interests, or that even if they sometimes diverge from the path of
self-interest the only rational course of action is that which advances the
agent's interests. It is clear that, on these premises, if justice is to have
the capacity to appeal, it cannot be advantageous to others at the expense of the agent. And, as before, the most plausible way of making
justice fit the requirements is to suggest that justice really is advantageous to everyone. Of course, if justice is to have content, it will be
necessary to define that content in such a way as to ensure that it really
is true that justice is advantageous to everyone, and there is no guarantee that justice so defined will correspond to what is commonly thought
of as justice.

It is important not to render this first approach in a way that makes it
appear cruder than it really is. Thus, Hobbes, the most famous exposi-
tor of the modern version of the first approach, has frequently been
interpreted as saying simply that "might makes right." But this is not
so. What justice consists in is, roughly speaking, carrying out undertakings that you consented to out of a sense of their advantage, and
Hobbes maintains that (under certain conditions that define the scope
of obligation) it is advantageous to carry out such undertakings.[1] The
neo-Hobbesian theory of David Gauthier is similar in this respect.[2]

I emphasize this point because I earlier defined the virtue of justice in
people as a disposition to do what justice demands voluntarily, and not
only under threat of sanctions. It is easy to assume that the Hobbes/
Gauthier line of analysis cannot accommodate this because it has to
make personal advantage the motive for cultivating the disposition. But
not every source of advantage is properly to be regarded as a sanction.
If we understand sanctions in a restrictive sense as evils formally and
deliberately visited on people for lack of compliance, we can see that
failures to be trustworthy may be disadvantageous in two ways that do
not involve sanctions.

First, failure to do your part in some cooperative venture may cause
it to collapse, or at any rate weaken it, so that you are eventually worse

off than you would otherwise have been. And, second, the cooperative scheme may continue after you fail to do your part but you may be excluded from this and perhaps other cooperative arrangements in future, to your long-run detriment. Hobbes makes both these points and also recognizes what the significance of formal sanctions is in this scheme. It is not that they are necessary to provide a reason for cooperating when others cooperate. Rather, what they do is to give greater assurance that others will in fact cooperate, thus ensuring that it will be advantageous to cooperate yourself.

It is worth getting clear what a sophisticated version of the first approach looks like so as to get the relation to the second approach straight. It is not the case that on the first approach anything that is advantageous for someone to do is just. Justice consists in playing one's part in mutually advantageous cooperative arrangements, where the standard of comparison is some state of affairs defined by absence of cooperation. Now in my view there is absolutely no question that this is at any rate a part of justice. Reciprocity is a core element in every society's conception of justice. The question is, rather, whether the first approach is adequate by itself. My answer is that it is not and that the second approach yields a general theory of justice which can incorporate the theory generated by the first approach as a special case. I shall explain at the end of the next section how this can occur, but I must now say something about the second approach itself.

It may be recalled that I defined the second approach more or less as the obverse of the first, saying that according to this approach the motivation for being just is the desire to act in ways that can be defended to oneself and others without appealing to personal advantage. Let me first follow along the line thus started by illustrating how this second approach differs from the first and then try to set out the foundational ideas underlying the second approach independently.

I have denied that the first approach is simply one of "might-makesright." This would be to ignore the contractual basis of the theory. Nevertheless, the charge is not wholly misplaced. For might can be transformed into right by the alchemy of consent. Thus, Hobbes insists on the validity of any agreement that a weak state makes with a strong one as the price of peace, however disadvantageous its terms may be. And this implies that it would be unjust to go back on it if the opportunity arose to do so with impunity. (Hobbes does allow that a new and just cause of fear would invalidate the agreement, but the case I am considering is one where fear is subsequently lessened rather than increased.)[3] Similarly, someone who is captured in a war and is spared his life in return for a pledge of servitude is obliged by this "covenant of obedience" to put his labor and that of his family at the disposal of the master.[4]

Gauthier, it should be said, attempts to ameliorate such results of the doctrine of justice as mutual advantage by ruling out threats as a way of creating the noncooperative alternative. As I argued in section 37, I do not think that he can do so compatibly with his premises. But in any cases he insists that natural advantages and disadvantages must be translated into unequal bargains by the method of splitting the difference, and that it is a disposition toward conformity with these bargains that constitutes the virtue of justice. (See especially sections 5 and 7.)

Now the alternative to this approach is to deny that the motivation for being just has to be its prospective advantageousness, and therefore to deny that the only basis of justice can be mutual advantage in comparison with the outcome if no agreement is reached. From this perspective, part of the point of justice is to provide a criterion for the redress of inequalities in bargaining power. Justice is not supposed to be merely a device for smoothing the path of exploitation, a way of ensuring that those with the stronger bargaining position are able to turn it automatically into an advantageous outcome.

How can we put the second approach positively rather than, as has been done so far, negatively? It is, I think, true to say that whenever someone wishes to deny that a distribution of benefits and burdens is just, while acknowledging that it is mutually advantageous to the parties in the situation as it actually exists, the same general kind of appeal is made. This is an appeal to what can be approved of from an impartial standpoint. Thus, if we call the first approach justice as mutual advantage we may call the second justice as impartiality.

The basic idea of justice as impartiality can be expressed in a variety of ways. One is the notion of an impartial observer: justice is seen as what someone with no stake in the outcome would approve of as a distribution of benefits and burdens. Another is to ask each of the parties, "How would you like to be treated in the way you are proposing to treat the other?" The object here is to get the party that stands to gain from an inequality of bargaining power to admit that it would not like to be on the losing end.

This basic idea of impartiality as a matter of putting oneself in the other's shoes can be fleshed out in a couple of different ways. One is to ask the parties what outcome they would favor if they did not know which position they occupied. The idea of this is to guarantee impartiality by preventing any party from giving the answer that suits itself. The other is to ask the parties to propose principles for the distribution of benefits and burdens that they think ought to be acceptable to everyone affected not merely as preferable to the outcome arising from lack of agreement but under conditions in which that kind of bargaining pressure is removed.

Each of these variants of the second approach can be formalized further and thus be made to constitute a separate version of justice as impartiality. Indeed, even saying this greatly underestimates the variety of theories that are possible—and that actually exist. For we must allow that each variant can be formalized in different ways, and the details of these differences can produce profound effects on the outcomes that the theory generates as constituting a just distribution of benefits and burdens. I shall return to this in the next section, which is concerned with the question of determining what is just. For the present purpose, it is sufficient if I have said enough about justice as impartiality to give a foundation for the discussion of motivation that is the business of this section.

What, then, is the motive for behaving in conformity with justice, conceived of along the lines of the second approach? To provide an answer it is necessary to challenge the theory of motivation that underlies the first approach. Whether in the Greek or the modern form, what the first approach comes down to is the claim that, if something's being just is to count as a good reason for doing it, justice must be shown to be in the interest of the agent. On the second approach this constraint on what can count as a good reason is abandoned. That something is just, as justice is understood by the second approach, can be in itself a good reason for doing it. The motive is the desire to act justly: the wish to conduct oneself in ways that are capable of being defended impartially.

No doubt it is simpler to appeal to one motive rather than two. This may account for the popularity of the first approach among undergraduates who are beginning to study moral philosophy. But a theory may be too simple to be adequate. It seems to be quite well established that human beings are and always have been moved by considerations of justice as impartiality. If it is said that they are irrational to give weight to such considerations, what exactly is the force of this? Presumably it is not being claimed that they are acting on some kind of factual error. And to say that it is irrational because the only rational motive is self-

Impartial.
human nature

interest merely assumes what needs to be proved. At the same time, I do not wish to endorse the claim made by some philosophers that it is irrational not to act in accordance with justice as impartiality. What I am saying is that the desire to be able to justify our conduct in an impartial way is an original principle in human nature and one that develops under the normal conditions of human life.

It may be said that, even if it is not irrational to be disposed to act according to the dictates of justice as impartiality, it is irrational to act on the assumption that others will do so, and irrational to create institutions that rely upon their doing so. For practical purposes should we not address ourselves to the universal motive of self-interest rather than to the weak and undependable force of justice as impartiality?

This claim can be effectively undermined, in my view, by bringing to bear a number of mutually reinforcing counterarguments. Suppose, to being with, that we were to concede the greater reliability of self-interest as a motive. The chain of reasoning that purports to show the long-run advantage of, say, keeping one's agreements is quite complex. Even if we were to concede its validity, we should have to say that it is going to be hard to harness self-interest to justice in the way proposed by Hobbes and Gauthier. The essence of justice as impartiality is encapsulated in the Golden Rule; the efforts of Hobbes and Gauthier require hundreds of pages of subtle reasoning. But I do not think that even then the chain of reasoning leading to justice as mutual advantage is completely secure. It is not really possible to prove that it is advantageous to be disposed to be just on all occasions—for example, to adhere inflexibly to a policy of keeping contracts that are, according to the terms of the theory, fairly entered into. As I suggested in section 19, there is no answer to Hume's "sensible knave" except the one that Hume himself offers, and that appeals to the force of the moral motive rather than to self-interest.

The notion that impartial justice is a weaker motive than that of self-interest should not, in any case, go without challenge. To see its importance we have only to contrast a world in which everyone accepts that the only rational motive is self-interest with one in which it is accepted that it can be rational to do things in pursuit of justice that are contrary to one's interest. In the first world, bargaining advantage is smoothly translated into outcome advantage. Each party dispassionately appraises the relative bargaining strengths and settles for the best deal it can hope to get. Now add the factor of a sense of justice that is not simply a device for ratifying inequalities of bargaining power. "Instead of everyone's wanting as much as he can get in a bargaining situation,

Justice rationality against interest

bargaining adv → outcome adv.

suppose there is some outcome such that everyone cares very much about getting his share under that outcome, but cares very little, not at all, or even negatively about getting more. Suppose also that each person prefers carrying out his threat to settling for less than his share under that outcome."[5] Then we can expect that outcomes in the second world will be different from those in the first.

There is no need to overstate the case. So long as one party has a large enough advantage in bargaining strength, it will still tend to finish up with more than justice as impartiality would give it unless it actually disvalues ill-gotten gains. But the overall effect of the sense of justice will be to shift outcomes in a just direction. If they believe their cause is just, armies will be less willing to surrender than a rational calculation of advantage would suggest. Similarly, trade unionists will be more willing to strike if they believe they have a just claim than they would be in the world of dispassionate calculation of relative bargaining advantage.

It is worth noticing that the determination to accept losses in the pursuit of just claims over and above what would be suggested by self-interested rational calculation actually itself changes the relative bargaining strengths of the parties: the other side is more likely to settle for the demands if they are backed by moral fervor derived from a sense of justice. But even if the threat has to be carried out—the soldiers carry on fighting, the union strikes—the outcome may still, at some cost to the weaker party, be closer to the just one than it would be in the world without a sense of justice.*

I cannot imagine what it would mean to say that, in the aggregate, the sense of justice has (say) 20 percent of the efficacy of self-interest. What can be said is, surely, that it conditions a vast number of everyday transactions in the world we live in, and that, where the sense of injustice is deep and pervasive, it can give rise to deeds of heroic self-sacrifice that prospects of personal gain could scarcely do. It would be hard to explain the political behavior of Palestinians or South African blacks by

---

* For what it is worth, we can see a parallel in a stylized version of fighting for territory within, for example, many species of birds. Suppose that a bird fights harder the closer it is to the center of its territory. Then territories will be more equal than they would be if birds fought equally hard wherever they met, though it is consistent with the model that a stronger bird should have a larger territory than a weaker one. Moreover, if it is common knowledge among adjacent birds that the outcome of a fight depends on its location, fights will occur, if at all, only at the boundaries of territories. The sense of justice functions in the same way as the sense of territory postulated here: what we are saying is that equal increments of gain will elicit unequal amounts of prospective loss to obtain them, depending on their perceived justice.

assuming that individual self-interest is the sole motivation. And those (mostly to be found in the United States) who are so wedded to that assumption that they dismiss everything that does not fit as "irrational" are condemned never to understand the rest of the world.[6]

There is a further point so obvious that it is sometimes overlooked when we talk about the motivation to do what justice requires. We may say, as I have done, that justice as a virtue is realized only in the voluntary compliance with what justice requires. And I think that impartial justice would be hard to instantiate if nobody ever regarded the injustice of an action as a reason for refraining from it. But I have now added that one can also be moved by a sense of justice to make strenuous efforts to satisfy just claims, and this is another and very important way in which justice as impartiality can be efficacious as a force among human beings. But we must add that voluntary compliance and self-help do not have to stand alone. The basis of justice is institutional, I have argued, and institutions normally deploy sanctions to provide an additional motive for compliance. It is not, therefore, necessary that everyone should be moved by a sense of justice so long as the gap can be filled by deliberately created incentives for compliance.

This point is of especial importance because I think that the sense of justice often has more free play at the stage when the forms of institutions are being decided on than at the stage when people are deciding whether or not to comply with the demands that institutions make on them. Self-interest cannot be expected to bring about just institutions in general, so it is crucial that the sense of justice should operate there. Fortunately, all that is often necessary is that those whose own interests are not directly affected should support the course of impartial justice. But people who are prepared, say, to vote for a fair system for assessing contributions to some collective project may not be sufficiently motivated to pay their contributions voluntarily. The solution here is, obviously, to vote also for a system of sanctions to ensure compliance.

45. THE CONTENT OF JUSTICE

The third and last question that I raised about justice is: How do we determine what justice requires? The answer will, naturally, depend on which of the two conceptions of justice we accept. Let me first ask how we can get from the general idea of justice as mutual advantage to some determinate conclusions about just institutions. In section 33 I presented it as a contractualist theory. The paradigm of mutual advantage is a contract: an agreement to move from some *status quo* to some new arrangement that is prospectively beneficial to both parties. Now it is an obvious and familiar objection to any kind of contractarian doctrine that institutions do not in fact rest upon agreements among millions of people, nor is it plausible that they should. And the response among sophisticated contract theorists has always been the same: that the social contract, unlike particular contracts, must be regarded as hypothetical. Thus, for Hobbes all specific social institutions are created and sustained by the fiat of the sovereign, but the sovereign's authority rests on a hypothetical contract: a "Covenant of every man, in such a manner, *as if* every man should say to every man" that he will give up his rights in favor of a sovereign provided everybody else does likewise.[7] And his disciple Gauthier similarly has social cooperation depend upon hypothetical rather than actual agreements.

This response is normally countered by a further objection, namely, that it is hard to see why hypothetical contracts should have any binding force. If I enter into a real contract, it is my voluntary decision that gives the contract its moral claim on me. Saying that it would have been advantageous to me to make some contract that I did not in fact make establishes no similar claim on me.

This objection would have a good deal of force against many versions of social contract theory, but it fails against the Hobbes/Gauthier version. For we must always recall that its initial premise is that the binding force of agreements rests in the sense of mutual advantage that presumptively underlies them. An actual agreement signalizes a recognition of mutual advantage but it cannot create a motive *de novo*; all it can do is channel the motive of self-interest. Justice thus underwrites mutually advantageous cooperative arrangements, whether they arise from explicit agreement or not. If the argument from long-term self-interest works in the one case, then it works as well in the other case. Cooperation is preferable to noncooperation—that is the central point. It is immaterial whether the cooperation arises from an actual contract or whether its basis lies in a convention that each should support cooperative arrangements on condition that others do the same.[8]

The question we are now confronted with is the following: given that we cannot appeal to actual agreements in relation to social institutions, how are we to establish what are the just terms of cooperation? The natural answer would seem to be that the just terms of cooperation are those that would have been agreed upon by people trying to do the best for themselves. For these are, presumably, precisely the terms that it is rational for self-interested people to support amd maintain here and now.

In order to give effect to this basic idea we need two things: a nonagreement point from which the hypothetical bargaining is to start, and a theory about the outcome of bargaining among rational self-interested agents. Thus, sticking to Hobbes as our example for a moment longer, we can say that he has an explicit answer to the first and an implicit answer to the second. His noncooperative baseline from which mutual advantage is to be reckoned is "the natural condition of mankind," which is a state of war where "the life of man" is, in the famous phrase, "solitary, poore, nasty, brutish, and short."[9] And his implicit answer to the question about the rational terms of cooperation is that any improvement over the nonagreement baseline is enough to warrant consent to the terms of cooperation. Thus, he admits that "of so unlimited a power" as he ascribes to the sovereign, "men may fancy many evil consequences." But he replies that "the consequences of the want of it, which is perpetuall warre of every man against his neighbour," are much worse.[10]

It is apparent that Hobbes's way of specifying the noncooperative outcome and his criterion for rational cooperation have the combined result that the range of just outcomes is extremely large. This is in fact Hobbes's intention: it is rational, according to Hobbes, to obey the sovereign unless doing so would constitute a direct threat to one's own life. If we want to get tighter constraints than these out of the notion of justice as mutual advantage we shall have to make the nonagreement point less abysmal and put more teeth into the criterion for rational bargaining outcomes.

Gauthier, as it happens, illustrates just how far the opposite position can be carried. On essentially Hobbesian psychological premises he erects a wonderful Lockean farrago which has fully developed market institutions all built into the noncooperative outcome. Overlooking Adam Smith's remark that, left to themselves, profit-seeking producers will collude to stifle competition, Gauthier supposes that a competitive equilibrium could in principle arise purely from the operations of self-interest in a state of nature. Thus, the only room left for cooperation is to deal with externalities and public goods. And here the second move to tighten up the constraints of justice on social institutions comes into play. It is not enough that everyone should be better off than at the nonagreement point. Rather, there is, according to Gauthier, a unique solution to every bargaining problem, and an institution is just only if it corresponds to that solution.

What kind of theory do we get when we try to operationalize the notion of justice as mutual advantage so as to elicit from it definite (and preferably unique) implications for the justice of institutions? I answer that what we get is a variety of constructivist theory. A constructivist theory (see above, section 33) tells us that, in order to get answers about the demands of justice, we must construct a model of human interactions in some specified context. The context includes the motivations of the actors and the rules of the game. The theory then says that what comes out of the hypothetical interactions is to be taken as constituting principles of justice. In the present instance, we have self-interest as the motive. We have some stipulations about the kinds of moves that can be made in establishing the nonagreement point. (For example, Hobbes admits but Gauthier excludes threats.) And we have some formula that tells us how rational self-interested actors move from the nonagreement point to the Pareto frontier—that is to say, how the gains from cooperation are to be divided up.

What, then, is to be said about the operationalization of the second approach, justice as impartiality? To answer this I can draw on the analysis of constructivist theories already sketched. For it will hardly have escaped notice that all the formulations of the notion of justice as impartiality that I ran through in the previous section included hypothetical elements: "How would you like it if. . . ?" "What would you say if. . . ?" and so on. And if we want to take such vague notions and generate definite implications from them about the requirements that must be met by just institutions, a constructivist theory of some sort seems like a natural recourse.

As before, a constructivist theory can be defined by the context that it sets up for the interactions of the hypothetical parties. As before, we are to identify what is agreed upon by the parties as the principles for just institutions. And, as before, we may leave it open whether the construction generates unique outcomes or only a range of acceptable outcomes. What is distinctive about the second approach is that a different set of considerations goes into the specification of the context.

Given the motivational assumptions of the first approach, it is clear that the construction must represent bargaining advantages and disadvantages; otherwise the principles derived from it would fail to elicit the allegiance of everyone. The second approach is distinguished from the first precisely by its denial of the assumption that people (or people insofar as they are rational) are moved only by self-interest. It rejects the idea that a theory of justice can have efficacy only to the extent that it makes the principles of justice reflect actual power relationships. It will therefore throw out the nonagreement point of a "state of nature" as a generally relevant place at which to start. It may have room for nonagreement points in a subordinate capacity, but these will be derived from the theory itself, rather than being imposed on it. And it will in one way or another block the translation of superior bargaining power into advantageous outcomes.

How can the context of interaction be specified so as to meet these desiderata? There are, broadly speaking, two routes that can be taken. The first is to retain from the first approach the postulate that the parties in the construction are pursuing their own advantage but to prevent them from abusing superior bargaining power by denying them various kinds of knowledge—most crucially, knowledge of their own identities. The other is to drop the postulate that the parties are to do the best for themselves that they can and instead to postulate that they are, under ideal hypothetical conditions, seeking to reach agreement on principles that nobody could reasonably reject.

The postulate of self-interest plays quite a different role when it is incorporated into a construction designed to formalize the second approach from that which it played earlier. It is no longer intended to represent people as they really are—the essence of the second approach is that people can be concerned with justice as impartiality—but is simply part of the context of interaction from which, it is claimed, justice as impartiality will arise. We might say, however, that the two constructions are similar in that they take agreements arising out of the pursuit of self-interest in suitably defined conditions to be constitutive of justice. Where they differ is in the specifications of the conditions.

But it is not enough to show that a veil of ignorance superimposed on self-interested choice will guarantee impartiality of a kind. We can still ask: Is it the right kind? What was said about the force of hypothetical agreements within the first approach applies also, *mutatis mutandis*, to the second approach as well. If we take justice to be a matter of mutual advantage, the only claim to be made for hypothetical agreements is that they function as a sign of where mutual advantage lies. Similarly, if we take justice to be a matter of impartial approval, the only claim to be made for hypothetical agreements is that they are a sign of what might be approved of impartially. As I argued in section 41, however, self-interested choices under uncertainty fail to capture the notion of justice as impartiality that originally attracted us.

The construction that I have been discussing starts by retaining the self-interest postulate from the construction corresponding to the first approach, and then adds a veil of ignorance with the object of mitigating its undesirable effects. The alternative route is to throw out the idea that the "agents of construction" should be assumed to be trying to maximize their gains. Instead we postulate that they are trying to reach agreement on terms that nobody could reasonably reject. The veil of ignorance that prevents them from knowing their own personal characteristics and positions is then no longer essential. It may still be useful as an *ad hoc* device: sometimes an argument can be advanced by asking, "What would you say about this if you didn't know how you'd be affected?" But this is now a part of the arsenal of persuasion rather than a move in a knockdown demonstration.

I have identified three kinds of construction, one corresponding to the first approach and two to the second approach. Each embodies a different decision process. The first construction creates a game: we ask what rational self-interested players would finish up with. As Anatol Rapoport put it in *Fights, Games, and Debates*, the parties in a game "co-operate in 'doing their best,' that is, in presenting to each other the greatest possible challenge. . . . [T]he *assumption* that the opponent will do 'his best' contributes to the validity of rational analysis, which both must accept."[11] The second construction, involving a veil of ignorance, has superficially the same game-like characteristics in that the parties are pursuing their own interests as effectively as possible. Moreover, they know that in real life they have conflicting interests. But the proviso that they do not know what these interests are prevents them from being able to advance their distinctive interests in the choice situation— the "original position," as Rawls dubs it. Each therefore in practice faces the same decision problem in an original position so defined. But with no conflict of interest in the original position we lose the characteristics of a game. What we have instead is a problem of individual choice-making under uncertainty which is posed in identical terms to the people in the original position. Finally, the third setting is one that Rapoport calls, in contrast to a game, a debate. "The objective is to *convince* your opponent, to make him see things as you see them."[12] But we should add that conviction must be conceived of as a two-way process. The parties in this third construction must debate in good faith, which means that they must be prepared to be convinced as well as to try to convince others. They must be willing to acknowledge a good argument, even if it runs against their interests to do so.

So far I have specified the third construction in two ways. The parties are concerned to reach agreement on principles that nobody can reasonably reject; and they do not operate behind a veil of ignorance, though they may invoke it in the course of argument. We should add that the parties are able to understand the implications of alternative proposals and are aware of a wide range of cultural and historical experiences. For some purposes it may help to think of the parties as representatives of the people in actual societies, but we should endeavor to avoid getting too hung up on details of this kind, since no claim is being made that conclusions can be demonstrated by using this apparatus. It is simply put forward as a way of thinking about justice as impartiality.

How does the construction connect up with the notion of impartiality? My answer is that impartiality enters in through the requirement that everybody's point of view must be taken into account. Each person in this original position has a veto over proposed principles, which can be exercised unless it would be reasonable for that person to accept a principle. To say that a principle could not reasonably be rejected by anyone covered by it is, I suggest, a way of saying that it meets the test of impartiality.

It has to be said that this construction is delicately poised between two poles, and that its integrity depends on maintaining an intermediate position. If it is pulled too far in either direction it turns into something else. On one side, we want to insist that the parties have interests and values that they are concerned, up to a point, to defend. But we do not want this to reduce the third construction to the first, where the parties utilize whatever strategic advantages they have in order to advance their interests. On the other side, we want to say that the parties are prepared to accept that it would be unreasonable to hold out against some proposal merely because it is relatively disadvantageous. But we do not want to say that their sense of what is reasonable is so strong that it leads them directly to identical conclusions about what is just. If we did this, we would lose the character of a debate, as the second construction lost the character of a game. Instead of a debate, we would again have an individual decision problem carried on in identical terms by all parties, and the requirement of consensus would once again be reduced to triviality. The only difference would be in the formulation of the decision problem: rather than an attempt to do the best for oneself under uncertainty it would now be an attempt to decide what justice requires.

46. ENVOI

"The Adventure of the Engineer's Thumb" is not one of the more distinguished items in the Holmesian canon, but it contains an incident that some readers of this book may regard as relevant. The engineer, having been engaged by a gang of forgers who are anxious to conceal their location, is met at a country railway station and driven for an hour through the night in a carriage with closed windows, finishing up at a house which is actually quite close to the starting point.[13] It may perhaps be felt that I have similarly taken a long way round to arrive at a destination which is scarcely exotic. People who have not been exposed to the arguments of a Hobbes or a Gauthier will naturally tend, I think, to reject out of hand the notion that justice is nothing more than a matter of mutual advantage. And it may be added that few of those who have studied the arguments have been persuaded either. It is true that the exact specification of justice as impartiality proposed here would not naturally occur to someone who had not given the question much thought. But at the same time I have myself emphasized the way in which the general idea of justice as impartiality is a systematization of everyday forms of moral argument.

I do not, however, think that it is sensible to demand originality in the general nature of the conclusions of a study such as this. To return to what was said in the opening section of this book, questions about the justice of institutions arise when the authority of custom weakens its hold on the minds of the members of a society. As it comes to be perceived that social, political, and economic inequalities are the product of human convention, the need for justification is felt. Two responses that have been developed deny that social inequality is based on convention. One seeks to found social inequalities in natural ones, a line of argument that can be traced from Aristotle's defense of slavery to modern "scientific" racism. The other seeks a metaphysical basis for social inequalities: from the elaborations of the Hindu system to the Church of England's complacent belief that God "ordered" the "estate" of rich and poor, the major religions have a remarkable record of supporting whatever system of inequalities happens to prevail at the time. This book has been premised on the assumption that neither of these forms of justification for inequality will do. Although some people believe them, of course, they are incapable of carrying any rational conviction to those who do not. They cannot therefore form an acceptable basis for the justification of inequality.

It may be said that this criterion itself rigs the question by stipulating that only certain kinds of doctrine can constitute a legitimate basis for inequality. I can see no alternative to pleading guilty on this charge. There is, I think, an inevitable circularity here. Asserting the demands of unbelievers to be given better reasons for accepting inequalities from which they suffer than those offered by the believers is necessarily deny-ing the claims that the believers themselves make to the effect that their beliefs provide all the justification that can be required.

Many philosophers think that it is possible to resort to higher-level arguments to show the superiority of the view that justifications of inequality should not appeal to inherently controversial empirical or metaphysical beliefs. I wish they were right but I can see no way of overcoming the problem that they must attribute to their adversaries premises that they manifestly do not believe in. Thus, suppose we were to expand Locke's argument for religious toleration and say that there are strong pragmatic grounds for not trying to impose a social order based on a particular set of religious beliefs. Even if this is a sound case in itself, its persuasive power can be no greater than the appeal of pragmatic considerations to the recipient. Any true believer prepared to regard them as decisive is already in effect a convert to the premises of secularism in politics.

For the purposes of this *Treatise*, and any other on the same subject, it is necessary at the outset for the author to commit himself to a position on the range of justifications to be seriously considered. My commit-ment is manifest from everything in this book. The point that now falls to be made is simply this: that if we set the problem up as one of justify-ing inequality on the assumption that it is the product of human con-vention and not underwritten by any deep natural or metaphysical inequality between human beings, there are not a lot of potential solu-tions. At the highest level of generality, there are perhaps only the two that have been discussed in this book. Both start from the idea that con-ventions that are adhered to are preferable to unrestrained conflict. They then diverge in what they ask of a satisfactory convention. One line says that the convention must be acceptable to each person when he consults his own advantage. The other says that it must be acceptable to everyone when he takes up an impartial standpoint. Leaping lightly over the centuries, we can trace the first tradition from the Sophists through Hobbes to Gauthier and the second from the Stoics through Kant to Rawls.

When the alternatives are stated in terms such as these, it is easy to maintain that philosophy never makes any progress and that the same basic ideas merely keep coming round in cycles. There is obviously something in this, but I believe that it conceals more than it reveals. Progress comes in the form of analytical techniques that enable us to state the grand alternatives with greater precision than before and to see more deeply into them. For the first alternative, the key development has been the invention of game theory and its increasingly flexible deployment in social analysis. For the second alternative, it has been the notion, put forward by Rawls, of an original position, conceived of as an ethically privileged choice situation. That these are genuine advances and not just changes of fashion is, I believe, evidenced by the way in which we can use these ideas to go back and shed fresh light on earlier versions of the theories. Thus, the level of sophistication with which Hobbes is treated has been raised immeasurably in the past two decades, and we are also beginning to see a reevaluation of the social contract tradition in the light of Rawls's work.

This book is offered as an attempt to consolidate and, more ambitiously, to carry further forward these advances of recent decades. I should like to believe that I have clarified a number of questions in the game-theoretical analysis of bargaining and have shown their relevance to the theory of justice as mutual advantage. I also hope that I have succeeded in following through on Rawls's passing suggestion that one might be able to construct a taxonomy of original positions within which Rawls's own version could be located as a special case. At the same time, I have tried to use the contrast between justice as mutual advantage and justice as impartiality as a way of probing the theories of justice put forward by Hume and Rawls. I do not want to make exaggerated claims for this exercise. No doubt by bringing some questions into sharp focus I have blurred others. But I feel confident of my basic claim that both approaches are implicit in the theories of both Hume and Rawls and I think it is illuminating to tease out the two approaches from their writings on justice.

In the end, however, it is true enough that the overall conclusions of the book can be stated in reasonably brief compass. The first three sections of this chapter are, indeed, designed to do precisely that. For the larger purposes of this *Treatise*, it would be very inconvenient if it were otherwise, since I wish in the two volumes that follow the present one to build on its conclusions. In the next volume, then, I shall take justice as impartiality to be my starting point and I shall then try to work through a number of problems that arise in its interpretation and application. In the third volume, I shall carry over the results of the second to address in detail one question: the application of the concept of social justice to the distribution of income and wealth.

Appendix A: Braithwaite's Solution and Rationale

In Figure A.1, the four points T_{11}, T_{12}, etc., correspond to the four possible outcomes on any given evening.[1] Figure A.2 reproduces Figure 1.2 with the addition of this system of reference to the outcomes. The straight line between T_{21} and T_{12} is, obviously, the Pareto frontier. At T_{21}, Luke plays solo every evening, and at T_{12} Matthew plays solo every evening. As we move along the line from T_{21} toward T_{12}, Matthew plays solo on an increasing proportion of evenings or has an increasing chance (generated by some random process) of playing solo on a given evening. This Pareto frontier represents the outcomes of what Braithwaite calls coupled strategies in that the points on it can be reached only if Matthew and Luke coordinate their actions so that on an evening when one plays the other does not.[2]

What about the hatched area? Every point in this space represents one of the possible payoffs to the two men that they could arrive at by acting independently. What "acting independently" means here is the following. We suppose each man to pick some strategy for each evening. This may be a pure strategy: he may choose to play every evening, or he may choose never to play at all. Alternatively, it may be a mixed strategy, which means that he elects to play some of the time. Suppose Matthew's strategy is to play on one evening in four: then he creates some device that will give him a random one in four chance of playing on any given evening. The randomizing device that Braithwaite envisages is a pack of cards marked "play" and "not play."[3] To give himself a one in four chance of playing on any given evening Matthew will have one-quarter of the cards marked "play." The point of saying that the strategies are independent is that each man has to make an unconditional choice of strategy. Neither can say, for example: "My strategy is to play whenever the other does not, and not to play when the other does." And, of course, there is no room here for "coupled" strategies—that is to say, those that are coordinated by agreement between the parties.

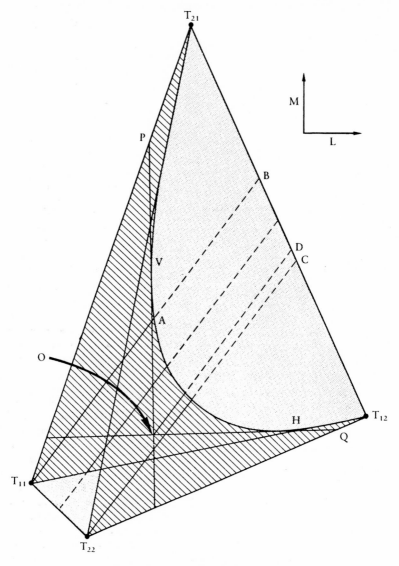

Figure A.1.   Braithwaite's Solution

Matthew

Play (1)   Not play (2)

	Play (1)	Not play (2)
Play (1)	1, 2 (T_{11})	7, 3 (T_{12})
Not play (2)	4, 10 (T_{21})	2, 1 (T_{22})

Luke

Figure A.2.   Payoff Matrix for Braithwaite's Problem,
with His Labeling of Solutions

The four corners of the hatched area are constituted by the payoffs arising from the conjunctions of pure strategies. All the rest of the space is arrived at by pitting one mixed strategy against one pure strategy or two mixed strategies against one another. The northeast frontier of the hatched area is a parabola—a fact which plays a role of some importance in the definition of Braithwaite's solution, as we shall see. The part of it between V and H forms a part of the Pareto frontier for outcomes arising from independently chosen strategies. (The complete Pareto frontier for such outcomes is PVHQ.)

Braithwaite's solution, like the Nash solution, has two stages, as was noted in the main text. In the first stage the baseline from which the move is to be made to the Pareto frontier has to be established. This is a pure struggle for relative advantage. "The outcome point resulting from each choosing his prudential strategy in the. . .competition [for relative advantage] is T_{11}, the base point farthest to the left; each of them will play his instrument every evening."[4]

The purely competitive first stage, with its struggle for relative advantage in the establishment of a baseline, is succeeded by a purely cooperative second stage, at which a move is made from the baseline to the Pareto frontier. Braithwaite's idea is this: if the two men could agree on a way of maintaining the relative advantages of the baseline position while moving up from it to the northeast, they would have nothing left to dispute about. For they would have a common interest in moving as far to the northeast as possible, until further movement was checked by their arriving at the Pareto frontier. Thus, once given a standard of equal gain over the baseline, the rest is a pure coordination game—a matter of both of them doing what is necessary to be on the unique point that maintains their relative positions at the baseline.

But how is such a standard to be found? Braithwaite somehow has to use the utilities to construct a criterion of equal relative advantage. And this he does. As I have mentioned, "the shape of the curved part of the boundary must be. . . a parabola," and this parabola is "uniquely determined by the four pure strategies available to the parties."[5] Braithwaite's next move, having pointed this out, is as follows:

The importance of the parabola arises from the fact that a definite direction is associated with it, namely, the direction of its axis; this direction, which is not an arbitrary one since it arises naturally out of the intrinsic logic of the situation, will give a method of comparing the preference scales of the two collaborators.[6]

We shall have to return later to Braithwaite's gnomic utterance about the "intrinsic logic of the situation" and puzzle over it. But let us for now follow Braithwaite's exposition.

Imagine a beam of lines ruled across the figure, all parallel to the axis of the parabola. [These are the lines from T_{11} to B, from T_{22} to C, and the others parallel to them.] Let us take the logic of the situation as determining that Luke's relative advantage over Matthew is constant along each line of the beam. The lines, that is, are contour lines of constant relative advantage: I will call them *isorrhopes*.[7]

If we are prepared to accept that "the logic of the situation" does generate the answer that the lines parallel to the axis of the parabola represent equal relative advantage, the rest is plain sailing. The result of the "competition" for "the most advantageous isorrhope" was the one that passes through T_{11}; "let us call it the *prudential isorrhope*."[8] Braithwaite continues:

It is unfortunate for both of them that the strategies which yield the prudential isorrhope also determine the outcome point as being the point which is both leftmost and lowest on this isorrhope, and so is least favourable to both. But if each of them will agree that the result of their isorrhopic competition has settled that, wherever the fair outcome point lies, it must lie on the prudential isorrhope, all that is left of the problem is that of collaborating to secure the best possible outcome point on this isorrhope. Since the isorrhope slopes upwards from left to right, this collaboration is wholly noncompetitive; both of them prefer a point as far up the isorrhope as possible, and the top end of the isorrhope where it runs into the upper right-hand frontier of the region of possible outcome points will be the point preferred. In our example this point (marked A on [Figure A.1]) lies on the parabola; to attain it each collaborator must choose the mixed strategy represented by the tangent to the parabola at this point. Luke's strategy will then be to play the piano on the average 23 evenings out of 68, Matthew's strategy will be to trumpet on the average 59 evenings out of 104; and if they consult me as to what strategies to adopt, I shall provisionally recommend these strategies to them jointly, delivering this lecture to them as my reason for this recommendation.[9]

This outcome is, however, only "provisionally recommended." It is the best that can be done in the way of moving up the "prudential isorrhope" from T_{11} subject to the proviso that the strategies are to be chosen independently. Note that it makes no difference to the independent status of the strategies that they are selected by agreement between the parties. The contrast is with coupled strategies, which make the decisions on particular evenings the subject of an agreement. By making use of coupled strategies, Matthew and Luke can continue to move up from point A to somewhere northeast of it on the straight line connecting T_{21} and T_{12}. This is the Pareto frontier, which represents all possible proportions of solo performance by the two men. (That point A is inefficient is brought out by observing, as Braithwaite does, that the results of the independent choices that define it will give Matthew and Luke either silence or cacophony almost half the time.)[10]

Suppose, then, that the rationality of moving first to point A and then beyond it to somewhere on $T_{21} T_{12}$ is accepted. Where should Matthew and Luke finish up? "My recommendation will be that [the chance mechanism that determines who plays solo on any given evening] should be adjusted so that the resulting outcome point on the boundary line $T_{21} T_{12}$ is the point (marked B [in Figure A.1]) where this line is cut by the upward continuation of the prudential isorrhope [from point A]."[11] This has the implication that "out of every 43 evenings over the long run, Luke will play the piano and Matthew refrain from trumpeting on 17 evenings, while Matthew will play the trumpet and Luke refrain from playing the piano on the remaining 26 evenings."[12] There is, incidentally, no particular reason for allocating playing time by using a chance mechanism on each evening. An obvious alternative would be to allocate the evenings so that Matthew gets exactly 26 out of every 43 evenings and Luke the remaining 17.

The argument for moving first to point A and only then onto point B adduces strategic considerations. Thus, Braithwaite says that "the merit in my eyes of the conjunction of strategies that I should provisionally recommend to them is that, since it is based upon the 'balance of power' between them, it requires the least degree of mutual confidence."[13] However, as he acknowledges, the two strategies are not in equilibrium. In fact, each man has an incentive to play more often than the outcome at A permits him to, so long as he can count on the other to stick to the strategy called for by the recommendation of point A. In fact, each man will do best to play on every evening provided the other plays no more than Braithwaite recommends. The potential gain for Matthew from departing from the "provisionally recommended" strategy is especially strong. By playing on every evening while Luke plays on about one evening in three, Matthew can increase his expected payoff from less than five units to more than seven units.

What, then, does Braithwaite count on to prevent either from reneging on this provisional agreement? Simply the implicit threat of retaliation: the fear on the part of each that, if he departs from the particular mixed strategy laid down in Braithwaite's recommendation and plays more often than it prescribes, the other will retaliate in kind and the situation will degenerate until they get back to cacophony every evening.

The obvious objection to this is that it does not distinguish A from a wide range of other points, all of which are superior to cacophony and attainable without coupled strategies. If we look at Figure A.1, we can see that these include the whole of the hatched area except for the corner of it south of T_{11}. (This corner contains outcomes that are worse for Matthew than cacophony.) The same rationale—that defection is prevented by the threat of retaliation—would seem, however, equally applicable to coupled strategies, in which case we should also include the area between the parabola and the line $T_{21} T_{12}$.

Braithwaite recognizes this. It is not enough, he says, simply to "ask them to consider whether it is really worth their while conducting a war whose result is to the disadvantage of both parties."[14] (In terms that I introduced in sections 23 and 37, the nonagreement point functions as more than a way of setting a threshold value that any agreement must surpass.) What he should be able to do, Braithwaite says, in order to demonstrate the uniquely stable properties of A, is to "point out to them that each has exactly the same advantage or disadvantage over the other [when they get back to the baseline of cacophony] as he had before agreement was broken, since T_{11} and the agreement point A lie on the same isorrhope." "Indeed," he adds parenthetically, "this was how the agreement point was fixed."[15] ("Isorrhope" is concocted from two Greek words meaning "equal advantage.")

The trouble with this, of course, is that it begs the question. For it assumes that the construction generating the isorrhopes does actually give us lines of equal relative advantage. If it does then Braithwaite has indeed produced a reason for our saying that the point A corresponds to the balance of bargaining power. Each man gains equally in moving from the noncooperative baseline to it, and so each would lose equally in moving back from it to the noncooperative baseline. But I do not see that Braithwaite has done anything to convince us that the isorrhopes do represent equal gain, in the relevant sense. To see what this sense is, let us think back for a moment to the Nash solution. There, we could see some real sense in which each party had an equal amount to lose from a collapse back to the nonagreement point. Harsanyi's approach brought this out clearly, as we may recall from section 2. But it seems to be pure fiat on Braithwaite's part to assert that all points on the line running parallel to the axis of the parabola represent equal relative advantage in the same strategically relevant sense. Airy talk of the "logic of the situation" does not help much.

A further difficulty Braithwaite gets himself into is one of consistency. He apparently does not believe that the rationale that he used to get from T_{11} to A will serve to get from A to B. Let me quote what he says on this score in full:

> I should not make this definitive recommendation to them until they had agreed upon the fairness and good sense of my provisional recommendation, when pairs of independent strategies were alone considered. This is because the Theory-of-Games argument for selecting the prudential isorrhope out of the beam of isorrhopes presupposes that the possible strategies of the two parties should be independent. When a coupled strategy is used the two parties are, from the standpoint of Theory of Games, conflated into one person, and the game ceases to be a two-person game. So the argument for the fairness and good sense of my definitive recommendation consists of three stages:
>
> (1) The von Neumann "solution" for the competition for relative advantage has an outcome represented by the prudential isorrhope;
>
> (2) The topmost point of this isorrhope is to be the outcome point when independent strategies are used;
>
> (3) The point where this isorrhope (continued upwards, if necessary, as in our example) cuts the upper right-hand boundary of the total strategic region is to be the outcome point when (as in our example) it is advantageous to both parties to use a coupled strategy.
>
> The argument for using the prudential isorrhope to determine the final outcome point is that this isorrhope yields what I believe both parties would agree to be an appropriate distribution of benefits in the region for which it is defined (the paired-strategies region where independent strategies are used), and there seems to me no good reason for departing from this principle of distribution when Luke and Matthew both increase their gains by agreeing together to use a coupled strategy.[16]

I do not understand the claim that agreement on coupled strategies takes us outside the sphere of the theory of games. Both points A and B require agreement (at least tacit agreement) to make them stick. As Braithwaite says of point A: "sufficient mutual confidence is required for Luke and Matthew to come to an agreement that they should each play their instruments in specified proportions, so that Luke can rely upon Matthew's not trumpeting more than 59/104ths of the time if Luke confines his playing to 23/68ths of the time, and vice versa."[17]

Both A and B, then, rest on an agreement: in that sense they both require trust. But B actually requires less trust than does A, because all the Pareto-optimal solutions to Braithwaite's problem (a set of which B is a member) have the characteristic that they are strong (i.e., Nash) equilibria. That is to say, if each man is sure that the other will not deviate from the agreement, he can deviate from it himself only by making himself worse off. Yet, as we saw, at point A each man gains by playing more than his allotted share if he can count on the other keeping to his.

As we have seen, Braithwaite wants to claim more for point A than that both men would lose by going back to cacophony from it. He wants to claim that what makes it stable is that both have an equally strong reason for preferring A to T_{11}. But then it is puzzling to me why Braithwaite should be reluctant to say that B has the same property. If there is a good argument for picking A as corresponding to the balance of bargaining power, why cannot exactly the same argument be deployed to assert that B similarly corresponds to the balance of bargaining power? It is, after all, a point further along the same isorrhope. The argument is simple. Either the isorrhopes genuinely represent lines of equal relative gain or they do not. If they do, then the case made by Braithwaite for the unique stability of A among points on the parabola ought to hold equally well to establish B as the uniquely stable point on the outer Pareto frontier. In both cases, it can be said that both men have the same incentive not to depart from it, namely, that both have the same relative amount to lose by a reversion to cacophony. Conversely, if that argument cannot be made for B then I do not see how it can be made for A either. Yet for some reason that I do not pretend to understand, Braithwaite argues that, while mutual prudence will underwrite the move from T_{11} to A, the continuation along the same isorrhope from A to B requires justification in terms of fairness.

Whatever his reasons for taking this line, Braithwaite's doubt about the possibility of a "balance of power" rationale for point B brings us to the second justification for his solution. According to this, the object is to get from the nonagreement point to the Pareto frontier in a fair way, and the criterion of fairness is equal utility gain. The problem then becomes how to determine equal utility gain when we do not have interpersonally comparable cardinal utilities. Somehow we must, if we are to get anywhere, find a way of bringing the utilities we are actually given into some alignment. What Braithwaite proposes is that we should look at the strategic situation created by the payoffs and see if anything suggests itself as a common measure. If we can find a plausible basis for equating the distance between some pair of Matthew's utilities with the distance between some pair of Luke's then we are in business: we can talk about equal utility gain because we have a basis for normalizing utilities.

Braithwaite moves to this line of analysis explicitly in the last third of his lecture. He imagines Luke saying that "he is not satisfied as to the fairness of this premiss, upon which my whole argument rests. Why should he be prepared to agree that motion of an outcome point up a line parallel to the axis should be supposed to benefit both him and Matthew equally?" He replies that "Luke is quite right in thinking that my choice of lines parallel to the parabola's axis as the isorrhopes is equivalent to an inter-personal comparison of utility scales."[18] But "since the relevant features in the situation are solely their two preference scales, clearly there is nothing that can be said about the advantage which one may have over the other by having a different preference scale that does not involve an inter-personal comparison, by one means or another, of the two preference scales."[19]

The main argument that Braithwaite makes for comparing the utilities in the way that he does involves a comparison between two alternative mixed strategies that could be the subject of independent choice. Luce and Raiffa, in a miracle of compression, describe Braithwaite's method of bringing the utilities into alignment as "a transformation in which the utility interval from a player's maximin strategy (based on his payoffs) to his minimax strategy (based on his opponent's payoffs), under the condition that his opponent uses his maximin strategy, is taken as the unit."[20]

The maximin strategy is one that guarantees the highest minimum payoff, whatever the other player does. For the utilities given us by Braithwaite this entails Matthew's playing one evening in every five and Luke's playing one evening in every four. It produces an average level of 2.8 utility units for Matthew and 3.25 utility units for Luke. This amount (the so-called security level) is not much, compared to what either could achieve by playing solo all the time; and it is less even than either could get by listening to the other play all the time. But it is more than either could count on from either of the pure strategies of playing all the time (in which case the worst outcome would be perpetual cacophony) or not playing any of the time (in which case the worst outcome would be perpetual silence).

Braithwaite confusingly calls both this maximin strategy and that of playing all the time so as to get an advantageous isorrhope the "prudential strategy," which is liable to cause misunderstanding. (This point is taken up in the text in section 7.) It should be clear that the motivations behind the two strategies are quite different. The maximin strategy pays no attention to what the other's payoff is. It is simply designed to get the guaranteed minimum payoff that one receives oneself as high as possible. In Figure A.1, "the vertical tangent of which OV is a part represents the von Neumann prudential strategy [i.e., the maximin strategy] for Luke; if Luke employs this strategy, the outcome point will lie on this tangent. . . . Similarly, the horizontal tangent of which OH is a part is the prudential strategy for Matthew."[21] What this means is that, when Luke plays his maximin strategy, the outcome will be somewhere on the line of which OV is a part. Where the outcome actually occurs depends on what Matthew does. But this will make no difference to Luke's utility, for he will always be the same distance to the right of the origin. (Recall that, in Figure A.1, Luke's utilities are measured along the horizontal axis.) Similarly, when Matthew plays his maximin strategy, Luke's actions determine where the outcome will lie on the horizontal line including OH. But the position will not affect the payoff that Matthew receives.

There is an important point here which is easily lost in Braithwaite's exposition. He says that the outcomes will lie on the tangents to the parabola including OV and OH. This is correct, but "including" should not be read loosely to mean "comprising." From the present point of view, V and H have absolutely no significance. They just happen to be points on the lines OP and OQ which contain the full range of outcomes that each can get from the other's maximin strategy. (The significance of this will become apparent at the end of this Appendix.) When both men play their maximin strategies, the outcome falls at the intersection of the two lines, marked 0 in Figure A.1. It will be seen that this is in fact the worst possible outcome for both men—the lowest utility on OP and OQ.

The minimax strategy is one that holds down the utility of the other to the lowest possible maximum, whatever he does. Matthew's minimax strategy is to play on five randomly chosen evenings in every eight. Matthew can thereby ensure that Luke will get an average of 3.25 units of utility whatever he does— so long as his choices on any given evening are not contingent in any way on Matthew's random decision to play or not play. And Luke can ensure, subject to the same condition, that Matthew gets an average of 2.8 units. He achieves this by playing an average of nine-tenths of the time. It will be noticed that the pair of payoffs that we get here are the same as the pair that we saw before. This implies that when Matthew plays his minimax strategy he holds Luke down to the utility that Luke gets from his maximin strategy, and vice versa.

In Figure A.1, the possible outcomes from Luke playing his minimax strategy (or "counter-prudential strategy," as Braithwaite calls it) are represented by the horizontal tangent OQ. This means that Luke can hold Matthew down to that level, whatever Matthew does. All that Matthew's choice of a strategy can do is to make Luke better or worse off by moving him along the line OQ. "Similarly, Matthew, by using his counter-prudential strategy represented by his taking the vertical tangent as strategy line, will ensure that Luke obtains no more and no less than what Luke himself would get by acting prudentially."[22] Once again, the result of both using their minimax strategies is 0, the point of intersection of the two tangents.

Now, the thing to observe is that the maximin strategies of the two players are not in equilibrium against one another. That is to say, if (for example) Matthew knew that Luke was going to use his maximin strategy, he could do better for himself by departing from his own. The maximin strategy, it should be recalled, is the most conservative possible: it is the one that does best out of all available strategies when the other does his worst. It can be improved on if the other does anything except his worst, and one player's maximin strategy is not the worst for the other.

It is this phenomenon that is exploited by Braithwaite to obtain the two utility levels that enter into his normalization procedure. The lower level in each man's utilities is to be given by point 0, which is each player's payoff when he uses his maximin strategy against the other's maximin strategy. The higher payoff is what each gets from playing his minimax strategy against the other's maximin strategy. As we have seen, if Matthew plays his own maximin strategy against Luke's maximin strategy, he gets an average of 2.8 units. But by moving to his minimax strategy and playing five-eighths of the time instead of one-fifth of the time he improves his payoff to 5.56 units. Similarly, if Matthew is playing his maximin strategy, Luke would do better to play nine evenings out of ten (his minimax strategy) for an average of 5.46 units than to play one evening in four (his maximin strategy) for an average of 3.25 units.

In Figure A.1, when Matthew switches from his maximin to his minimax strategy against Luke's maximin strategy he moves the outcome from O to V; and when Luke switches from his maximin to his minimax strategy against Matthew's maximin strategy he moves the outcome from O to H. "Thus each will gain by transferring from a prudential strategy to a counter-prudential strategy while the other keeps to a prudential strategy, and the lengths OV and OH represent the increments of M-utility or of L-utility which Matthew and Luke respectively will gain in this way."[23]

The two lines OV and OH become the basis for comparing Matthew's and Luke's utilities:

> The choice of the direction of the parabola's axis for the direction of the isorrhopic beam is thus equivalent to agreeing to compare Luke's and Matthew's utility scales by taking the increment in the former represented by the length of OH as being on a parity with the increment in the latter represented by the length of OV. To put the matter another way, it corresponds to taking the lengths of OH and OV as representing the natural units of the L-utility scale and of the M-utility scale respectively, these natural units being imposed by the logic of the collaboration situation, and of agreeing to equate these units for the purpose of determining the fairness of a recommendation. . . . To treat the L-utility natural unit as equivalent in fairness to the M-utility natural unit is to agree that, there being no other satisfactory criterion for interpersonal fairness, each collaborator should be regarded as benefiting equally by a change from a prudential to a counter-prudential when his colleague is holding to his prudential strategy.[24]

Braithwaite goes on to say that "this, in fact, was the first criterion for interpersonal fairness which I came upon when I started working on the subject."[25] Only the technical problem that there are not always a vertical and a horizontal tangent forced him, he says, to turn to the axis of the parabola as a basis for relating the utilities. "This restriction, however, would have to be considered as not affecting the fairness of treating the natural utility units as equivalent."[26]

But what is there that is interpersonally fair about treating the lengths of the lines OH and OV as representing equal amounts of interpersonally comparable utility? Why *should* we treat as equal the utility that the two men get by shifting from a maximin to a minimax strategy against the other's maximin strategy? Braithwaite doesn't tell us and I can see no possible answer. Perhaps he would fall back on saying that something beats nothing and this is at any rate something. But we do not have to adopt a criterion of equal utility gain in the first place. And even if we do, there is no shortage of alternatives, as section 5 indicated.

It will help to make clear how arbitrary Braithwaite's equation of OH and OV is to point out that the minimax strategy of one man has no special significance as a reply to the other's maximin strategy. We should observe that it is not the *best* strategy for each to use against the other's maximin strategy. With Luke playing the piano on one-quarter of the evenings so as to carry out his maximin strategy, Matthew does better the more often he plays. It follows trivially that he does better with his minimax strategy against Luke's maximin strategy than he would with his maximin strategy, simply because his minimax strategy has him playing more often than does his maximin strategy. He will go up from playing one-fifth of the time to playing five-eighths of the time. But he would do even better if he played even more often, and his best possible reply to Luke's maximin strategy is not to use a mixed strategy at all but simply to play on every evening. His average payoff would then move up from the 5.56 utility units yielded by his minimax strategy to 8.0 units. In Figure A.1, he moves from V to P. Similarly, against Matthew's maximin strategy of playing one-fifth of the time, Luke would do best to play all the time. This would give him an average of 5.8 utility units as against 5.46 units from his maximin strategy. (The gain for him is modest because his minimax strategy already has him playing nine-tenths of the time.) In Figure A.1 he moves from H to Q.

I thus conclude that neither of the lines of argument in favor of his solution that Braithwaite puts forward will hold water. Insofar as point B is recommended as a bargaining solution, it suffers from the lack of any real effort to show that moving up the isorrhopes preserves the balance of bargaining power at the nonagreement point. And insofar as it is recommended as fair, it suffers from the lack of any remotely plausible rationale for normalizing the utilities so that the distance from O to V and the distance from O to H should be equated.

Appendix B:
Splitting the Difference
as a Bargaining Solution

David Gauthier's argument for the superiority of splitting the difference over the Nash solution as a way of simulating rational bargaining is that the former "enables us to capture directly the relevant maximizing considerations."[1] His reason for making this claim for splitting the difference is that it gives a central role to what he calls the "ideal point," which is defined for each party as the maximum amount that it could possibly get compatibly with the other party's receiving its nonagreement payoff. Gauthier explains why "the introduction of the ideal point enables us to capture directly the relevant maximizing considerations" as follows: "Each individual bargainer seeks to do as well for himself or herself as possible; each therefore seeks his or her greatest utility given that a bargain is possible at all. And so each seeks the utility he or she would receive at the ideal point. In rejecting the relevance of the ideal point, [the Nash] solution excludes the individual maximizing concerns of the bargainers in favour of an ungrounded joint maximizing concern. [Splitting the difference] makes no such error."[2]

This attack on the Nash solution seems to me totally misguided. The Nash solution is to be conceived of as a bargaining solution: it starts from the assumption that the parties are trying to do as well for themselves as they can. (Harsanyi's account, which I followed in section 2, makes this clear.) Far from being "ungrounded," the Nash solution grows directly out of strategic considerations. It happens to call for maximizing the product of utilities, but this does not mean that the parties are to be thought of as aiming at any particular outcome. The Nash solution cannot be distinguished in this respect from splitting the difference.

Gauthier has a positive argument in favor of splitting the difference, which also appeals to the role that the ideal point plays in it. This runs as follows: "Each person wants as big a slice of the pie for himself as possible. [Splitting the

388

difference] divides the pie into slices, each of which represents the same proportion of its recipient's maximal share—the share one could get leaving others
with as much pie as in the absence of agreement. And no pie is left over—the
slices are as large as possible, given that each is to be the same proportion of its
recipient's maximum as every other slice."[3] However, it simply does not follow
from the assumption that the parties are individual maximizers that the bargaining solution should be responsive to what Gauthier calls their ideal points
in the manner dictated by the formula for splitting the difference.

Let us return for a moment to a case (discussed in section 5) where we have
two well-matched parties dividing a hundred dollars. Since the parties are well
matched we should expect that the money will be divided equally between
them. Now introduce the stipulation that one of the parties is restricted to a
maximum of ninety dollars. This means that his ideal point has been lowered.
But is an aspiration to get ninety dollars out of this game distinguishable in any
serious way from an aspiration to finish up with the whole hundred dollars to
oneself? Surely both are so unrealistic that it is absurd to allow the person with
the slightly more unrealistic aspirations to gain an advantage from that. The
independence of irrelevant alternatives does not have to rest its appeal on considerations of mathematical esthetics: it continues to be attractive as a demand
on outcomes simulating the results of bargaining by individually maximizing
agents.

The defenders of splitting the difference can respond to this along the following lines. If we look at actual cases of bargaining where the parties succeed in
reaching an agreement, we find that the process almost invariably takes the
form of offers and counteroffers converging toward a single agreed point. It
looks as if the positions taken by the parties determine the course, and ultimately the outcome, of the negotiations. Reaching a compromise between the oppos-
ing demands is thus intrinsic to bargaining, and this is captured, it may be
argued, by the notion of splitting the difference.

Now, it can be pointed out that Harsanyi's analysis of the rationale of the
Nash solution made use of the idea of offers and counteroffers converging on a
single point. But Gauthier is quite correct in saying that all of this is purely
heuristic. Since the party with the largest amount to lose (calculated in the
appropriate way) always makes the next concession, the parties will finish up at
the Nash point whatever the actual course of bargaining. The outcome is unaffected by the points at which the parties start or the way in which they move
subsequently, provided only that neither party makes a concession that leaves it
with less than the Nash solution offers it. Thus, for example, if one party's
opening offer corresponds exactly to the Nash solution, the theory tells us that
the other party should close with it immediately, since this is the best outcome it
can realistically hope to obtain. "The series of proposals and concessions seems
to model a process of bargaining, but, given that the proposals play no role in
determining the outcome, the concessions, from meaningless proposals, are
equally meaningless, and so the modeling is entirely spurious."[4]

Now in saying this Gauthier is, I believe, pushing at an open door. He is not
denying anything that Harsanyi, say, would wish to affirm. The Nash solution

produces a path-independent outcome, by which I mean that its location is not affected by the route by which it is arrived at.* I shall ask later if it is a fault in a bargaining theory that the solution is path-independent. Before doing that, however, I wish to observe that if it is a fault then it is one that splitting the difference also suffers from. For the solution of splitting the difference is path-independent in exactly the same way as the Nash solution is. If we accept splitting the difference as an accurate way of simulating the outcome then we are committing ourselves to the proposition that the outcome of bargaining can be predicted in advance of any process of bargaining from a bare knowledge of the utility functions of the parties. The actual course of bargaining plays no part in the theory. We can say of splitting the difference everything we could of the Nash solution. Thus, if one of the parties makes an initial offer that corresponds exactly to the solution of splitting the difference, the other party will have to move from whatever was its initial offer so as to close immediately with the offer of the first party.

When we consult a book such as Howard Raiffa's *The Art and Science of Negotiation*,[5] which is based on the analysis of anecdotes about actual (or in some cases fictitious) negotiations and the results of pencil-and-paper experiments with students, we do indeed find that there is a tendency for an agreed outcome to reflect the actual history of bids made on each side. Specifically, Raiffa claims that "once two offers are on the table . . . , the best prediction of the final contract is the midpoint [the initial offers on each side added together and the sum divided by two]—provided that the midpoint falls within the zone of agreement."[6] By "the zone of agreement" Raiffa means the same as I do when I speak of the feasible set of outcomes: the possible agreements that would be preferred by both parties to the nonagreement point.

If the midpoint lies outside this range, all bets are off, according to Raiffa. "It is not true that [the agreement point] will be near the reservation point that is

---

*Aficionados of social choice theory should understand that by "path independence" I mean to refer to just the feature that we can determine the equilibrium outcome once we know the feasible set and have the relevant utility information. A simple example of the violation of path-independence so defined is a case where there exist cyclical majority preferences over three outcomes (x is preferred by a majority to y, y to z, and z to x) and where the decision procedure is the common one of putting two of the alternatives against one another and then taking a vote between the winner of that and the remaining alternative. It is easy to see that under this arrangement the outcome depends on the order in which the alternatives are voted on, and in a quite systematic way: whichever alternative is left out of the first round must be the one chosen. (Thus, if x and y are paired against one another first, x wins and is then beaten by z; if y and z are paired, y wins and is beaten by x; and if x and z are paired, z wins and is then beaten by y.) This is a classic failure of path-independence, in that the outcome cannot be derived from knowledge of the feasible set and the preferences of the actors over it but is contingent on the moves actually made.

For a clear exposition, see Charles R. Plott, "Axiomatic Social Choice Theory," in Brian Barry and Russell Hardin, eds., *Rational Man and Irrational Society? An Introduction and Sourcebook* (Beverly Hills, Calif.: Sage, 1982), pp. 231–45. As Plott says of the phenomenon: "The outcome is y, x, or z, depending only upon . . . the agenda sequence. . . . This is true in theory and in fact [Plott here refers to an article summarizing experimental work by himself and a colleague]. Now, what kind of social philosophy would depend on that?" (ibid., p. 233).

closer to the midpoint. The reason is that [if the midpoint is outside the zone of agreement] the concessions will have to be lopsided, and it's hard to predict the consequences."[7] Thus, going back to our case of the house sale in the main text (section 5), let us say that the seller's reservation price (the price below which he would prefer to keep the house) is $140,000 and the buyer's reservation price (the price above which he would prefer to keep his money) is $160,000. The "zone of agreement" is thus the range from $140,000 to $160,000. Raiffa's empirical generalization about the relation of bids to outcomes has the implication that each should frame his opening bid at whatever level will get the midpoint as close as possible to the other's reservation price without going past it. But how to do that?

Most often neither party knows the other's reservation price in such a situation—indeed, commonly one has only a vague idea of one's own reservation price, let alone the other's. Waiving this difficulty, the problem remains that, with simultaneous opening bids, the right bid to make depends on what you expect the other party to bid. If you are the buyer and you expect the seller to ask $200,000, for example, you should offer just over $80,000 so as to get the midpoint between the two bids a little above his reservation price of $140,000. But how are you to form an expectation?

In practice, this problem of coordinating expectations is largely solved by the existence of cultural norms that establish the rough degree to which bids should be overpitched and underpitched. These will vary from place to place and may well in a given place be different for different kinds of objects. In Britain and the United States, sellers ask perhaps 10 percent more than they expect to get for houses—they do not, for example, ask twice as much as they expect to get in anticipation of being offered nothing and splitting the difference. In fact, overpricing in relation to the norm tends to put off potential purchasers and also to discourage real estate agents from putting effort into trying to make a sale. In these countries, shopkeepers are not generally amenable to bargaining about prices, but in other places it is customary in relation to some classes of merchandise (not everyday foodstuffs, for example) for a trader to start by asking for a multiple of the price he expects to get. Here the seller will, indeed, make most of the concessions but one has to assume that traders know their own business best and that in such a context that is the most advantageous way to proceed. It seems plausible that the best predictor of the price at which the sale is made will then be the midpoint of the "last offers" on each side rather than the midpoint of the opening bids. This illustrates the cultural relativity of Raiffa's generalization.

There are, I believe, three conclusions to be drawn here. In ascending order of importance they are as follows. First, the actual process of offers and counteroffers has nothing in common with Gauthier's formula for splitting the difference. To the extent that Raiffa is right about the way in which negotiations actually take place, there is indeed a phenomenon of splitting the difference. But the difference that is split is between bids, not between reservation prices as the splitting-the-difference formula would have it. In fact, it is implicit in what Raiffa says of the bargaining process that normally opening bids will lie outside the "zone of agreement." Someone who never asked for more than the maximum as defined by splitting the difference (i.e., the most favorable boundary of the "zone of agreement") would clearly do very badly in bargaining conducted according to the norms elicited by Raiffa.

The second point to be made in the light of Raiffa's analysis is that to explain the actual sequence of offers and counteroffers we need two things: some notion of the relevant cultural norm for exaggeration, and an idea of the amount the buyer and the seller think it reasonable to expect to settle for. It follows from this that there is no possibility of having a general theory of the bargaining process with predictive capacity.

The third and most significant point is that, given the use we want to make of a bargaining theory in this book (and it is the same as the use that Gauthier wants to make of one), we do not really want a theory of the bargaining process designed to explain how people get to initial bids and from there to agreements. We have no interest in the process by which the outcome is reached. What we want is in fact exactly what the Nash solution (and splitting the difference, too) delivers. That is to say, we want a predicted outcome of bargaining that reflects the bargaining power of the parties. To the extent that people can actually get more than the theory predicts by playing their cards skillfully, this is something that we (and Gauthier) deliberately wish to abstract from.

Appendix C:
Economic Motivation
in a Rawlsian Society

In *A Theory of Justice* Rawls himself introduces the topic of economic motivation by asking why the people who are in the original position should be prepared to consider a move from an equal distribution of income to an unequal one. The answer he offers is as follows:

> If there are inequalities in the basic structure that work to make everyone better off in comparison with the benchmark of initial equality, why not permit them?... If, for example, these inequalities set up various incentives which succeed in eliciting more productive efforts, a person in the original position may look upon them as necessary to cover the costs of training and to encourage effective performance.[1]

Rawls then goes on to address himself to the possible objection that material incentives should not be necessary in a society whose members are committed to justice.

> One might think that ideally individuals should want to serve one another. But since the parties are assumed not to take an interest in one another's interests, their acceptance of these inequalities is only the acceptance of the relations in which men stand in the circumstances of justice. They have no grounds for complaining of one another's motives. A person in the original position would, therefore, concede the justice of these inequalities.[2]

This reply begs the question it is supposed to answer. We want to know why it should not be regarded as a requirement of justice that people should work without reward for the common good, and Rawls simply asserts that in the original position it would be accepted that people should be motivated in economic affairs by self-interest. But why should that be accepted in the original position? The reference to the circumstances of justice does nothing to advance the case. Let us concede that actual societies are marked by "confin'd generosity." As Rawls puts it, we should "not presuppose...extensive ties of natural sentiment."[3] All that is ruled out by this is the possibility that principles of

393

justice would be otiose because people would be so attached to one another's interests spontaneously that conflicts of interest would never arise. We thus start from the presumption that conflicts of interest will occur, and that principles of justice will therefore be needed to adjudicate between conflicting demands. This still leaves open the nature of the principles of justice that are to settle such conflicts. Nothing Rawls has said has any implication that they cannot prescribe that everyone should work for the common good without being paid for it. We shall have to look further for the roots of Rawls's position on economic motivation.

It is instructive at this point to compare Rawls with Bentham. Bentham assumes a single kind of motivation: people pursue their self-interest in all spheres of life. It is then the task of institutions to ensure that as far as possible individual self-interest will be channeled into the furtherance of the general interest. Thus, for example, political institutions should be set up so as to steer the self-interest of all concerned—voters, candidates, bureaucrats, and so on—in the direction stipulated by the utilitarian principle. An appropriate constitutional code would function in the political realm analogously to a competitive market in the economic.

Although many American political theorists and political scientists have subscribed to this conception, it is not Rawls's. Rawls maintains, I believe quite correctly, that there is no constitutional machinery, however ingeniously designed, that can be expected to produce passably just outcomes unless the citizens want such outcomes and the politicians pursue them.[4] There is a "natural duty of justice...to support and to further the arrangements that satisfy [the two] principles [of justice]."[5] This entails not only that we should "support that party or favor that statute which best conforms to the two principles of justice" but also that we should accept a duty to obey just laws.[6] "Citizens generally are bound by the duty of justice."[7] Thus, a Rawlsian would not simply regard a law as a tariff setting out the penalty for certain conduct if he is caught and convicted; rather, he would be moved to compliance by the sense of justice.

The point that all this is intended to make is simply that Rawls does not posit a single kind of motivation in a just society. Most institutions require that people internalize norms of justice that require them sometimes to act in a way contrary to their interests. When it comes to economic institutions, however, we get a division of motivation. The institutions themselves (for example, the tax and transfer system) are to be created with the conscious objective of realizing the principles of justice. But the people who are to act within these institutions will, it is assumed, pursue self-interest.

Now, it may be said at once that Rawls is by no means peculiar in this regard. On the contrary, his outlook is quite characteristic of those who support a market system (whether capitalist or socialist or with some mix of public and private ownership) plus a system of taxes and benefits designed to provide a "safety net" or to increase equality as an end in itself. Thus, James Meade, who clearly functions as something of an economic guru for Rawls in A Theory of Justice, wrote the following two years later, in 1973: "In my view the ideal society would be one in which each citizen developed a real split personality, acting selfishly in the market place and altruistically at the ballot box. . . . [I]t is, for example, only by such 'altruistic' political action that there can be any alleviation of 'poverty' in a society in which the poor are in a minority."[8]

It was suggested by Thomas Grey in a percipient review of Rawls's book that the schizophrenia attributed to people in a Rawlsian society—making whatever amount of money they can get in the market and then voting for a government pledged to instantiate the difference principle—is reflected in the real world by the fact that "the concept of income redistribution as such has found no strong political favor in any country whose economy is based largely on a market system."[9] This is, I think, too sweeping a statement, given the degree of support for avowedly egalitarian ends found in market societies such as Norway and Sweden. But even there the strains are apparent and it does seem plausible to suggest that the rise of anti-tax movements in a number of countries in recent years may well have something to do with a conflict between the spirit of individual self-interest fostered by the market and the spirit of collective responsibility for the worst off that is required to maintain support for redistributive programs.

It is important here to distinguish between two claims. One is that there is as a matter of fact a psychological difficulty in switching from self-interested bargaining in the market to the pursuit of equality (or maximizing the minimum) in the voting booth. This seems undeniable. The stronger claim, which Grey also wants to make, is that there is also a moral inconsistency in that the principled rationale for the market determination of incomes is incompatible with the principled rationale for redistribution.

Grey's idea here is that there are two conflicting notions, one of which underwrites equality, the other an entitlement to whatever one makes on the market. On the socialist view, "bargaining for extra income on the basis of superior productive capacity" is "a species of extortion." "This approach implies a social duty to work, and to work to one's full capacity, without bargaining for extra income in exchange." The upshot would be "an equal division of the social product," which would be compatible with maximum production, "since everyone would work to the limit of his ability without regard to pay."[10] The second view is "the free market principle" that "the person of superior productive capacity is justified in extracting in return for his labors what the market will bear. Under proper market conditions his return will equal his marginal contribution to society."[11]

That these two views are inconsistent seems patent. But is it really true that they are the only ones in the field? Grey apparently thinks so, and hence regards Rawls's difference principle as an unconvincing attempt to mediate between them. "Rawls's attempt to describe the bare bones of an ideal market redistributist state based on moral principles may show the internal inconsistency of the ideal even more clearly than our own frustrating political experience."[12]

Fairly obviously, as a sheer matter of exegesis, one could scarcely attribute either of the alternative positions to Rawls, since he does not put forward the notion of a moral duty to work at maximum capacity without thought of reward and he does not accept any notion of an entitlement to one's market earnings. But what Grey apparently believes is that there is no way of backing differential earnings without the market principle and no way of backing redistribution without the socialist moral outlook.

"How can I justly bargain for more than an equal share by threatening to withhold my scarce talents? It must be because I have some special claim on these talents and their fruits. But if they are considered a social asset—as Rawls apparently regards them—I can have no such special claim. On the other hand, if my talents and the fruits of the use I choose to make of them belong to me, then there can be no justified coercion of me if I do not choose to share them with others."[13]

Let me put this in terms of the discussion of the difference principle in chapter 6. The claim of inconsistency can be expressed in the following way. On the one hand, when he is seeking to establish equality as the baseline from which departures have to be justified, Rawls relies on the premise that whatever makes people more or less capable of producing is morally arbitrary. On the other hand, in the course of making his move from equality to the difference principle he makes use of the premise that people in a just society will respond to material incentives. But the implication of any system of material incentives is that those who produce more will finish up with more. The charge is that, if it is accepted that productive advantages are unjust, there should be no need for material incentives. For the members of a just society should be motivated by thoughts of the injustice of inequality to work loyally in pursuit of the goal of maximum income equally distributed.

Reasoning along these lines, Jan Narveson has devoted a couple of articles to the proposition, outlined at the end of section 28, that Rawls faces a dilemma. If the first principle, which establishes the basic liberties, includes economic liberty in some full-bodied sense, then there is no room for the difference principle, for in that case people are entitled to what they make in the market. If, alternatively, there is to be a duty to work without reward in order to make the worst off as well off as possible, then again there is no room for the difference principle, for in that case there is no reason for admitting any departure from equal distribution.[14]

So far, Narveson's claim amounts to the same as Grey's: the only internally consistent theories of distribution are the free-market one of entitlement to what one makes and the socialist one of a duty to contribute to social wealth. Narveson goes on to say (surely undeniably) that Rawls plainly does not intend to attribute to everyone a right to the full value of his own product. If he is correct in asserting that there is no middle way between the horns of the dilemma that he seeks to foist on Rawls, Narveson can obviously conclude from this that (in spite of any appearances to the contrary) Rawls must adhere to the second position: that in a truly just society there would be no room for inequality. "The motives of justice would always direct one to sharing equally with one's fellows."[15] So saying that incentives will be needed to get people to produce the optimal amount is simply admitting that they will be actuated not by justice but by greed.[16]

This of course means sweeping away Rawls's stipulation that people are not to complain about one another's motives in the economic sphere. The question, Narveson says, is precisely whether or not self-interested motivation should be "'accepted' in the sense that it is allowed as a reason for justifying differentials

incentive ~ greed

th of dist
free-market; entitlement to what one makes
Socialist: duty to contribute to social wealth

in social reward."[17] It should not be so allowed on Rawls's premises, according to Narveson.

> If it is the case that socially distributable goods ought to be distributed equally unless an unequal distribution is required to improve the prospects of the worst off, and if we all have the option, if we so choose, of sharing equally with others, then does it not follow that if we don't take this option, we are being *unjust*? For in effect, my claim that I 'need' more as an 'incentive' is just a misleading way of saying that I *want* more and that I'm not willing to do as much if I don't get it.[18]

One possible answer that might be given (as Narveson admits) is that, ideally, a just distribution would be an equal one, but that unfortunately we cannot count on people to work at their best without material incentives. John Stuart Mill took this view in the *Principles of Political Economy*. Noting that attempts to realize socialism in France by associations of working men had begun with equal distribution and moved to payment by the piece, he observed that "the original principle appeals to a higher standard of justice, and is adapted to a much higher moral condition of human nature. The proportioning of remuneration to work done, is really just, only in so far as the more or less of the work is a matter of choice: when it depends on natural difference of strength or capacity, this principle of remuneration is in itself an injustice: it is giving to those who have; assigning most to those who are already most favoured by nature."[19] Mill defended it, however, as "a compromise with the selfish type of character formed by the present standard of morality, and fostered by the existing social institutions."[20] It is "highly expedient"—but the expedient is here to be contrasted with the ideally just.

Mill himself implied that if education were "entirely regenerated" the ideal would be attainable,[21] but this is not an essential feature of the view in question. The critical point is that, as Narveson puts it, inequalities might be *excused* by our saying that we cannot ask for too much from people, but they would not be *justified*.[22] In paying people to do things that they should, as a matter of justice, be willing to do without special reward, we would be in the position of citizens in a country where it is necessary to bribe officials to issue documents—licenses, passports, and so forth—which it is supposed to be their job to do anyway. One pays up, recognizing that it is better than the alternative, but one does not accept the justice of being faced with the choice.

Now, it would of course be quite in accord with this view of incentives as a necessary evil to reintroduce the difference principle as a principle of *relative* justice. We could say: once we abandon ideal justice, we still want to distinguish between more or less just departures from equality. The difference principle can then reasonably be interpreted as the least obnoxious concession to the necessity of incentives. For, although it licenses greed, it at least insists that greed should be harnessed to the improvement of the position of the worst off.

We must be clear that this is not the line Rawls takes. It is true, as I have already noted, that he considers an "ideal" possibility that people would not require incentives, but the state of affairs he has in mind there is one in which justice would not be necessary because people would work for the common good spontaneously.[23] He does not ever suggest that ideal *justice* would require people to work for the common good.

Again, it is true that Rawls makes use of the notion of the "strains of commitment" in *A Theory of Justice*.[24] This is the idea that people who are choosing principles of justice should check to see if some set of principles in other respects attractive is liable to issue in calls on people to make extraordinary sacrifices. Prudence should, Rawls argues, lead to the rejection of principles that may be too hard to live up to. The "strains of commitment" are deployed as an argument against the principle of maximizing aggregate utility. It is, Rawls says, asking too much of people to expect them to put up with hardship for themselves merely in order to confer somewhat greater benefits on people who are already very well off.

The only alternative to the utilitarian principle considered in this context is the two principles of justice. Rawls argues that these can be lived with by everyone because the worst-off position will be acceptable and "a fortiori everyone would find the other positions acceptable."[25] There is no suggestion here that what is required by strict justice has to be modified to take account of the problems posed by the strains of commitment. Rather, the difference principle, with its attendant inequalities, *is* the principle of ideal justice.

The argument for the difference principle as a second-best principle of justice could be fitted together with the derivation of the difference principle that I gave in chapter 6. It would then enable us to explain quite easily how we get from the premise that all inequalities based on differential productive ability are morally arbitrary to a conclusion in which there are inequalities corresponding to productive contributions. We would simply say that these inequalities are not ideally just, but that, once we concede the need for incentives, inequalities permitted by the difference principle are the only defensible ones. However, we must be clear that this argument is not Rawls's. Our question now must be whether Rawls can consistently defend the difference principle not as a second best but as what justice really demands.

I believe that he can. In order to develop my ideas on this score, I shall attend to another critic of Rawls, Alan Donagan. Donagan, like Narveson, claims that Rawls's theory entails a duty to work for the common benefit, not merely up to some limit defined by the requirement that all receive some minimum income (say, one sufficient to satisfy basic needs) but up to the point at which the worst off are as well off as they can possibly be made. Therefore "it . . . requires a social structure that takes away the option of idleness when one's own needs and the demands of beneficence have been met."[26]

Donagan's primary concern is that this moral duty might open the way to coercion. He argues that, although Rawls's own opinion is that the difference principle would not entail the direction of labor, there is nothing in the theory to rule it out.[27] Donagan notes that the basic liberties listed by Rawls as having priority (at any rate in an economically advanced society) are

> political liberty (the right to vote and to be eligible for public office) together with freedom of speech and assembly; liberty of conscience and freedom of thought; freedom of the person along with the right to hold (personal) property; and freedom from arbitrary arrest and seizure as defined by the concept of the rule of law.[28]

Donagan comments that "*these* basic liberties would not directly exclude the conscription of labour in time of peace."[29] This is obviously true.

It is less clear that Donagan is correct in dismissing the relevance of the second half of Rawls's second principle: that the operation of the difference principle is to be subject to the constraint that social and economic inequalities should be "attached to offices and positions open to all under conditions of fair equality of opportunity."[30] Donagan says simply that this would not exclude conscription of labor any more than anything on the list of basic liberties would do.[31] But it is hard to see how it could be consistent with the stipulation that places must be "open on a fair basis to all" for labor to be conscripted.[32] If someone is conscripted into a job, it is not open to competition by others, nor can that person compete for other jobs which he might prefer.

It must be emphasized that Rawls insists on the implementation of open access to positions even in cases where this is not required by the difference principle. It is not merely put forward as a means to the realization of the difference principle—if it were, one might indeed ask why it is worth stating separately. Rather, those excluded from competition "would be right in feeling unjustly treated . . . not only because they were excluded from certain external rewards of office such as wealth and privilege, but because they were debarred from experiencing the realization of self which comes from a skillful and devoted exercise of social duties. They would be deprived of one of the main forms of human good."[33] This looks like a pretty strong statement of the importance of occupational choice, and I think that, even if Rawls does not list it among the "basic liberties," the best interpretation of his theory is that he regards it as having priority over the difference principle.

It may be noted that "the liberties of equal citizenship" are said by Rawls to include, in addition to the list quoted above, "fair (as opposed to formal) equality of opportunity," and that this not only entails appropriate educational provision but "also enforces and underwrites equality of opportunity in economic activities and in the free choice of occupation."[34] We may also recall from section 38 that Rawls lists as one of the main virtues of the market as an economic mechanism its "protect[ing] the important liberty of free choice of occupation."[35]

That the difference principle is not one of maximizing the income of the worst off at all costs is made plain when Rawls sums up his discussion of it in the following terms: "Whether the principles of justice are satisfied, then, turns on whether the total income of the least advantaged (wages plus transfers) is such as to maximize their long-run expectations (consistent with the constraints of equal liberty and fair equality of opportunity)."[36] And if I am right, the free choice of occupation and the absence of coercion to work are covered by the words in parentheses.

The important question, however, is not so much whether or not Rawls does make the difference principle subject to free choice of occupation but whether or not he is entitled to do so, given his egalitarian premises. Conscription—directing people into certain jobs and, presumably, applying sanctions to make them work—is not the only point at issue here. Even if people were legally free to choose their occupations, it would make a big difference to the way in which that choice were exercised if it were widely accepted that one had a duty to work hard at the most socially valuable occupation one could successfully follow, even if it paid no more than any other (or than doing nothing at all, perhaps).

Now, I do not see that there is any way of showing that Rawls is being inconsistent in positing the priority of freedom of occupation. The priority of the first principle, equal liberty, over the second principle is built into the theory. And within the second principle, the clause stipulating that positions are to be open to all under conditions of "fair equality of opportunity" is stated by Rawls to have priority over the difference principle. I can therefore see no problem of internal coherence for Rawls's theory if we understand the application of the difference principle to be limited by the constraint of respecting freedom of occupational choice.

The interpretation offered by Narveson and Donagan, according to which the difference principle is read as a mandate to do whatever makes the lot of the worst off as eligible as it can possibly be made, is also undeniably consistent. It gives us a simple maximizing theory according to which justice requires doing whatever is necessary to maximize the income of those with least. And this, with some combination of coercion and moral suasion taking care of the incentive problem, may be expected to entail dividing the maximum total income equally among all the members of the society.

We should be clear, however, that in *A Theory of Justice* the difference principle has to fit round the constraints introduced by the first principle of justice and the half of the second principle that mandates equal opportunity. And this, I have argued, entails that the only thing which it is legitimate to do to further the difference principle is to set the tax and transfer system so as to produce the best results when the members of the society consult their own interests about their line and amount of work.

Notes

PREFACE

1. These were as follows: "Justice between Generations," in P. M. S. Hacker and J. Raz, eds., *Law, Morality and Society: Essays in Honour of H. L. A. Hart* (Oxford: Clarendon Press, 1977), pp. 268–84; "Circumstances of Justice and Future Generations," in Richard Sikora and B. M. Barry, eds., *Obligations to Future Generations* (Philadelphia: Temple University Press, 1978), pp. 204–48; "Do Countries Have Moral Obligations? The Case of World Poverty," in Sterling McMurrin, ed., *The Tanner Lectures on Human Values*, vol. 2 (Salt Lake City: University of Utah Press, 1981), pp. 2–44; "Humanity and Justice in Global Perspective," in Roland Pennock, ed., *NOMOS 24: Ethics, Economics and the Law* (New York: New York University Press, 1982), pp. 219–52; and "Intergenerational Justice in Energy Policy," in Douglas Maclean and Peter G. Brown, eds., *Energy and the Future* (Totowa, N.J.: Rowman and Littlefield, 1983), pp. 15–30.

2. Robert M. Pirsig, *Zen and the Art of Motorcycle Maintenance* (New York: Bantam, 1975), pp. 296–306.

CHAPTER 1

1. Thucydides, *The Peloponnesian War*, trans. Benjamin Jowett (New York: Bantam, 1960), bk. 5, p. 342.

2. Charles S. Beitz, *Political Theory and International Relations* (Princeton, N. J.: Princeton University Press, 1979).

3. Adam Smith, *The Theory of Moral Sentiments* (Indianapolis, Ind.: Liberty Classics, 1969), p. 238.

4. See David Gauthier, *Morals by Agreement* (Oxford: Clarendon Press, 1986) for a comprehensive statement of his position. Different aspects of

Gauthier's position are taken up in chapters 2, 3, 7, 8, and 9 and Appendix B. Two recent expositions of Hobbes which draw upon game-theoretical reasoning are Jean Hampton, *Hobbes and the Social Contract Tradition* (Cambridge: Cambridge University Press, 1986), and Gregory Kavka, *Hobbesian Moral and Political Theory* (Princeton: Princeton University Press, 1986).

5. Plato, *The Republic*, trans. and ed. Raymond Larson (Arlington Heights, Ill.: AHM, 1979), bk. 2, section 359 on p. 32.

6. John Rawls, *A Theory of Justice* (Cambridge, Mass.: Harvard University Press, 1971).

7. Gauthier, pp. 129–30.

8. J. F. Nash, "The Bargaining Problem," *Econometrica* 18 (1950): 155–62.

9. R. B. Braithwaite, *Theory of Games as a Tool for the Moral Philosopher* (Cambridge: Cambridge University Press, 1955).

10. John von Neumann and Oskar Morgenstern, *The Theory of Games and Economic Behavior* (Princeton, N. J.: Princeton University Press, 1944).

11. A discussion of Pareto's original treatment of the concepts and of developments may be found in Brian Barry and Russell Hardin, eds., *Rational Man and Irrational Society? An Introduction and Sourcebook* (Beverly Hills, Calif.: Sage, 1982), pp. 139–43.

12. See Russell Hardin, *Collective Action* (Baltimore: Johns Hopkins University Press, 1982), pp. 141–42, for a more extended argument on this head.

13. More precisely, Harsanyi picked up a theory of concessions in bargaining developed much earlier by Frederik Zeuthen (*Problems of Monopoly and Economic Warfare* [London: G. Routledge and Sons, 1930]) and pointed out its equivalence to the Nash solution. The most extensive statement and defense of this approach is to be found in chapter 8 of John C. Harsanyi, *Rational Behavior and Bargaining Equilibrium in Games and Social Situations* (Cambridge: Cambridge University Press, 1977). There is a brief account in section 6.7 (pp. 135–37) of R. Duncan Luce and Howard Raiffa, *Games and Decisions* (New York: Wiley, 1957). Sections 6.5 and 6.6 (pp. 124–34) contain an accessible discussion of Nash's axiomatic approach.

14. Hardin, pp. 141–42.

15. The most extensive presentation of this rationale is Harsanyi, pp. 153–59.

16. Ibid., p. 154 (italics in original).

17. Anatol Rapoport, *Fights, Games, and Debates* (Ann Arbor: University of Michigan Press, 1960), p. 194.

18. Thomas C. Schelling, *The Strategy of Conflict* (Cambridge, Mass.: Harvard University Press, 1960), p. 290.

19. See Appendix B of *The Strategy of Conflict*, "For the Abandonment of Symmetry in Game Theory," esp. pp. 288–90.

20. Oscar Wilde, *The Works of Oscar Wilde: Epigrams* (Boston: C. T. Brainard, 1909), vol. 11, pp. 251–65. The quotation is taken from pp. 258–59.

21. George F. Willison, *Here They Dug the Gold* (3rd ed. New York: Reynal & Hitchcock, 1946), p. 218.

22. Lewis Smith and Henry Justin Smith, *Oscar Wilde Discovers America*

(1882) (New York: Harcourt Brace, 1936), p. 317. Wilde's visit to Leadville is described on pp. 308–19.

23. Ibid., p. 314.

24. Phyllis Flanders Dorset, *The New Eldorado: The Story of Colorado's Gold and Silver Rushes* (New York: Macmillan, 1970), p. 263.

25. Willison, p. 220.

26. Ibid., pp. 220–21.

27. Braithwaite, p. 28.

28. For an analysis of the notion of optimal threats, see Harsanyi, pp. 169–79.

29. Luce and Raiffa, pp. 145–50.

30. Braithwaite, p. 57 n. 5.

31. Ibid., pp. 38–39.

32. Ibid., pp. 36–37.

33. Rawls, pp. 134–35 n. 10.

34. Braithwaite, p. 39.

35. Ibid., p. 41.

36. Nash, p. 158, quoted in Luce and Raiffa (with a number of small errors) on pp. 128–29 (italics in original).

37. Otomar J. Bartos, *Simple Models of Group Behavior* (New York: Columbia University Press, 1967), pp. 253–59.

CHAPTER 2

1. Thomas Hobbes, *Leviathan*, ed. with an introduction by C. B. Macpherson (Harmondsworth, England: Penguin, 1968), chap. 15, pp. 208, 212.

2. Indeed, the sixteenth Law of Nature is "that they that are at controversie, submit their Right to the judgment of an Arbitrator" (ibid., chap. 15, p. 213).

3. Ibid., chap. 15, pp. 212–13.

4. "Nature hath made men so equall, in the faculties of body, and mind; as that . . . the difference between man, and man, is not so considerable, as that one man can thereupon claim to himselfe any benefit, to which another may not pretend, as well as he" (ibid., chap. 13, p. 183).

5. David Gauthier, "Justice and Natural Endowment: Toward a Critique of Rawls' Ideological Framework," *Social Theory and Practice* 3 (1974): 3–26. The quotation is from p. 23.

6. J. R. Lucas, "Moralists and Gamesmen," *Philosophy* 34 (1959): 1–11. The quotation is from p. 9.

7. David Gauthier, *Morals by Agreement* (Oxford: Clarendon Press, 1986), p. 200.

8. Ibid.

9. Ibid.

10. Ibid.

11. This can be inferred from Lucas's characterization of the point on p. 9 of "Moralists and Gamesmen." In Figure A.1 in Appendix A, we are to take the point 0 as the nonagreement point and then follow the "prudential isorrhope"

that runs through it up to the Pareto frontier at point D. For David Gauthier, see "Reason and Maximization," *Canadian Journal of Philosophy* 4 (1975): 411–33, esp. p. 428. This article is excerpted and discussed in Brian Barry and Russell Hardin, eds., *Rational Man and Irrational Society? An Introduction and Sourcebook* (Beverly Hills, Calif.: Sage, 1982), pp. 90–106.

12. David Gauthier, "Rational Cooperation," *Nous* 8 (1974): 53–65. The quotation is from p. 57.

13. Lucas, p. 10.

14. Ibid.

15. R. Duncan Luce and Howard Raiffa, *Games and Decisions* (New York: Wiley, 1957), p. 149. The quotation is from R. B. Braithwaite, *Theory of Games as a Tool for the Moral Philosopher* (Cambridge: Cambridge University Press, 1955), p. 37.

16. Braithwaite, p. 37. As Braithwaite explains, "the outcome point where this [new] prudential isorrhope intersects the upper right-hand boundary $T_{21} T_{22}$ will be as far below the midpoint of this line as the outcome point of the original situation was above the midpoint" (ibid.). (See Appendix A.)

17. Gauthier notes this feature as the relevant one, saying that in his solution (splitting the difference from a joint maximin baseline) "Matthew's advantage arises because he makes a greater concession in listening to Luke play than Luke makes in listening to him play" ("Rational Cooperation," p. 64).

18. John Rawls, "Justice as Fairness," *Philosophical Review* 67 (1958): 164–94. The quotation is from p. 175 n. 10.

19. John Rawls, *A Theory of Justice* (Cambridge, Mass.: Harvard University Press, 1971), pp. 134–35 n. 10.

20. Ibid., p. 134.

21. Ibid.

22. Ibid., pp. 134–35.

23. Ibid., p. 134.

24. Amartya K. Sen, *Collective Choice and Social Welfare* (San Francisco: Holden-Day, 1970), p. 122.

25. Ibid., pp. 120–21.

26. Ibid., p. 121. There is a more extended discussion of Harsanyi on pp. 141–46.

27. See John C. Harsanyi, "Cardinal Welfare, Individualistic Ethics, and Interpersonal Comparisons of Utility," *Journal of Political Economy* 63 (1955): 309–21; "Can the Maximin Principle Serve as a Basis for Morality? A Critique of John Rawls's Theory," *American Political Science Review* 69 (1975): 594–606; and *Rational Behavior and Bargaining Equilibrium in Games and Social Situations* (Cambridge: Cambridge University Press, 1977), discussed in chapter 1.

28. Sen, p. 122.

29. See, for example, Rawls, *A Theory of Justice*, pp. 180–81.

30. Holly Smith Goldman, "Rawls and Utilitarianism," in H. Gene Blocker and Elizabeth H. Smith, eds., *John Rawls' Theory of Social Justice: An Introduction* (Athens, Ohio: Ohio University Press, 1980), pp. 346–94.

31. Lucas, p. 10.

32. Gauthier, "Rational Cooperation," pp. 62–63.

33. Gauthier, "Justice and Natural Endowment," p. 23.

34. Gauthier, *Morals by Agreement*, p. 341.

CHAPTER 3

1. Arthur L. Caplan, "Can Applied Ethics Be Effective in Health Care and Should It Strive to Be?" *Ethics* 93 (1983): 311–19. The quotation is from p. 312.

2. Ibid.

3. R. B. Braithwaite, *Theory of Games as a Tool for the Moral Philosopher* (Cambridge: Cambridge University Press, 1955), p. 8.

4. Ibid., pp. 8–9.

5. Ibid., p. 9.

6. Ibid., pp. 22–23.

7. Ibid., p. 9.

8. Ibid., p. 14.

9. R. Duncan Luce and Howard Raiffa, *Games and Decisions* (New York: Wiley, 1957), p. 134.

10. Paul Slovik, Baruch Fischhoff, and Sarah Lichtenstein, "Regulation of Risk: A Psychological Perspective," in Roger G. Noll, ed., *Regulatory Policy and the Social Sciences* (Berkeley and Los Angeles: University of California Press, 1985), pp. 241–78. The quotation is from p. 249.

11. Ibid., pp. 250–52. The work referred to is A. Tversky and D. Kahneman, "The Framing of Decisions and the Psychology of Choice," *Science* 211 (1973): 1453–58.

12. Slovik et al., pp. 248–56, provides a compact survey. See also D. Kahneman, P. Slovik, and A. Tversky, *Judgment under Uncertainty: Heuristics and Biases* (New York: Cambridge University Press, 1982).

13. See, for a protest by a behaviorist against drawing too sweeping conclusions from Tversky-style experiments, Richard A. Winett, "Comment," in Noll, ed., pp. 278–83.

14. See David M. Grether, "Financial Incentive Effects and Individual Decision Making," Social Science Working Paper 40, California Institute of Technology, September 1981.

15. Braithwaite, p. 14.

16. A. C. Pigou, *The Economics of Welfare* (4th ed. London: Macmillan, 1932).

17. Braithwaite, p. 5.

18. Lionel Robbins, *An Essay on the Nature and Significance of Economic Science* (London: Macmillan, 1932; 2d ed., 1935).

19. The *locus classicus* is A. J. Ayer, *Language, Truth and Logic* (2d ed. Harmondsworth, England: Penguin, 1946).

20. Luce and Raiffa, p. 146.

21. Anatol Rapoport, *Fights, Games, and Debates* (Ann Arbor: University of Michigan Press, 1960), pp. 186–90.

22. Ibid., p. 190.

23. Ibid., p. 192.

24. Ibid., pp. 192–94.

25. Braithwaite, pp. 39–40.

26. Ibid., p. 21.

27. Ibid., pp. 46–47.

28. Philip Pettit, *Judging Justice: An Introduction to Contemporary Political Philosophy* (London: Routledge & Kegan Paul, 1980), p. 126.

29. Montaigne, "Of Friendship," *Essays*, trans. Donald M. Frame (Stanford, Calif.: Stanford University Press, 1965), p. 141.

30. Richard Flathman, *The Practice of Rights* (Cambridge: Cambridge University Press, 1976), pp. 189–90.

31. Richard A. Posner, *Economic Analysis of Law* (Boston: Little, Brown, 1972).

32. *Smoking and Health—A Report of the Surgeon General* (Washington, D.C.: U.S. Department of Health, Education, and Welfare, 1979). Quotation from James L. Repace, "Risks of Passive Smoking," in Mary Gibson, ed., *To Breathe Freely: Risk, Consent, and Air* (Totowa, N.J.: Rowman & Allanheld, 1985), p. 6.

33. Ibid., pp. 5–6.

34. The story is told in *The Mill News Letter* 10, no. 2 (Summer 1975): 16–18.

35. Repace, p. 3.

36. Ibid., p. 6.

37. Michael Walzer, *Spheres of Justice: A Defense of Pluralism and Equality* (New York: Basic Books, 1983), p. 87.

38. Repace, p. 7.

39. See ibid., pp. 7–9, for a review of the evidence.

40. Thomas Scanlon, "Preference and Urgency," *Journal of Philosophy* 72 (1975): 665–69.

41. J. R. Lucas, "Justice," *Philosophy* 47 (1972): 229–48. The quotation is from p. 243. See also Lucas's *On Justice* (Oxford: Clarendon Press, 1980).

42. Lucas, "Justice," p. 243.

CHAPTER 4

1. David Hume, *A Treatise of Human Nature*, ed. L. A. Selby-Bigge, 2d ed., ed. P. H. Nidditch (Oxford: Clarendon Press, 1978); John Rawls, *A Theory of Justice* (Cambridge, Mass.: Harvard University Press, 1971).

2. Jonathan Harrison, *Hume's Theory of Justice* (Oxford: Clarendon Press, 1981), p. ix.

3. Hume, p. 579.

4. David Hume, *Enquiries Concerning Human Understanding and Concerning the Principles of Morals*, ed. L. A. Selby-Bigge, 3d ed., ed. P. H. Nidditch (Oxford: Clarendon Press, 1975), p. 305.

5. Ibid., pp. 305–6.

6. Harrison, p. 61.

7. Ibid., p. 66.

8. Hume, *Treatise*, p. 526.

9. John Rawls, "Kantian Constructivism in Moral Theory: The Dewey Lectures," *Journal of Philosophy* 77 (1980): 515–72. The quotation is from p. 564.

10. Hume, *Enquiries*, p. 188.

11. Hume, *Treatise*, p. 495 (italics suppressed).

12. Hume, *Enquiries*, p. 188.

13. Ibid., p. 184.

14. For a strong statement of the point that a society can be "affluent," in the sense that its members' wants are well satisfied at a low material level, see Marshall Sahlins, *Stone Age Economics* (New York: Aldine, 1972). Chapter 1 is entitled "The Original Affluent Society." The gist is contained in the following statement: "The hunter, one is tempted to say, is 'uneconomic man.' At least as concerns nonsubsistence goods, he is the reverse of that standard caricature immortalized in any *General Principles of Economics*, page one. His wants are scare and his means (in relation) plentiful" (p. 13). See also Norman Lewis's account of the indigenous inhabitants of Liberia in *A View of the World* (London: Eland, 1986), p. 95: "The Liberian tribesman has always been accustomed to gain the mere necessities of life with a minimum of effort. . . . It is natural enough that such a villager is extremely reluctant to exchange this lotus-eating existence for that of a plantation labourer working up to twelve hours a day for a wage of 30 cents, and what are called 'fringe benefits,' i.e., free housing, medical supervision, and so on."

15. Hume, *Enquiries*, pp. 186–87.

16. Ibid., p. 187 (my italics).

17. See Jay Katz and Alexander Morgan Capron, *Catastrophic Disease: Who Decides What? A Psychosocial and Legal Analysis of the Problems Posed by Hemodialysis and Organ Transplantation* (New York: Russell Sage Foundation, 1975), for a discussion of this issue. More generally, see Guido Calabresi and Philip Bobbitt, *Tragic Choices* (New York: Norton, 1978), and Steven E. Rhoads, ed., *Valuing Life: Public Policy Dilemmas* (Boulder, Colo.: Westview Press, 1980).

18. Hume, *Enquiries*, p. 186.

19. Interview with Belding Scribner, in Renée C. Fox and Judith P. Swazey, *The Courage to Fail: A Social View of Organ Transplants and Dialysis* (Chicago: University of Chicago Press, 1974), p. 328.

20. Hume, *Treatise*, pp. 496–97.

21. Ibid., p. 487.

22. Ibid., p. 488.

23. Ibid., p. 492.

24. Ibid.

25. H. L. A. Hart, *The Concept of Law* (Oxford: Clarendon Press, 1961), p. 192.

26. Hume, *Enquiries*, p. 185.

27. Philip Mercer, *Sympathy and Ethics: A Study of the Relationship between Sympathy and Morality with Special Reference to Hume's Treatise* (Oxford: Clarendon Press, 1972).

28. Hume, *Enquiries*, p. 219 n. 1.

29. Ibid., pp. 301–2.

30. Ibid., pp. 190–91.

31. Ibid., p. 191.

32. See Dee Brown, *Bury My Heart at Wounded Knee: An Indian History of the American West* (London: Barrie & Jenkins, 1971).

33. Ibid., p. 187.

34. See, for example, David Gauthier, "The Unity of Reason: A Subversive Reinterpretation of Kant," *Ethics* 96 (1985): 74–88.

35. Hume, *Treatise*, pp. 533–34 (italics in original).

36. Ibid., pp. 522–23.

37. Hume, *Enquiries*, p. 228.

38. Hume, *Treatise*, pp. 583–84.

39. Ibid., p. 472.

40. Mercer, p. 53.

41. Hume, *Treatise*, p. 499 (italics in original).

42. Alternative (manuscript) reading of pp. 499–500; in Nidditch ed. of the *Treatise*, p. 670 (italics in original).

43. Hume, *Enquiries*, p. 282.

44. Ibid., p. 284.

45. Ibid., p. 283.

46. Ibid.

47. Ibid., pp. 293–94.

48. The discussion of public enterprises occurs in Hume's discussion of the functions of government (*Treatise*, pp. 538–39).

49. See Brian Barry, *Political Argument* (London: Routledge & Kegan Paul, 1965), pp. 190–206.

50. Hume, *Treatise*, p. 529.

51. Ibid., p. 496; cf. p. 529.

52. J. L. Mackie, *Hume's Moral Theory* (London: Routledge & Kegan Paul, 1980), pp. 153–54.

53. Hume, *Treatise*, p. 503.

54. Ibid., p. 502.

55. Ibid.

56. Ibid., p. 579.

57. Ibid., p. 502. Cf. Mackie, p. 91: "Hume . . . may have meant that the particular acts in question actually *are* beneficial, given the existence of the system and their tendency to support it, though they *are not* beneficial *apart from* their long-range tendency and *would not be* so if the system were not working" (italics in original).

58. Hume, *Treatise*, p. 497.

59. Ibid., p. 503.

60. Harrison, p. 92.

61. Ibid., p. 93.

62. Hume, *Enquiries*, pp. 195–96.

63. Ibid., pp. 194–95. Harrison, indeed, says of the *Treatise* that "Hume himself implicitly allows that there are some criteria by which what he calls rules of justice may be assessed, for he claims that they are useful, and the habit

of observing them is a virtue because it is a useful habit" (pp. 30–31). But this is still consistent with the utility lying in *there being* rules rather than in their specific content.

64. Hume, *Enquiries*, p. 193.

65. Ibid., p. 194.

66. Ibid.

67. Ibid.

68. James Boswell, *The Life of Samuel Johnson*, ed. R. W. Chapman, rev. J. D. Fleeman (London: Oxford University Press, 1970), p. 1215.

69. David Gauthier, "David Hume, Contractarian," *Philosophical Review* 88 (1979): 3–38. "In 'David Hume: Contractarian,' he sought to win over utilitarian opponents of contractianism by showing that Hume, often regarded as a proto-utilitarian, actually held a contractarian theory of justice. After all, they might think, if David Hume is a contractarian, then why shouldn't I be one also?" (Stephen Darwall, "Kantian Practical Reason Defended," *Ethics* 96 [1985]: 89.)

70. The parallelism has been well worked out by Michael Taylor in chap. 6 of *The Possibility of Cooperation* (Cambridge: Cambridge University Press, 1987).

71. See especially on the origions of property Winston Bush, "Individual Welfare in Anarchy," in Gordon Tullock, ed., *Explorations in the Theory of Anarchy* (Blacksburg, Va.: Center for the Study of Public Choice, 1972), pp. 5–18; Winston Bush and L. S. Mayer, "Some Implications of Anarchy for the Distribution of Property," *Journal of Economic Theory* 8 (1974): 401–12.

72. J. M. Buchanan, *Freedom in Constitutional Contract* (College Station, Texas: Texas A & M Press, 1977), pp. 82–83.

73. John Stuart Mill, *Principles of Political Economy*, vols. 2 and 3 in J. M. Robson, ed., *Collected Works of John Stuart Mill* (Toronto: University of Toronto Press, 1965).

74. John Stuart Mill, *Autobiography and Literary Essays*, vol. 1 in the *Collected Works*, ed. John M. Robson and Jack Stillinger (Toronto: University of Toronto Press, 1981), p. 239: "Education, habit, and the cultivation of the sentiments will make a common man dig or weave for his country, as readily as fight for his country."

75. A. C. Pigou, *The Economics of Welfare* (4th ed. London: Macmillan, 1932; 1st ed. 1920). Quotations will be drawn from the 1932 edition.

76. This line of argument was first set out formally by the economist Abba Lerner in *The Economics of Control* (London: Macmillan, 1944), though it is foreshadowed in Pigou's *The Economics of Welfare*. It has recently been revived by the utilitarian philosopher Richard Brandt in his *A Theory of the Good and the Right* (Oxford: Clarendon Press, 1979).

77. Lerner, p. 32 (italics suppressed).

CHAPTER 5

1. John Rawls, *A Theory of Justice* (Cambridge, Mass.: Harvard University Press, 1971), p. 127. Cf. n. 3 on p. 126: "My account largely follows that of Hume."

2. Ibid., pp. 126–27.

3. All expressions are quoted from ibid., p. 127.

4. Ibid., p. 128.

5. See especially Michael Sandel, *Liberalism and the Limits of Justice* (Cambridge: Cambridge University Press, 1982).

6. Rawls, p. 126.

7. Ibid., p. 129.

8. Ibid., p. 134.

9. Ibid., p. 134–35.

10. Ibid., p. 378.

11. Ibid.

12. Ibid., p. 379.

13. Ibid., p. 128.

14. Ibid.

15. Ibid., p. 121.

16. Ibid., p. 128.

17. Ibid., p. 292.

18. Ibid., p. 128.

19. See ibid., pp. 284–93, section 44 on "The Problem of Justice between Generations."

20. Ibid., p. 288.

21. Ibid., pp. 291–92.

22. Ibid., pp. 139.

23. Ibid.

24. Gregory S. Kavka, "Rawls on Average and Total Utility," *Philosophical Studies* 27 (1975): 237–53.

25. David J. Richard, *A Theory of Reasons for Action* (Oxford: Clarendon Press, 1971), p. 81 (italics in original).

26. G. R. Grice, *The Grounds of Moral Judgment* (Cambridge: Cambridge University Press, 1967).

27. Richards, p. 81, quoting Grice, p. 150.

28. Richards, p. 307 n. 13, quoting Grice, p. 95.

29. Richards, p. 110.

30. Rawls has denied this explicitly. But his denial seems to me simply a flailing of the air. See "Reply to Alexander and Musgrave," *Quarterly Journal of Economics* 88 (1974): 633–55; quotation from p. 651.

31. Rawls, *A Theory of Justice*, p. 287.

32. See, for example, R. M. Hare, *The Language of Morals* (Oxford: Clarendon Press, 1952); *Freedom and Reason* (Oxford: Clarendon Press, 1963); and *Moral Thinking: Its Levels, Method and Point* (Oxford: Clarendon Press, 1981).

33. Hare, *Freedom and Reason*, pp. 217–24.

34. Rawls, *A Theory of Justice*, p. 287.

35. Ibid., p. 292.

36. Ibid., p. 289.

37. Ibid., pp. 289–90.

38. Ibid., p. 289.

39. Ibid.

40. Peter Singer, *Animal Liberation: Towards an End to Man's Inhumanity to Animals* (London: Granada Books, 1977), p. 230.

41. See ibid., p. 35, and also Peter Singer, *Practical Ethics* (Cambridge: Cambridge University Press, 1979), p. 53.

42. Hare, *Freedom and Reason*, p. 223.

43. Singer, *Practical Ethics*, p. 89.

44. Singer, *Animal Liberation*, p. 35.

45. Richards, p. 182.

46. Ibid.

47. Ibid.

48. Ibid.

49. Ibid.

50. Ibid.

51. Ibid., p. 82.

52. Ibid., p. 83 (italics in original).

53. Ibid.

54. Ibid., p. 88.

55. Rawls, *A Theory of Justice*, section 77, pp. 504–12

56. Ibid., p. 510.

57. Ibid., p. 505.

58. Ibid., p. 512.

59. Ibid.

60. Ibid., p. 509–10.

61. Ibid., p. 509.

62. Ibid., p. 512.

CHAPTER 6

1. The standard bibliography, which runs up to 1981, lists over three hundred items in its index under the heading "Difference principle" and I have sampled enough to be sure that almost all of them are critical of it. See J. H. Wellbank, Denis Snook, and David T. Mason, *John Rawls and His Critics: An Annotated Bibliography* (London: Garland, 1982), pp. 663–64, s.v. "Difference principle." A large amount of criticism—probably the largest body of work on any one aspect of *A Theory of Justice*—has been directed against Rawls's attempt to derive the difference principle as a rational self-interested choice in an original position characterized by an appropriate veil of ignorance. The popularity of this line of criticism is evidenced by the two hundred or so entries under "Maximin" in the same bibliography (ibid., pp. 671–72, s.v. "Maximin"; the numbers of entries cannot simply be added, due to overlap).

2. John Rawls, *A Theory of Justice* (Cambridge, Mass.: Harvard University Press, 1971), p. 302.

3. Ibid., p. 60.

4. Ibid., p. 72.

5. Ibid.

6. Ibid.

7. Ibid. Rawls also calls it "the liberal interpretation of the two principles [of justice]" (p. 73), which I find less perspicuous.

8. Ibid., p. 73.

9. Ibid.

10. See, for example, A. H. Halsey, A. F. Heath, and J. M. Ridge, *Origins and Destinations: Family, Class, and Education in Modern Britain* (Oxford: Clarendon Press, 1980), pp. 201–5.

11. Rawls, p. 66.

12. Ibid., p. 73.

13. Ibid., p. 74.

14. Ibid., pp. 73–74.

15. Christopher Jencks et al., *Inequality: A Reassessment of the Effect of Family and Schooling in America* (London: Allen Lane, 1973), p. 73. (First published in the United States in 1972.)

16. Rawls, p. 75.

17. Ibid., p. 60.

18. Ibid., p. 75.

19. This is true, for example, of James S. Fishkin, *Justice, Equal Opportunity, and the Family* (New Haven, Conn.: Yale University Press, 1983).

20. "*Naturall Power*, is the eminence of the Faculties of Body, or Mind: as extraordinary Strength, Forme, Prudence, Arts, Eloquence, Liberality, Nobility. *Instrumentall* are those powers, which acquired by these, or by fortune, are means and Instruments to acquire more: as Riches, Reputation, Friends, and the secret working of God, which men call good Luck." (Thomas Hobbes, *Leviathan*, ed. C. B. Macpherson [Harmondsworth, England: Penguin, 1968], chap. 10, p. 150.)

21. I include in this chapters 9 to 11 of my own critique of Rawls, *The Liberal Theory of Justice* (London: Oxford University Press, 1973), but it is just one of many.

22. Rawls, p. 155.

23. Ibid., p. 60.

24. Ibid., p. 62.

25. Ibid.

26. Ibid.

27. Ibid., p. 80.

28. Ibid., section 17, "The Tendency to Equality," pp. 100–108.

29. Ibid., pp. 105–6.

30. Ibid., p. 4.

31. John Rawls, "Kantian Constructivism in Moral Theory: The Dewey Lectures," *Journal of Philosophy* 77 (1980): 515–72. The quotation is from p. 526.

32. John Rawls, "The Basic Structure as Subject," in Alvin I. Goldman and Jaegwon Kim, eds., *Values and Morals: Essays in Honor of William Frankena, Charles Stevenson and Richard B. Brandt* (Dordrecht: Reidel, 1978), p. 60.

33. Ibid., p. 56.

34. Rawls, *A Theory of Justice*, p. 96.

35. Rawls, "The Basic Structure as Subject," p. 61.

36. Rawls, "Kantian Constructivism," p. 536.

37. Rawls, *A Theory of Justice*, p. 539.

38. Rawls, "The Basic Structure as Subject," p. 65.

39. Rawls, *A Theory of Justice*, p. 102.

40. Ibid., p. 88.

41. Ibid.

42. Ibid.

43. Ibid., p. 84.

44. Ibid., p. 4.

45. Ibid., p. 103.

46. Ibid.

47. Rawls, "Kantian Constructivism," p. 546.

48. Ibid.

49. Ibid.

50. Rawls, *A Theory of Justice*, p. 512.

51. Rawls, "The Basic Structure as Subject," p. 62.

52. Rawls, *A Theory of Justice*, pp. 496–97.

53. David Gauthier, *Morals by Agreement* (Oxford: Clarendon Press, 1986), p. 268.

54. Ibid., p. 218.

55. David Gauthier, "Justice and Natural Endowment: Toward a Critique of Rawls' Ideological Framework," *Social Theory and Practice* 3 (1974): 3–26. Some of the same points are made in Gauthier, *Morals by Agreement*, pp. 245–57.

56. Gauthier, "Justice and Natural Endowment," p. 14.

57. Ibid.

58. Ibid., pp. 15–16.

59. Ibid., p. 19.

60. Ibid.

61. Ibid., p. 22.

62. Ibid.

63. David Gauthier, "Justified Inequality?" *Dialogue* 21 (1982): 431–43. The quotation is from p. 439.

64. Ibid., p. 433.

65. Gauthier, *Morals by Agreement*, p. 13.

66. Ibid.

CHAPTER 7

1. Kenneth Arrow, *Social Choice and Individual Values* (New Haven, Conn.: Yale University Press, 1951). For discussion of the significance of this result and others like it, see Part II of Brian Barry and Russell Hardin, eds., *Rational Man and Irrational Society? An Introduction and Sourcebook* (Beverly Hills, Calif.: Sage, 1982).

2. Henry Sidgwick, *The Methods of Ethics* (7th ed. London: Macmillan, 1907; reprint, 1967), p. 214. (Rather awkwardly, Sidgwick splits his discussion

between two chapters, both entitled "Intuitionism" Bk. 1 Ch. 8 and Bk. 3 Ch. 1.)

3. Ibid., pp. 98–99.

4. Ronald Dworkin, "The Original Position," in Norman Daniels, ed., *Reading Rawls: Critical Studies of A Theory of Justice* (New York: Basic Books, 1975), pp. 16–53. The quotation is from p. 28.

5. Ibid., p. 29.

6. John Rawls, "Kantian Constructivism in Moral Theory: The Dewey Lectures," *Journal of Philosophy* 77 (1980): 515–72.

7. Ibid., p. 522.

8. Ibid., p. 523.

9. Ibid.

10. Ibid.

11. Ibid.

12. John Rawls, "The Basic Structure as Subject," in Alvin I. Goldman and Jaegwon Kim, eds., *Values and Morals: Essays in Honor of William Frankena, Charles Stevenson and Richard B. Brandt* (Dordrecht: Reidel, 1978), pp. 47–71. The quotation is from p. 58.

13. John Rawls, *A Theory of Justice* (Cambridge, Mass.: Harvard University Press, 1971), p. 86.

14. Rawls's original position is, of course, an example of this, and it has often been pointed out that its features "mean that the deliberators reason alike from the exact same premises. An incidental effect is that this is a 'contract argument' in the most attenuated sense, since no room is left for disagreement, bargaining, or even relevant differences among the parties" (David Lyons, "Nature and Soundness of the Contract and Coherence Arguments," in Norman Daniels, ed., p. 151).

15. Sidgwick, p. 498.

16. Ibid., p. 497.

17. Rawls, *A Theory of Justice*, pp. 34–40.

18. Rawls, "Kantian Constructivism," pp. 554–72. "Rational intuitionism" is the view that there is a "moral order" that "is given by the nature of things and is known, not by sense, but by rational intuition" (p. 557).

19. Rawls, *A Theory of Justice*, p. 104.

20. Dworkin, p. 28.

21. Ibid. See pp. 30, 31, 37, and 46 for other occurrences of the expression "constructive model." Apparently as a stylistic variant with no distinctive significance, Dworkin also employs the expression "constructivist model" on p. 44. The word "constructivism" itself does not appear anywhere in the article.

22. Ibid., p. 28.

23. Ibid.

24. Ibid.

25. Ibid., pp. 28–29.

26. Ibid., p. 28 n. 3.

27. Lyons, p. 158.

28. Rawls, "Kantian Constructivism," pp. 554–72.

29. Lyons (p. 145 n. 9) lists the following passages as relevant here: pages 19–21, 46–53, and 578–82 of *A Theory of Justice*.

30. John Rawls, "Outline of a Decision Procedure for Ethics," *Philosophical Review* 60 (1951): 177–97.

31. Ibid., p. 182.

32. Ibid., p. 183.

33. Ibid., p. 184.

34. Ibid., p. 188.

35. Ibid.

36. Ibid., pp. 188, 189.

37. Rawls, *A Theory of Justice*, p. 19.

38. Ibid., p. 20.

39. Ibid.

40. Ibid., p. 19.

41. Ibid., pp. 311.

42. Section 47, "The Precepts of Justice," pp. 303–10 of *A Theory of Justice*.

43. See especially bk. 3, chap. 11, of Sidgwick, pp. 337–61.

44. T. M. Scanlon, "Contractualism and Utilitarianism," in Amartya Sen and Bernard Williams, eds., *Utilitarianism and Beyond* (Cambridge: Cambridge University Press, 1982), pp. 103–28. The quotations are from p. 116 and p. 116 n. 12.

45. See, for a critique of Kant on these lines, David Gauthier, "The Unity of Reason: A Subversive Reinterpretation of Kant," *Ethics* 96 (1985): 74–88.

46. See Alan Gewirth's *Reason and Morality* (Chicago: University of Chicago Press, 1978), and his *Human Rights: Essays on Justification and Applications* (Chicago: University of Chicago Press, 1982).

47. Gewirth claims that the "denial or violation" of "the supreme principle of morality and of human rights"—a version of the Golden Rule—"commits every agent to self-contradiction" (*Human Rights*, p. 26).

48. Ibid., pp. 81–82.

49. Ibid., pp. 79–99 (originally published in 1970).

50. Ibid., p. 87.

51. Ibid., p. 88.

52. Ibid., p. 91.

53. See ibid., pp. 88–89.

54. Adam Smith, *The Theory of Moral Sentiments* (Indianapolis, Ind.: Liberty Classics, 1976), p. 235. Cf. David Hume, *Enquiries Concerning Human Understanding and Concerning the Principles of Morals*, ed. L. A. Selby-Bigge, 3d ed., ed. P. H. Nidditch (Oxford: Clarendon Press, 1975), pp. 227–28. It may be noted that Jonathan Harrison, in *Hume's Moral Epistemology* (Oxford: Clarendon Press, 1976), writes that "Hume was close to holding an 'ideal observer' theory of moral judgments" (p. 114).

CHAPTER 8

1. David Gauthier, *Morals by Agreement* (Oxford: Clarendon Press, 1986), p. 205.

2. Ibid., pp. 211–12.

3. Ibid., pp. 214–17.

4. Ibid., p. 222.

5. Ibid.

6. See ibid., pp. 223–27.

7. David Luban, "Bargaining and Compromise: Recent Work on Negotiation and Informal Justice," *Philosophy and Public Affairs* 14 (1985): 397–416, quotation from p. 406.

8. John Rawls, *A Theory of Justice* (Cambridge, Mass.: Harvard University Press, 1971), p. 89.

9. Ibid., pp. 85–86.

10. Ibid., p. 85.

11. Ibid.

12. Ibid., p. 89.

13. Ibid., p. 85.

14. Ibid., p. 86.

15. Ibid., pp. 274–75.

16. Ibid., pp. 86–87.

17. Ibid., p. 87.

18. Ibid., p. 88.

19. Ibid.

20. Ibid., p. 274.

21. Ibid., p. 304.

22. Ibid., p. 275.

23. See ibid., sections 18 and 19, pp. 108–17.

24. Ibid., pp. 134–35 n. 10.

25. For a general discussion of the peculiarities of labor markets, see David Marsden, *The End of Economic Man? Custom and Competition in Labor Markets* (Brighton, Sussex: Wheatsheaf, 1986).

CHAPTER 9

1. John Rawls, "Justice as Fairness," *Philosophical Review* 67 (1958): 164–94. The quotation is from pp. 171–72.

2. Ibid., p. 170.

3. Ibid., p. 171.

4. Ibid., pp. 181–82.

5. Ibid., p. 179.

6. Ibid., p. 172.

7. Ibid., p. 170.

8. II Samuel 12: 1–13.

9. John Rawls, *A Theory of Justice* (Cambridge, Mass.: Harvard University Press, 1971), p. 138.

10. Ibid., p. 140.

11. Ibid., p. 141.

12. Ibid., p. 587.

13. John Rawls, "Kantian Constructivism in Moral Theory: The Dewey Lectures," *Journal of Philosophy* 77 (1980): 515–72.

14. Ibid., p. 547.

15. Ibid., p. 525.

16. Ibid.

17. Ibid., p. 527.

18. Ibid., p. 569.

19. Gilbert Harman, *The Nature of Morality: An Introduction to Ethics* (New York: Oxford University Press, 1977), p. 162.

20. Ibid., p. 111 (italics in original).

21. Ibid., pp. 111–12.

22. Rawls, *A Theory of Justice*, pp. 289–90.

23. T. M. Scanlon, "Contractualism and Utilitarianism," in Amartya Sen and Bernard Williams, eds., *Utilitarianism and Beyond* (Cambridge: Cambridge University Press, 1982), pp. 103–28. The quotation is from p. 116 n. 12.

24. Thomas C. Schelling, *The Strategy of Conflict* (Cambridge, Mass.: Harvard University Press, 1960), chapter 4, pp. 83–118. See also David Lewis, *Convention* (Cambridge, Mass.: Harvard University Press, 1969).

25. See, for a discussion of this idea, Karol Soltan, *The Causal Theory of Justice* (Berkeley and Los Angeles: University of California Press, 1987).

26. David Hume, *A Treatise of Human Nature*, ed. L. A. Selby-Bigge, 2d ed., ed. P. H. Nidditch (Oxford: Clarendon Press, 1978), bk. 3, section 3, pp. 501–13.

27. David Hume, *An Enquiry Concerning the Principles of Morals* in *Enquiries Concerning Human Understanding and Concerning the Principles of Morals*, ed. L. A. Selby-Bigge, 3d ed., ed. P. H. Nidditch (Oxford: Clarendon Press, 1975), pp. 195–96.

28. Rawls, *A Theory of Justice*, p. 584.

29. Ibid.

30. Ibid., p. 585.

31. Ibid.

32. Colin Turnbull, *The Mountain People* (New York: Simon and Schuster, 1972).

33. J. H. Wellbank, Denis Snook, and David T. Mason, *John Rawls and His Critics: An Annotated Bibliography* (London: Garland, 1982), p. 3, item A2.

CHAPTER 10

1. See Brian Barry, "Warrender and His Critics," *Philosophy* 48 (1968): 117–37; reprinted in Maurice Cranston and Richard S. Peters, eds., *Hobbes and Rousseau* (Garden City, N.Y.: Doubleday, 1972).

2. David Gauthier, *Morals by Agreement* (Oxford: Clarendon Press, 1986).

3. The passage runs as follows: "And if a weaker Prince, make a disadvantageous peace with a stronger, for feare; he is bound to keep it; unlesse (as hath been sayd before) there ariseth some new, and just cause of feare, to renew the war" (Thomas Hobbes, *Leviathan*, ed. with an introduction by C. B. Macpherson [Harmondsworth, England: Penguin, 1968], chap. 14, p. 198).

4. Ibid., chap. 20, p. 256.

5. Allan Gibbard, "Human Evolution and the Sense of Justice," in Peter A.

French, Theodore E. Uehling, Jr., and Howard K. Wettstein, eds., *Midwest Studies in Philosophy*. vol. 7: *Social and Political Philosophy* (Minneapolis: University of Minnesota Press, 1982), pp. 31–46. The quotation is from p. 37. I should point out that Gibbard's conception of a sense of justice is, in my terms, an emotional attachment to a bargaining solution.

6. The belief that everyone can be counted on to respond mechanically to a balance of advantage and disadvantage led to many of the barbarities of American policy in the Vietnam war such as the massive bombing of North Vietnam and Cambodia. See Alexander George and Richard Smoke, *Deterrence in American Foreign Policy: Theory and Practice* (New York: Columbia University Press, 1974).

7. Hobbes, chap. 17, p. 227 (my italics).

8. See, for the notion of contract by convention, Russell Hardin, *Collective Action* (Baltimore: Johns Hopkins University Press, 1982).

9. Hobbes, chap. 13, p. 186.

10. Ibid., chap. 20, p. 260. Compare the similar passage in chap. 18, pp. 238–39.

11. Anatol Rapoport, *Fights, Games, and Debates* (Ann Arbor: University of Michigan Press, 1961), p. 9.

12. Ibid., p. 12.

13. Sir Arthur Conan Doyle, "The Adventure of the Engineer's Thumb," in William S. Baring-Gould, ed., *The Annotated Sherlock Holmes* (New York: Clarkson N. Potter, 1967), vol. 2, pp. 209–24.

APPENDIX A

1. Based on diagram V (p. 29) of R. B. Braithwaite, *Theory of Games as a Tool for the Moral Philosopher* (Cambridge: Cambridge University Press, 1955).

2. Ibid., pp. 34–35.

3. Ibid., p. 34.

4. Ibid., p. 30.

5. Ibid., pp. 26, 27.

6. Ibid., p. 27.

7. Ibid., p. 28.

8. Ibid., p. 30.

9. Ibid., pp. 30–31.

10. Ibid., p. 33.

11. Ibid., p. 35.

12. Ibid.

13. Ibid., p. 32.

14. Ibid., p. 33.

15. Ibid., pp. 32–33.

16. Ibid., pp. 35–36.

17. Ibid., p. 32.

18. Ibid., p. 39.

19. Ibid., p. 40.

20. R. Duncan Luce and Howard Raiffa, *Games and Decisions* (New York: Wiley, 1957), p. 154.

21. Braithwaite, pp. 42–43.

22. Ibid., pp. 43–44.

23. Ibid., p. 44.

24. Ibid., pp. 44–45.

25. Ibid., p. 45.

26. Ibid., p. 46.

APPENDIX B

1. David Gauthier, "Bargaining and Justice," *Social Philosophy and Policy* 2 (1985): 27–47. The quotation is from p. 34. Most of the same points are made in *Morals by Agreement* (Oxford: Clarendon Press, 1986), pp. 130–50, though the criticism of the Nash solution is less developed.

2. "Bargaining and Justice," p. 34.

3. Ibid., p. 35.

4. Ibid., p. 34.

5. Howard Raiffa, *The Art and Science of Negotiation* (Cambridge, Mass.: Harvard University Press, 1982).

6. Ibid., p. 48.

7. Ibid., p. 49.

APPENDIX C

1. John Rawls, *A Theory of Justice* (Cambridge, Mass.: Harvard University Press, 1971), p. 151.

2. Ibid.

3. Ibid., p. 129; see also pp. 281–82.

4. See ibid., section 36, "Political Justice and the Constitution," pp. 221–28.

5. Ibid., p. 335.

6. Ibid.

7. Ibid., p. 350.

8. J. E. Meade, *Theory of Economic Externalities: The Control of Environmental Pollution and Similar Social Costs* (Leiden: Sijthoff, 1973), p. 52.

9. Thomas C. Grey, "The First Virtue," *Stanford Law Review* 25 (1973): 286–327; quotation from p. 324.

10. Ibid., p. 323.

11. Ibid.

12. Ibid., p. 325.

13. Ibid.

14. Jan F. Narveson, "A Puzzle about Economic Justice in Rawls' Theory," *Social Theory and Practice* 4 (1976): 1–27; and "Rawls on Equal Distribution of Wealth," *Philosophia* 7 (1978): 281–92.

15. Narveson, "Rawls on Equal Distribution of Wealth," p. 287.

16. Ibid., pp. 287–89.

17. Narveson, "A Puzzle," p. 15.

18. Ibid., p. 12.

19. John Stuart Mill, *Principles of Political Economy*, bk. 2, chap. 1, section 4, in J. M. Robson, ed., *Collected Works of John Stuart Mill*, vol. 2 (Toronto: University of Toronto Press, 1965), p. 210.

20. Ibid.

21. Ibid.

22. Narveson, "A Puzzle," p. 16.

23. Rawls, p. 151.

24. Ibid., esp. pp. 176–78.

25. Rawls, "Reply to Alexander and Musgrave," *Quarterly Journal of Economics* 88 (1974): 633–55, quotation from p. 653.

26. Alan Donagan, *Morality, Property and Slavery*, The Lindley Lecture, 1980 (Lawrence, Ks.: Philosophy Department of the University of Kansas, 1981), p. 21.

27. Ibid., pp. 18–19.

28. Rawls, *A Theory of Justice*, p. 61.

29. Donagan, p. 19.

30. Rawls, *A Theory of Justice*, p. 83.

31. Donagan, p. 19.

32. Rawls, *A Theory of Justice*, p. 84.

33. Ibid.

34. Ibid., p. 275.

35. Ibid., p. 274.

36. Ibid., p. 277.

Index

Printed in the United States
1067100007B